Information
and *Emotion*

ADVANCE PRAISE FOR *INFORMATION AND EMOTION*

"This book tackles the important role that emotions play in our interaction with information systems. ... Until now this domain has been neglected in information behavior research, leaving a gap in our full understanding of information interaction. This book fills that gap and is essential reading for anyone who wants the full picture."

—Carol Tenopir, Professor, School of
Information Sciences, University of Tennessee

"A timely and valuable compilation of theory and research on the important influence of the affective domain on information behavior."

—Carol C. Kuhlthau, Professor Emerita,
Library and Information Science, Rutgers University

"We knew about motivation and frustration, but now the vast territory of affective responses has been charted, opening up many possibilities for future researchers. Readers will more clearly see the path to making information seekers happier and more successful."

—Ben Shneiderman, *Designing the User Interface:
Strategies for Effective Human–Computer Interaction*

"Nahl and Bilal's broad-ranging collection on the affective issues associated with information behaviors has opened new research territory, and will significantly influence future information behavior research."

—Barbara M. Wildemuth, Professor, School of Information and
Library Science, University of North Carolina at Chapel Hill

"This excellent volume brings together the most recent research on the role of affect in the way people select, use, and process information. ... a nice balance of advanced theorizing, cutting-edge empirical research, and real-life applications. This book should be on the reading list of all researchers and practitioners interested in the fascinating role of affectivity in human thinking and behavior."

—Joseph P. Forgas, Scientia Professor
of Psychology, University of New South Wales

Information
and *Emotion*

The Emergent Affective Paradigm
in Information Behavior
Research and Theory

Edited by
Diane Nahl
and
Dania Bilal

ASIST Monograph Series

Published on behalf of the American Society for
Information Science and Technology by

Medford, New Jersey

First Printing, 2007

Information and Emotion: The Emergent Affective Paradigm in Information Behavior Research and Theory

Library of Congress Cataloging-in-Publication Data

Information and emotion : the emergent affective paradigm in information behavior research and theory / edited by Diane Nahl and Dania Bilal.
    p. cm. -- (ASIS&T monograph series)
  Includes bibliographical references and index.
  ISBN-13: 978-1-57387-310-9
 1. Information Behavior. I. Nahl, Diane. II. Bilal, Dania, 1956-
  ZA3075.I53 2007
  025.5'24--dc22

2007030581

Printed and bound in the United States of America

President and CEO: Thomas H. Hogan, Sr.
Editor-in-Chief and Publisher: John B. Bryans
Managing Editor: Amy M. Reeve
ASIST Monograph Series Editor: Samantha Hastings
VP Graphics and Production: M. Heide Dengler
Cover Designer: Shelley Szajner
Book Designer: Kara Mia Jalkowski
Proofreader: Dorothy Pike
Copyeditor: Barbara Brynko
Indexer: Sharon Hughes

Contents

v

PART II: Macro-Emotional Information Environment

PART III: Micro-Emotional Information Environment

PART IV: Special Information Environments

Figures and Tables

Figures

Tables

Acknowledgments

Information and Emotion is a collaborative work of the information behavior research community. We extend our deepest thanks to the 24 contributors who made this volume possible. We especially thank graduate student Caitlin Nelson, from the Library and Information Science Program at the University of Hawaii, for her dedicated editorial work on the manuscript. Special recognition goes to our excellent editor Samantha Hastings, who expertly guided this work through the publication process. Royalties from the publication of this work will be used to support the future activities of the American Society for Information Science and Technology Special Interest Group on Information Needs, Seeking and Use (ASIST SIG USE).

Foreword

Hooray and congratulations to Diane Nahl and Dania Bilal for bringing together a prominent group of authors to write this book. The title *Information and Emotion: The Emergent Affective Paradigm in Information Behavior Research and Theory* at first seems unusual. We are used to "information" being associated with searching, retrieving, transferring, displaying, and communicating information. We talk about information and information science, suggesting utilitarian and logical approaches that dominate the way we think about information. Yet, we react emotionally to information all the time, whether it is in newspapers, books, databases, films or online. Skillful authors, designers, illustrators, marketing professionals, and filmmakers use their expertise to present information in ways that heighten our emotions. They want us to "feel" their message.

Recently, I was disturbed by the manipulative character of Briony in Ian McEwan's *Atonement*. How did this 13 year old manage to dupe the adults into thinking that Robbie abused Lola, ruining his life and giving rise to complex emotional interpretations that perplex readers? In contrast, I was charmed and reassured by the honest characters of Fannie and Edward in Jane Austin's *Mansfield Park*, and I was enthralled, bemused, and amused by the teenage characters in J. K. Rowling's *Harry Potter and the Deathly Hollows*. When asked by a friend to identify a memorable book, I immediately singled out John Fowles' *Collector*, even though it has been more than 25 years since I read it. Why? Because this book played on my emotions, chilling me to the bone with fear, tantalizing me with the promise of freedom for the heroine—a young woman who was stalked, "collected," and kept captive by a crazed person who treated her like a butterfly to be collected and admired. Being of similar age myself at that time, it was natural to empathize with this character as though it was me. Would I now react like this? Would a man react like this? Empathy is a powerful emotional force.

Though potent, fiction is not the only trigger of affective responses. Data displays delight, fascinate, alarm, or frustrate us, depending on their content. For example, Minard's graph published in 1861[1] on the subject of Napoleon's[2] disastrous Russian campaign of 1812[3] is seen by many as an anti-war statement. Salgado's photographs raise our awareness of poverty in developing countries, and the World Wildlife Fund's appealing panda symbol raises hope that these and other magnificent creatures can be saved by our donations. Children, and adults too, select books by their titles and covers because they appeal to their emotions. During the last 25 years, increasingly complex data visualization tools allow us to search and display data in different ways. Depending on the color, size, type font, and display techniques, our search strategies are influenced, including our affective responses. Smells and sounds can evoke warm feelings of childhood experiences long forgotten or rivet us with fear depending on the associations they conjure.

How we respond depends on the information content and context. Instinctively we know that there is an inherent emotional and affective quality to information. Diane Nahl and Dania Bilal have chosen an appropriately bold title that emphasizes how little information scientists and knowledge workers have focused on users' emotions as they interact with information. By bringing together chapters that cover theoretical frameworks and macro-, micro-, and special emotional environments, Nahl and Bilal remind us that the emotional states that we bring to a task and those that the information induces influence choices we make and, ultimately, how well we perform the task and how we feel about it. Recent studies have tended to emphasize the role of computers in determining users' affective responses and the impact of different media in promoting affective responses. It is refreshing to read a book that goes beyond the technology to recognize the centrality of information content and context.

Readers will learn about the theoretical basis of emotion in Diane Nahl's impressively authored first chapter, which provides a solid foundation for chapters about affective responses to search tasks, children's book selection, the relationship between constructivism and emotion, emotion and culture, and much more. Anyone who values the affective component of the human spirit will welcome this book. It will stimulate novel research and contribute to classes on information retrieval and sense-making by encouraging students and researchers to pay attention to affective responses as well as cognition. This book deserves a prominent place on the shelf of every researcher, student, scholar, and manager who seeks to understand users' information behavior.

Jennifer Preece
Dean, College of Information Studies
University of Maryland

ENDNOTES

1. "1861" retrieved July 23, 2007 from en.wikipedia.org/wiki/1861.
2. "Napoleon I of France" retrieved July 23, 2007 from en.wikipedia.org/wiki/Napoleon.
3. French invasion of Russia (1812)" retrieved July 23, 2007 from en.wikipedia.org/wiki/French_invasion_of_Russia_%281812%29.

Introduction

Diane Nahl
University of Hawaii

The purpose of this book is to establish a focus on affective and emotional dimensions in information behavior (IB) research, based upon recent theoretical developments and research findings in information science and the cognate fields of cognitive science, psychology, business, education, ethnomethodology, communication, neuroscience, and computer science. The affective paradigm established in this book traces its origins to early work in education and cognitive science. In 1950, Erik Erikson published his still-influential theory of socio-emotional development from birth to old age. In 1956, Benjamin Bloom, David Krathwohl, and Bertram Masia published the taxonomy of the affective domain that is still used to develop instruction according to the principle of internalization. In the late 1960s, Herbert Simon (1967) identified emotion as a major challenge to cognitive science due to emotion's determining effect on cognition.

This book introduces the emerging research areas of affective issues in situated information seeking and use, and the affective paradigm applied to IB in a variety of populations, cultures, and contexts. The book is primarily concerned with IB research findings on the user perspective, the user experience, and how emotional aspects can be interpreted, mitigated, or enhanced through design that is informed by use and by users who directly participate in information design. The chapters in the book present IB research relating to a variety of theories, Web technologies, everyday settings, populations, communities, ages, ethnicities, and cultures that are engaged in information seeking and use, and the research employed a variety of qualitative and quantitative methodologies that demonstrate how emotion can be measured in diverse settings.

Over the past 35 years, social sciences research has developed ethnographic, observational, and self-reporting methodologies capable of examining the higher mental and emotional processes involved in naturalistic or situated behavior. This user-based methodological trend is driven by the need to reduce artificiality by obtaining concurrent process data that is collected as behavior occurs, as well as to obtain user discourse about information, information systems, and information settings. Cognitive and affective data that is inherent in actual situations is needed to create information environments, systems, and services that are truly responsive to the needs of the individuals inhabiting and using these settings. Such data permit analyses of situated cognitive and affective processes, yielding much needed knowledge of the dynamic role of motivation, emotions, feelings, values, and preferences in influencing choice-making and decision-making.

While it can be said that there has been inattention to affect in information science, a cadre of key researchers has pursued the examination of the domain of affect, emotion, feeling, mood, sentiment, affection, disposition, preference, interest, value, motivation, intention, and goals with respect to information seeking and use. One could say that this work began with Herbert Simon (1967, p. 29) who defined this research area for information science when he wrote, "Since in actual human behavior motive and emotion are major influences on the course of cognitive behavior, a general theory of thinking and problem solving must incorporate such influences." Over the past 25 years, information scientists have applied these process- and context-rich methodologies to examine situated information processing and use in order to gain a fuller understanding of IB. This research has revealed the vital role of emotions and affect in information processing and use. Early studies include: Belkin, 1980; Dervin, 1983; Ingwerson, 1992; Kuhlthau, 1988; Mellon, 1986; Nahl & Jakobovits, 1985; Wilson, 1981; among others.

This peer-reviewed volume evolved through a confluence of scholarly activities, including the first panels on Emotional Design organized by Diane Nahl at the ASIST 2004 and 2005 annual meetings that drew crowds of interested IB researchers, generating synergy around the topic. In 2005, Carol Collier Kuhlthau was awarded the ASIST Information Science Research Award, recognizing her work on the information search process model, a holistic information behavior model with a significant emphasis on affective information behavior. The inception for this book occurred at the conclusion of the 2005 panel because it was clear that there existed a community of researchers exploring the role of affect in information behavior (IB) and that the group's work could benefit from dissemination and collaboration. The Special Interest Group on Information Needs, Seeking and Use (SIG USE) decided to make affect and IB the focus of the next Research Symposium organized by Nahl and Bilal. The focal moment to introduce this book to the IB research community was the 6th Annual SIG USE Research Symposium at the 2006 annual meeting of the American Society for Information Science and Technology (ASIST), titled Information Realities: Exploring Affective and Emotional Aspects in Information Seeking and Use. The symposium drew applications from more than 40 information behavior researchers who have taken the affective turn in their data analysis and research design, some of whom are contributors to this volume.

This work demonstrates the deepening realization in information science that technology is deployed within a mental environment of emotions and thoughts. The "information environment" is actually the interactional sphere of a group of people enacting in social life the emotions and intentions they choose to exercise with each other. An information community differs from another by the quality of such choices. Members differ in the satisficing of particular emotions that attach value to a set of choices, and they differ in the intentions through which they wish to optimize an information facility. This is the emotional reality upon which the entire edifice of information technology is constructed.

The chapters in this volume represent the efforts of information behavior researchers who are in the process of charting the emotional quality of the information environment in a wide variety of social spheres and in diverse populations. The contributions are divided into four parts: The first examines theoretical treatments of the role of emotion in information behavior, the second and third represent empirical studies distinguished by methodological level of analysis of emotion, and the fourth is characterized by analyses of disturbances in the information environment. As a whole, these chapters define the role of affect in information behavior and serve as the forerunners of future research into the emotional information environment. The benefits of a holistic approach to studying IB in context will include the development of new design principles that enable the creation of humane interfaces, services, and information settings. The development of new information systems and services, as well as theoretical and empirical investigations, must take into account emotional and affective factors. This volume represents an effort to develop a holistic approach to the human-centered paradigm.

The four chapters in Part I create a theoretical context for integrating emotions into the information environment to reflect the centrality of the affective domain in all human activity. In the socio-cultural sphere of information ecology, *information reception* is keyed to "user acceptance," and this individual judgment to accept or reject information is the consequence of a prior emotional value that the individual accepts in common with others in a particular community of practice. *Information use* is keyed to the feeling of wanting to do something with the information that has been received, such as telling someone else, or buying it, or selling it, or using it to achieve something more effectively, and so on. Both information reception and use are therefore grounded in social feelings, emotions, and intentions. Further, emotion concerning information is manifold, dynamic, situation-bound, context-dependent, and representative of group practices with information. This is the affective reality to which technology responds in the era of emotional design. Adults and children experience systems emotionally and cognitively, but children's experience differs at various developmental stages.

Chapters 5–9 in Part II present a wide variety of details on how the flow of emotions is actualized in the information practice of people on their daily round. It charts the macro-emotional information environment of adults and children as observed in their social and mental activities while striving to adapt and cope, and thus meet their goals. The chapters report on global measures of affect as they apply to situated information behavior. Every technological detail is deemed a pleasure or a pain, a breeze or a headache, a barrier or an assist.

Chapters 10–14 in Part III detail the micro-components of emotionality that shape the information experience and condition its behavioral manifestations in a variety of settings. Human beings keep track of their emotions and feelings in specific information settings and in relation to particular information content. From the perspective of users, there is no clear distinction between emotional reactions during information reception and the technological environment that provides access to participate. These chapters show that emotion and feeling are general terms for a variety of affective activities during information reception and use. Discovering these micro-human operations has become essential to emotional design.

Chapters 15–17 in Part IV present studies documenting the emotional intensification of the information environment when a break occurs in human symbiosis with technology, due to physical disability or demographic estrangement from the information culture. Being blind, foreign, and poor are biographical states that displace the ordinary solutions available to others. Emotion, feeling, value, and identity are virtual gatekeepers that condition what people are willing to notice or ignore, to accept or to oppose, to engage or avoid.

In Chapter 1, Diane Nahl presents a theoretical context suitable for discussing the details of how the emotional information environment is created by the symbiotic interaction between technological systems and the user's feelings and intentions. Both information reception and use involve all three biological systems: the affective, the cognitive, and the sensorimotor. Receiving information is identified as a process of adaptation or coping with the information environment. This involves the ways people notice information (sensorimotor) when interacting with a system through *satisficing affordances* or features that people can use to receive information. After noticing the information, users then appraise it (cognitive), and then attach value to it by emotional or consummatory processing (affective).

During the second phase of information use, people form an intention or motivation (affective) that directs their thinking into a plan (cognitive) that is executed (sensorimotor) by interacting with the system's *optimizing affordances* or features that allow users to enter commands. Evidence is presented from discourse analysis of user self-reports, which shows that information behavior viewed at both the macro and micro levels is a regulated flow of cognitive-affective procedures that the user operates in conformity with the group norms in a community of practice.

In Chapter 2, Dania Bilal presents major child-development theories, outlining the cognitive and affective abilities of children as they mature through stages of growth. Because information system design for children is based on adults, design has not taken child development into account. Bilal presents data from a number of studies that have identified areas of difficulty that can be addressed developmentally in system design, through corrective feedback and mediator functions, including taxonomy development, engaging and concrete visual representations, spell-checking, context-driven help, clear levels of complexity for appropriate learning challenge, and other features to support children in different developmental stages.

In Chapter 3, Brenda Dervin and CarrieLynn Reinhard make it clear that the affective dimension of emotions has "always been incorporated into the framework" of "universals of human sense-making" and "sense-unmaking." The authors describe themselves as "entering the study of emotions through different doors" by conceptualizing emotions and feelings as inner mental activities "arising out of situations, tasks, or contexts or their sub-parts." Affective mental states are defined as "attributes of persons" such as sociocultural personality features that are the source of the motivations, goals, and purposes people have when performing information behavior acts. Furthermore, the awareness of one's own mental states and their quality (positive or negative for example) has information value to the person.

Because information seeking and use are highly situated, it follows that the role of emotions in information behavior varies with the situation. Informants in the study described the details of recent situations of scholarly or personal research using electronic resources, and focusing especially on experiences that they found "challenging, important, confusing, emotional, unfamiliar, and contradictory." The "person-in-situation sense-making analysis" of the "informant narratives" indicates a highly complex confluence of emotions in each situation in relation to people's assessment of the outcome. Still, positive emotions are associated with better outcomes, confirming a solid trend noted throughout the other chapters as well. This chapter makes it clear that further research is needed to clarify what Dervin and Reinhard call "the ebb and flow of situational assessments" that people perform throughout their information seeking efforts.

In Chapter 4, Nicola Parker and Jennifer Berryman take the theoretical position that "affect is conceptualized as a system that activates cognitive, physiological and behavioral components, or actions." Since information behavior involves a sequence of actions constructed by the individual in real time, it becomes important to understand how a subsequence ends and another begins. Parker and Berryman monitored these critical directional choice points, which they termed 'What is enough?', an expression used by Herbert Simon in defining "bounded rationality" or what constitutes "satisficing" to a decision-maker. Parker and Berryman differentiate "the action of stopping or continuing ... from the evaluations that precede that action."

Content analysis of extensive interview tapes and transcripts uncovered several distinctive types of affective evaluations in relation to when post-graduate searchers decided they have "enough" information to complete an assignment. The affective components of "enough" in an information processing task emerged as (1) the feeling of wanting to gain control and wanting to finish, (2) the desire to optimize the search effort, (3) seeking the feeling of interest and pleasure through engagement and understanding, (4) the feeling of satisfaction that marks the completion of the process, and (5) experiencing the inherent desire for generation and creation, and its growth producing self-satisfaction. As Parker and Berryman aptly put it: "Affect infused everything."

In Chapter 5, Lesley Farmer examines how personality features of users impact their motivation for information seeking and the "mechanisms used in engaging with information." One of the issues addressed is whether affective personality traits are "permanent, or do they grow and change developmentally?" For instance, confidence, coordination, control, composure, and persistence are personality traits that impact information behavior. One way to measure information behavior in a new context is to use established sets of information literacy competencies, which include such skills as "problem identification and solving, communication skills, and social skills of cooperation and help-seeking. Thus, as students exhibit positive social-emotional behavior, they may be more likely to achieve information literacy competency."

What is the basis for expecting correlations between personality traits and information behavior? Consider a searcher's motivation to enact persistence, which is the affective energy to postpone quitting. Searchers with less persistence quit too soon, losing the motivation to continue searching. Searchers who persist are more successful. Persistence in searching is best measured directly through observing how people search under various conditions and for various purposes, and especially, when they quit a task or procedure.

Correlational research may be helpful in identifying the factors that need to be studied more directly. Farmer provides modest correlational evidence that high school students who rate themselves higher on socio-emotional scales also exhibit more successful information behavior patterns such as wanting to share information activities by communicating with others, or making a greater effort to be organized. Other traits identified include a greater willingness to check work when finished and to "participate in new activities and to try even when schoolwork is hard."

Further research is needed to determine how socio-emotional traits vary for the same individuals across a variety of information settings and tasks in which they regularly participate as members of a community of practice. Research must explain theoretically how these affective traits intervene and produce the variation in the observed information behavior.

In Chapter 6, Michelynn McKnight presents findings on information behavior in an "intense information ecology" with life and death consequences. "Professional nurses must pay close attention to everyone's affective behaviors, including their own." Critical care nursing involves both direct patient care and information management of multiple medical data on each patient known as "the chart." The progressive increase in the complexity of patient charts is known to be a source of intense stress on nurses. The feelings they express are similar to those of searchers who are intimidated by the technological complexity of the experience in time pressure, frustration, uncertainty, and self-doubt.

McKnight discovered that the negative affect of both male and female nurses freely expressed during the information management task is typically inhibited or transformed into positive enactments when giving direct patient care. Frustration was overtly expressed during records management in the presence of other nurses. Recurrent problems included interruptions (e.g., phone, call button), illegible handwriting, unavailability of people with the needed information, navigation difficulty in online systems, multitasking demands, social protocol barriers, malfunctioning of ancillary equipment, misplacing of a document or slip of paper, missing items on a record, and disappearing records or printouts.

When nurses switched tasks to direct patient care, they "were observed stopping before the door, taking a deep breath and waiting a beat to compose themselves. The nurses consistently made this conscious change in their outward demeanor." Nurses presented an affective demeanor that contrasted with what they were expressing with each other moments before in the records management setting. The reverse happens when nurses exit the patient's room.

Chapter 7 by Sheri Massey, Allison Druin, and Ann Carlson Weeks shows that the emotions children feel while reading help them construct an intuitive scheme for categorizing books they are reading, discussing, and recommending to each other. The authors used a longitudinal approach to observe the behavior of children from several countries while they wrote and shared their views of self-selected and preselected books from the International Children's Digital Library (ICDL), which makes it possible "to explore patterns in readers' responses to identical works in multiple international settings."

Reader response research reviewed in the chapter suggests "in order to understand response it is necessary to explore attributes of not only the text and the reader, but also of the socio-cultural context in which the reading transaction occurs." This "anthropological" view of the reader states that "emotions are cultural artifacts and must be analyzed within the social and cultural contexts in which they are experienced."

In this study, children were provided with laptop computers and access to the digital library. Children were asked to rate each book they read along several dimensions of feeling and emotion (e.g., How does this book make you feel? Happy, sad, scared, funny, or other. This book made me feel this way because ..."). An interesting finding from content analysis of the children's book reviews is children's emotional experiences change frequently during the reading transaction. Another interesting finding is "in books with strong morals or messages, the children's emotional responses were remarkably similar across study sites." One important recommendation of this research is to point to the need for a classification scheme that "allows children to search for books by how it might make them feel."

In Chapter 8, Lisa Given explores the "emotional underpinnings of students' information behaviors" as a social context for constructing information services that support their academic activities. The use of affective traits as an internal context for information behavior is part of the ecological, holistic, and experiential approaches in information science. Information behavior becomes part of the individual's life strategy for inclusion and approval in the never-ending effort of constructing one's social identity. The external public information ecology interlocks with the internal private affective and cognitive ecology.

In Given's "model of the affective information behavior ecology," human feelings and information technology become inextricably linked or intermeshed. Campus academic policies and services have an impact on both the students' emotions and how or when they make use of the available information technology. Given identifies the "macro-emotional context" that shapes students' information behaviors. For example, students on a fast-track program experience frustration and anger when discovering that online courses will not be supported. In the experience of the student, the affective "micro-information sphere" (e.g., joy, surprise, anger, fear, frustration, alienation, resentment) conflicts with the "macro-information sphere" (what is available and accessible, and what is not). Understanding this relationship can guide information policy.

In Chapter 9, Rich Gazan reports on a study about the affective behavior of participants in an online community who "violate the community's rules or spirit." Rogue information behavior has been observed in online communities and is attributed to the desire to exert control over group attitudes and communication practices. Rogue behaviors observed include vindictive rating of others' contributions, the use of abusive language, flooding suggestion boxes, excessive contact with administrators, and creating separately registered identities.

Gazan was interested in characterizing the negative affective features that are infused into the information environment by the action of rogue behaviors. They are a source of negative emotions expressed by other group members and influence the pattern of community participation. The data show a change in the emotional environment of the online community when a new information facility was provided allowing users "to construct enhanced personal profile pages on the site." Rogue behaviors diminished. Interestingly, while only a few members have availed themselves of this new facility, the majority of former rogues have.

Chapter 10 by Lynne (E. F.) McKechnie, Catherine Sheldrick Ross, and Paulette Rothbauer shows that affective responses during "pleasure reading" that have an influence on information behavior of children are confirmed and extended to adults. Readers of books talk about their "emotional connections to textual worlds" and describe books as "emotional touchstones." Information behavior with books is connected to the affective reactions and evaluations that readers experience while interacting with a book.

An important theme is that the feelings or emotions that readers experience appear subjectively as being exclusively one's own private reaction, though they are tied to group practices. When children and adult readers discover their own private feelings accurately described as the feelings of a character, the result is a strengthening of the acculturation process by which an individual becomes a participant and practitioner of a group community process. The authors conclude that "the affective significance of reading" is that the "elicitation of emotions can yield a part of the information transformative insights." The authors recommend that affective variables be made part of the information retrieval approach.

In Chapter 11, Helena Mentis reviews the literature on how negative emotions are ordinary in people's experience with information technology. It is clear that people experience frustration in routine interaction with systems that "thwart" some immediate goal (e.g., "specific bugs in the software, systems freezing or crashing, auto-formatting, pop-up windows, slow system response"). These incidents cause an interruption in the workflow, which is experienced as frustration since "they take control away from the user."

Mentis concludes that "unanticipated interruptions" are more critical to users than the designer's concept of system "efficiency." Users retain a vivid "memory of emotions" associated with particular systems such as the frustration experienced when the computer takes control, and especially when the user is uncertain how to regain control. Mentis concludes "in order to design for emotion, we need a better understanding of the occurrence of particular emotions in an information systems environment."

Chapter 12 by Karen Fisher and Carol Landry shows that "affect is a major factor in determining" how the information needs of stay-at-home mothers are created and shared. They trace the expanding literature that attempts to empirically describe how feelings, emotions, and intentions shape the information environment in real life contexts by providing emotional support and promoting community building. Affect associated with information seeking and sharing plays a decisive role due to the overwhelming nature of intense emotions, whether positive, such as feeling safe or empowered, or negative, such as revulsion or resentment.

In monitoring the information behavior of stay-at-home mothers, the researchers identified 25 particular positive and negative emotions associated with their information behavior (e.g., anticipation, curiosity, gratitude, optimism, and empowerment vs. fear, doubt, confusion, anger, worry, and frustration). Some of the social settings identified in the study as rich information grounds for stay-at-home mothers include structured children's activities, shopping in stores, park playgrounds, and planned neighborhood activities. A theoretically important focus of this research is its motivation to trace the "sociodemographic characteristics" that shape everyday information behavior in a technological environment.

In Chapter 13, Nahyun Kwon explores further the known relationship among college students between "library anxiety" and "critical thinking disposition," focusing on the "motivation to decide what to believe and what to do when one approaches problems, ideas, decisions, or issues." A variety of negative emotions allied to anxiety may occur during an initial encounter with the formalized procedures of an academic library. Part of successfully coping in this emotional information environment consists of constructing workable cognitive justifications for what is happening.

One of the consequences of experiencing intense negative affect in the library environment is the disruption of and interference with cognitive procedures that could be helpful in coping with overwhelming anxiety. On the other hand, the desire to be inquisitive, the motivation to be well informed, or the readiness to ask for help are positive affective procedures that lead to more precise cognitive distinctions—for instance, making a cognitive separation between a momentary emotional challenge one feels, and the value and convenience of the library one knows. The affective procedures constructed by successful students to cope with their library anxiety are affective coping skills that can be taught as part of information literacy.

In Chapter 14, Heidi Julien explores a new angle on information literacy instruction that has long been integral to academic libraries. As indicated in the chapter, public libraries are increasingly adopting this same perspective on education for information literacy. Julien confirms by empirical observation that "affective issues such as confidence are primary variables in people's use of online information sources." The affective component of information use skills includes "self-perceptions of one's own literacy." Julien examines how these reflexive self-evaluations influence users' information behavior related to online access.

Analysis of tape-recorded interviews of public library patrons in Canada indicated a variety of emotional involvement in their Internet use. There was a feeling of personal empowerment when people were able to use the Internet on their own at will, and a sense of satisfaction at being able to do so independently without having to ask for help. Interestingly, Julien also found the opposite emotional involvement with some people who appeared to focus negatively on their own traits, such as feeling impatient, inadequate, or anxious. One of Julien's conclusions is that "since self-efficacy and success are related, developing learners' positive feelings about their information literacy skills could become a standard objective of training efforts."

Chapter 15 by Susan Hayter examines information reception and sharing as an interpersonal process, showing how information behavior is conditioned by the quality of the "support systems" that are operative in a particular community or group context. This is particularly visible in the case of "marginalized groups and settings" such as the working poor, a retirement community, or female prisoners. Information access is inhibited or facilitated by people's socio-cultural perceptions of the information source and its affective context.

Hayter examines some life conditions that create a social category of people referred to as "information poor," who face intellectual barriers stemming from their "disadvantaged" relationship to information access. Social setting features that created barriers to access included "insularity, cultural issues, and everyday problems." Information trust is limited to group members and is not extended to "strangers" such as information professionals. Availability of sources of help was not a sufficient condition for accessing that source due to negative social expectations associated with them.

According to Hayter, the "affective elements determined many aspects of the participants' information behaviour." The word "information" was associated with the threatening perception of societal attempts to breach the privacy of socially marginal people. Trusted information sources included friends, family, and "trusted expert workers in the community centre." Outside help with a personal problem was considered only in extreme situations. According to Hayter, who spent significant ethnographic time with a community, "Information that many of us would access easily was very difficult for the residents of this community because of affective issues of fear and anxiety." Some methods are identified for developing a "trusting relationship with information providers." These include working in partnership with community workers and using interpersonal approaches that built cumulative trust.

In Chapter 16, Wooseob Jeong reviews the research on information seeking behavior of the visually impaired. "The Internet is an important part of visually impaired people's information seeking no less than sighted people's." The Web's visual and spatial construction through multiple hypertext links provides a deep challenge to blind people forced to perform "information seeking in linear mode." The visually handicapped are routinely excluded from participating in information communities as social equals since interactive technology incorporates a strong visual approach. Consider the feelings of alienation and bewilderment when clicking on a link to land unexpectedly on a foreign page whose script offers no clues as to the meaning of the content.

Jeong discovered that when adequate technology for the visually impaired is available, there is active participation in a full variety of Internet activities, including daily email and Web surfing, instant messaging (IM) and chat, and online community projects. The visually impaired also play computer games cued to sound in a linear mode, which is why it is difficult for sighted onlookers to follow what's going on.

In Chapter 17, Bharat Mehra focuses on the "intersections between emotions, actions, and learning as a process of construction during 'sense making' in a culturally alien information environment." International LIS students studying in the U.S. have to learn to function in such information environments. Mehra's narrative interviews of international doctoral students at one university brings to fore the affective, cognitive, and sensorimotor strategies they use in the attempt to cope with information elements and procedures that raise conflicting emotions and doubts.

Although there was significant variation among students in relation to their country of origin, nevertheless they shared some overlapping experiences and challenges. These "commonalities" are related to the social setting requirements of being a foreign graduate student, which involves completing a sequence of enculturating procedures over several months or longer. These include anticipation jitters prior to program initiation, followed by "overwhelming information clutter" as the students gradually acquire the "dominant American way of doing things," which demands that they "de-condition" their past information experiences. Mehra describes the final stage as "enlightened adaptation." The cross-cultural setting of this study has global implications for facilitating information sharing. The "internationalization" of LIS education in the U.S. may become an important factor in promoting "global interconnectedness and interdependence" by creating "globally dispersed knowledge networks."

It is hoped that this volume will inspire those working in information behavior and the related areas of human–computer interaction, information system design, and social informatics, to examine data in the light of the theories and findings presented, and to design studies that focus on the central role of affect in information needs, seeking, reception, design, and use. A focus on affect in information behavior can breathe new life into research by expanding research environments to include every setting where people use and exchange information, including the mental and social information environment, and promote a cumulative and holistic approach to understanding human engagement with information.

REFERENCES

Belkin, N. J. (1980). Anomalous state of knowledge for information retrieval. *Canadian Journal of Information Science, 5*, 133–143.

Dervin, B. (1983, May). *An overview of sense-making research: Concepts, methods and results*. Paper presented at the annual meeting of the International Communication Association, Dallas, TX.

Erikson, E. H. (1950). *Childhood and society*. New York: Norton.

Ingwerson, P. (1992). *Information retrieval interaction*. London: Taylor Graham.

Krathwohl, D. R., Bloom, B. S., & Masia, B. B. (1964). *Taxonomy of educational objectives: The classification of educational goals. Handbook II: Affective domain*. New York: David McKay.

Kuhlthau, C. (1988). Perceptions of the information search process in libraries: A study of changes from high school through college. *Information Processing & Management, 24*(4), 419–427.

Mellon, C. (1986). Library anxiety: A grounded theory and its development. *College & Research Libraries, 47*(2), 160–165.

Nahl, D., & Jakobovits, L. A. (1985). Managing the affective micro-information environment. *Research Strategies, 3*(1), 17–28.

Simon, H. A. (1967). Motivational and emotional controls of cognition. *Psychological Review, 74*(1), 29–39.

Wilson, T. D. (1981). On user studies and information needs. *Journal of Documentation, 37*(1), 3–15. Accessed December 5, 2006, from informationr.net/tdw/publ/papers/1981infoneeds.html.

PART I

Theoretical Frameworks

CHAPTER 1

The Centrality of the Affective in Information Behavior

Diane Nahl
University of Hawaii

INTRODUCTION

This chapter presents a social-biological information technology model of information behavior, provides a theoretical justification, and presents evidence for the model from user studies. The literature review covers research from several fields that examine the affective aspects of behavior, including cognitive science, affective neuroscience, affective computing, affective human–computer interaction, and information science. The approach taken here is holistic, constructionist, and integrative. The information environment is increasingly incorporated in daily life through technology. The accelerated deployment of more encompassing information architectures depends on people's willingness to adapt to them, and thus to receive information through them, and to use them in the practice of social communication. This more pervasive information environment tends toward becoming ubiquitous, encompassing social and personal purposes in daily life. Therefore, there is a distinct need to develop a unified theoretical framework that would encourage discussion of the full range of information behavior studied from specific perspectives and in specific contexts and situations.

A unified theoretical framework needs to integrate the three intersecting zones of the information environment as it exists today, namely, the intersection of technology, human biology, and social structures that define group practices and community values. An information behavior theory should therefore describe a symbiotic integration of technological affordances, social practices, and biological activity such as the user's sensorimotor, cognitive, and affective procedures during information reception and use. These biologically based information behaviors interact with technological affordances and are the embodiments of the community's social life.

The social-biological information technology model presented here is essentially constructionist (Nahl, 2007a, 2007b). The model shows that information behavior and interaction with information systems consists of a continuous dynamic flow of individual biological procedures in an attempt to adapt and cope within a context. Individuals perform sensorimotor, cognitive, and affective procedures in unique adaptation to information ecology.

These unique procedures, or operations, are individually constructed by each person according to that person's participation in group practices. The biological procedures are thus embodiments of group practices.

Another essential feature of the ecological constructionist model is that it applies in a similar way to both micro- and macro-information behaviors. The biological reductionism of the model does not detract from the social constructionism inherent in information behavior. For instance, larger social issues raised by social constructionists in information theory (Tuominen & Savolainen, 1997) are also made visible by the analysis of user discourse, sometimes referred to as interpretive discourse.

There has been a consistent increase in the pace of research on the emotions and feelings people experience while interacting with a variety of information systems and social settings. Designers have incorporated the affective dimensions of technology to the extent that the expression "emotional design" has become identified in ergonomics as "Kansei Engineering" or "pleasurable engineering" (Green & Jordan, 2002; Grimsaeth, 2005; Jordan, 2000). According to Don Norman, "the focus of emotional design [is] to make our lives more pleasurable" (Van Hout, 2004). Examination of papers given at the first Kansei engineering conference of 2006 reveals that designing for pleasurable experiences extends to a wide variety of domains and information settings, including theme park attractions, computer games, automobile driving, image retrieval systems, e-commerce, and recommender systems, among others. This focus on human affective, emotional, or social components of information systems is driving innovative system design in the 21st century.

The central focus of a unified theory of information behavior is the process by which users adapt to the information environment and make use of it for personal and social purposes. By making this adaptation process explicit, the model reveals how the ubiquitous information environment can be viewed as an *affective* information environment because all information needs, seeking, reception, and use is processed through emotions. Discovering the workings of affective information behavior permits designers to apply affective design principles that will spur innovation in humane information system design (Friedman, 1997; Raskin, 2000). This chapter proposes the beginnings of a general framework that could allow researchers to begin discussing information behavior with a common conceptual language, while retaining specific research contexts, and inspiring a focus on the role of emotional aspects in information behavior.

CHARTING THE DYNAMIC FLOW OF INFORMATION RECEPTION AND USE

There are two basic biological functions of the human affective system in relation to information behavior. One function is adapted for reception and evaluation of information, while the other has evolved for the use of information in the purposeful planning of tasks:

> Type I: affective information reception (evaluative and consummatory)

> Type II: affective information use (conative and motivational)

Information reception is an adaptive behavior that involves all three biological systems: sensorimotor, cognitive, and affective. The sensorimotor system functions as a symbiotic interface with the technological system: A computer screen, mouse, and keyboard interact symbiotically with the eyes and hands as we compute. The sensorimotor system transforms the complex physical signal into a coherent and recognizable sensation that we may call "noticing something." We don't notice just anything in the signal. We only notice those aspects of the information that coalesce into some familiar unit, and the rest is ignored. Once we have noticed some information, we immediately strive to make sense of it. This activity is called "appraising" the incoming information.

Noticing information is a group practice that individuals perform through sensorimotor activity, while appraising information that has been noticed is a group practice performed through an individual's cognitive activity. When this cognitive operation is completed, the meaning assigned to the information, including its context or implications, is next processed by the affective system for evaluation or consummation of the appraised information. Evaluation of meaningful information is the cultural or group process of attaching value to received information. This involves the application of group norms about what deserves our love (importance, validity, acceptance), when to be satisfied (needs, attachments, desires, entertainment), or what is deemed preferable at the time (options, priorities, preferences). These evaluative and consummatory feelings and emotions that people attach to information constitute the end point of information reception and adaptation involving the three biological systems.

This dynamic flow involving noticing the information, appraising it, and attaching value to it is continuous throughout information reception, both at the micro and macro levels of information behavior. For instance, when a Web user inspects a screen, continuous eye movement takes place to allow the user to notice what is displayed. These are micro-level sensorimotor adjustments of information reception. Similarly, micro-level cognitive adjustments occur while appraising the meaning of the words and images, and finally affective adjustments as each unit is evaluated in terms of group values or norms. Various details are evaluated as important or unimportant, pleasant or unpleasant, etc. Macro-level units are also processed through the dynamic flow of this biological activity. For instance, users may notice a new logo on a familiar site. The cognitive activity appraises the new item as an announcement for another site, and the affective activity marks it as something intriguing or interesting, arousing emotions of surprise or curiosity.

In general, biological organisms adapt to the environment by noticing information in their daily foraging grounds (Gibson, 1986). Once something is detected by the senses, the sensory information is passed to cognitive appraisal, so that it may be evaluated according to established parameters of survival value. Human organisms adapt to the information environment by interacting with a technological system that displays the information for human reception. These technological devices may be called *satisficing affordances* because they allow humans to consummate the displayed information according to their affective needs and interests. All information reception is completed as a process when the person assigns some value to it. Satisficing affordances are technological devices designed to make information reception possible. They include display screens and computer sounds, as well as directory folders or email notifications.

For example, when we click the "Add to Cart" link during Web shopping, we expect the item to be there on the final list after we click the "Checkout" link, and when we do not find it there, might blurt out, "It's not there. It should be there. Something is wrong." This spontaneous verbalization illustrates the three-step biological procedure of information reception. First, through a sensorimotor procedure, we notice the absence of the expected item on the listing. Second, through a cognitive procedure, we interpret this information as meaning that it's not there when it should be there. Third, through an affective procedure, we evaluate and consummate this information ("Something is wrong."). This adaptation process to information reception and consummation is similar whether the satisficing device is a computer screen or the person we talk to while waiting in a doctor's office. The human agent's verbalizations and the computer's display screens function similarly as satisficing affordances for information reception.

Biological organisms have evolved sensorimotor, cognitive, and affective systems that are not merely receptive of information but are conative or purposive in function (Type II) (Martin & Tesser, 1996). Not only do humans notice, appraise, and evaluate information, they use it to optimize current intentions and goals. For example, when we scroll through a list of search returns, we don't just satisfice the titles of the links by noticing each, appraising its meaning, and evaluating it as wanted or not wanted. We also optimize the information by intending to do something with it, such as forgetting about it, clicking on it, saving it as a favorite for possible later use, clicking on it just to see what it looks like, or clicking on it to read it, etc. There is a multiplicity of momentary goal intentions, or feelings of wanting to engage the system, that we spontaneously experience upon completing the process of information reception. This affective intentionality for optimizing the information after it has been received, is the first step in information use.

The first *optimizing phase* of information use is the affective procedure that we experience as having an intention or purpose in relation to the information that has been satisficed. For example, when verbalizing, "It's not there. It should be there. Something is wrong." we experience the feeling of wanting to do something about it. This is the biological process of affective engagement. It is the operation of intentionality with regard to a technological affordance. We want to tell the computer that something is wrong. We want to tell the computer to fix it. When the affective procedure of intentionality occurs, it spontaneously arouses relevant problem-solving activity in the cognitive system. This affective-cognitive interaction procedure results in a plan that is executable by the sensorimotor action on the system interface. This part of the technological system is called an *optimizing affordance*, because it is designed so a user can influence the system and thus change what it is doing or providing. Information use begins with the intention or motivation to engage the system through its available optimizing affordances, and it is completed when our sensorimotor system acts upon it by touching, clicking, or keyboarding within the limits provided.

For example, the Back button may be called an optimizing affordance because it allows the user's intentional plan to be put into effect by inputting the command to the system. Now the system responds by providing a new display and new affordances, both satisficing and optimizing, re-initiating the flow of information reception by satisficing (noticing, appraising, evaluating), and then through the flow of information use by optimizing (intending, planning, executing). This recurrent dynamic flow of information behavior in the context of reception and use is depicted in Figure 1.1.

Don't make me think!

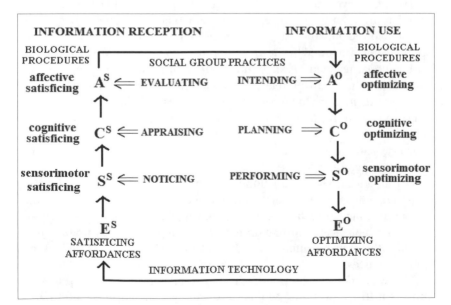

Figure 1.1   Social-Biological Information Technology

As discussed earlier, information reception is a recurrent dynamic flow involving a three-step process during which information is first *noticed*, then *appraised*, and then *evaluated or consummated* in accordance with group practices. This is shown in Figure 1.1 by the ascending path traced as [$E^SS^SC^SA^S$]. These steps describe explicitly how technology supplies a satisficing affordance [E^S] such as a screen display or sound that a user can process in three connected biological procedures within the limits that satisfice existing group standards. To count as noticing the expected features of a display screen, such as images, link titles, and screen positions, each user constructs personal and unique *sensorimotor procedures* [S^S] to satisfy the social requirements of group practice regarding what counts as having been noticed or not. Novice users construct eye movements that are ineffective compared to the habituated eye movements of a skilled user. Web designers regularly use font size, appearance, and screen position to facilitate noticing.

Besides noticing the expected features or affordances, the members of a communication group or work team acquire *cognitive procedures* [C^S] that count in the group as appraising the information appropriately. When we land fortuitously on a Web page in a language foreign to us, we become aware that our normal eye movements are not providing much to appraise with meaning. We can notice font colors and images, if there are any, and possibly links, if they are underlined. Our cognitive procedures cannot satisfice the requirements of group practices on that page. Even Web pages that the user can read may be difficult to appraise meaningfully if they are designed for a technical audience.

There is an evolutionary interdependence among the three biological systems during information reception and adaptation. The cognitive procedures involved in appraising information that was noticed [$E^SS^SC^S$] are spontaneously followed by the *affective procedures* [A^S] that we experience as an emotional reaction or value judgments that have intensity and bipolar directionality (nice-awful, relevant-useless, etc.). It is common to consider feelings and emotions to be personal, yet they are socialized reactions of the affective system in accordance with group values. Since every individual is biologically unique with a unique set of subjective experiences, people spontaneously learn to acquire control over their biological procedures to fit into the group practices.

Learning to survive or function in the information environment involves acquiring biological procedures that satisfice group requirements in a community of practice or task team. All information technology is therefore social and biological. Information reception is a process of symbiotic interaction with satisficing affordances that is kept within the limits set by social group practices.

Figure 1.1 depicts information use in similar terms, as the three-step process in the descending sequence, during which satisfied information [$E^SS^SC^SA^S$] prompts the *motivated intention* [A^O] to engage the optimizing affordance [E^O], through some *planning or directing* [C^O], and then *performing* it [S^O]. The three-step optimizing process is charted in Figure 1.1 by the descending sequence [$A^O C^O S^O E^O$]. Information use is the process of optimizing information that has been received. It is the process of engaging the system actively, by acting on it to achieve a wanted result. Each individual performs information use in three steps. First, there must be present a biological state of conation or motivation to do something about the received information. Lacking this, the information dissipates.

The intention [A^O] to remember the information for later is a minimal way in which people optimize received information. Or, the optimizing intention may go further into formulating a plan of action [$A^O C^O$]. This involves cognitive procedures called optimizing because the cognitive operations are directed by the affective intention or goal one desires to achieve. For instance, you notice [$E^S S^S$] that the text field for your credit card number on a Web site is not on a secure page [C^S], and you react with alarm [$C^S A^S$]. You immediately feel motivated [A^O] to figure out another plan [C^O], executed by clicking back to another page [$S^O E^O$]. Functioning in an information setting requires alternating between steps of reception and steps of use in a continuous dynamic flow.

In the process of performing mental procedures, people make these procedures conform sufficiently to the social meanings, norms, and values they share with a community of practice. Table 1.1 provides additional terms that identify important components of group practices that govern an individual's biological procedures during the three satisficing and three optimizing steps of information reception and use.

Table 1.1 entries show which group practices are performed within each of the three biological systems. For instance, the first step is marked as *noticing practices*, which includes recognizing or perceiving information that is displayed or presented. The specific ways in which an individual performs noticing practices through sensorimotor procedures [S^S] is controlled by the group practices for what people notice in that information context. What is being noticed and ignored is dictated by group norms, and the individual learns these norms by being a participant. The verbal expressions and sentences an individual constructs may be unique according to personal style, but every sentence is generated by commonly known grammatical rules that people use. Similarly, what we notice on a display [$E^S S^S$] or how we appraise [C^S] and evaluate [A^S] incoming information is dictated by social practices in the context of people's information behavior.

EVIDENCE FOR THE MODEL

Traditionally, the field of cognitive science has relied on overt indices of thought processes and feelings. Two successful approaches in information science have been the *think aloud method* and the *concurrent report method* (Ericsson & Simon, 1993). Nahl (2005a, 2006) analyzed the sentences that

Table 1.1   Additional Terms Referring to the Social Group
Practices Portrayed in Figure 1.1

Step 1 [S^S] Noticing Practices (by performing sensorimotor satisficing procedures)	Step 2 [C^S] Appraising Practices (by performing cognitive satisficing procedures)	Step 3 [A^S] Evaluating Practices (by performing affective satisficing procedures)
identifying ignoring locating perceiving recognizing sensing attending orienting etc.	interpreting or categorizing justifying or giving reasons attributing cause comparing or limiting explaining or listing etc.	value-attaching or rating applying reference norms prioritizing or ranking accepting vs. avoiding feeling satisfied vs. not consummating or filling a need feeling attracted or interested vs. not etc.
Step 6 [S^O] **Performing Practices** (by performing sensorimotor optimizing procedures)	**Step 5** [C^O] **Planning Practices** (by performing cognitive optimizing procedures)	**Step 4** [A^O] **Intending Practices** (by performing affective optimizing procedures)
performing or acting keyboarding or texting verbalizing or languaging inspecting or reading purchasing or waiting clicking or moving the mouse etc.	predicting or problem-solving designing or scheduling inventing or extending imagining or picturing managing or setting objectives etc.	purpose or goal-setting regulating or directing striving or persisting intending or wanting to engaging or making use of implementing or adopting looking for or searching etc.

people typed to describe concurrently what they are in the process of doing while shopping on the Web and performing other online tasks. The discourse analysis of hundreds of such samples showed that users invariably describe what they are doing online in terms of sensorimotor interactions with technological devices, cognitive-affective processing of information, and the social constraints of the context.

Consider the following brief illustration, consisting of a discourse sample from an adult user who was instructed to type notes while carrying out a Web shopping session. The notes were kept to help future students to perform the same task. The two-sentence fragment is typical of what people write in such self-reports. In this type of *user discourse* (Nahl 1993, 2005a, 2006, 2007a, 2007b), every sentence is first segmented into smaller units called *information speech acts*, each being categorized, if possible, into one of the three biological domains of information behavior: affective, cognitive, and sensorimotor. Next, the fragment was categorized as either satisficing or optimizing. Finally, the sequence was charted on Figure 1.1.

> *After searching for the first article, I had clicked on new search to look for the second article, but the steps became more confusing. Therefore, I found that it was much easier to just back space all the way back to the main page of the electronic database and search the second article from the beginning as if it was the first one.*
>
> *After searching for the first article,*
> > [C^O] cognitive optimizing procedure – <u>planning</u> the sequence of search strategy
>
> *I had clicked on new search*
> > [S^O] sensorimotor optimizing procedure – <u>clicking</u> on an optimizing affordance
>
> *to look for the second article,*
> > [A^O] affective optimizing procedure – <u>motivated intention</u> to search for something
>
> *but the steps became more confusing.*
> > [A^S] affective satisficing procedure – <u>evaluating</u> the uncertainty in the search process
>
> *Therefore,*
> > [C^O] cognitive optimizing procedure – <u>planning</u> the sequence of the search strategy
>
> *I found that it was much easier*
> > [A^S] affective satisficing procedure – <u>evaluating</u> the difficulty in the search process
>
> *to just back space all the way back to the main page of the electronic database and search the second article from the beginning*
> > [C^O] cognitive optimizing procedure – <u>planning</u> the sequence of the search strategy
>
> *as if it was the first one.*
> > [C^S] cognitive satisficing procedure – <u>appraising</u> the sequence of the search strategy
> > Charting the Dynamic Flow: [$C^O S^O A^O A^S C^O A^S C^O C^S$]
> > Or: [planning, performing, intending, evaluating, planning, evaluating, planning, appraising]

This charted flow indicates the characteristics of the mental processes that the person performs while engaged in the described information behavior. The charted flow shows that using the computer to search a database consists of a string of micro-behaviors involving the three biological domains of information behavior (Nahl, 2006). Each domain participates in a string of either a receptive-adaptive function (satisficing) or an active-engaging function (optimizing). Figure 1.1 illustrates the sequence of such activities. The model shows how information behavior is constructed out of information micro-behaviors in which the affective system plays a pivotal role for information reception and use. Not all components of the model are mentioned in any single sample of user discourse, but they are all mentioned in larger discourse segments.

Information behavior can be understood more completely and holistically when viewed as an activity at the intersection of information technology, biological mental procedures, and social practices in communicative exchanges. Information technology is designed to provide ways in which people's biological operations can interact with information transmitted within a social context or community. For instance, instant messaging (IM) systems are technological devices that allow real time social exchanges between any two individuals over the Internet. IM information behavior consists of typing sentences to each other within this social context. Of course, keyboarding and reading the screen are merely the overt visible components of the information behavior. Typed sentences are sensorimotor acts generated by cognitive operations of thinking, remembering, connecting facts, interpreting intentions, etc. But what we recall from memory or which facts we connect together at a particular time depends on the purpose or intention. These are affective states of motivation, need, interest, and value.

Lewis and Fabos (2005) report that "IM offered the excitement of successfully staying on top of the information flow" while it "assuaged social relations, making all potentially threatening exchanges (such as face to face or telephone) less so." These young people preferred IM instead of chatrooms because "communicating with strangers was not nearly as engaging as communicating with one's peers." Figure 1.1 offers a framework for depicting and understanding information behavior at both the macro and micro level. For instance, at the macro level, IM may be viewed globally as a series of normalized exchanges between individuals known to each other.

The flow of these macro exchanges rendered in Figure 1.1 involves the threefold biological mental micro procedures each individual performs in accordance with the group practices and norms regarding what to *notice or ignore* [S^S] (e.g., normal vs. special markers), how to *appraise* it [C^S] (e.g., how will others take this), and how it measures up to the *evaluative norms* of the group [A^S] (e.g., is it exciting or innovative). Once a message is satisficed through this sequence of mental micro-behaviors, the receiver engages the optimizing affordances of the system, using the threefold mental biological procedures in the reverse sequence from reception. First, the satisficed information is affectively optimized [A^O] by forming the *intention* to reply, or to contact someone else about it, through the cognitive formulation of a *plan* [C^O] and its immediate *sensorimotor* execution [S^O] by manipulating the appropriate optimizing affordances (e.g., send message mode, attach or insert other things, etc.).

According to Lewis and Fabos (2005), "literacy involves the designing and redesigning of social futures. The core concept here is that in order to make meaning, one must have access to available resources for designs (semiotic systems), ways to engage in design (semiotic processes), and the means to transform designs (a combination of received meanings and the agency to redesign them)." Figure 1.1 describes the process of constructing meaning $[C^S]$ as dependent on two types of affective procedures: $[A^S]$ and $[A^O]$. One involves consummatory and evaluative feelings of information reception vs. rejection $[A^S]$. The other involves feelings of intentionality $[A^O]$ toward optimizing affordances $[E^O]$. Receiving information through the available satisficing affordances and engaging the system through the optimizing affordances that are provided are the two general components of information behavior during computer-mediated interaction. These two types of technological devices are the "available resources" for users to carry out their intentions in "design and redesign" within their community of practice. Technology thus becomes a symbiotic extension of human feelings. It is the user's feelings that dictate how information is received, that is, the specific appraising and value-attaching procedures $[E^S S^S C^S A^S]$, and likewise, it is feelings that dictate how information is used for planning, performing, and languaging $[A^O C^O S^O E^O]$.

Information behavior viewed at both the macro and micro levels is a regulated flow of cognitive-affective procedures that the person operates in conformity with the group norms practiced in common. Consider another illustration in the following brief discourse segment, constructed by a young adult upon agreeing to help his friend learn to use eBay. The exchange was tape recorded and transcribed:

> AC: *Delete the current web address* $[S^O]$ *shown on your browser* $[S^S]$ *and type "ebay".* $[S^O]$ *Press enter.* $[S^O]$ *This should* $[A^S]$ *then* $[C^O]$ *take you to the eBay website.* $[C^S]$ *What do you want to search for* $[A^O]$ *or bid on?* $[A^O]$
>
> MC: *Let's say* $[A^O]$ *a Prada jacket* $[A^O]$
>
> AC: *If you have something in particular* $[C^O]$ *you want* $[A^O]$ *you should be more specific* $[A^S]$ *such as white small Prada jacket* $[C^S]$ *just* $[A^S]$ *to narrow down the search* $[A^O]$

Clearly the information behavior involved in using eBay is governed by specific group practices, such as how to phrase a query for a wanted object, or what it means to "bid" for one, and what is the appropriate sequence for doing it. The user discourse constructed by this individual reveals the information behavior micro units that he constructs to enact the community information practices of eBay. His information behavior is partly constructed out of his symbiotic interactions with the technological affordances involved (navigation, searching, bidding, email). The sensorimotor optimizing procedures he performs [S^O] consist of engaging the keyboard (delete, type, enter), while the sensorimotor satisficing procedures he performs [S^S] concern what he should be noticing on the screen, both the general aspects, such as recognizing where one is, and the particular aspects of where one has access to certain information or actions.

Besides these symbiotic sensorimotor procedures, there are cognitive procedures being performed, such as appraising whether this is the right site you want to be on now [C^S] or else planning the search sequence or navigation sequence [C^O]. In the sample discourse segment just discussed, the user focuses on the affective procedures more than the other two, with several affective optimizing procedures [A^O] in evidence, such as intending to search or bid for something specific, as well as some affective satisficing procedures [A^S], such as evaluating the search parameters to conform to group norms in context (e.g., *Prada jacket* is not as good as *small white Prada jacket*).

Analysis of hundreds of samples from a variety of contexts (Nahl, 1995, 2005a, 2006, 2007a) shows that *user discourse* reflects the basis for human–computer interaction because it corresponds to how users recognize, think, feel, intend, and execute plans while performing information behavior to conform to group practices in interaction with technological affordances.

MEASURES OF AFFECTIVE SATISFICING AND OPTIMIZING PROCEDURES

Affective states have a variety of biologically based characteristics:

- *Bipolarity* (e.g., this is fun vs. boring; I feel engaged vs. disconnected)

- *Intensity* (e.g., it is very relevant vs. only somewhat relevant)

- *Steady state* (e.g., being optimistic; having a need; being motivated)

- *Ambivalence or uncertainty* (e.g., it's good in some ways but not in others)

- *Neutrality* (e.g., I'm neither accepting nor rejecting it)

Bipolar self-rating scales have been frequently used to measure an individual's affective states. Nahl (1993, 2001, 2005a) used bipolar semantic differential scales (Osgood, Suci, & Tannenbaum, 1957) to measure searchers' affective load, search self-efficacy feelings, optimism, time pressure, frustration, affective uncertainty, system loyalty, expected effort, and degree of motivation for completion. The individual is the objective source of those mental states indexed by user discourse. Part of becoming information literate is to understand and produce user discourse. Help instructions are commonly cast as user discourse, for instance, in Microsoft Word Help:

> *To insert a manual page break* [A^O], *click* [S^{O}E^O] *where you want* [A^O] *to start a new page* [C^O]. *On the Insert menu* [E^{S}S^S], *click Break* [S^{O}E^O]. *Click Page break* [S^{O}E^O].
> Charting the entire flow: [A^{O}S^{O}E^{O}A^{O}C^{O}E^{S}S^{S}S^{O}E^{O}S^{O}E^O]
> Or: [intending, performing, intending, planning, noticing, performing, performing]

The reason help instructions follow the dynamic flow elements charted in Figure 1.1 is that help instructions model how users notice, think, and intend when interacting with technological affordances. The instructions are understandable to users to the extent that the discourse realistically models the user's biological procedures.

Since affective and cognitive information behavior cannot be observed directly, operational definitions of these biological procedures may be given in terms of concurrent structured self-reports, in spontaneous user discourse, and in bipolar ratings provided concurrently with users' performance of information tasks. It is generally accepted that the ability to self-monitor a person's affective, cognitive, and sensorimotor procedures during information tasks is a form of literacy. People who have not acquired this self-witnessing ability are less likely to understand and follow instructions, and they will be less capable of describing a problem when requesting help. People have the ability to report what they are thinking at any particular moment, as well as what feelings, moods, and intentions they actively or consciously maintain, such as how motivated they are, how much frustration they are experiencing and willing to tolerate, what their preference rankings are for a list of options, and what is the goal hierarchy in their motivation, and they are able to state satisficing norms for what is to count as enough.

Affective Measures with Self-Ratings

Nahl (2004, 2005a) used the combined scores of two or more scales to increase the reliability of affective measures. Such compounded measures reduce the variance and stabilize the mean at a significantly lower standard error. The following are some examples:

Task Completion Motivation (TCM) [A^O] on Figure 1.1

This is an affective optimizing procedure involving intensity of motivation that a user has for completing a computer task and is measured by structured self-monitoring items such as:

> How important to you is this task today? Not important (1) to Extremely important (10).

> How upset would you be if you found nothing today? Not upset (1) to Extremely upset (10).

Uncertainty Feelings in Information Seeking *(U)* [A^S] on Figure 1.1

This is an affective satisficing procedure that is generally experienced as negative or distressing when it is intense. The escalating emotionality is defined through four intensity phases of *affective uncertainty*, namely, irritation, anxiety, frustration, and rage, as measured by such items as:

> How much irritation [anxiety, frustration, rage] did you feel in today's search task? No irritation (1) to Extremely irritated (10).

Time Pressure *(TP)* [A^S] on Figure 1.1

This is an affective satisficing procedure that intensifies the uncertainty component. For instance, when time pressure is low, uncertainty may not reach beyond irritation and anxiety. But when time pressure is high, the person is affected by frustration and even rage. Time pressure is measured by subtracting "Felt Length" at task completion from "Expected Length" at the start (anticipatory affect):

$$TP = Expected\ Length - Felt\ Length$$

Expected Length is measured by this item given at the beginning of the session:

> How long do you think this task will actually take today? Much less than others (1) to Much more than others (10).

At the end of the session, this item measures actual Felt Length:

> If you compare this task to other search tasks you've done, how long did it take? Much less than others (1) to Much more than others (10).

Affective Load *(AL)* [A^S] on Figure 1.1

This affective satisficing procedure refers to uncertainty multiplied by time pressure:

$$AL = U \times TP$$

When affective load is relatively high in a task, the person requires adequate coping skills to avoid quitting, along with experiencing negative feelings of dissatisfaction or failure. When affective load is low, the user is not as challenged by the negative consequences of uncertainty.

User Coping Skills *(UCS)* [A^S] on Figure 1.1

This affective satisficing procedure is defined by two affective subcomponents acting together: Self-Efficacy (SE) and Search Optimism (Op):

$$UCS = SE + Op$$

Self-efficacy is measured by these three items given at the beginning of the session:

> How sure are you that you will succeed in this task? Doubtful (1) to Almost certain (10).

> How likely is it that you will become good at this type of task? Pretty doubtful (1) to Almost certain (10).

> How much luck do you have in searching in comparison to other types of tasks? I have bad luck (1) to I always find something useful (10).

Search optimism is measured by the following three items given at the beginning of the session:

> How motivated are you to keep on trying today until you succeed? Slightly motivated (1) to Very highly motivated (10).

> Computers and search engines make it easy for people to find what they're looking for. I strongly disagree (1) to I very much agree (10).

> How likely is it that there will be something specific on what you're looking for? Not likely (1) to Very likely (10).

Evaluation of Search Episodes [A^S] on Figure 1.1

This affective satisficing procedure is measured by the extent to which users feel that they have met their search goal for the task. Since goals for a task may be complex and multiple, several sub-components need to be measured. Evaluation is defined by two sub-components: Worthwhile and Relevance.

Worthwhile = Expected Effort – Felt Effort

Expected Effort is an affective satisficing procedure measured by self-ratings prior to beginning the task. The affective satisficing procedure Felt Effort is measured at the completion of the task. If the Expected Effort (pre) is greater than the Felt Effort (post), users feel that the time and effort were Worthwhile (i.e., a positive feeling of reward). But if the Felt Effort is greater than the Expected Effort, there is an accompanying feeling of dissatisfaction or ambivalence:

> How much effort do you expect this task to take today? Not much (1) to A tremendous amount (10).

> How much effort did this task require of you today compared to other search tasks in your experience? Much less than others (1) to Much more than others (10).

Relevance is measured by users' rating of the search results on a scale of relevance to what they had been hoping to find. Satisfaction is defined by the summation of Worthwhile and Relevance:

Satisfaction = Worthwhile + Relevance

Acceptance of Search Environment [A^S] on Figure 1.1

This affective satisficing procedure is measured by the amount of support the user feels for the system environment through which the search was performed. This is measured by items given at the end of the session:

> How supportive are you of the search engine or computer facility you used today? Not supportive (1) to Very supportive (10).

> How easy was it to use the search engine or computer facility today? Very easy (1) to Very difficult (10).

There is need for a variety of measures of affective information behaviors since the affective domain of human life is so complex and vast, including values that are attached to emotions, and intentions that are based on what people want and seek.

AFFECTIVE MEASURES USING DISCOURSE ANALYSIS AND TAXONOMIC CLASSIFICATION

Nahl (1993, 2006, 2007a, 2007b) has shown that the interpretive discourse constructed by users in their structured self-reports can be segmented into minimal meaningful units termed *information speech acts*. As shown in the user discourse analyses, information speech acts correspond to sensorimotor, cognitive, and affective procedures carried out in the user's interaction with information affordances. Nahl (1993) analyzed the information speech act units constructed by librarians in point of use instructions for "How to Print" or "Search Tips." It was discovered that increasing the affective to cognitive ratio of speech acts in the written instructions had significant positive effects for novice users. By inserting additional affective information speech acts that gave encouragement and reassurance, the instructions were significantly more helpful and easier to understand, as evidenced by student ratings.

Nahl (1995) examined the information speech acts of college students that they constructed in interpretive discourse as concurrent self-reports ("This is what I am doing now"). Students were assigned various search tasks to perform using electronic resources. Based on the segmented analysis of user discourse, Nahl discovered three levels of focus in learning the Internet (see Table 1.2).

Taxonomy of Technophobia

The taxonomic approach illustrated in Table 1.2 can serve as an objective method for discovering the biological procedures that users perform while

Table 1.2 Developmental Levels of Learning the Internet

Levels of Internet Adaptation	Affective Procedures	Cognitive Procedures
Level 1 Achieving Focus	Striving for accuracy on Internet tasks	Observing and noting differences
	Having the motive to persist with Internet tasks	Identifying one's problems on Internet
Level 2 Achieving Engagement	Feeling self-confident	Predicting and expecting Internet functions
	Having the desire for mastery of Internet tasks	Making inferences about what leads to what
Level 3 Achieving Acceptance	Having the desire to complete Internet tasks	Evolving an Internet map as a context for new tasks
	Feeling symptoms of attraction to Internet tasks (love, excitement)	Finding Internet personally relevant

interacting with information affordances. To illustrate this possibility, the generic ACS biological taxonomy (Jakobovits & Nahl, 1987, 1990; Nahl, 1993, 1995) was applied to an extensive set of user errors collected over several years while observing online searching of novices in an academic library. Items were selected that referred in some way to technophobia and were defined as expressing an affective information problem. The results are summarized in Table 1.3 (based on Nahl, 2001).

Affective information procedures that users construct at developmental level 1 consist of elementary but essential activities such as exercising a person's willingness [A^O] to engage in cognitive activity like figuring out the directions [C^S] and executing them [S^O], or pulling down a menu of resources, and highlighting and selecting one. Or, they must overcome their fear [A^S] before they can fully comprehend the instructions. Level 1 technophobic behaviors occur in information settings where people are learning unfamiliar systems and making adjustments to new demands imposed by the information environment. Technophobic behaviors, such as expressing fear, avoiding doing something required, or feeling pessimistic, are negative affective satisficing procedures that inhibit the processing of the instructional information, and instead facilitate the processing of competing information supplied by the person's imagination, such as "I can't do this" or "This thing never works for me."

Negative affective information procedures that people construct at developmental level 2 consist of putting up various types of resistance to becoming an independent user. Individuals sometimes resist or avoid [A^O]

Table 1.3 Affective Taxonomy of Technophobia Experienced by Novice Searchers

Problem Level	Affective Procedures of Technophobia
1 Information Adjustment Problems	Unwilling to receive assistance when needed
	Averse to reading screen instructions
	Shyness, cultural norms, shame
	Feeling overwhelmed, intimidated, time-pressured
2 Search Process Problems	Low self-efficacy evaluation
	Resistance to viewing searching as an iterative problem-solving process
	Lacking confidence as a searcher, feeling inadequate
	Mental inertia, mental chaos
3 Personal Information Problems	Avoiding exchanges with information professionals
	Distrusting the system
	Fear of rejection, fear of disapproval, cultural norms, shame
	Pessimism, cynicism, feeling depersonalized

controlled vocabulary [C^O] in composing search queries [S^{O}E^O] and continue to use natural language that creates difficulty in result sets. Some lack confidence as a searcher or adopt pessimistic expectations or anticipations that discourages them [A^O] from continuing with the learning activity, or they skip a specific activity, such as being told to carefully inspect a menu, due to the desire to show resistance to stepping through the process [A^O]. Search process problems (problem level 2) are more advanced or serious than information adjustment problems (level 1), but both types occur and recur throughout the learning stages, as evidenced by longitudinal self-reports.

Even more serious are the negative affective information procedures that people construct at developmental level 3, which consist of various affective procedures that become a liability to functioning adequately in the information environment. In other words, *there is an unwillingness* [A^O] *to adopt group practices in information reception and use.* One example is someone who persistently clings to negative attitudes about technology [A^S], resulting in the intention to avoid using the available technology [A^O]. Some people maintain a long-held aversion for technical details, procedures, and requirements [C^O], resulting in reduced performance and productivity [S^{O}E^O]. They avoid asking questions, refrain from seeking help, and don't trust the system. In short, they remove themselves from information literacy practices and do not learn.

Learned Affective Norms (LANs)

An essential part of the framework of ecological constructionism portrayed in Figure 1.1 is the controlling interaction between social group practices and the individual's biological procedures during the dynamic flow of information behavior. Nahl (1997, 1998a) used the method of *accounted ratings* to observe the nature of the interaction effect between cognitive and affective procedures that users reported while carrying out assigned online tasks. Table 1.4 presents some data obtained from concurrent self-ratings of college students regarding one particular, often reported, affective satisficing procedure: *feeling anxious* [A^S] about successfully completing course-integrated online information assignments.

How anxious did you feel in today's search task?

| 1 | 2 | 3 | 4 | 5 | 6 | 7 | 8 | 9 | 10 |

not anxious   extremely anxious

Please type an explanation for your answer:

The intensity and polarity of the self-rating is taken as an index of the intensity and quality of the affective procedure involved [$A^S A^O C^O S^O E^O$]. In other words, the rating score itself [$S^O E^O$] is produced by the person's affective state of felt anxiety [A^S], which leads to the motivation [A^O] to select from the available choices and definitions [C^O] given on the scale. Selecting a rating of "2" [$S^O E^O$] is produced by a different affective motivation [A^O] than a rating of "9" [S^O]. Table 1.4 is ordered by the intensity of ratings for which the explanations were given (each rating in the table represents a different student). The third column presents the LANs of anxiety [A^S] as rated by intensity in the first column and their cognitive justifications [C^S]. LANs are learned affective norms or procedures that students construct in conformity with group practices. Since a college classroom brings together people from a variety of distinct communities of practice, the data reflect these differences in the social area of feeling anxiety (i.e., when, how much, and with what consequences).

Table 1.4 presents the cognitive justifications student searchers give for the affective norm of feeling anxious and how strongly. The table may be summarized for greater clarity as follows:

Feeling anxious—None: affectivity 1–2

- No time pressure
- Search success not required

Feeling anxious—Somewhat: affectivity 3–4

- Uncertainty of success
- First user of this system

Feeling anxious—Quite a bit: affectivity 5–7

- Rushing due to closing hour

- Pressure to come up with something

Feeling anxious—Extreme: affectivity 8–10

- It's taking too long

- Pressure to finish even though sleepy

- Pressure to meet deadline

There are two main categories of justifying the LAN of anxiety in information searching: *affective uncertainty* and *time pressure*. Both of these affective

Table 1.4 Learned Affective Norms (LANs) of Feeling Anxious and Their Cognitive Justifications

SELF-RATING	EXPLANATIONS CONSTRUCTED BY DIFFERENT SEARCHERS	LEARNED AFFECTIVE NORMS [A^S]	COGNITIVE JUSTIFICATION [C^S]
1	I was not anxious at all. I feel better that I am working on this research weekly so not to get stressed out later. It is not due till next week, which helps me not be anxious.	NONE	When there is no time pressure
2	The results of this particular search did not have a very high level of importance to me (only at this particular time).	NONE	When search success is not required
3	I felt a little anxious hoping to find a useful article.	SOMEWHAT	When there is uncertainty of success
4	This is the first time that I used the library catalog and its databases.	SOMEWHAT	When being a first time user of a system
6	The computer lab is closing soon so I feel rushed.	QUITE A BIT	When rushing due to time pressure
7	I was a little anxious because it was in the back of my mind that I needed something to use in my research.	QUITE A BIT	When feeling pressure to get something
8	Because it took forever to find something relevant.	QUITE A BIT	When it takes longer than expected
9	I am extremely anxious at this point because I want to finish writing up my report but I am sleepy and just want to go to bed, but I know when I wake up I would not have finished my task, and all day at school I am going to be stressed out because it is going to be at the back of mind that I did not complete my task.	EXTREMELY	When feeling pressure to finish even though sleepy
10	The due date is extremely near.	EXTREMELY	When feeling pressure due to a close deadline

factors were significantly related in prior research to coping skills, satisfaction, and self-efficacy (Nahl, 2004).

HISTORY OF THE AFFECTIVE REVOLUTION IN INFORMATION SCIENCE

Research in cognitive science, affect control theory, affective neuroscience, affective computing, and affective human–computer interaction provides foundational concepts, principles, and findings to inform information science and information behavior research. These research areas exemplify the ferment in the field regarding the examination of and the significance of the role of affect in human endeavors.

Cognitive Science

The expression "affective revolution" has been used to mark a change in discourse practices regarding feelings. Investigators in social history and culture have used the expression "affective revolution" in connection with the 19th-century paradigm shift in viewing the family from a "utilitarian to a more emotive bond" (Burrell, 1997). Sadl (1996) examined the content of interpretive discourse in turn-of-the-century parenting manuals showing how "feeling norms" and "feeling rules" were promoted as standards of evaluation in a particular society (Slovenia), during a particular period (1850–1930) regarding a specific emotion such as *anger*. The social environment of people as human information affordances to each other involves "social arrangements" or interactional norms and practices, which specify the appropriate or permissible ranges of expressing particular affective procedures such as anger. In this situation, government-produced instruction booklets advised parents when to allow their children to express anger and in what way, and how to punish the children when they went beyond these satisficing bounds.

The affective procedure of value-attaching [A^S] involves applying community promoted frames of evaluation. Sadl argues that "we can understand the full significance of feeling norms in a society only if we accept that emotions are functional or subversive in the maintenance of the existing social order" (Sadl, 1996, p. 958). In this historical instance, mothers were instructed "to be sure not to smile at the child if he is angry" or "If he doesn't stop to express anger, scare him." Children were to be informed, "anger is the dark side of your heart" and "must be suppressed." Sadl proposed the term "emotiology" for the new awareness in the social sciences of the importance of emotions in maintaining social systems and calls it the "affective revolution."

Currently, the affective revolution is active in the fields of business and economics. Ashkanasy and Daus (2005) review the literature and conclude that "emotional intelligence is attracting deserved continuing research interest as an individual difference variable in organizational behavior related to the way members perceive, understand, and manage their emotions." The application of emotional intelligence principles has been successfully implemented in motivational and leadership training for business managers (Huang, Law, & Wong, 2006). In U.S. public schools, a "self-science curriculum" has been used to reduce conflict and aggression among students by teaching them to recognize and regulate their affective procedures while interacting with other children, and thus establishing the bounds of group practices (McCown, Freedman, Jensen, & Rideout, 1998). Emotional intelligence training teaches more adaptive affective satisficing procedures [A^S] and more effective affective optimizing procedures [A^O].

According to Dervin (2003), "Sense-Making asks informants to talk in terms of their real material conditions and situations and the ideas, conclusions, emotions, feelings, questions, confusions they had and the connections between these and their past horizons (past experiences, lived conditions) and their future horizons (hopes, dreams, plans)." In their appraisal theory of emotions, Ortony and Turner (1990) consider the issue of the "cognitive-emotion interface." They define emotion as an "affective reaction" [A^S] to "cognitive appraisal of the situation in terms of likely consequences" [C^S]. "Event based emotions" are reactions [A^S] to what we observe in our environment [$E^S S^S C^S$]. "Attribution emotions" [$C^S A^S$] are reactions to what we notice others are doing [$E^S S^S$] or have done. At the same time, Ortony and Turner (1990; Ortony, Clore, & Collins, 1988) recognize that the "appraisal mechanism that underlies emotion" [C^S] is necessary for the affective reaction [A^S] "but not sufficient."

Affect Control Theory

Affect control theory insists that cognitive processes cannot be understood without recognizing the mechanism by which feelings and emotions control the parameters of every cognitive operation. Frijda, Manstead, and Bem (2000) examine current research on the "belief-emotion" relation, concluding that the "impact of emotion on beliefs has been unduly neglected in the past" (p. 8), and they encourage more research in the disciplines on this causal connection. According to Nahl (1998a), "The searcher's affective filters are set to keep out or let pass anything that is felt to be not relevant to the currently defined search topic. The *affective filter* delineates the scope of the cognitive content for inclusion or exclusion within the query formulation" (p. 60). For instance, when browsing, what we are interested in [A^S] determines our intention [A^O], our strategy [C^O], and our execution [S^O], consequently what we ignore and don't notice [S^S], what we look at more closely, where we stop, and what we click [$S^O E^O$]. The affective system [$A^S A^O$] is clearly in charge of all aspects of information processing and use.

People make use of a diversity of evaluative frames of reference by which they attach particular types of value to incoming information [A^S]. *Each distinct evaluative frame of reference is a social repertoire of information practices in a particular information ecology.* Adapting and functioning in a new group context requires learning the procedures already practiced by the regulars in that setting. This means that new emotions and feelings must occur, reflecting the commonly agreed upon evaluative frame of reference in that setting.

An individual is not a fully engaged participant until the information environment occasions the new feelings and the individual resonates affectively with the other members of the group. In the ecological constructionism framework of Figure 1.1, the individual, the group, and the information system form one interdependent modular unit embodied in the practices of the group regarding the noticing $[S^S]$, appraising $[C^S]$, and evaluating $[A^S]$ of satisficing affordances $[E^S]$, and the use of optimizing affordances $[E^O]$ for intentional goal-setting $[A^O]$, planning $[C^O]$, and executing $[S^O]$.

According to MacKinnon (1994), "after cognitive processes have narrowed the choice of behavior to a smaller set, affective processes kick in to narrow the choice to a single option." The basic principle of affect control theory is that evaluative and consummatory feelings $[A^S]$ are spontaneously occasioned when people appraise $[C^S]$ the information they can notice $[E^S S^S]$. These emotional-evaluative feeling procedures $[A^S]$ are adaptive to the ecology or "appropriate" to the situation. When certain feelings, emotions, and mood states $[A^S]$ are present or active prior to the appraising procedure $[C^S]$, they may not be appropriate to the situation $[E^S]$; if they persist during the appraising procedure $[C^S]$, they promote maladaptive behavior, like the levels of technophobia discussed earlier. The individual is then unable to cope effectively with the optimizing affordances in the information environment $[E^O]$, and consequently, the individual is not engaging, using, or practicing them. When there is failure in coping with the incoming information, the satisficing evaluation procedure $[A^S]$ will be negative, avoidant, or aversive. This maladaptive condition occurs in information seeking when the affective load felt by users overwhelms coping skills (Nahl, 2004, 2005b).

Scheutz and Sloman (2001) explicitly recognize the satisficing and optimizing functions of affect control, though they use other terms. They refer to "two aspects that are relevant to a variety of architectures, namely direction and evaluation." What they term *evaluation* is referred to in Figure 1.1 as an affective satisficing procedure $[A^S]$, and what they term *direction* is an affective optimizing procedure (goal feelings or intentions) $[A^O]$. "Either way affective states are examples of control states" (Scheutz & Sloman, 2001, p. 2). They indicate that the affective domain $[A^S A^O]$ is capable of "detecting mismatch" between the incoming information and the desired goal state. When this occurs, there is a "disposition" to reset the goal to allow for the mismatch—and this is a satisficing procedure. This is achieved by revising the appraisal, which is a cognitive satisficing procedure $[C^S]$. The entire process is traceable on Figure 1.1 as the path $[A^O C^O C^S A^S A^O]$, or [intending, planning, appraising, evaluating, intending].

Alice Isen (2004), a strong proponent of the affective revolution in cognitive psychology, reviews the extensive evidence accumulated in that field regarding how "affective states [A] can markedly influence everyday thought processes [C], and do so regularly" (p. 417). Positive feelings have the power to "cue positive material in memory ... making it more likely that positive material will 'come to mind'" (p. 417). The evidence overwhelmingly demonstrates that "common positive feelings are fundamentally involved in cognitive organization and processing" (p. 417). Isen hypothesizes that the enhancing influence of positive affect on cognition, including openness to information reception and greater levels of aspiration and exploration, may be related to neurotransmitters like dopamine being present in greater quantities during positive affect states (p. 430).

"Negative affectivity" (Watson & Clark, 1984) can be defined in terms of Figure 1.1, as a predisposition to performing affective satisficing procedures [A^S] that apply a self-critical value frame of reference, which evokes inhibitory and diffused optimizing goal-setting [A^O] and planning [C^O]. This maladaptive optimizing procedure [A^{O}C^O] occasions maladaptive cognitive procedures during appraising that highlight the threatening features of a situation. The chain continues with new maladaptive optimizing goal feelings that lead to threat-avoidant behavior that inhibits engagement and intentionality, reducing a person's ability to be productive and effective in the situation. Negative affectivity research in organizational settings generally supports its relationship to job stress, role conflict, and turnover intentions (Barsky, Thoresen, Warren, & Kaplan, 2004).

Dania Bilal (2004, pp. 278–280) reviews the research on children's information seeking on the Web and finds that children experience similar coping issues and find searching both challenging and delightful. Bilal recommends taking a developmental approach, involving children in designing interfaces and search engines for children. Children in these studies enjoyed a sense of mastery, self-confidence, and satisfaction with relevant results [A^S], but expressed negative feelings when they experienced difficulty with deep subject hierarchies and advanced vocabulary, keyword searching, and irrelevant or advanced results.

Affective load theory (Nahl, 2005b) states that successful information behavior depends on counterbalancing procedures to regulate the negative and positive affective forces operating on individuals in information intense environments. The negative forces are aversive affective evaluations [A^S] and are occasioned during appraising by a cognitive procedure that ends with *cognitive* uncertainty [C^S], which frequently accompanies particular phases of information seeking (Kuhlthau, 2004; Spink, Wilson, Ford, Foster, & Ellis, 2002; Wilson, Ford, Ellis, Foster, & Spink, 2000). *Affective* uncertainty manifests itself in negative feelings such as irritation, frustration, stress, and even rage.

Nahl (2005a) discovered that searchers who have strong, positive affective coping skills, such as high self-efficacy and optimism, make use of satisficing procedures with less variability than searchers who obtain lower optimism and self-efficacy scores. Affective variability was measured by the standard error of affective self-ratings over weekly search sessions. This finding "indicates that less affective variability, or more affective stability, is part of the dynamic property of affective coping" (p. 33). Nahl predicts that the information environment will be able to provide design features that occasion a more stable affective environment supported by effective coping skills. Results show that these coping skills provide a "significant affective advantage as indicated by higher optimism, stronger self-efficacy, lower uncertainty, higher support and acceptance of the system, and smaller affective load" (Nahl 2005b, p. 25).

Affective Neuroscience

Panksepp (1998) discusses the effort to introduce into cognitive science the "evolutionary antecedents, such as the neural systems for the passions, upon which our vast cortical potentials are built and to which those potentials may still be subservient" (p. 5). In other words, the newer cognitive capacities ("cortical potentials") that have evolved as higher information systems are still connected to and founded upon the older emotional brain ("neural systems for the passions"). In cumulatively evolving organic systems such as inherited genes and neurological networks, the older system forms the basis upon which the newer system depends for critical optimizing control functions (Forgas, 2000; Frijda et al., 2000; Solomon, 2004). This explains biologically why the affective system, being older or primary in evolution, retains control over the cognitive system, which is newer or later (Evans, 2001).

For instance, an affective intention, such as wanting to send an email to a person [A^O], initiates planning thoughts regarding how to obtain the email address of that person [C^O]. Then, after typing the message [$S^O E^O$], the person feels obligated to check a fact mentioned in the email [A^O] and decides to postpone sending it [C^O]. Later, the optimizing feeling of goal-persistence [A^O] initiates new planning thoughts [C^O] as to how to check the fact, and when to go back to finishing the task of sending the email message [$S^O E^O$]. The entire dynamic flow of these events can be charted on Figure 1.1 as the path of procedures [$A^O C^O S^O E^O A^O C^O S^O E^O$] (i.e., [intending, planning, performing and interrupting with optimizing affordance, intending new goal, changing plan, performing new plan with optimizing affordance]).

The ecological constructionist model in Figure 1.1 defines the information environment as constructed out of the organized practices of people in a social group. These ecological information systems are cumulatively evolving in organic steps with the neurobiology of the brain and the biology of mental states (feelings, thoughts, sensations, muscle action determinations). The same evolutionary laws that act upon the brain also act upon information systems that are designed to interact with people's feelings [$A^S A^O$], thoughts [$C^S C^O$], and sensations or actions [$S^S S^O$]. Consequently, affective neuroscience and information science are allied fields of investigation.

Damasio (1999) explains that a particular feeling or emotion is "represented within the brain as neural 'object'" (p. 79). Brain activity is a necessary but not sufficient condition for experiencing an emotion [A^S]. If there is malfunctioning of normal neural activity, affective life [$A^S A^O$] is restricted because it does not have an intact neural basis to thrive and proceed. Damasio states that whatever happens in one locality of brain action influences adjacent regions. This neurobiological ecology creates the specific brain activity necessary for sustaining the affective states that are involved in value-attaching feelings [A^S] and goal-striving feelings [A^O].

Individual differences in "affective style" have been discussed in terms of "affective reactivity" and "dispositional mood" (Davidson, 2003; Davidson, Scherer, & Goldsmith, 2000). Since their focus is on neuroscientific indices of emotions, they concentrate on the sensorimotor system [$S^S S^O$], including physiological response, muscle tension, sensory acuity, eye blink-startle magnitude, rate of execution, and recovery time. It is known that affective regulation involves both "state-like" and "trait-like" properties. Nahl (1996) has shown that self-efficacy evaluation of searchers and their feelings of optimism [A^S] persist "trait-like" across weekly search sessions. However, this positive coping style may be eclipsed by negative satisficing feelings (uncertainty, anxiety, frustration, doubt) when the information setting is unfamiliar or novel. Students were optimistic about Web search engines that they were used to but pessimistic when contemplating a new task such as uploading files to a designated server (Nahl, 2004).

Affective Computing and Affective HCI

Newell and Simon (as quoted in Simon, 1967, p. 31) state that "the obvious way to govern the behavior of a serial processor is by a hierarchy of subroutines, with an interpreter capable of executing the instructions in the proper order" (Simon, 1967, p. 31). Simon's (1967) examples of how humans govern cognitive processes through affective control mechanisms include "aspiration achievement" [A^O], "satisficing" [A^S], "impatience" [A^S], and "discouragement" [A^O]. Simon referred to these affective procedures as "goal completion subroutines." He used the term "satisficing" to refer to an affective subroutine that terminates a cognitive routine "when its sub-goal has been achieved '*well enough*'" (p. 32). However, if only negative satisficing occurs, another affective subroutine called "discouragement" [A^O] then "terminates" the problem-solving activity [C^O].

Although Simon's (1967) use of "satisficing" appears to have applied to the affective system, it receives a more extended usage in ecological constructionism, as is clear from Figure 1.1. This makes explicit the fact that satisficing procedures are involved in all the steps of information reception. Every user is unique in information reception because this is a biological procedure constructed uniquely by each individual. However, users must succeed in keeping their personal procedures within appropriate limits defined by group practices. Hence, the sensorimotor procedures must be "good enough" to be categorized by others as noticing. The cognitive procedures cannot be idiosyncratic but must be trained to function within limits defined by group practices in appraising information during reception. Similarly, the technological devices that make up an information system are designed to relate to the sensorimotor system—either they provide sensory input or they allow motor action on them. In both cases, they are affordances in the information ecology, either satisficing affordances in the reception phase or optimizing affordances in information use or engagement.

Don Norman (1981) proposed 12 issues central to information science. The first phase of the cognitive revolution, which Norman terms the "conventional view," conceptualizes humans as biological organisms possessing "separable subsystems of information processing mechanisms" [C^SC^O], "perceptual systems (including pattern recognition)" [E^SS^S], "motor or output systems" [S^OE^O], "memory systems" [C^S], and systems for internal reasoning and deduction [C^SC^O], which includes thinking [C^SC^O], problem-solving [C^SC^O], and languaging (verbalizing or texting) [S^OS^S]" (p. 265). All of the elements in Figure 1.1 are mentioned in Norman's definition of the cognitive viewpoint except the affective system.

Norman (1981) describes his increasing unease with this "pure cognitive system" (p. 274) perspective on human beings and ultimately entered the affective revolution by adding the theoretical element he terms the "emotional system" (p. 276). According to Norman, the cognitive system [C^SC^O] must have a regulatory system [A^O], and the two must be interfaced through the emotional system [A^S]. In this revised form, the affective revolution in Norman's perspective is complete, since the affective takes on the primary role as a regulatory system [A^O] and an emotional system [A^S], while the cognitive [C] is evaluated [A^S] and regulated [A^O] by feelings [A]. Norman's influential turnabout shows clearly in the title of his book, *Emotional Design* (2004).

Eva Hudlicka (2003) reviewed "the role of affect in human–computer interaction" concluding that an "effective HCI" is an "affective HCI." The "emerging research area of affective HCI" is about "the ability of systems to address *user affect*" (p. 1). This means two things. First, users can act upon the system [S^OE^O] by having the system recognize user affect [E^OE^S]. "Affect sensing and recognition" by computers is defined in Figure 1.1 as an optimizing affordance of the information environment that allows the user to act upon the system to promote an intention [$A^OC^OS^OE^O$]. Second, "to address user affect" means to equip the system with the ability to express appropriate affect in return, thus insuring "reciprocity" between human and computer. This affective expressive ability of computers is represented in Figure 1.1 as satisficing affordances

[E^S] because the computer's quasi-feelings can now be noticed by the user [E^{S}S^S] and satisfied through cognitive procedures of empathy [C^S], as well as through affective procedures of reassurance and attachment [A^S].

Hudlicka (2003) considers the modeling of user affect as "critical for the successful completion of a task, for avoiding (often disastrous) errors, for achieving optimal performance, or for maintaining reasonable user stress levels" (p. 6). The "broad aim of affective HCI" is to develop the knowledge that system designers need to "assess the range of possible affective states the users may ... experience during interactions with the system, and that they understand their effects on the user, and thus on task performance. Such understanding then allows informed decisions regarding which affective considerations must be addressed, when and how" (p. 7). The expression "affective state" is defined as "a range of conditions, including simple bipolar 'reactions' such as like and dislike, boredom and excitement, or approach and avoid; basic emotions such as joy, sadness, frustration, anger, fear and anxiety; complex emotions such as shame, guilt, jealousy; and long term moods (see Davidson, 1994). These signatures depend both on the individual ... and on the situational context" (pp. 7–8).

Hudlicka (2003) traces some of the history of the study of emotion in HCI, reflecting on the "marginal status of emotion research": "This is exemplified, for example, by the almost complete denial of affective influence on cognition during the 'cognitivist revolution' that began in the 1960s. Although notable dissenting opinions existed even then, e.g., Simon, 1967" (p. 10). The varieties of ways in which emotions or *affective states* influence cognitive and sensorimotor activity, as reviewed by Hudlicka, include mechanisms for:

- "Communicating intentions" [A^O]

- "Goal-management" [A^{O}C^O]

- Determining "optimal resource allocation" during "cognitive redirecting" [C^{O}C^{S}A^S]

- Disrupting "attentional processes" [A^{S}A^{O}S^S]

- Facilitating and inhibiting "perceptual categorization biases" [A^{O}S^{O}S^S]

- Influencing the effectiveness of "memory encoding and recall" [A^{S}A^{O}C^{O}C^S]

- Influencing "reasoning, judgment, and decision making" [A^{O}C^{O}C^S]

Preece, Rogers, Sharp, and Benyon (1994) and Green and Jordan (2002), among others, make a distinction between "usability" and "user experience" in discussing information design. *Usability studies* are concerned with optimizing affordances of the system [E^O], such as "efficient to use" or "easy to remember how to use." *User experience* studies are concerned with satisficing affordances of the system [E^S], such as helpful, fun, or aesthetically pleasing. Usability refers to the built-in functionality of optimizing affordances [E^O], while user experiences are adaptations to satisficing affordances. Making this distinction has become a design priority (Diller, Shedroff, & Rhea, 2006).

Affective computing has driven the tremendous expansion of research on the affective aspects of system use and users (Hudlicka, 2003). MIT Media Lab researchers have designed "affective processors" that have brought the affective revolution to computer architecture (Picard & Klein, 2002). Media Lab researchers describe their research as "investigating, designing, building, and evaluating relational agents that may act as intelligent tutors, virtual peers, or a group of virtual friends to support learning, creativity, playful imagination, motivation, and pursue the development of meta-cognitive skills that persist beyond interaction with the technology" (Burleson & Picard, 2004). These "affective learning companions" promote satisficing strategies that allow children to accept [A^S] and understand [C^S] uncertainty and failure as they progress to becoming expert at something through optimizing intentions [A^O] and strategies [C^O]. Picard and her colleagues in affective computing rely on evidence produced by researchers of feelings in cognitive psychology, such as Isen (2004) and Seligman and Csikszentmihalyi (2000), who have demonstrated that "positive affect" facilitates cognitive processing, while negative affect inhibits and disturbs it.

These and related efforts in design development and research have actualized the affective revolution in information science. The understanding that motivates this effort is that humanizing the information environment means connecting it to feelings. Figure 1.1 establishes this connection by defining the information environment in terms of biological satisficing and optimizing, both carried out within socially practiced limits. Every technological device and each functionality in a system that constitutes the totality of the information ecology is designed to be either a satisficing affordance [E^S] for information reception or an optimizing affordance [E^O] for information use and engagement. The dialogue box on the Format menu in a word processor is a satisficing affordance [E^S] because it displays a list of options at the user's disposal. Appropriate satisficing procedures allow the user to notice, appraise, and evaluate this information [E^{S}S^{S}C^{S}A^S], and once this process is completed, different optimizing affordances such as selecting Font, Paragraph, Borders and Shading, etc., allow the user to engage the system, to modify the information environment to fit his or her optimizing intentions and desires according to his or her understanding and execution [A^{O}C^{O}S^{O}E^O].

SUMMARY AND CONCLUSION

This chapter offers an integrating perspective that unifies technology and humans in a symbiotic relationship. It shows in concrete terms that biology

and technology form an inseparable synergy operating within a social context of meanings, norms, rules, and values. Every individual has a unique private world of subjective experiences, but membership in a group delimits our
thoughts and feelings so that we may conform to group practices in the way
we receive and use information. The model makes explicit what people do
mentally when they receive and use information. This explanation describes
how the three human biological systems interact with each other and with
technology in order to satisfy the expectations of other participants. These
expectations or norms are embodied in their group practices.

During information reception, users construct sensorimotor procedures,
like eye movements, in such a way as to enact the normal noticing practices
of the group. For example, when inspecting an online bank statement, the
screen may at first look like organized and formatted gibberish. Our eyes
don't follow an effective pattern, getting lost in scanning loops, missing large
zones, not seeing patterns of bolded subtitles in rows and columns. It takes a
few practice sessions before eye movements are adapted to the information
elements on the screen, knowing where to look and focus. Once practiced, we
have become members of a community of practice involving people who do
online banking. This permits expanding to several banks and credit cards, all
different in some ways, yet the sensorimotor procedures we follow are
adapted to noticing pertinent things in each sub-setting. We can now notice
what other online bank customers can notice.

Once we notice an item, we perform cognitive procedures to assign meaning and context to it. All practiced members of some setting appraise what
they notice through cognitive procedures that harmonize with other participants. For instance: *This is a login button. That's what I need to get to my
account. This is a next button. I need that to go on*, etc. All the elements that
have been noticed are spontaneously appraised. Members can do this from
practice. They can also perform standard cognitive procedures like, "*If I click
on it and it's not what I want, I can press back and not lose my place.*" But in
some settings, such as on secure sites, this cognitive procedure does not
work, and performing it will result in the user losing his or her place and
things have to be redone or restarted.

Once information has been noticed and appraised, it must be value-
attached. This is done by affective procedures, not cognitive. For example,
when practiced searchers notice the cursor flashing in a search box, they
understand that it's ready for them to type, and that it's not necessary to click
in the field, as novices often do. We receive the information as a final step by
attaching value to it, in this case, "*I can go ahead and type now.*" This is the
value of the blinking cursor. Information that has no value is not received. The
value of information depends on two types of affective satisficing procedures.
One is consummatory based on need, and the other is evaluative based on
judgment. The feeling of "*I love this. I enjoy this ...*" is a consummatory affective procedure, while the feeling of "*This is useless. This is too little ...*" is an

evaluative affective procedure that counts in group practices as making a judgment. Information reception is therefore the process of noticing, appraising, and value-attaching.

Once information has been received, it is spontaneously connected to a feeling of intention or motivation. For instance, *"I want to avoid clicking on that"* or *"I'll ask someone about it."* This intentionality is an affective procedure that involves conative or motivational components of the affective system, rather than consummatory or evaluative. The interdependence of these three types of affective systems forms the pivot point around which information technology revolves between the end point of reception and the beginning point of use. Affective intentions or purposes spontaneously evoke cognitive strategies for executing or performing a goal intention. The execution requires sensorimotor procedures in interaction with optimizing affordances.

Two types of evidence are presented to support the face validity of the model. One is from think-aloud protocols and transcripts of user discourse. The other is from written self-reports. Both methods involve segmenting user discourse into information speech act units. The data show that users make things comprehensible to themselves and to others by constructing sentences about their information behavior. This is also the basis of help instructions. When these sentences are analyzed, one can clearly see that they are constructed of information speech act units that refer to some biological procedure, sensorimotor, cognitive, or affective. All three have been found to be involved in hundreds of independent discourse samples.

The evidence from written self-reports indicates that the way people talk about their experiences in the information environment can be categorized into three taxonomic levels of affective and cognitive activity. It is evident from analysis that the affective and cognitive procedures people construct during information behavior are learned skills of membership practices and that it involves an adaptation period during which negative procedures interfere with learning and must be modified to fit group practices. Learned affective norms (LANs) define the user's emotional reactions and feelings during this process of adaptation to information reception and initiation of information use.

The face validity of the model was demonstrated by a literature review in several sub areas of HCI and IS showing that some of the principal concepts of the literature on users are represented on the model. Perhaps the main value of the model is to show explicitly that information behavior is a dynamic flow of biological procedures constructed by users to fit the practices of the group. Charting this dynamic flow through the analysis of user discourse makes it very evident that cognitive operations cannot occur independently but must be kept goal-coherent by the affective operations.

It remains to be demonstrated that the model can be useful in examining specific content, setting, and purpose. It is evident to the researchers of feeling in this volume that users of information systems of all kinds in different community settings and information grounds operate within a social environment through what they are doing, thinking, and feeling. The model may help us see how one research focus is related to another.

REFERENCES

Ashkanasy, N. M., & Daus, C. S. (2005). Rumors of the death of emotional intelligence in organizational behavior are vastly exaggerated. *Journal of Organizational Behavior, 26*(4), 441–452.

Barsky, A., Thoresen, C. J., Warren, C. R., & Kaplan, S. A. (2004). Modeling negative affectivity and job stress: A contingency-based approach. *Journal of Organizational Behavior, 25*(8), 915–936.

Bilal, D. (2004). Research on children's information seeking on the Web. In M. Chelton & C. Cool (Eds.), *Youth information-seeking behavior: Theories, models, and issues* (pp. 271–291). Lanham, MD: The Scarecrow Press.

Burleson, W., & Picard, R. W. (2004, August). *Affective agents: Sustaining motivation to learn through failure and a state of "stuck."* Paper presented at the Social and Emotional Intelligence in Learning Environments Workshop in conjunction with the 7th International Conference on Intelligent Tutoring Systems, Maceio—Alagoas, Brasil. Accessed December 13, 2006, from affect.media.mit.edu/pdfs/04.burleson-picard.pdf.

Burrell, D. (1997). *From sanctity to property: Dead bodies in American society and law, 1800–1860.* Accessed December 13, 2006, from www.historicalinsights.com/dave/bodyasproperty.html.

Damasio, A. (1999). *The feeling of what happens: Body and emotion in the making of consciousness.* New York: Harcourt.

Davidson, R. J. (1994). Complexities in the search for emotion-specific physiology. In P. Ekman, & R. J. Davidson, (Eds.), *The nature of emotion: Fundamental questions* (pp. 237–242). New York: Oxford University Press.

Davidson, R. J. (2003). Affective neuroscience and psychophysiology: Toward a synthesis. *Psychophysiology, 40*, 655–665. Accessed December 13, 2006, from www.sprweb.org/articles/Davidson03.pdf.

Davidson, R. J., Scherer, K. R., & Goldsmith, H. H. (2000). *The handbook of affective sciences.* Oxford: Oxford University Press.

Dervin, B. (2003). Human studies and user studies: A call for methodological interdisciplinarity. *Information Research, 9*(1) paper 166. Accessed December 13, 2006, from InformationR.net/ir/9-1/paper166.html.

Diller, S., Shedroff, N., & Rhea, D. (2006). *Making meaning: How successful businesses deliver meaningful customer experiences.* Berkley, CA: New Riders.

Ericsson, K. A., & Simon, H. A. (1993). *Protocol analysis: Verbal reports as data.* Cambridge, MA: MIT Press.

Evans, D. (2001). *Emotion: The science of sentiment.* Oxford: Oxford University Press.

Forgas, J. P. (Ed.). (2000). *Feeling and thinking: The role of affect in social cognition.* Cambridge: Maison des Science de l'Homme & Cambridge University Press.

Friedman, B. (1997). *Human values and the design of computer technology.* Stanford, CA: CSLI Publications.

Frijda, N. H., Manstead, A. S. R., & Bem, S. (2000). *Emotions and beliefs: How feelings influence thoughts.* Cambridge: Cambridge University Press.

Gibson, J. J. (1986). *The ecological approach to visual perception.* Mahwah, NJ: Lawrence Erlbaum Associates.

Green, W. S., & Jordan, P. W. (Eds.). (2002). *Pleasure with products: Beyond usability.* New York: Taylor & Francis.

Grimsaeth, K. (2005). *Kansei engineering: Linking emotions and product features.* Accessed December 13, 2006, from www.ivt.ntnu.no/ipd/fag/PD9/2005/artikler/ PD9%20Kansei%20Engineering%20K_Grimsath.pdf.

Huang, G. H., Law, K. S., & Wong, C. S. (2006). Emotional intelligence: A critical review. In L. V. Wesley (Ed.), *Intelligence: New research* (pp. 95–113). New York: Nova Science Publishers.

Hudlicka, E. (2003). To feel or not to feel: The role of affect in human–computer interaction. *International Journal of Human–Computer Studies, 59,* 71–75.

Isen, A. M. (2004). Positive affect and decision making. In M. Lewis & J. Haviland-Jones (Eds.), *Handbook of emotions.* New York: Guilford Press.

Jakobovits, L. A., & Nahl-Jakobovits, D. (1987). Learning the library: Taxonomy of skills and errors. *College & Research Libraries, 48,* 203–214.

Jakobovits, L. A., & Nahl-Jakobovits, D. (1990). Measuring information searching competence. *College & Research Libraries, 51,* 448–462.

Jordan, P. W. (2000). *Designing pleasurable products: An introduction to the new human factors.* Philadelphia: Taylor & Francis.

Kuhlthau, C. C. (2004). *Seeking meaning: A process approach to library and information services* (2nd ed.). Westport, CT: Libraries Unlimited.

Lewis, C., & Fabos, B. (2005). Instant messaging, literacies, and social identities. *RRQ Reading Research Quarterly, 40*(4), 470–501. Accessed December 13, 2006, from www.reading.org/Library/Retrieve.cfm?D=10.1598/RRQ.40.4.5&F=RRQ-40-4-Lewis.html.

MacKinnon, N. J. (1994). *Symbolic interactionism as affect control.* Albany: State University of New York Press.

Martin, L. L., & Tesser, A. (1996). *Striving and feeling: Interactions among goals, affect and self-regulation.* Mahwah, NJ: Lawrence Erlbaum Associates.

McCown, K., Freedman, J. M., Jensen, A., & Rideout, M. (1998). *Self science.* San Mateo, CA: Six Seconds Press.

Nahl, D. (1993). *CD-ROM point-of-use instructions for novice searchers: A comparison of user-centered affectively elaborated and system-centered unelaborated text.* Unpublished doctoral dissertation, University of Hawaii, Honolulu. Accessed December 13, 2006, from www2.hawaii.edu/~nahl/articles/phd/phdtoc.html.

Nahl, D. (1995). Affective elaborations in Boolean search instructions for novices: Effects on comprehension, self-confidence, and error type. *Proceedings of the 58th ASIS Annual Meeting, 32,* 69–76.

Nahl, D. (1996). Affective monitoring of Internet learners: Perceived self-efficacy and success. *Proceedings of the 59th ASIS Annual Meeting, 33,* 100–109.

Nahl, D. (1997). Information counseling inventory of affective and cognitive reactions while learning the Internet. In L. E. M. Martin (Ed.), *The challenge of Internet literacy: The instruction-Web convergence* (pp. 11–33). New York: Haworth Press.

Nahl, D. (1998a). Ethnography of novices' first use of Web search engines: Affective control in cognitive processing. *Internet Reference Services Quarterly, 3*(2): 51–72.

Nahl, D. (1998b). Learning the Internet and the structure of information behavior. *Journal of the American Society for Information Science, 49*(11), 1,017–1,023.

Nahl, D. (2001). A conceptual framework for defining information behavior. *Studies in Multimedia Information Literacy Education (SIMILE), 1*(2). Accessed December 13, 2006, from www.utpjournals.com/simile/issue2/nahlfulltext.html.

Nahl, D. (2004). Measuring the affective information environment of Web searchers. *Proceedings of the 67th annual meeting of the American Society for Information Science & Technology, 41,* 191–197.

Nahl, D. (2005a). Affective and cognitive information behavior: Interaction effects in Internet use. *Proceedings of the 68th annual meeting of the American Society for Information Science & Technology, 42.* Accessed December 13, 2006, from eprints. rclis.org/archive/00004978/01/Nahl_Affective.pdf.

Nahl, D. (2005b). Affective load theory (ALT). In K. E. Fisher, S. Erdelez, & L. E. F. McKechnie, (Eds.), *Theories of information behavior* (pp. 39–43). Medford, NJ: Information Today, Inc.

Nahl, D. (2006, January). *A symbiotic human-machine model for tracking user micro-attributes.* Paper presented at the Hawaii International Conference on System Sciences (HICCS), Kauai, Hawaii. Accessed December 13, 2006, from www.itl.nist.gov/iaui/vvrg/hicss39/HICSS-2006-Nahl1.doc.

Nahl, D. (2007a). A discourse analysis technique for charting the flow of micro-information behavior. *Journal of Documentation, 63*(3): 323–339.

Nahl, D. (2007b). Social-biological information technology: An integrated conceptual framework. *Journal of the American Society of Information Science* (JASIST), *58*(13): 1–26.

Norman, D. A. (1981). Twelve issues for cognitive science. In D. A. Norman (Ed.), *Perspectives on cognitive science* (pp. 265–295). Hillsdale, NJ: Erlbaum, Basic Books.

Norman, D. A. (2004). *Emotional design: Why we love (or hate) everyday things.* New York: Basic Books.

Ortony, A., & Turner, T. J. (1990). What's basic about basic emotions? *Psychological Review, 97,* 315–331.

Ortony, A., Clore, G. L., & Collins, A. (1988). *The cognitive structure of emotions.* Cambridge: Cambridge University Press.

Osgood, C. E., Suci, G., & Tannenbaum, P. (1957). *The measurement of meaning.* Urbana, IL: University of Illinois Press.

Panksepp, J. (1998). *Affective neuroscience: The foundations of human and animal emotions.* Oxford: Oxford University Press.

Picard, R. W., & Klein, J. (2002). Computers that recognize and respond to user emotion: Theoretical and practical implications. *Interacting with Computers, 14*(2), 141–169.

Preece, J., Rogers, Y., Sharp, H., & Benyon, D. (1994). *Human–computer interaction.* Boston: Addison-Wesley Longman.

Raskin, J. (2000). *The humane interface: New directions for designing interactive systems.* Boston: Addison-Wesley.

Sadl, Z. (1996). *The 'affective' revolution: Cognitive turn in contemporary social sciences. Emotiology in Slovenia (1850–1930). The European Legacy, 1*(3): 958–963.

Scheutz, M., & Sloman, A. (2001). Affect and agent control: Experiments with simple affective states. In N. Zhong, J. Liu, S. Ohsuga, & J. Bradshaw (Eds.), *Intelligent agent technology: Research and development. Proceedings of the 2nd Asia-Pacific Conference on IAT Maebashi City, Japan 23–26 October 2001.* Singapore: World Scientific. Accessed December 13, 2006, from www.cs.bham.ac.uk/research/cogaff/scheutz.sloman.affect.control.pdf.

Seligman, M. E. P., & Csikszentmihalyi, M. (2000). Positive psychology: An introduction. *American Psychologist, 55,* 5–14.

Simon, H. A. (1967). Motivational and emotional controls of cognition. *Psychological Review, 74*(1), 29–39.

Solomon, R. C. (2004). *Thinking about feeling: Contemporary philosophers on emotions.* Oxford: Oxford University Press.

Spink, A., Wilson, T. D., Ford, N. J., Foster, A. E., & Ellis, D. (2002). Information-seeking and mediated searching: Part 1. Theoretical framework and research design. *Journal of the American Society for Information Science and Technology, 53*(9), 695–703.

Tuominen, K., & Savolainen, R. (1997). A social constructionist approach to the study of information use as discursive action. In P. Vakkari, R. Savolainen, & B. Dervin

(Eds.), *Information seeking in context: Proceedings of an International Conference on Research in Information Needs, Seeking, and Use in Different Contexts (Aug. 14–16, 1996, Tampere, Finland)* (pp. 81–96). London: Graham Taylor.

Van Hout, M. (2004). Getting emotional with ... Donald Norman. *Design & Emotion.* Accessed December 13, 2006, from www.design-emotion.com/2004/12/15/getting-emotional-with-donald-norman.

Watson, D., & Clark, L. A. (1984). Negative affectivity: The disposition to experience aversive emotional states. *Psychological Bulletin, 96,* 465–490.

Wilson, T. D., Ford, N., Ellis, D., Foster, A. E., & Spink, A. (2000). Uncertainty and its correlates. *The New Review of Information Behaviour Research, 1,* 69–84.

CHAPTER 2

Grounding Children's Information Behavior and System Design in Child Development Theories

Dania Bilal
University of Tennessee

INTRODUCTION

Many theorists and researchers have emphasized connecting affective, cognitive, and psychomotor aspects to construct a unified framework for studying the user as a whole individual during the information seeking process (Bilal, 2005; Kuhlthau, 1993, 2004; Nahl, 1996). The significant role of affect has been recognized in theory for decades (Bruner, 1986; Dewey, 1933; Kelly, 1963; Simon, 1967). In their seminal review of information needs and uses research, Dervin and Nilan (1986) viewed users from a holistic perspective that focuses on cognitive and psychological states. They identified a paradigm shift from the system-centered to the user-centered and provided seven key dimensions for understanding users: how to view information, the view of the user, how to predict user behavior, the view of user experience, how to determine information needs, dealing with individuals, and research approaches to undertake. These dimensions have had a significant influence on developments in the field of information science. The shift from the physical paradigm (system-based) to the cognitive paradigm (user-oriented) has guided much research for the last 20 years. The user has become the center of the information seeking process.

Today, children are brought up in the age of digital information. Computer use and surfing the Web have become the norm for many children in schools and at home. The ubiquitous nature of digital information and its sheer volume raises many issues about children's interactions with digital interfaces and the appropriateness of the design of these interfaces for them, both cognitively and affectively.

For children, using technology can be intellectually challenging, gratifying, and motivating, but affectively frustrating (Bilal, 2000). Picard (1997, 1999) notes that no matter how hard researchers perfect computers and interface design, frustration can happen during the interaction. Decades ago, Simon (1967) emphasized that thinking and problem solving are influenced by emotions. Emotion theorists have also argued about the pivotal role of emotion in thinking, learning, perception, decision-making, and creativity (Bandura, 1997; Isen, et al., 1987). Emotions cannot be separated from cognition because human development is ingrained in cognitive, affective, physical, and social domains, which are interwoven within each individual. Therefore, understanding children's interaction with information systems and assessing the utility of digital interfaces for them should be grounded in cognitive, emotional, and social child development theories. These theories have implications for teaching, mediation, and learning, as well as system design that supports children's developmental levels. However, before describing these theories, we need to give an overview of research on children's information seeking.

CHILDREN AND INFORMATION SEEKING (LIT REV)

Researchers have examined various dimensions of children's interactions with the Web and digital libraries. The results of these studies have been reported in Bilal (2005). This section provides an overview of the purposes of these studies and the commonality among the results.

Watson (1998) explored children's feelings about and perceptions of using the Web. Bilal (2000, 2001, 2002) examined children's use of the Yahooligans! to locate information for different types of tasks, assess their success, and elicit their affective states. Large and Beheshti (2000) gathered children's reactions to specific search engines in terms of usefulness and interface design. Bilal (2003) involved children in the design of Web search engines, explored their information needs, and analyzed their affect for the interfaces they developed. Reuter and Druin (2004) and Druin (2005) investigated children's use of the International Children's Digital Library (ICDL) but did not examine their affective states. Most recently, Bilal and Bachir (2007a, 2007b) examined Arabic-speaking children's interaction with the ICDL and their success in finding information on various types of tasks. They elicited children's affective experience and uncovered the role of culture in assessing the usability of the ICDL as an international interface.

In summary, the cited research provided understanding of children's information seeking behaviors in using a variety of digital interfaces. Despite the disparity among the grade levels, prior experience, and culture of the children involved in these studies, findings showed that these young users experienced difficulty in using digital interfaces including those that were specifically developed for them, mainly due to the inadequate design of the interfaces, age, and insufficient level of knowledge in how to use the interfaces. Researchers suggested that system developers build interfaces that support children's developmental levels, affective states, and information seeking behaviors. "Information seeking is a dynamic process that involves the whole individual" (Bilal, 2005, p. 205).

THEORETICAL CONCEPTIONS

During the early decades of the 20th century, constructivist theorists recognized the significant roles that thoughts, feelings, and actions play in the process of learning and seeking understanding. Dewey's theory of Reflective Thinking (1933), Kelly's five Phases of Construction (1963), and Bruner's theory of the Interpretive Task (1986) together provided the cornerstone of the constructivist learning process on which most user-centered research in the field of information science has been built.

Kuhlthau (1993) developed an integrated model of the Information Search Process that encompassed students' thoughts, feelings, and actions as they engaged in information seeking activities. The six-stage model describes feelings of uncertainty, confusion, anxiety, and apprehension during the initial stages of the process. As users' thoughts are formulated and foci are found, these negative affective states diminish depending on the user's level of satisfaction or dissatisfaction and the level of cognitive enrichment in meeting the information need. Kuhlthau suggested diagnosis of the user's information problem and professional intervention to mediate the user's information problem. Kuhlthau's model is user-centered and grounded in the writings of John Dewey (1933), George Kelly (1963), Jerome Bruner (1986), and Lev Vygotsky (1978).

In her conception of the user-centered revolution, Nahl (1996) focused on understanding users and their information needs from different perspectives (affective, cognitive, and physical). In an effort to express the connectivity between the cognitive, affective, and sensorimotor domains, she proposed a three-dimensional model of learning information structure called the ACS (Affective, Cognitive, Sensorimotor) Matrix. The model emphasizes that every information skill—from the smallest to the most general—is constructed from affective, cognitive, and sensorimotor behaviors acting together as a unit within a hierarchical behavioral system (Jakobovits & Nahl-Jakobovits, 1990).

Most recently, Nahl described her Affective Load Theory (ALT) for measuring several dimensions of affect in information behavior (2004; 2005a). Affective Load was defined as uncertainty intensified by felt time pressure (U*TP) (2004, p. 195), while uncertainty was measured by combining ratings on irritation, anxiety, frustration and rage scales (U = I + A + F + R). She also introduced the Affective Coping Skills (ACS) measure combining both self-efficacy (SE) and optimism (Op) measures. Nahl notes that "high self-efficacy and optimism have been found to significantly and beneficially influence success in a variety of information tasks, by counteracting the effects of negative emotions such as irritation and frustration" (2005b, p. 1). Nahl's model of Information Reception and Use (2007) combines social, biological, and technological systems. The biological systems include affective, cognitive, and sensorimotor procedures, as well as satisficing and optimizing affordances.

The recent rise of the Affective Paradigm (Bilal, 2005) further validates the pivotal role affect plays in shaping users' information seeking behaviors. This paradigm is founded on two main premises: the existing cognitive paradigm and the ongoing work in affective computing. "Affective computing expands human–computer interaction by including emotional communication together with appropriate means of handling affective information" (Picard, 1999, p. 1). Intelligent applications in affective computing are being implemented at the MIT Media Lab. The aim of these applications is to reduce user frustration, enable communication of user emotion, and build devices and gather, communicate, and express emotional information during human–computer interaction (Picard, 1997).

These theoretical conceptions provide the basis for understanding the connection among a user's cognitive, affective, and physical behaviors in seeking information. However, to interpret behaviors, we must understand significant child development theories.

CHILD DEVELOPMENT THEORIES

Child development theories describe the socio-emotional, cognitive, and physical developments that occur from birth to adolescence. These theories explain observations and discoveries and provide a broad framework for understanding how children feel, think, and act at different stages of development. Underlying these theories is our ability to analyze and interpret children's information needs, information seeking behaviors, information use, and knowledge structures in relation to their developmental levels. Many development theories portray child development in a relatively ordered sequence. Each phase of growth has its own distinct emotional, intellectual, and social abilities that establish the foundation for the next phase (Erikson, 1963; Piaget & Inhelder, 1969). The following section summarizes the significant emotional, cognitive, and socio-cognitive developmental theories.

Children and Emotion

Erikson's theory of socio-emotional child development (1963; 1968) provided a perspective on eight stages of sequential development, starting with infancy and ending with older adulthood. In Erikson's view, both the social environment and biological development provide each individual with a specific set of crises that must be resolved before moving to the next stage. The first stage, Trust vs. Mistrust, begins in infancy. The infant's sense of trust is derived from the mother and the surrounding environment. The second stage, Autonomy vs. Shame and Doubt, is found in the toddler years. During this phase, the child establishes interpersonal patterns "that are united in the social modality of taking and holding on to things" (Erikson, 1968, p. 100). The child learns to develop a sense of self-control without loss of self-esteem. Loss of self-control results in doubt and shame. A firmly developed trust at the first stage is necessary for the growth of autonomy. The third stage, Initiative vs. Guilt, occurs in the early childhood years. The child learns to move around and explore, and his or her sense of language becomes perfected. These aspects expand the child's imagination. Initiative is governed by conscience, and a sense of guilt is awakened. Guilt is expressed as rage that is often directed toward younger siblings and the child's failure to secure a favorite position with one of the parents leads to anxiety. At this stage, the child's imagination is expansive.

The fourth stage, Industry vs. Inferiority, is in the middle childhood years. Erikson (1968) also identifies this stage as School Age and Task Identification because the child is more ready to learn quickly, share obligations, discipline, and performance than at the end of the former stage. The child is eager to work with others and begin to imitate other people. He or she becomes attached to teachers and the parents of other children. A child becomes dissatisfied for not being able to do things perfectly and develops a sense of industry. He or she may build a sense of estrangement from tasks that may result in a sense of inferiority, the danger at this stage of development. The fifth stage, Identity and Identity Confusion, occurs in adolescence. The adolescent establishes a sense of self-identity and begins to form relationships with others that he or she has faith in. However, when trusted relationships fail, the adolescent becomes cynical and mistrusting. The adolescent is "mortally afraid of being forced into activities in which he [or she] would feel exposed to ridicule or self-doubt" (Erikson, 1968, p. 129). The adolescent's sense of identity is highly significant at this stage and radical deprivation of all forms of expression may result in the highest form of resistance. Inability to identify one's role and settle on an occupational identity becomes disturbing and creates identity confusion.

The sixth stage, Intimacy vs. Isolation, occurs during the young adulthood years. The young adult experiences a crisis of intimacy. He or she develops a true and mutual psychosocial intimacy with another person and is able to give and receive love. When the young adult's identity is formed well, he or she can experience true intimacy. An identity crisis leads to intimacy crisis. The seventh stage, Generativity vs. Stagnation, is the middle adulthood years. The adult is concerned about establishing and guiding the next generation. Generativity includes productivity and creativity. "Regression to an obsessive need for pseudo-intimacy takes place, often with a pervading sense of stagnation, boredom, and interpersonal impoverishment" (p. 138).

The eighth stage, Ego Integrity vs. Despair, is the older adulthood years. The older adult develops a sense of integrity-accrued ego integration about life and its meaning. The older adult develops acceptance of one's life as it was lived and accepts the people who have become significant in his or her life (e.g., parents) as they are. Accumulated knowledge, mature judgment, and inclusive understanding are attributes to a meaningful life of an older adult. Lack or loss of accrued ego integration results in disgust, despair, displeasure, and disapproval of one's self.

Implications of Erikson's Theory

Erikson's theory details the affective and social states an individual passes through from infancy to older adulthood. His theory has implications for teaching, research, and mediation. Pre-school children, for example, are in the stage of developing a hardy personality. Activities should relate to children's interests and the choices they make for themselves. Because children's learning is intrusive and vigorous, researchers should assign tasks that allow children to show initiative. Working in small groups that focus on role play and switching roles will give children a chance to lead. Adult guidance plays a significant role in helping children overcome their limitations and move into a world of future possibilities.

At school age, children are eager to make things together and experience success. They need to trust the people they interact with, especially mediators such as teachers. Similarly, they need to develop a trusted relationship with researchers in order to achieve tasks successfully. Erikson noted that "one teacher can be credited with having kindled the flame of hidden talent" (p. 125). Therefore, tasks children are to achieve should be goal-oriented, of interest to them, and challenging, but at the same time they should be at their level of difficulty. When children begin to receive systematic instruction, they are able to use structured information systems. Systems that provide visual representations for browsing, spell-checkers, and simple interface design that children will enjoy rather than endure will allow them to experience success and increase self-confidence. Erikson believed that technology "must reach meaningfully into [a child's] life, supporting in every child a feeling of competence—that is, the free exercise of dexterity and intelligence in the completion of serious tasks unimpaired by an infantile sense of inferiority" (1968, p. 126).

Children and Cognition

Like Erikson, Piaget provided a perspective on children's sequential development in his four stages of cognitive development. He identified four primary cognitive structures that underlie specific types of intelligence: sensorimotor stage, preoperational stage, concrete stage, and formal operations stage. These stages are associated with characteristics based on age spans that vary for each individual. Each stage lays the foundation for the next and may be divided into substages.

The sensorimotor stage occurs from birth to age 2. At this stage, development takes the form of motor actions. Children learn through their senses and physical interaction with the environment. Children are limited to "thinking in action," that is, they have an inability to think before acting or engaging in certain behavior (Campbell, 1997). The end of this stage concludes with a full understanding of permanent objects, and the ability to imitate someone else's action on the basis of memory alone (Campbell, 1997).

The pre-operational stage occurs from age 2 to 7. Children are able to think about the consequences of their actions. However, they cannot think abstractly and need more concrete physical situations. They are egocentric in that they understand the world from their own perspectives and are unable to understand how the perspectives of others might be different from theirs. Children's intelligence is intuitive in nature.

The concrete stage spans from age 7 to 11. Children start to conceptualize and create logical structures, classify objects, form relationships among objects, and organize objects based on specific criteria. Understanding time, measurements, and numbers begin at this stage. Children are able to perform basic mathematical operations on numbers, but the level of abstract thinking is limited.

The formal stage begins after age 11. Cognitive structures involve abstraction, analogical and conceptual reasoning, formulating hypotheses, and generating multiple possibilities. Children can provide inferences, design and test experiments, and perform an advanced level of logical operations.

Implications of Piaget's Theory

Piaget distinguished between younger and older children's abilities while working on one of his experiments. He found that younger children answered questions differently from older ones. He explained this difference as pertaining to different thought processes between younger and older children rather than to difference in intelligence. Thus, children are not short adults; they are different from adults due to their cognitive developmental abilities. Accordingly, tasks and other learning activities designed for children should be developmentally appropriate and challenging but not beyond the children's abilities to achieve them. Activities should ignite children's interest, and engage and motivate them. Children who are at the concrete stage and moving toward the early formal stage (e.g., ages 11 to 13), for example, should be provided with a mix of concrete and abstract tasks along with examples illustrating how to accomplish them. In addition, certain tasks should be freely selected by children based on their interest. Children can be more successful in completing tasks that they generate because these tasks provide them with a sense of authority, independence, and control that could lead to higher satisfaction, certainty, and achievement (Bilal, 2002).

Piaget's theory provides interpretation of certain phenomena that should influence system design. Research reveals that children browse more than they search by keyword on the Web, although they prefer keyword searching (Bilal, 2000; Large, Beheshti, & Moukdad, 1999). Children who are in transition to the formal stage of development (ages 11 to 13) have limited vocabulary and recall knowledge. The fact that most of children's vocabulary does not match the vocabulary implemented in information systems (Abbas, Norris, & Soloway, 2002; Bilal, 1998; Bilal, 2000; Bilal & Wang, 2005; Cooper, 2005) moves children toward browsing. While this option is logical, the design of many subject categories and hierarchies may not be cognitively appropriate for children. Bilal and Wang (2005), for example, found that middle school children's cognitive structures of science concepts did not match the structures of those implemented in the Yahooligans! and KidsClick! taxonomies. Children had more difficulty with abstract concepts that were profound in nature, and they structured these concepts based on experience, situation, and perception, which is not surprising at this age of development (Piaget & Inhelder, 1969). Understanding children's cognitive structures and developmental stages should lead to designing interfaces that are highly supportive of their mental structures.

Children and Social Cognition

Vygotsky (1978) asserted that a child learns in the context of culture and that social interaction influences the changes in a child's thinking, behavior, and knowledge level. Social agents, such as family, teachers, and peers, as well as the surrounding environment, are the tools that significantly contribute to a child's learning. Vygotsky (1978) distinguished between lower and higher mental functions. Lower functions are those that a child genetically inherits such as natural mental abilities; higher functions are those that a child acquires through social interaction. He believed that intelligence, reasoning, personality, perception, madness, emotions, memory, and language rest on "cultural means" (Ratner, 1991). Memory is culturally reconstructed from a natural process to a psychological one. Young, preschool children directly memorize items before them. However, school-age children use socially devised mnemonic devices in the form of symbolic associations and reminders. The transition from natural forms of memory (direct memorization) to the cultural ones (acquired through schooling and social interaction) constitutes development of memory from child to adult (Lauria, 1979; Vygotsky, 1962).

One of the major principles that underlie Vygotsky's theory is the Zone of Proximal Development (ZPD). A child performs a task that he or she cannot do alone with the help of skilled agents such as teachers, peers, and family members. Vygotsky (1978) describes the ZPD as "the distance between the actual development level as determined by independent problem solving and the level of potential development as determined through problem solving under adult guidance or in collaboration with more capable peers" (p. 86). He notes "The central fact about our psychology is the fact of mediation" (Vygotsky, 1982, p. 166).

Implications of Vygotsky's Theory

Vygotsky's conceptualization of how culture, semiotic activity (signs, symbols, and language), and mediation shape learning and development has an impact on teaching and learning, as well as the design of digital interfaces. Since children learn best through social interaction, learning activities (e.g., information seeking tasks) should be designed to emphasize interaction among children. Small group work and role play will contribute to children's construction of knowledge and learning. Because learning occurs through mediation, children's tasks should be designed at a higher level of complexity and unfamiliarity so that children move from the current level to a higher level of mental functions.

The ZPD supports children's learning through mediation and social interaction. Researchers who interact with children should provide guidance to ensure that these young users can accomplish difficult tasks that they are incapable of achieving on their own. Kuhlthau's Zones of Intervention (1993) is a variation of the ZPD influenced by Vygotsky's framework. Mediators who interact with users to identify information needs should diagnose problems during the information seeking process and provide appropriate assistance in solving these problems. Another variation of the ZPD is the Proximal Zone of System Intervention (PZSI) that is conceptualized by the author of this chapter. The user-centered approach to system design emphasizes the development of information systems that support users cognitively and affectively. For example, systems that provide corrective feedback to recover from breakdowns (e.g., spelling suggestions, recommendations on search refinement, context-driven help) serve as "mediators" whose purpose is to move the user from the current state to a state they could not have recognized or performed on their own. The PZSI suggests the development of intelligent intervention mechanisms to support user interaction with information systems.

Vygotsky's theory has another significant implication for system design: the connection between semiotic activity and learning activity. As children's learning moves from a semiotic to a logical form of thinking (driven by the use of language and other symbols), their preference for signs and representations changes gradually. Making meaning out of signs is central to the development of semiotic activity. Prior studies have shown that young children in the early grades can be involved in semiotic activities (finding the relationship between a sign and its meaning), if this activity is based on the construction and use of self-made diagrams of real-life situations and objects (Van Oers, 1994). To support children's use of information systems, system designers should incorporate iconic representations and symbols that are developmentally appropriate, concrete, meaningful, and based on children's preferences.

CONCLUSION

Children of the 21st century are growing up in a digital society and their lives are saturated with Web-bound information. Using the Web to locate information has become a first choice for the majority of children and young adults (Bilal, 2000). In schools, curricula and supporting materials are based on children's developmental levels. Conversely, most of the systems children interact with on the Web do not capitalize on their cognitive and affective states in seeking information. The connection of a child's thoughts, feelings, and actions are pivotal to understanding information seeking behaviors and information needs. Grounding these behaviors in socio-emotional, cognitive, and social theories will help researchers, mediators, and system designers to conceptualize, understand, and interpret how children perceive the world, how they learn, and "why they act the way they do." Providing human and system interventions will allow children to construct knowledge, meaning, and understanding that will strengthen higher mental functions. "Constructing understanding is a process of interrogating multiple ideas, perspectives, and interpretations, and philosophical frameworks; confronting the ideational challenges of ... world views ... and shaping new perspectives and understandings" (Todd, 2003, p. 42).

REFERENCES

Abbas, J., Norris, C., & Soloway, E. (2002). Middle school children's use of the ARTEMIS digital library. *Proceedings of the 2nd Joint Conference on Digital Libraries*, 98–105.

Bandura, A. (Ed.). (1997). *Self-efficacy: The exercise of control*. New York: W.H. Freeman.

Bilal, D. (1998). Children's search processes in using World Wide Web search engines: An exploratory study. *Proceedings of the 61st annual meeting of the American Society for Information Science and Technology, 35*, 45–53.

Bilal, D. (2000). Children's use of the Yahooligans! Web search engine: I. Cognitive, physical, and affective behaviors on fact-based search tasks. *Journal of the American Society for Information Science and Technology, 51*, 646–665.

Bilal, D. (2001). Children's use of the Yahooligans! Web search engine: II. Cognitive and physical behaviors on research tasks. *Journal of the American Society for Information Science and Technology, 52*, 118–136.

Bilal, D. (2002). Children's use of the Yahooligans! Web search engine: III. Cognitive and physical behaviors on fully self-generated search tasks. *Journal of the American Society for Information Science and Technology, 53*, 1170–1183.

Bilal, D. (2003). Draw and tell: Children as designers of Web interfaces. *Proceedings of the 66th annual meeting of the American Society for Information Science and Technology, 40*, 135–141.

Bilal, D. (2005). Children's information seeking and the design of digital interfaces in the affective paradigm. *Library Trends, 54*, 197–208.

Bilal, D., & Bachir, I. (2007a). Children's interaction with cross-cultural and multilingual digital libraries. I. Understanding interface design representations. *Information Processing & Management, 43*, 47–64.

Bilal, D., & Bachir, I. (2007b). Children's interaction with cross-cultural and multilingual digital libraries. II. Information seeking, success, and affective experience. *Information Processing & Management, 43*, 65–80.

Bilal, D., & Wang, P. (2005). Children's Conceptual Structures of Science Categories and the Design of Web Directories. *Journal of the American Society for Information Science and Technology, 56*, 1303–1313.

Bruner, J. (1986). *Actual minds: Possible worlds*. Cambridge: Harvard University Press.

Campbell, R. N. (1997). Expertise and cognitive development. In L. Smith, J. Dockrell, & P. Obeying (Eds.), *Piaget, Vygotsky and beyond: Developmental psychology and education issues for the future* (pp. 159–164). London: Routledge.

Cooper, L. Z. (2005). Developmentally appropriate digital environments for young children. *Library Trends, 54,* 286–302.

Dervin, B., & Nilan, M. (1986). Information needs and uses. *Annual Review of Information Science and Technology, 21,* 3–33.

Dewey, J. (1933). *How we think.* Lexington, MA: Heath.

Druin, A. (2005). What children can teach us: Developing digital libraries for children with children. *Library Quarterly, 75,* 20–41.

Erikson, E. H. (1963). *Youth: Change and challenge.* New York: Basic Books.

Erikson, E. H. (1968). *Identity: Youth and crisis.* New York: WW. Norton & Company.

Isen, A. M., Daubman, K. A., & Gorgoglione, J. M. (1987). The influence of positive affect on cognitive organization: Implications for education. In R. E. Snow & M. J. Farr (Eds.), *Aptitude, learning, and instruction.* Vol. 3: *Cognitive and affective process analyses* (pp. 143–164). Hillsdale, NJ: Lawrence Erlbaum Associates.

Jakobovits, L. A., & Nahl-Jakobovits, D. (1990). Measuring information searching competence. *College & Research Libraries, 51*(5), 448–462.

Kelly, G. A. (1963). *A theory of personality: The psychology of personal constructs.* New York: W.W. Norton & Company.

Kuhlthau, C. C. (1993). *Seeking meaning: A process approach to library and information services.* Westport, CT: Libraries Unlimited.

Kuhlthau, C. C. (2004). *Seeking meaning: A process approach to library and information services.* (2nd ed.). Westport, CT: Libraries Unlimited.

Large, A., & Beheshti, J. (2000). The Web as a classroom resource: Reactions from the users. *Journal of the American Society for Information Science, 51,* 1069–1080.

Large, A., Beheshti, J., & Moukdad, H. (1999). Information seeking on the Web: Navigation skills of grade-six primary school students. *Proceedings of the 62nd annual meeting of the American Society for Information Science and Technology, 36,* 84–97.

Lauria, A. R. (1979). *The making of mind.* Cambridge, MA: Harvard University Press.

Nahl, D. (1996). The user-centered revolution: 1970–1995. *Encyclopedia of Microcomputing* (vol. 19, pp. 143–200). New York: Marcel Dekker.

Nahl, D. (2004). Measuring the Affective Information Environment of Web Searchers. *Proceedings of the 67th annual meeting of the American Society for Information Science and Technology, 41,* 191–197.

Nahl, D. (2005a). Affective load theory (ALT). In K. E. Fisher, S. Erdelez, & L. E. F. McKechnie (Eds.), *Theories of information behavior* (pp. 39–43). Medford, NJ: Information Today.

Nahl, D. (2005b). Affective and cognitive information behavior: Interaction effects in Internet use. *Proceedings of the 68th annual meeting of the American Society for Information Science and Technology, 42.* Accessed December 13, 2006, from eprints.rclis.org/archive/00004978/01/Nahl_Affective.pdf.

Nahl, D. (2007). A discourse analysis technique for charting the flow of micro-information behavior. *Journal of Documentation, 63*(3): 323–339.

Piaget, J., & Inhelder, B. (1969). *The psychology of the child.* New York: Basic Books.

Picard, R. W. (1997). *Affective computing.* Cambridge, MA: MIT Press.

Picard, R. W. (1999). Affective computing for HCI. Accessed December 15, 2006 from affect.media.mit.edu/pdfs/99.picard-hci.pdf.

Ratner, C. (1991). *Vygotsky's sociohistorical psychology and its contemporary applications.* New York: Plenum.

Reuter, K., & Druin, A. (2004). Bringing together children and books: An initial descriptive study of children's book searching and selection behavior in a digital library. *Proceedings of the 67th annual meeting of the American Society for Information Science and Technology, 41,* 339–348.

Simon, H. (1967). Motivational and emotional controls of cognition. *Psychological Review, 74,* 29–39.

Todd, R. J. (2003). Adolescents of the information age: Patterns of information seeking and use, and implications for information professionals. *School Libraries Worldwide, 9,* 27–46.

Van Oers, B. (1994). On the narrative nature of young children's iconic representations: Some evidence and implications. Accessed November 12, 2006 from www.psych.hanover.edu/vygotsky/vanoers.html.

Vygotsky, L. (1962). *Thought and language.* Cambridge, MA: MIT Press.

Vygotsky, L. (1978). *Mind in society: The development of higher psychological processes.* Cambridge, MA: Harvard University Press.

Vygotsky, L. (1982). *Collected works, vol. 1: Problems in the theory and history of psychology.* Moscow: Isdatel'stvo Pedagogika.

Watson, J. S. (1998). If you don't have it, you can't find it. *Journal of the American Society for Information Science, 49,* 1024–1036.

CHAPTER 3

How Emotional Dimensions of Situated Information Seeking Relate to User Evaluations of Help from Sources: An Exemplar Study Informed by Sense-Making Methodology

Brenda Dervin and CarrieLynn D. Reinhard
Ohio State University

Since its early inception, Dervin's Sense-Making Methodology has conceptualized information seeking and use as a sub-set of human "sense-making" and "sense-unmaking." "Emotions" have always been incorporated into its framework (Dervin, 1983; Dervin & Foreman-Wernet, 2003). Despite this long history, this chapter offers the first explicit interrogation of how the methodology conceptually handles the concept. The reason for this apparent neglect speaks, in fact, to the heart of the difference in how Sense-Making conceptualizes "emotion."

In the metaphoric picture of the Sense-Making triangle (Figure 3.1) that serves as the foundation of the approach, emotion is specified explicitly as a bridging sense-making element, along with other elements (e.g., intuition, thoughts, attitudes) that have been traditionally treated separately in sometimes quite distant social science discourse communities. Emotion is also incorporated implicitly at each of the converging vectors of the triangle. Thus, if we examine the empirical work guided by the Methodology, we see that all the anchoring concepts in the Sense-Making triangle incorporate elements usually defined in extant literatures as "emotions" (e.g., outcomes incorporate what are typically called "emotional" helps and hinders; gaps include questions usually defined as "emotional"); bridges encompass "learnings" relating to emotions as well as the explicitly specified "feelings"; situations and their histories may be described by sense-makers as imbued with "emotion."

Of course, concepts such as emotions, cognitions, attitudes, values, learnings, and so on—the collection of "elements" that Sense-Making pulls

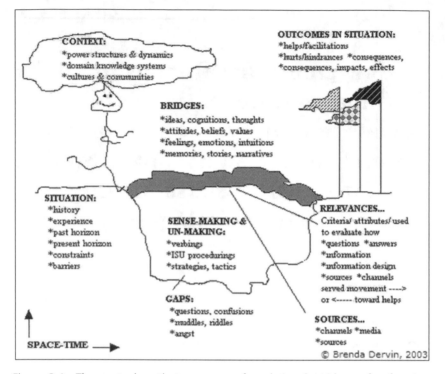

Figure 3.1 The metaphor that serves as foundational guidance for framing research questions, interviewing, and analyzing data in Sense-Making guided studies

together into a deliberately undistinguished and undefined group—are the focal centers for most traditional social science treatments of human beings and their internal-external behaviors. It is an important distinction in the development of Sense-Making Methodology that energies have not been put into defining and theorizing emotions or cognitions or any of these traditional concepts used to categorize and compartmentalize human internal and external behaviors.

In Sense-Making, the foundational metaphor, drawn from philosophical sources (Dervin, 2003), is used to provide methodological guidance for research analytics including question formation, data collection, and analysis. In the most general sense, the metaphor provides guidance for a way of looking at users (and intended users) by whatever names they may be called. In its most used application, the triangle is used to inform an approach to interviewing informants who are asked: What were your questions? Confusions? Muddles? Feelings? Thoughts? Conclusions? Ideas? Learnings? What happened in your situation? What stood in the way? What did you struggle with? What helped and how? What hindered and how? If you could have got any help you wanted, what would that have been?

In this naturalistic and holistic approach to interviewing, it is the inform-ant—not the researcher—who is left free to define terms such as emotions or learnings or muddles. While many dominant theories of interviewing attempt to structure interviewing in such a way that the goal is to constrain informant interpretations to researcher intent, Sense-Making draws on dif-ferent theories of communicating and enters into the relationship with interviewees in the mode of collaboration—treating interviewees as knowl-edgeable informants on their life situations, capable of theorizing events, causes, and outcomes.

Working in a trajectory shared by a number of social scientists who have been experimenting with ways to develop approaches to making sense out of the chaotic edifices of social science literature and to make the social sci-ences "matter" in the practical worlds of the everyday, Sense-Making has deliberately eschewed the definitional baggage that is the important collat-eral of most social science work.[1] This has not been an act of rejection but rather a quest to find a way to pursue a mode of research that physicist Feynman (1999) proposed the social sciences must pursue if they are to mat-ter—to observe, observe, observe. Observe the phenomenon of our interest on its own terms without a priori definitional and propositional notions—no matter how valuable they may have proved in the past and may still be in the present.

Sense-Making Methodology has been, thus, at its highest level of abstrac-tion, an attempt to free us of some assumptive legacies from the traditional social sciences by developing a framework that has been intended to be about no particular real-world context but focused instead on universals of human sense-making and sense-unmaking. The attempt has been to refocus attention from the nouns, which have been the collateral of the social sci-ences, to verbs (Dervin, 1993).

ENTERING THE STUDY OF EMOTIONS
THROUGH DIFFERENT DOORS

For purposes of this chapter, we will start by accepting the generally agreed upon idea that emotion—whatever the potential variety of ways it is or might be heuristically defined—is a state of being that occurs inside indi-viduals and is associated in some way with those host states of being that laypeople call "feelings." This is perhaps the only premise agreed upon throughout the various literatures that attend to emotions; although as the concept gets explicated, the observational traces of this internal state of being are defined as observable in a dizzying array of possibilities—as multi-ple variations of causes, manifestations, and consequences. Unraveling these complexities is beyond the aims of this chapter. For our purposes here, we will simplify markedly.

Figure 3.2 does this for us by encapsulating in eight miniature portraits what we see as the essential thrusts of the theorizing about emotions and their relationships to information seeking and use, broadly defined, as used in the field of library and information science, and as this field is informed by communication and psychology.[2] Each of these theoretic thrusts, and the work guided by them, is informative to our collective efforts to understand emotions. Admittedly, there are numerous nuances and details that Figure

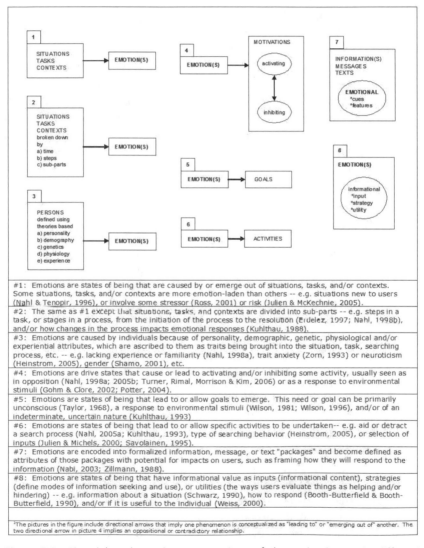

#1: Emotions are states of being that are caused by or emerge out of situations, tasks, and/or contexts. Some situations, tasks, and/or contexts are more emotion-laden than others -- e.g. situations new to users (Nahl & Tenopir, 1996), or involve some stressor (Ross, 2001) or risk (Julien & McKechnie, 2005).

#2: The same as #1 except that situations, tasks, and contexts are divided into sub-parts -- e.g. steps in a task, or stages in a process, from the initiation of the process to the resolution (Erdelez, 1997; Nahl, 1998b), and/or how changes in the process impacts emotional responses (Kuhlthau, 1988).

#3: Emotions are caused by individuals because of personality, demographic, genetic, physiological and/or experiential attributes, which are ascribed to them as traits being brought into the situation, task, searching process, etc. -- e.g. lacking experience or familiarity (Nahl, 1998a), trait anxiety (Zorn, 1993) or neuroticism (Heinstrom, 2005), gender (Shamo, 2001), etc.

#4: Emotions are drive states that cause or lead to activating and/or inhibiting some activity, usually seen as in opposition (Nahl, 1998a; 2005b; Turner, Rimal, Morrison & Kim, 2006) or as a response to environmental stimuli (Gohm & Clore, 2002; Potter, 2004).

#5: Emotions are states of being that lead to or allow goals to emerge. This need or goal can be primarily unconscious (Taylor, 1968), a response to environmental stimuli (Wilson, 1981; Wilson, 1996), and/or of an indeterminate, uncertain nature (Kuhlthau, 1993)

#6: Emotions are states of being that lead to or allow specific activities to be undertaken-- e.g. aid or detract a search process (Nahl, 2005a; Kuhlthau, 1993), type of searching behavior (Heinstrom, 2005), or selection of inputs (Julien & Michels, 2000; Savolainen, 1995).

#7: Emotions are encoded into formalized information, message, or text "packages" and become defined as attributes of those packages with potential for impacts on users, such as framing how they will respond to the information (Nabi, 2003; Zillmann, 1988).

#8: Emotions are states of being that have informational value as inputs (informational content), strategies (define modes of information seeking and use), or utilities (the ways users evaluate things as helping and/or hindering) -- e.g. information about a situation (Schwarz, 1990), how to respond (Booth-Butterfield & Booth-Butterfield, 1990), and/or if it is useful to the individual (Weiss, 2000).

²The pictures in the figure include directional arrows that imply one phenomenon is conceptualized as "leading to" or "emerging out of" another. The two directional arrow in picture 4 implies an oppositional or contradictory relationship.

Figure 3.2   Pictorial and word representations of the main thrusts in different conceptualizations of "emotion(s)" in the current library and information science and communication literature

3.2 leaves behind, and many authors combine two or more of the thrusts in their projects. Further, Figure 3.2 glosses over two major bifurcations in the literature: (a) While some researchers treat emotion in the singular, others treat it as multidimensional, although there are many disagreements about what these dimensions are, and (b) while some researchers impose their definitions of emotions a priori (mostly quantitative researchers), others impose them after data is collected (mostly qualitative researchers).

Despite these overlooked complexities, Figure 3.2 allows us to position how Sense-Making focuses on "emotion(s)" in as brief an explication as possible. In Figure 3.2, we offer both graphic and verbal pictures of the eight theoretical thrusts that show the relationships posited between emotions and other phenomena. For brevity's sake, we have summarized the literature review that supports Figure 3.2 in an extensive footnote.[3]

Briefly stated, Figure 3.2 suggests that emotions have been conceptualized as: being caused by or arising out of situations, tasks, or contexts or their subparts (pictures 1 and 2, in Figure 3.2); being attributes of persons—their personalities, demography, genetics, physiology, or past experiences (picture 3); being causes of inhibiting or activating motivations (picture 4); causing or leading to specific actor goals or activities (pictures 5 and 6); being encoding traces left in information, message, or text packages (picture 7); and serving as states of being that have informational value (picture 8).

As one looks at the literature, it is fair to say that picture 4 has what can best be termed a foundational role: It is often assumed to be operating no matter what other thrust a project adopts. Most frequently, emotion has been conceptualized as a constant or changing state of being that limits or hinders information seeking and use (broadly defined and including source use, media use, search capacities, and so on). Because of how Sense-Making has conceptualized emotions and related concepts using interpretive and phenomenologically grounded theorizing tools, over the years, one or more Sense-Making studies have empirically advanced in ways that could be described as working within each of the eight pictures in Figure 3.2. It is important to note, however, that examining studies through the lenses provided by this or that theoretical thrust pictured in Figure 3.2 ends up unintentionally co-opting work from one thrust into another. It is as if apples are used to define oranges and vice versa.

Most of the extant work on emotions and information has, in fact, been primarily concerned with positioning information seeking and use as an "outcome," examining how emotions come out of prior conditions or lead to consequent conditions to in some way impact information seeking and use in good and/or bad ways. In contrast, Sense-Making Methodology has been most closely aligned from the beginning with what is now emerging as theory 8. Sense-Making positions "emotions" as a situated sense-making orientation in a confluence of sense-making orientations—in effect, as a potentially transitory orientation toward a moment in time-space that could potentially be motivating or inhibiting, helpful or hindering, facilitating or interfering, but always informing to greater or lesser degrees.

Further, because Sense-Making deliberately mandates consideration of time-space as central to all theorizing, by definition, Sense-Making would assume that the journey from an emotional orientation of some kind is not assumed to be written in advance. Nor is the longevity of its presence or influence—it might be elusively short or habitually long, it might be triggered by a single event or a confluence, or it might itself be the force that leads to situational definition. It might also have impacts of short or minor consequence, or impacts that endure far beyond its time-space. Sense-Making assumes, however, that hidden in this complexity are discernible patterns that will help us understand information seeking and use. The trick is applying research frameworks that allow complexities to show in systematic ways.

RESEARCH FOCUS FOR AN EXEMPLAR STUDY

In the remainder of this chapter, we present a small exemplar study of the relationships described by users of the "emotional" characteristics of the situations they were in and the ways they saw the sources of input they turned to in these situations as helping them. In executing this study, we implemented the following explicit assumptions drawn from Sense-Making Methodology:

1. Information seeking and use are at least in part highly situated and, thus, the relationships between "emotion" and information seeking and using behaviors will vary across time-space in situated ways.

2. Aspects of situations normatively thought of as "emotional" may or may not be seen as such by users.

3. There are universals of human situation facing we can address methodologically, which will let us capture systematically explanatory aspects of situated information seeking and use.

4. Users can usefully be turned to as "theorists" of their own information seeking and use and inform us about how they saw their emotional and cognitive states and their consequences.

5. Everywhere that expertise assumes particular bridges across time-space gaps (e.g., between particular kinds of situations or states or inputs and particular outcomes), we can explicitly ask users to articulate how they saw themselves as bridging these gaps and use this interpretive input as evidential fodder for enlarging our understandings of users.

Our study looked at how 409 informants-in-situations evaluated 2,030 situations on a series of situational assessment scales that tapped "emotional" dimensions as found in the extant literatures on emotion. We then looked at how these situational assessments related to informant reports of how much and how sources helped them. The study was executed via deep qualitative interviewing that incorporated some quantitative aspects, followed by systematic content analysis, and, for this report, statistical analyses.

METHOD[4]

The Sample

The data used to implement the purposes previously set forth were collected as part of a large scale study of information seeking and use conducted with three random samples of faculty, graduate students, and undergraduates from 44 colleges and universities in central Ohio.[5] For purposes here, we will focus only on the portions of the project that inform this chapter. Informants were brought into the sample in proportion to population counts at each of the 44 institutions. The goal was to achieve approximately equal sub-sample sizes. The final sample consisted of 118 faculty, 142 graduate students, and 149 undergraduates.

Data Collection

Sampled informants were asked to complete an online survey describing five recent situations in which they sought input of some kind to answer a question, resolve a problem or confusion, or had to pay extra attention in some way. The five critical entries were: (1) troublesome academic life situation, (2) situation involving scholarship or research, (3) troublesome personal life situation, (4) mostly electronic source use in an academic situation, and (5) mostly electronic source use in a personal situation.

The follow-up to the online survey was a phone interview in which informants were asked to describe each of their five situations in detail. They were asked, following Sense-Making's mandates, how they saw their situations, what questions they had, what learnings they achieved, what "helps" they sought and gained, what sources they turned to, and what prevented them from getting complete help.

Taken together, the online survey and phone interview took an average of about 90 minutes to complete. The particular sub-sets of informant narratives used in this study involved informant assessments of their situations in a series of six close-ended situational evaluation scales and informant explanations of how and to what extent the sources they used in their situations helped them. These measures were elicited as attributes of situations as experienced by informants. These variable clusters will be explicated more fully later in this chapter. The specific nature of the situations informants faced (i.e., the nouns of their situations) was analyzed and is reported elsewhere. Our analysis here purposively focused on the verbs of situation-facing.

Units of Analysis

The Sense-Making's unit of analysis has long been conceptualized as person-in-situation.[6] Each of the study's 409 informants completed narrative descriptions of five situations. Of the targeted goal of 2,045 situation descriptions, 2,030 were obtained. These were the units of analysis used for this study.

Measurement of Situation Assessment Scales

The situational assessments, which we positioned in our earlier purpose statement as our address of aspects of situations traditionally defined as emotion-based, consisted of a series of six close-ended scales. Informants were asked the extent to which they saw each particular situation as challenging, important, confusing, emotional, unfamiliar, and contradictory. Each of these attributes have been applied in the emotion-focused literature as describing emotional aspects of situations, texts, messages, and information as well as the emotional states of people. The concepts have had a long history of use in Sense-Making studies and have been applied here because they address a cluster of concepts that have traditionally been treated in various ways as "emotional" indicators in the literature but have been frequently confounded. For this reason, in this study, we have deliberately treated these assessments as six independent dimensions, both to attempt to isolate a less confounded and thus purer phenomenological measure of affect and to examine how the six scales differentially relate to information seeking and use outcomes. These situational assessment scales are the predictor variables in the analyses presented here.

As predictor variables, we used each scale in two different forms, the purpose of which is explained in our statistical tests section that follows. In one form, the measures are used as continuous mathematic scales with ranges from 01–10, tapping the extent to which informants saw each scale as applying to a particular situation "not at all" to "very much so." Results showed that the average ratings for the six scales across all 2,030 informants-in-situations were: challenging, 6.71; important, 8.21; confusing, 4.96; emotional, 5.21; unfamiliar, 6.06; and contradictory, 4.05.

The second form of each measure was a reconstructed three-category predictor collapsing the original 10-point scales into three groups with as near-equal numbers of cases as possible. For each measure, the resulting categories were labeled as low, medium, and high on the particular situational assessment attribute.

Measurements of How Sources Helped and How Much

The criterion measures for this study focus on informant reports of how sources help in their situations and how much. In their online self-interviews, informants checked off from a roster of 25 which input sources they used in their situation. These sources incorporated sources typically used in prior studies of everyday information needs (e.g., Dervin et al., 1976) and included such categories as: own observations or thinking; family, friends, or neighbors; college and university libraries; library catalogues; journal articles; fiction books; commercial advertisements; electronic databases; and personal Web pages.[7]

In follow-up phone interviews, informants were asked to indicate the extent to which each source used was helpful on a 10-point scale (no help at all to maximum help) and to describe in their own words how the sources helped. The content of these narrative descriptions of help was analyzed using the help categories that have been used in Sense-Making studies since the 1970s. For purposes here, the five categories used are illustrated in Figure 3.3 with both pictorial and verbal pictures. The categories included: Got Pictures, Got or Kept Moving, Got Support, Got Control, and Got There. Each category is meant to tap metaphorically how the informants evaluated their sources as facilitating their situational journeys. In terms of traditional studies on emotion, the Got Support and Got Control categories would be considered most relevant.

Tables 3.1 and 3.2 illustrate how these measures of helpfulness and qualities of help were extracted from informant interviews. Table 3.1 provides excerpts from an interview with a female associate professor at a small liberal arts college as she discussed her troublesome academic situation, her struggle as a department chair with a disrespectful colleague, and her use of six sources, including nonfiction books. Table 3.2 provides a second example in the interview with a doctoral student at a large public university discussing his efforts to finish a paper in one night that he had barely started and his use of an array of nine sources, including libraries, journals, and the Internet.

In these tables, we see, for example, that the assistant professor evaluated her situation as 10, 10, 10, 10, 10, and 8, respectively, on the challenging, important, confusing, emotional, unfamiliar, and contradictory scales. In contrast, the doctoral student showed scale ratings of 10, 10, 5, 10, 3, and 9. The variability in these patterns across our informants was marked and was a primary reason that we opted not to attempt to use any conceptual or statistical data reduction tools on the six situational assessment scales.

While the informants applied these scale ratings directly to their situations, our measures of source helpfulness levels and qualities were extracted by content analysis and computation across all the sources an informant used in a situation. Thus, for example, the assistant professor in Table 3.1 used six sources with helpfulness grades on the 10-point scale of 10, 9, 10, 5, 10, 10, and 10, with an average of 8.8. In contrast, the doctoral student in

CATEGORY NAME	CATEGORY PICTURE	CATEGORY DEFINITION	CATEGORY EXAMPLES
	got pictures	informant got: *ideas, pictures *choices, directions *hows, methods *to find and choose directions to travel in *to learn how to get on with it	*they showed me how to use the database and gave me some ideas *the Web site gave me a chance to explore my options
	got or kept moving	informant got: *connected to sources *started down a chosen road *help continuing traveling, staying on track, making progress *traveling made easier, quicker, more convenient, timelier	*she came in and did some of the work for me so that it would be done on time *from writing other research papers I was able to figure out what I had to do next
	got support	informant got: *support, praise, understanding, listening *a sense of traveling a road with others, or that others have traveled a similar road before	*they listened to me, helped me talk this out *I could talk to them about the project, share experiences on the training workshop
	got control	informant got: *inner/self control, refuge, peace *out of, controlled, or avoided a bad situation *rest, respite, escape *pleasure, joy, happiness	*it reminded me that sometimes things change and you've got to move on and deal with things as they come best you can *maybe sort of as an outlet, let my feelings and frustration out
	got there	informant got: *specific resource(s) needed for completing the journey *to the end of the journey, the destination set out for	*the library gave me the slides to show to my students *they were able to fix my computer, stop it from crashing

Figure 3.3 Pictorial and word representations of the five qualitative categories of helps used as evaluations of sources of inputs—the criterion variables in this study

Table 3.2 used nine sources with helpfulness grades of 10, 8, 7, 7, 10, 5, 10, 10, and 10, with an average of 8.5. These average source helpfulness scores became one of our six criterion measures. The average of these averages across all 2,030 informants-in-situations was 7.38, with informant-in-situation scores occupying the possible range of 1.00 to 10.00.

Table 3.1 Excerpts from a Female Associate Professor's Responses to a Troublesome Academic Situation Illustrating How Situation Scales Were Ascribed to the Situation and How Source Evaluation Data Was Collated Across All Sources Used in That Situation

INFORMANT E001: female, associate professor, single, age 44, works at small private primarily liberal arts college, student enrollment 15% graduate students at master's level
SITUATION #1 (troublesome academic:): ... *with a co-worker who treated me without respect ... I am acting chair, and this new co-worker treated me like I am subservient to her.*

THE INFORMANT'S SITUATION SCALE RATINGS ...		
CHALLENGING: 10	IMPORTANCE: 10	CONFUSING: 10
EMOTIONAL: 10	UNFAMILIAR: 10	CONTRADICTORY: 9

AVERAGE HELPFULNESS SCORE FOR 6 SOURCES LISTED BELOW: 8.8		
WAS EACH HELP CATEGORY USED 1+ TIMES TO EVALUATE SOURCES IN THE SITUATION ...		
GOT PICTURES: Yes	GOT OR KEPT MOVING: Yes	GOT SUPPORT: Yes
GOT CONTROL: Yes	GOT THERE: No	

SOURCE EVALUATION DATA FROM WHICH HELPFULNESS SCORE & HELP CODES WERE EXTRACTED:
OWN OBSERVATIONS, THINKING, REFLECTION: helpfulness grade – 10 *... I had to think about everything she said ... I had to think about her position ... about the email and I just spent a lot of time thinking and sorting through ... the situation and observing her behavior ... [GOT PICTURES, GOT OR KEPT MOVING]*
FAMILY, FRIENDS, OR NEIGHBORS: helpfulness grade – 9 *... they pray about a situation I feel it gives me input in how I should act ... how does a Christian act ... this is emotional help and a reminder ... [GOT PICTURES, GOT SUPPORT]*
CO-WORKERS OR COLLEAGUES: helpfulness grade – 10 *... they helped me by giving different perspective ... by discussing with me their own observations ... [GOT PICTURES, GOT CONTROL]*
PROFESSORS, ADVISORS, TEACHERS, MENTORS: helpfulness grade – 5 *... he told me what he [had] told her he wanted her to do but did not address [everything] ... [GOT PICTURES]*
OTHER PROFESSIONALS: helpfulness grade – 10 *... he basically listened and I kind of worked through my own thoughts [GOT SUPPORT, GOT OR KEPT MOVING]*
OTHER NON-FICTION BOOKS: helpfulness grade – 10 *... I started reading books on leadership and teamwork and communication ... they gave me advice about ... how to deal with situations and how to speak to people ... so I could handle myself better [GOT PICTURES, GOT OR KEPT MOVING, GOT CONTROL]*

Informant qualitative assessments of how sources helped them were also computed across all the sources an informant used in a situation. This was done by content analyzing informant narratives into the specified help categories[8] and then calculating whether each category was used one or more times in evaluating sources in a particular situation. For example, Table 3.1 shows that the assistant professor was coded as: Got Pictures, Got or Kept Moving, Got Support, and Got Control. Across her six sources, the assistant professor specified each of these helps 5, 3, 1, and 2 times, respectively. In

Table 3.2   Excerpts from a Male Doctoral Student's Responses to a Scholarship, Research Situation Illustrating How Situation Scales Were Ascribed to the Situation and How Source Evaluation Data Was Collated Across All Sources Used in That Situation

INFORMANT E002: male, doctoral student, married, age 34, works at large public university, student enrollment at 26% graduate students		
SITUATION #3 (scholarship, research): *... one paper was due like tomorrow ... however, I had no idea [how] to figure it out so I had to stay up all night to work on it ...*		
THE INFORMANT'S SITUATION SCALE RATINGS ...		
CHALLENGING: 10	IMPORTANCE: 10	CONFUSING: 5
EMOTIONAL: 10	UNFAMILIAR: 3	CONTRADICTORY: 9
AVERAGE HELPFULNESS SCORE ACROSS 9 SOURCES: 8.5		
WAS EACH HELP CATEGORY USED 1+ TIMES TO EVALUATE SOURCES IN THE SITUATION ...		
GOT PICTURES: Yes	GOT OR KEPT MOVING: Yes	GOT SUPPORT: No
GOT CONTROL: No	GOT THERE: Yes	
SOURCE EVALUATION DATA FROM WHICH HELPFULNESS SCORE & HELP CODES WERE EXTRACTED:		
OWN OBSERVATIONS, THINKING, REFLECTION: helpfulness grade – 10 *... my thinking directed me to the general idea to solve the problem ... what I should ask or what I should find online so my thinking is very important ... [GOT PICTURES]*		
COLLEGE OR UNIVERSITY LIBRARIES: helpfulness grade – 8 *... I got the books and we still have lots of online things [GOT THERE]*		
OTHER KINDS OF LIBRARIES: helpfulness grade – 7 *they have some of the information I can't find in this library but I can get this information fast through OhioLink ... I can get the books or some journals ... [GOT PICTURES, GOT OR KEPT MOVING, GOT THERE]*		
LIBRARY CATALOGUES: helpfulness grade – 7 *... they make it easy to find information in books and journals into different categories ... [GOT OR KEPT MOVING, GOT PICTURES]*		
JOURNAL ARTICLES OR BOOK CHAPTERS: helpfulness grade – 10 *... I found some free and immediate information from journals, they are just new journals so they refreshed my memory very quick ... [GOT THERE, GOT OR KEPT MOVING, GOT PICTURES]*		
GOVERNMENT, NON PROFIT ORGS, INSTITUTIONS: helpfulness grade – 5 *... not a lot but ... I need some figures, some numbers from the government ... [GOT PICTURES, GOT THERE]*		
ELECTRONIC DATABASE SEARCHING SYSTEMS: helpfulness grade – 10 *... they give me all kinds of information ... yeah, I can get almost anything ... [GOT PICTURES, GOT OR KEPT MOVING]*		
INTERNET SEARCH ENGINES: helpfulness grade – 10 *... gave me easy and quick response and I can find almost anything there ... [GOT OR KEPT MOVING, GOT PICTURES]*		
WEB DIARIES, JOURNALS OR BLOGS: helpfulness grade – 10 *... I easily found the journals and created my paper ... I needn't buy and go to the library so it was very convenient [GOT OR KEPT MOVING, GOT THERE]*		

contrast, the doctoral student was coded as: Got Pictures, Got or Kept Moving, and Got There. Across his nine sources, he specified each of these helps 7, 6, and 5 times, respectively. Final computations of the criterions for each informant-in-situation were reduced to a dichotomous code: Yes, the informant named this help one or more times across the sources used in this situation; or no, the informant did not. Results showed that across the five help qualities, percentages of informants-in-situations reporting each help were: Got Pictures, 85.9 percent; Got or Kept Moving, 87.9 percent; Got Support, 77.9 percent; Got Control, 53.9 percent; and Got There, 47.8 percent.

Interview Transcriptions and Coding

During the interviews, interviewers were trained to re-anchor their interviewees' attentions to each particular situation being discussed. Interviews were tape-recorded, verbatim transcripts constructed, and narratives content analyzed using standard quality control procedures. Interjudge coding reliabilities for each of the helps coding was 90 percent agreement or above, using both the percentage agreement index and correction for chance.[9]

Statistical Analyses

We have attempted here to present statistical analyses in a way that will be of interest to a variety of readers. We combine two different statistical approaches. The first is one-way analyses of variance in which we use the three-category versions of the situational scales as predictors of the help measures. This method allows us to attach policy-articulate figures to the results (e.g., naming the percentages of informants-in-situations who reported their helps in significantly different ways). The second method is the use of multiple regression correlational models in which we focused on how much variance in each "criterion help measure" was accounted for by each predictor scale when it was acting alone versus when it was entered into the equation last, after all the other scales combined were allowed to grab all the variance they could. It is this last measure that provides the best entry point for comparing the predictive power of the different situational assessment scales.[10]

Using two statistical approaches—one which assumes linear relationships (regression) and one which assumes potential curvilinearity—allowed us to enlist statistics as complementary tools. Clearly, regression as an approach provides the most parsimonious array of findings, but examination of curvilinearities opens up more potential future research questions.

Before proceeding with our results, it is useful to reference findings from studies that have already been conducted using this same database. The results are illustrative of the possibilities for looking at emotion and information that Sense-Making as a methodology was designed to make possible.

One study used informants in their situations as units of analysis to look at how academic rank (faculty, graduate students, undergraduates) and situation entry (the five situation collection entry points used in this study) worked as predictors of both the six-situation assessment scales and the qualitative and quantitative judgments of how sources used in situations helped. Briefly stated, findings showed that both academic rank and situation entry related to the six situation assessment scales in ways that face validity logics would predict. For example, graduate students saw situations as more challenging and emotional, undergraduates as more unfamiliar, and faculty as more contradictory; troublesome personal situations were rated highest on all scales except contradictory, for which it was troublesome academic situations that received high ratings. This summary leaves out important nuances, of course, but the most important for our considerations were that no two situational assessment scales showed the same patterns in results.[11]

A second study[12] reported on source-using instances as a predictor of how informants saw sources as helping. The 11,319 source-using instances of the 409 informants in their 2,030 situations were grouped into source categories (e.g., libraries versus family, friends, and neighbors). Major patterns in results showed that every category of sources was evaluated at least some of the time as helping in all possible ways. Thus, for example, both interpersonal sources and library sources were evaluated at least some of the time as giving support or providing pictures. While some sources were evaluated as helping more than others, every category of sources showed at least 25 percent of its source-using instances evaluated as low in helpfulness and at least 25 percent evaluated as high in helpfulness. Differences between source categories in helpfulness ratings were small compared to differences in how many different kinds of help were reported as helping. Some of the least named helps (e.g., Got There, Got Control) were evaluated as the most helpful. In contrast, the most used evaluator (Got Pictures) was evaluated as among the least helpful. In general, results suggested that sources wishing to serve their users more effectively might look less at overall assessments of how they compared to other sources, and more at what users evaluated as particularly helpful in their sense-making journeys.

In terms of relevance to our focus here, the results also showed that the two dimensions of helps tapped by our criterion measure under a variety of other labels in the emotions literature (Got Control and Got Support) behaved quite differently from each other. Furthermore, Got Pictures, which was traditionally seen as bedrock for information seeking assessments, was more likely to act like a necessary but not sufficient condition for evaluating source-using encounters as highly helpful. Finally, all source-using categories were evaluated as highly helpful under some conditions. In particular, libraries—feared to be losing ground when compared to Internet sources—held their own.

RESULTS

Results for each of the six criterion variables are reported in the following section, tapping how much and how informants-in-situations saw sources used in their situations as helping them.

Average Source Helpfulness Ratings

Figure 3.4 shows the results for the analysis of the six situational assessment scales as predictors of average source helpfulness scores. Results show that each of the scales was a significant predictor accounting for variance explained ranging from 0.6 percent (challenging) to 2.6 percent (important). When tested last in the regression model, two of the scales—challenging and

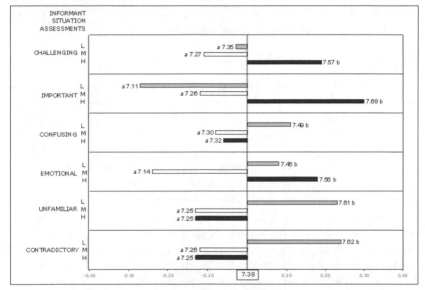

INFORMANT SITUATION ASSESSMENTS	SITUATION ASSESSMENT LEVEL ns (total n=2030)			REGRESSION MODEL		
	L	M	H	DIRECTION	R² ALONE	R² LAST
CHALLENGING	809	688	533		0.6***	0.2
IMPORTANT	588	658	784		2.6****	1.6****
CONFUSING	789	521	720		0.4**	0.1
EMOTIONAL	761	673	596		1.3****	0.7****
UNFAMILIAR	726	688	616		1.2****	1.0****
CONTRADICTORY	703	658	669		1.3****	0.7****
				ALL SIX SCALES	6.0****	

In graph above, marginal means were tested with a one-way analysis of variance, with unlike letter scripts a, b, c significantly different at p<.05, all tested with Games-Howell. In table above, significant R² last for the situation assessment subgroup on a regression model with all other situation assessment subgroups are indicated by: * <.10 n.s.; ** <.05; *** <.01; **** <.001.

Figure 3.4   How average helpfulness scores given to all sources used in a situation varied by low, medium, and high scores on the situational assessment six scales

confusing—dropped out as significant predictors. None showed increases in predictive strength. Working together, all six scales accounted for 6.0 percent of variance in average source helpfulness ratings.

The overall average helpfulness rating was 7.38 on a 10-point scale. After examining the four scales that remained significant after regression control, we see that situations seen as high on the important scale had significantly higher source helpfulness ratings (7.68 compared to 7.11 and 7.26 for low and medium). The opposite was true for the unfamiliar and contradictory scales: Situations rated low on these scales showed significantly higher source helpfulness ratings—mean ratings of 7.61 and 7.62 respectively compared to lows of 7.25–7.26. The emotional scale showed a more complex pattern. Here, the situations rated medium on the emotional scale showed lowest source helpfulness ratings (7.14 compared to highs of 7.46 and 7.56 for the low emotional and high emotional groups).

Got Pictures

Figure 3.5 reports the results for the analysis of the six situational assessment scales as predictors of the help—Got Pictures. Results showed that three of the scales—challenging, important, confusing—were not significant predictors either when analyzed alone or last. The scale—contradictory—was significant at $p<.05$ alone, but dropped to nonsignificant when it was entered into the regression equation last. Working together, all six scales accounted for 2.1 percent of the variance in Got Pictures.

The strongest predictor for Got Pictures was the emotional scale, showing that situations rated as high in emotion related to significantly lower uses of Got Pictures as an evaluation category for sources. Eighty-one percent of high-emotion situations used this evaluation compared to 86.9–88.8 percent for situations rated as medium or low in emotion. This relationship, significant at $p<.001$ when operating alone, became stronger after regression control. The second scale showing a significant relationship that endured after control was unfamiliar, where situations rated high on the unfamiliar scale related to significantly fewer Got Picture evaluations but only when compared with situations rated medium on the unfamiliar scale.

Got or Kept Moving

Figure 3.6 reports the results for the analysis of the six situational assessment scales as predictors of the help—Got or Kept Moving. Results showed, again, that three of the scales—challenging, important, confusing—were not significant predictors. The important scale became significant after regression control. Though our analyses do not precisely identify how the scales interacted with each other to yield this change, an examination of the underlying correlation matrix suggested that the relationship shown in the one-way analysis of variance became stronger. Situations evaluated as high in

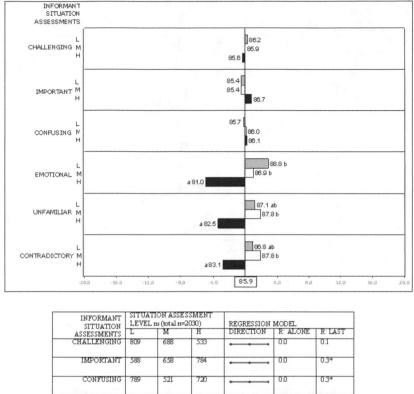

Figure 3.5   How percentage of Got Pictures coded for all sources used in a situation varied by low, medium, and high situation assessment scores on six scales

importance exhibited more use of the Got or Kept Moving help as a source evaluation criterion than the low and medium groups. As shown in the predictive pattern for the Got Pictures help, the situational assessment scale—contradictory—was significant at $p<.05$ alone, but dropped to nonsignificant when entered into the regression equation last in predicting Got or Kept Moving. Working together, the six scales accounted for 2.3 percent of the variance in Got or Kept Moving.

Two situational scales showed significantly different uses of the Got or Kept Moving help depending on scale level. Situations rated high and

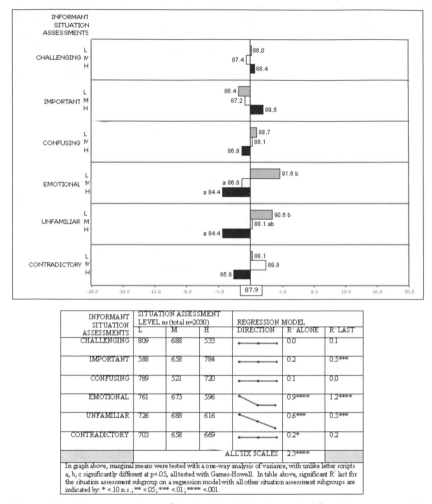

Figure 3.6   How percentage of Got or Kept Moving coded for all sources used in a situation varied by low, medium, and high situation assessment scores on six scales

medium on the emotional scale related to reports of less use of Got or Kept Moving as an evaluation for sources—84.4–86.8 percent compared to a 91.6 percent for situations rated low in emotion. The emotional scale was the strongest predictor and became a bit stronger after regression control. The unfamiliar scale also showed a negative relationship—the more unfamiliar the situation, the less the use of Got or Kept Moving. Here the relationship was linear, with percentages of the use of Got or Kept Moving as a source evaluation criterion ranging from a low of 84.4 percent to a high of 90.6 percent.

Got Support

Figure 3.7 reports the results for the analysis of the six situational assessment scales as predictors of the help—Got Support. Here results showed a very different pattern. All the situational assessment scales showed positive relationships with the use of Got Support as a source evaluation criterion. Working together, the six scales accounted for 5.9 percent of variance overall. The regression control analysis interestingly shows that every one of the situational assessment scales became a weaker predictor after control, indicating that for this criterion help, the scales showed strongly overlapping

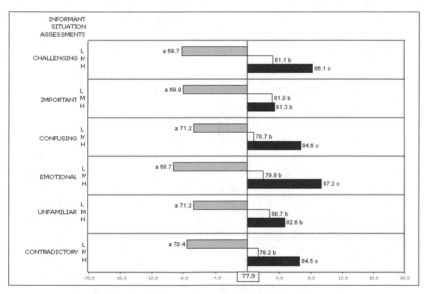

INFORMANT SITUATION ASSESSMENTS	SITUATION ASSESSMENT LEVEL ns (total n=2030)			REGRESSION MODEL		
	L	M	H	DIRECTION	R² ALONE	R² LAST
CHALLENGING	809	688	533		2.8****	0.3**
IMPORTANT	588	658	784		1.5****	0.3**
CONFUSING	789	521	720		1.9****	0.0
EMOTIONAL	761	673	596		3.4****	0.6***
UNFAMILIAR	726	688	616		1.5****	0.8****
CONTRADICTORY	703	658	669		2.0****	0.5***
				ALL SIX SCALES	5.9****	

In graph above, marginal means were tested with a one-way analysis of variance, with unlike letter scripts a, b, c significantly different at p<.05, all tested with Games-Howell. In table above, significant R² last for the situation assessment subgroup on a regression model with all other situation assessment subgroups are indicated by: * <.10 n.s.; ** <.05; *** <.01; **** <.001.

Figure 3.7   How percentage of Got Support coded for all sources used in a situation varied by low, medium, and high situation assessment scores on six scales

predictive patterns in the midst of independent involvement. Only one scale became nonsignificant in its relationship after control: confusing, dropping from 1.9 percent variance, accounted for less than 0.09 percent. The strongest scales were emotional before control (3.4 percent) and unfamiliar after control (0.8 percent).

By examining the one-way analyses of variance graphs, we see in all cases the group of situations classified as high on each scale exhibited percentages of use of the Got Support criterion ranging from 81.3 percent (important) to 87.2 percent (emotional), in contrast to the percentages for situations classified as low on each scale, 68.7 percent (emotional) to 71.2 percent (confusing and unfamiliar). The relationships were for the most part linear, although the precise significance patterns showed some nuances.

Got Control

Figure 3.8 reports the results for the analysis of the six situational assessment scales as predictors of the help—Got Control. The pattern here mirrors to some extent that shown on Got Support but with important differences. All six situational assessment scales showed significant positive relationships when working alone with the use of Got Control as a criterion for evaluating source encounters in situations. Working together, the six scales showed their highest variance accounted for on this measure—9.1 percent overall. Here, the emotional scale was strongest both alone (6.8 percent variance accounted for) and last (3.1 percent). The contradictory scale was second strongest—4.1 percent alone and 1.3 percent last. Two scales—challenging and confusing—became nonsignificant, and all scales lost predictive power after control.

Not surprisingly since the given variance was accounted for overall, the bar graphs show the highest deviations in the percentages of situations reporting use of the Got Control help for evaluating source encounters, depending on how they were categorized as high versus medium versus low on each scale. Situations rated low on the scale values showed percentages ranging from 37.3 percent (low situation emotion rating) and 41.8 percent (low situation contradictory rating), while those rated high showed percentages upwards of 66.8 percent (high situation emotion rating) and 66.5 percent (high situation contradictory rating). The relationships were for the most part linear although the precise significance patterns again showed some nuances.

Got There

Figure 3.9 reports the results for the analysis of the six situational assessment scales as predictors of the help—Got There. Here, working together, the six situational assessment scales accounted for 3.8 percent of variance in the

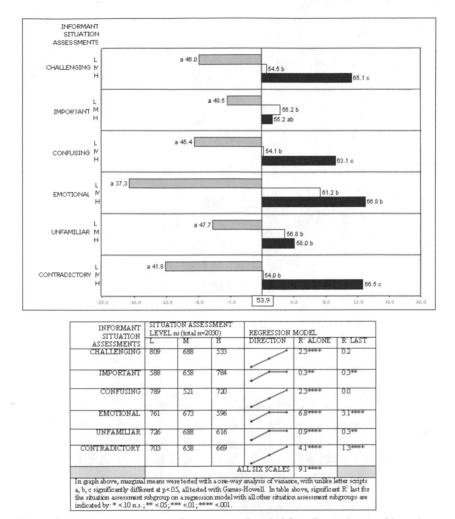

Figure 3.8   How percentage of Got Control coded for all sources used in a situation varied by low, medium, and high situation assessment scores on six scales

criterion variables, and the general pattern across the scales was negative—with high-scale values relating to less use of the Got There help criterion. The results exhibit many complexities, however, this was the most complex of all the criterion measures.

Two of the situational scale assessments—challenging and important—were not significant when working alone but became so (or nearly so) after situational control. The most marked change was for the challenging scale with only 0.1 percent of variance accounted for in the Got There help before control and 0.7 percent after. Both these scales showed curvilinear patterns

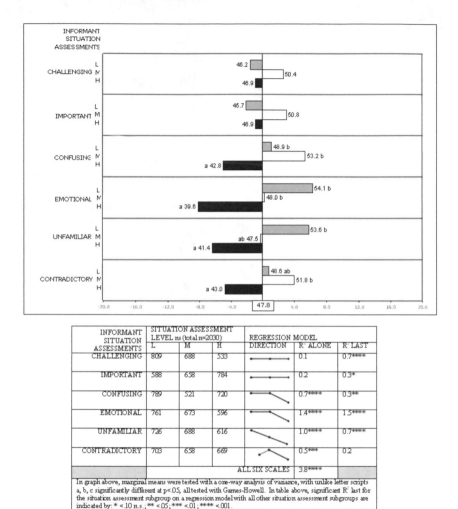

Figure 3.9 How percentage of Got There coded for all sources used in a situation varied by low, medium, and high situation assessment scores on six scales

in the one-way analysis of variance display of means with situations rated medium challenging and medium important exhibiting higher use of this help criterion. While the differences are not large, the significance pattern was clear. Of course, we cannot specify precisely how the scales operating together impacted each other. In general, though, the pattern suggests a positive relationship that reached a threshold beyond which it became negative. The same pattern showed for contradictory, although it became not significant after controls. In all, four of the six situational assessment scales show this curvilinear relationship for the Got There help.

Of the remaining three situational assessment scales, emotion showed the strongest relationship both before and after control (1.4–1.5 percent variance accounted for) with situations rated high in emotion having their sources evaluated less often on Got There—39.6 percent versus a high of 54.1 percent for situations rated low in emotion. The same pattern showed for the unfamiliar scale although with less strength. The percentages using Got There as an evaluation criterion for sources ranged from 41.4 percent (in high unfamiliar situations) to 53.6 percent (in low unfamiliar situations). The confusing category was the third scale in predictive strength both before and after controls. Here, however, results showed a curvilinear relationship with situations rated medium on the confusing scale exhibiting the greatest use of the Got There criterion for evaluating sources (53.2 percent for medium confusing situations compared to 48.9 percent for low and 42.8 percent for high).

CONCLUSION

In interpreting these results, it is important to emphasize that the five categories of helps, coded with informant narratives about how sources helped them, are all conceptualized in Sense-Making as part of the confluence of orientations that constitute information seeking and use processes. Data from prior analyses on this same database showed, for example, that all sources, including libraries and database systems, were evaluated on all help criterions some of the time. Further, those help criterions seen as most helpful did not include Got Pictures—the help category that taps the traditional Got Information and understanding dimensions of situation-facing.

Figure 3.10 presents a summary portrait of results. It encapsulates briefly pictures of the relationships between the six situational assessment scales and the six criterion measures of how informants-in-situations saw sources as helping them. The six scales were selected because each tapped dimensions of "emotion(s)" that have been addressed in a variety of ways in the extant literature of emotions and information behavior. Results with implications follow. In general, as intended, the findings open up far more questions than they answered.

All six situational assessment scales working together accounted for a significant portion of variance in all six help criterions. Got Control was predicted best with 9.1 percent variance accounted for, followed by: average helpfulness ratings, 6.0 percent; Got Support, 5.9 percent; and Got There, 3.8 percent. The two remaining criterions—Got Pictures and Got or Kept Moving—showed total variance accounted for as 2.1 percent and 2.3 percent, respectively. The fact that Got Pictures was lowest in variance while at the same time being the most used evaluator (used in 85.9 percent of all informant-in-situation reports) seems to give additional support for the finding obtained in prior Sense-Making studies—that getting information is a necessary but not sufficient condition for all the other helps to be activated. This proposition needs explicit test in future work.

	average source helpfulness	got pictures	got or kept moving	got support	got control	got there
CHALLENGING	(line)			(line)	positive	*curvilinear*
IMPORTANT	(line)		*positive*	(line)	(line)	
CONFUSING	(line)			positive	positive	(line)
EMOTIONAL	(line)	≈ (line)	≈ (line)	(line)	(line)	(line)
UNFAMILIAR	(line)	(line)	(line)	(line)	(line)	(line)
CONTRADICTORY	(line)	curvilinear		(line)	(line)	curvilinear
informants-in-situations	7.38	85.9	87.9	77.9	53.9	47.8
R2 - all six scales	6.0%	2.1%	2.3%	5.9%	9.1%	3.8%

Cells with relationship lines pictured indicate situational assessment scales that had significant relationships with the indicated help measure both before and after regression control. For the two cells marked with an ≈, the emotional scale became substantially stronger after control. Cells with the italicized words "positive" or "curvilinear" indicate scales that had significant relationships only after control; cells with arabic words indicate significant relationships only before control. Blank cells indicate scales with relationships that were significant neither before nor after control.

Figure 3.10   Summary portrait of the results of all six situation assessment scales as they relate to the six criterions of source evaluation in a given situation

Of the six situation scales, only emotional and unfamiliar had significant relationships with Got Pictures and Got or Kept Moving. In both cases, these relationships were overall negative (i.e., the more emotional and unfamiliar, the less use of Got Pictures and Got or Kept Moving in evaluating sources). Emotional, in particular, was a strong predictor here and substantially stronger after being controlled for the other scales. Of all the findings, this is perhaps the most interesting, given how the emotional scale played such an overlapping role for other criterion measures. For Got Pictures and Got or Kept Moving, the emotional scale was both strongest and operating almost alone. This finding confirms in one sense the generalization from prior emotions literature that emotional states relate to less information processing. Yet, the data for the other help categories suggests this may not be so. Got There, for example, included in its coding many instances of getting a particular document that was essential for completing a project or task. As a second example, Got Support included many instances of learning there was a struggle shared by others. An alternative explanation that itself requires testing is that the time-space materiality of situations that lead to generalized Got Pictures and Got or Kept Going evaluations of sources tend to occur at moments when informants are beginning to articulate information seeking and use. It may be that analyses anchored in time-space movement could tease out the contiguous relationships between the help qualities and show how Got Pictures and Got or Kept Moving fit into the flows of journey-facing.

All six situational scales showed significant positive relationships before and/or after regression control with Got Support and Got Control. These two help evaluations were predicted best. At the same time, all six predictors dropped substantially in variance accounted for after regression control, suggesting that the six scales had important overlapping as well as independent involvements for informants in their orientations toward their situations. Also, the positive and overlapping relationships between the six scales and these two helps suggest that they fit the a priori judgment that they are relatively more affective than the other three helps and, at the same time, affective in multidimensional ways.

Three of the scales—confusing, emotional, and unfamiliar—related generally negatively to Got There. The more confusing, the more emotional, the more unfamiliar, then the less use of Got There as a criterion for evaluating sources. Our explanation of these results is that they pertain mostly to how informants saw the actual material conditions of their situations. Getting there in difficult situations can be a very hard thing to do. The fact that this help quality showed two curvilinear relationships may also provide a hint. For both, there was a positive relationship between low and medium situation scale values and Got There, and then a negative one once the situation was rated as high on that assessment. It seems as if for these relationships—but also spattered throughout the entire set of relationships shown in Figure 3.10—there is some kind of threshold operating, beyond which informants evaluate things as either getting better (e.g., the relationship between the emotional scale and average source helpfulness) or worse (e.g., the relationship between the challenging scale and Got There after regression control, as suggested by Figure 3.9).

Relationships between the six scales and average source helpfulness were both positive and negative. The more challenging and important, the higher the helpfulness ratings given to sources; on the other hand, the more confusing, unfamiliar, and contradictory, the lower. The emotional scale showed a U-curve relationship with both low and high emotional categories relating to higher helpfulness scores. This is another of the more interesting findings, both for its complexity and because it raises interesting questions. Why, for example, the U-curve relationship for the emotional scale? And why do the scales operate diversely here when they hang together so much for the help qualities?

In terms of the most general overall pattern, we see the following: For the more stereotypical information seeking and use outcomes (Got Pictures, Got or Kept Moving, and Got There), the more affective or emotional assessments saw less help when rated high (i.e., the more emotional, confused, unfamiliar or contradictory the situation was judged as, then the less likely informants were to report getting these help qualities). On the other hand, the less typical outcomes (Got Support and Got Control) showed the opposite, where higher emotional assessments were related to judging sources as providing more of these help qualities. However, this does not mean that the one grouping of helps was seen as more helpful than the other, because the pattern of results for the average helpfulness of sources showed a more complex relationship. While confusing (unfamiliar and contradictory showed the pattern of higher levels relating to lower helpfulness ratings), the emotional scale was higher on both extremes. Seeing the situation as being either high or low on emotional related to higher average helpfulness scores. This finding may have particular significance if we can conceptualize the emotional scale used in this study as being a purer measure of affect than that offered in many prior treatments, where aspects of all six situational assessments are often confounded in measurements.

Overall, our findings seem to indicate that both groupings of helps—those traditionally defined as cognitive end goals of information seeking and use, and those traditionally defined as more affective—were important in how helpful the source was perceived. This adds further support to the line of Sense-Making studies that have suggested that it is not the nature of the source or what the source has to offer, but the need of the person-in-situation that is driving how users use sources and how they evaluate them as being useful and helpful.

Finally, it is important to emphasize that Sense-Making guided studies are not intended to present essentialist pictures of user behavior as concrete aspects of reality, but rather phenomenological pictures of how users construe their worlds. When an informant applies a specific attribute in a narrative account to their evaluations of sources, it does not mean that in an essentialist sense the other evaluations were not operating. Rather, it means that given how informants were asked to share narratives of their situation-facing, certain dimensions were salient and others were not.

It becomes a methodological and theoretical challenge to zone in on the most useful directions for further research. From this study, for example, we would suggest that examining situational assessments as they are altered and changed at different moments in situation facing will be extremely important because it will allow us to begin to understand how the ebb and flow of situational assessments relate to source use and evaluations. Additionally, the complex interactions and overlappings seen in how these six scale assessments related to evaluations of source helpfulness indicates a need to further understand how people are characterizing their situations. This will require grounded-theorizing research approaches to flesh out the nuances in affective and cognitive evaluations of situations.

ACKNOWLEDGMENTS

This chapter is one of the outcomes from the project "Sense-Making the information confluence: The whys and hows of college and university user satisficing of information needs." Funded by the Institute of Museum and Library Services, Ohio State University, and the Online Computer Library

Center, the project was implemented by Brenda Dervin (Professor of Communication and Joan N. Huber Fellow of Social & Behavioral Science, Ohio State University) as Principal Investigator; and Lynn Silipigni Connaway (OCLC Consulting Research Scientist III) and Chandra Prahba (OCLC Senior Research Scientist), as Co-Investigators. More information can be obtained at imlsproject.comm.ohio-state.edu.

The authors thank Karen Fisher for encouraging the development of a chapter for this book. In addition, they thank these student research assistants for their invaluable contributions to coding and data analysis: Zack Y. Kerr, Noelle M. Karnolt, Mei Song, Elizabeth M. Kelley, Teena Berberick, Kasey L. Martini, Sarah Adamson, and Jonathan Racster.

ENDNOTES

1. Dervin (1994, 2003) presents much of this underpinning. See, in particular, Briggs (1986), Denzin & Lincoln (2000), Flyvberg (2001), Freire (1970), Lather (1991), Richardson (2002), Scheurich (1995), Yankelovich (1996).

2. This approach to picturing bodies of theoretical work is informed by Richard F. Carter's (2003) development of an iconic language intended to allow comparisons between theories free of the constraints of defining one theory as a shadow of the other (Dervin, 1975/2002, 2003).

3. Our literature review focused most centrally on research in the field of library and information science, covering all the major journals and literature databases for the past five years. Additional forays were made into other fields' treatments of emotion(s)—particularly the fields of communication and psychology—if they received prominent attention in LIS. From this review, we extracted eight conceptualizations of emotions and their relationships to information seeking and use. These conceptualizations were sometimes used by researchers separately or in combinations. For purposes of this literature review, we discuss each conceptualization separately and cite example works that exemplify each thrust. The examples are presented as illustrations and not as a comprehensive list.

   Of those conceptual thrusts focusing on what "causes" or "leads to" emotion(s), No. 1 focuses on the nature of the situation or task (the context) that may contain stimuli that would elicit emotional responses. Tasks may include using the Internet or other technology for the first time (Dalyrumple & Zweizig, 1992; Nahl, 1998a) or searching for information to complete a project (Bilal, 2002, 2005). Situations may include health or other risk-related contexts (Julien & McKechnie, 2005), or coping with some stressor (Ross, 2001). Oftentimes, the situation or task is conceptualized as eliciting a level of uncertainty and anxiety in the individual due to a gap in understanding, which initiates the searching behavior (Kuhlthau, 1993; Wang & Tenopir, 1998; Wilson, Ford, Ellis, Foster, & Spink, 2002); however, searching behavior may also be used to prolong positive emotions that are occurring (Zillmann, 1988).

   No. 2 differs from No. 1 only in that the situation or task has been broken down into its component steps or stages, such as the steps undertaken during a searching process (Kuhlthau, 1988, 1991, 1993; Tenopir, 1994). Again, the steps are conceptualized as eliciting positive or negative emotions, which in turn conceptualized as having subsequent impacts on the overall searching process (Nahl, 1998b, 2005b). This may occur during any step of the process, from the initiation to the resolution of the task (Dalyrumple & Zweizig, 1992; Erdelez, 1997).

Whereas No. 1 and No. 2 describe characteristics of the situation the individual is facing that may differ across time and space, No. 3 conceptualizes the impetus of emotion(s) as derived from some internal trait of the individual that exists across situations. Traits have included: personality aspects, such as the general tendency to be "emotional" (Booth-Butterfield & Booth-Butterfield, 1990; Heinstrom, 2005; Savolainen, 1995; Zorn, 1993); demographic aspects, such as gender (Knobloch-Westerwick & Alter, 2006; Shamo, 2001); and, experience levels with any tool or step in the searching process (McCreadie, 1998; Nahl, 1998a; Wang & Tenopir, 1998; Wilson et al., 2002). An individual's general interests, lifestyles, and motivational states have also been ascribed as being cross-situational (Kracker & Wang, 2002; Nahl, 2005a; Nahl-Jakobovits & Jakobovits, 1985). While other fields (e.g., Condit, 2000; Damasio, 1999) have conceptualized physiological and genetic origins for emotion(s), no research in library and information sciences was found specifically focused here.

What has been found consistently, in combination with the three conceptualizations of causes, is emphasis on the central idea that emotion(s) impact information searching behavior. No. 4 conceptualizes emotion(s) as a drive state that leads to motivations that either activate or inhibit searching. In library and information science, research has largely seen negative emotion(s), such as anxiety, as the main activation to seek information (Kuhlthau, 1991, 1993; Nahl, 1998a, 2005a; Powell, 2004), whereas other fields have theorized the opposite—that emotions lead individuals to avoid information (Turner, Rimal, Morrison, & Kim, 2006; Zorn, 1993). Generally, the consensus is that emotions motivate internal and/or external behavior (Gohm & Clore, 2002; Potter, 2004; Schwarz, 1990).

In the same sense, motivations are conceptualized as arising from emotional needs the individual has, arising from contextual and/or personal requirements. No. 5 conceptualizes emotion(s) as informing the goal of the individual. An individual's emotional need, such as for support or pleasure, has also been conceptualized as an unconscious desire, triggered by environmental stimuli, to serve as the foundation and direction for information seeking behavior—even if the nature of the need itself is vague and uncertain (Bilal, 2002; Kuhlthau, 1993; Nahl, 2005a; Roe, 1985; Taylor, 1968; Wilson, 1981, 1996; Zillmann, 1988). Thus, the goal elicited by an emotional need has been variously conceptualized as providing the motivation that impacts whether or not the search proceeds, as seen in No. 4, and/or dictating the methods undertaken to fulfill that need, as seen next in No. 6.

The conceptualization in No. 6 suggests that emotions may orient individuals toward specific activities or behaviors in order to accomplish their information seeking and use (Heinstrom, 2005; Raghunathan & Corfman, 2004; Tenopir, 1994). Just as No. 2 theorizes how the process may impact emotion(s), No, 6 suggests that feedback from emotion(s) may impact subsequent steps during searching (Nahl, 2005a, 2005b). Emotion has also been conceptualized as impacting the selection of sources of input (Choo, Detlor, & Turnbull, 2000; Julien & Michels, 2000; Kuhlthau, 1991; Potter, 2004; Savolainen, 1995; Wilson, 1981; Zillmann, 1988), which, in turn, has consequences on the end-result, or the sought-for goal. Emotion(s) has thus been conceptualized as an impetus to behavior, from vague need to impetus for each step of the process to fulfill that need.

The final two pictures show emotion(s) as being conceptually linked to information. No. 7 conceptualizes emotion(s) as being encoded into the nature of the information, message or text "package" that the individual is interpreting. These "emotional cues" may then impact how the information is perceived and thus used by the individual (Nabi, 2003; Potter, 2004). This conceptualization comes largely out of the communication field, from work done on information-processing of messages (Nabi, 2003), and from work focusing on the uses and gratifications audiences derive from media. The latter work has focused on the use of media content to manage mood states (Zillmann, 1988), where the features of particular media texts are conceptualized as interacting with the users' mood state in consistent and predictable ways to influence the mood state (Chang, 2006; Hansen, 2003; Knobloch-Westerwick & Alter, 2006; Roe, 1985).

In a related conceptualization, No. 8 shows how emotion(s) can be construed as another source of information for the individual to use, if judged applicable (Beer, Knight, & D'Esposito, 2006; Schwarz, 1990). One variant suggests that emotion(s) is related neurologically to memory, telling the individual what to attend to, how to attend to it, and what to remember for the future (Booth-Butterfield & Booth-Butterfield, 1990; Gohm & Clore, 2002; Schwarz, 1990; Weiss, 2000). Another variant (Dervin, 2003) proposes emotions or feelings as themselves information bearers in a confluence of sense-making elements a user brings to bear in satisficing an information need. While Dervin (2003) is the one example we found of a researcher focusing on information seeking and use who has explicitly positioned emotions as informational, across our entire review picture No. 8—referred to in the social psychology literature as affect-as-information—has played an implied role in how researchers have theorized the nature of emotion(s) in the process of information seeking and use.

4. Detailed accounts of the various methods used in this study are available in the formal report of this study (Dervin, Reinhard, Kerr, Song, & Shen, 2006).

5. The initial sample included four sub-samples: faculty, graduate students, undergraduates, and netLibrary subscribers. When the proposal for the project was written in 2002, it was projected that netLibrary subscribers could be classified as diffusion-of-technology innovators and would, thus, behave differently than others. Given the speed of technology diffusion, the actual results showed few differences between the netLibrary subscribers and others, and no differences on our variables of interest here. Since a qualitatively based study should rest on as large a foundation of qualitative input as possible, and since our purposes here are conceptual and not population estimation, we collapsed the netLibrary sample into our three base samples. A comparison of the netLibrary sub-sample to the non-netLibrary sample is available in the report cited in footnote 4 above.

6. The earliest use is reported in Dervin et al. (1976). An extensive example of the use of source-using instances as units of analysis is available in a research paper drawn from the data being used here: 409 informants in 2,030 situations reported experiencing 11,319 source-using instances. Each of these was analyzed in terms of source type as predictor of average helpfulness and qualities of help. See Dervin, Reinhard, Kerr, Connaway, et al. (2006). For works addressing statistics as theory rather than merely method, see as examples: Dervin (2003), Desrosières (1998), Murdock (199), Porter (1995), and Tufte (1997).

7. The roster included: own observations or thinking; family, friends, or neighbors; students or classmates; co-workers or colleagues; professors, educational advisors, teachers or mentors; other professionals (e.g., pastors, social workers); college or university libraries; public libraries; other kinds of libraries; library catalogues; journal articles or book chapters; reference books (e.g., dictionaries, encyclopedias); other non-fiction books; fiction books; newspaper articles or content; radio programs of content; television programs or content; museum exhibitions or materials; government, nonprofit organizations or institutions; commercial advertisements or materials; electronic database searching systems; Internet search engines (such as Google, Yahoo!); Internet chatrooms or listservs; personal Web pages; and Web diaries, journals, or blogs.

8.   The actual coding operations involved an extended set of 15 help categories, which for this article were collapsed into five major categories.
9.   See, in particular, Krippendorff (2004), Scott (1955), and Stempel (1955).
10.   All statistical analyses were computed with SPSS 14.0. An especially helpful statistical reference was Hayes (2005). The senior author thanks Peter Shields (Eastern Washington University) and Melissa Spirek (Bowling Green State University) for discussions that generated this "policy-articulate" approach to analysis. An example of another analysis using this approach in another context—telecommunication policy user studies—is available as Dervin & Shields (1999).
11.   Reported in Chapters 5 and 10 of Dervin, Reinhard, Kerr, Song, et al. (2006).
12.   Available online in Dervin, Reinhard, Kerr, Connaway, et al. (2006).

REFERENCES

Beer, J. S., Knight, R. T., & D'Esposito, M. (2006). Controlling the integration of emotion and cognition: The role of the frontal cortex in distinguishing helpful from hurtful emotional information. *Psychological Science, 17*(5), 448–453.

Bilal, D. (2002). Perspectives on children's navigation of the World Wide Web: Does the type of search task make a difference? *Online Information Review, 26*(2), 108–117.

Bilal, D. (2005). Children's information seeking and the design of digital interfaces in the affective paradigm. *Library Trends, 54*(2), 197–208.

Booth-Butterfield, M., & Booth-Butterfield, S. (1990). Conceptualizing affect as information in communication production. *Human Communication Research, 16*(4), 451–476.

Briggs, C. L. (1986). *Learning how to ask: A socio-linguistic appraisal of the interview in social science research.* Cambridge: Cambridge University Press.

Carter, R. F. (2003). Communication: A harder science. In B. Dervin & S. Chaffee (Eds.), *Communicating, a different kind of horse race: Essays honoring Richard F. Carter* (pp. 369–376). Cresskill, NJ: Hampton Press.

Chang, C. (2006). Beating the news blues: Mood repair through exposure to advertising. *Journal of Communication, 56*(1), 198–217.

Choo, C. W., Detlor, B., & Turnbull, D. (2000). *Web work: Information seeking and knowledge work on the World Wide Web.* Boston: Kluwer Academic Publishers.

Condit, C. M. (2000). Culture and biology in human communication: Toward a multicausal model. *Communication Education, 49*(1), 7–24.

Dalrymple, P. W., & Zweizig, D. L. (1992). Users' experience of information retrieval systems: An exploration of the relationship between search experience and affective measures. *Library and Information Science Research, 14*(2), 167–181.

Damasio, A. (1999). *The feeling of what happens: Body and emotion in the making of consciousness.* San Diego, CA: Harcourt Press.

Denzin, N. K., & Lincoln, Y. S. (2000). *Handbook of qualitative research* (2nd ed.). Thousand Oaks, CA: Sage Publications.

Dervin, B. (1975/2002). *Communicating ideas: An adapted guide to Richard F. Carter's early picturing language.* Unpublished manuscript. Accessed November 24, 2006, from communication.sbs.ohio-state.edu/sense-making/art/artabsdervin75pic lang.html.

Dervin, B. (1983, May). *An overview of sense-making research: Concepts, methods and results.* Paper presented at the annual meeting of the International Communication Association, Dallas, TX.

Dervin, B. (1993). Verbing communication: Mandate for disciplinary invention. *Journal of Communication, 43*(3), 45–54.

Dervin, B. (1994). Information <—> democracy: An examination of underlying assumptions. *Journal of the American Society for Information Science, 45*(6), 369–385.

Dervin, B. (2003). Sense-making's journey from metatheory to methodology to method: An example using information seeking and use as research focus. In B. Dervin & L. Foreman-Wernet (Eds.), *Sense-Making Methodology reader: Selected writings of Brenda Dervin* (pp. 133–164). Cresskill, NJ: Hampton Press.

Dervin, B., & Foreman-Wernet, L. (Eds.). (2003). *Sense-Making Methodology reader: Selected writings of Brenda Dervin.* Cresskill, NJ: Hampton Press.

Dervin, B., Reinhard, C. D., Kerr, Z. Y., Connaway, L. S., Prabha, C., & Normore, L. et al. (2006, November). *How libraries, Internet browsers, and other sources help: A comparison of sense-making evaluations of sources used in recent college/university and personal life situations by faculty, graduate student, and undergraduate users.* Poster presented at the annual meeting of the American Society for Information Science & Technology, Austin, TX.   Accessed November 24, 2006, from http://imlsproject. comm.ohio-state.edu/imls_papers/asist06poster_list.html.

Dervin, B., Reinhard, C. D., Kerr, Z. Y., Song, M., & Shen, F. C. (Eds.). (2006). *Sense-Making the information confluence: The whys and hows of college and university user satisficing of information needs. Phase II: Sense-making survey.* Report on National Leadership Grant LG-02-03-0062-03, to Institute for Museums and Library Services, Washington, D.C. Columbus, Ohio: School of Communication, Ohio State University. Accessed November 24, 2006, from imlsproject.comm.ohio-state.edu/imls_reports_list.html.

Dervin, B., & Shields, P. (1999). Adding the missing user to policy discourse: Understanding US user telephone privacy concerns. *Telecommunications Policy, 23,* 403–435.

Dervin, B., Zweizig, D., Banister, M., Gabriel, M., Hall, E. P., Kwan, C. et al. (1976). *The development of strategies for dealing with the information needs of urban residents: Phase 1: Citizen study.* Washington, DC: U.S. Office of Education. (ERIC Document Reproduction Service No. ED125640).

Desrosières, A. (1998). *The politics of large numbers: A history of statistical reasoning.* Cambridge, MA: Harvard University Press.

Erdelez, S. (1997). Information encountering: A conceptual framework for accidental information discovery. In P. Vakkari, R. Savolainen, & B. Dervin (Eds.), *Information seeking in context: Proceedings of an International Conference on Research in Information Needs, Seeking, and Use in Different Contexts (Aug. 14–16, 1996, Tampere, Finland)* (pp. 412–421). London: Graham Taylor.

Feynman, R. P. (1999). *The pleasure of finding things out: The best short works of Richard P. Feynman.* Cambridge, MA: Perseus Publishing.

Flyvbjerg, B. (2001). *Making social science matter: Why social inquiry fails and how it can succeed again.* Cambridge: Cambridge University Press.

Freire, P. (1970). *Pedagogy of the oppressed* (M. Bergman Ramos, Trans.). New York: Seabury Press.

Gohm, C. L., & Clore, G. L. (2002). Affect as information: An individual-differences approach. In L. F. Barrett & P. Salovey (Eds.), *The wisdom in feelings: Psychological processes in emotional intelligence.* New York: The Guilford Press.

Hansen, R. A. (2003). *Coping with loss: The use of media and entertainment as a mood-management device.* Unpublished master's thesis, California State University, Fullerton.

Hayes, A. (2005). *Statistical methods for communication science.* Mahwah, NJ: Lawrence Erlbaum Associates.

Heinstrom, J. (2005). Fast surfing, broad scanning and deep diving: The influence of personality and study approach on students' information-seeking behavior. *Journal of Documentation, 61*(2), 228–247.

Julien, H., & McKechnie, L. (E. F.). (2005). What we've learned about the role of affect in information behaviour/information retrieval. In J. Gascón, F. Bruguillos, & A. Pons, (Eds.), *Proceedings of the 7th ISKO (International Society for Knowledge Organization)-Spain Conference. The Human Dimension of Knowledge Organization* (pp. 342–356). Barcelona, July 6–8, 2005.

Julien, H., & Michels, D. (2000). Source selection among information seekers: Ideals and realities. *Canadian Journal of Information and Library Science, 25*(1), 1–18.

Kalbach, J. (2006). I'm feeling lucky: The role of emotions in seeking information on the Web. *Journal of the American Society for Information Science and Technology, 57*(6), 813–818.

Knobloch-Westerwick, S., & Alter, S. (2006). Mood adjustment to social situations through mass media use: How men ruminate and women dissipate angry moods. *Human Communication Research, 32*(1), 58–73.

Kracker, J., & Wang, P. (2002). Research anxiety and students' perceptions of research: An experiment. Part II: Content analysis of their writings on two experiences. *Journal of the American Society for Information Science and Technology, 53*(4), 295–307.

Krippendorf, K. (2004). Reliability in content analysis. *Human Communication Research, 30*(3), 411–433.

Kuhlthau, C. C. (1988). Developing a model of the library search process: Cognitive and affective aspects. *RQ, 28*(2), 232–242.

Kuhlthau, C. C. (1991). Inside the search process: Information seeking from the user's perspective. *Journal of the American Society for Information Science, 42*(5), 361–371.

Kuhlthau, C. C. (1993). A principle of uncertainty for information seeking. *Journal of Documentation, 49*(4), 339–355.

Lather, P. (1991). *Getting smart: Feminist research and pedagogy with/in the postmodern.* New York: Routledge.

McCreadie, M. (1998). *Access to information: A multidisciplinary theoretical framework.* Unpublished doctoral dissertation, Rutgers, The State University of New Jersey, New Brunswick.

Murdock, G. (1997). Thin descriptions: Questions of method in cultural analysis. In J. McGuigan (Ed.), *Cultural methodologies* (pp. 178–192). Thousand Oaks, CA: Sage Publications.

Nabi, R. L. (2003). Exploring the framing effects of emotion: Do discrete emotions differentially influence information accessibility, information seeking, and policy preference? *Communication Research, 30*(2), 224–247.

Nahl, D. (1998a). Ethnography of novices' first use of Web search engines: Affective control in cognitive processing. *Internet Reference Services Quarterly, 3*(2), 51–72.

Nahl, D. (1998b). Learning the Internet and the structure of information behavior. *Journal of the American Society for Information Science, 49*(11), 1017–1023.

Nahl, D. (2004). Measuring the affective information environment of Web searchers. *Proceedings of the 6th ASIS&T Annual Meeting, 41*, 191–197.

Nahl, D. (2005a). Affective and cognitive information behavior: Interaction effects in Internet use. *Proceedings of the 67th annual meeting of the American Society for Information Science & Technology, 41.*

Nahl, D. (2005b). Affective load theory (ALT). In K. E. Fisher, S. Erdelez, & L. E. F. McKechnie, (Eds.), *Theories of information behavior* (pp. 39–43). Medford, NJ: Information Today, Inc..

Nahl, D., & Tenopir, C. (1996). Affective and cognitive searching behavior of novice end-users of a full-text database. *Journal of the American Society for Information Science, 47*, 276–289.

Nahl-Jakobovits, D., & Jakobovits, L. A. (1985). Managing the affective micro-information environment. *Research Strategies, 3*(1), 17–28.

Porter, T. M. (1995). *Trust in numbers: The pursuit of objectivity in science and public life.* Princeton: Princeton University Press.

Potter, W. J. (2004). *Theory of media literacy: A cognitive approach.* Thousand Oaks, CA: Sage Publications.

Powell, M. C. (2004). *To know or not to know? Perceived uncertainty and information seeking and processing about contaminated great lakes fish.* Unpublished doctoral dissertation, University of Wisconsin, Madison.

Raghunathan, R., & Corfman, K. P. (2004). Sadness as pleasure-seeking prime and anxiety as attentiveness prime: The "different affect–different effect" (DADE) model. *Motivation and Emotion, 28*(1), 23–41.

Richardson, L. (2002). Poetic representation of interviews. In J. F. Gubrium & J. A. Holstein (Eds.), *Handbook of interview research: Context and method* (pp. 877–892). Thousand Oaks, CA: Sage Publications.

Roe, K. (1985). Swedish youth and music: Listening patterns and motivations. *Communication Research, 12*(3), 353–362.

Ross, C. S. (2001). What we know from readers about the experience of reading. In K. D. Shearer & R. Burgin (Eds.), *The reader's advisor's companion* (pp. 77–95). Englewood, CO: Libraries Unlimited.

Savolainen, R. (1995). Everyday life information seeking: Approaching information seeking in the context of 'way of life.' *Library and Information Science Research, 17*(3), 259–294.

Scheurich, J. J. (1995). A postmodernist critique of research interviewing. *International Journal of Qualitative Studies in Education, 8*(3), 239–252.

Schwarz, N. (1990). Feelings as information: Information and motivational functions of affective states. In E. T. Higgins & R. M. Sorrentino (Eds.), *Handbook of motivation and cognition: Vol. 2. Foundations of social behavior* (pp. 527–561). New York: Guilford Press.

Scott, W. A. (1955). Reliability in content analysis: The case of nominal scale coding. *Public Opinion Quarterly, 19*, 321–325.

Shamo, E. (2001). *University students and the Internet: Information seeking study.* Unpublished doctoral dissertation. University of North Texas, Denton, Texas.

Stempel, G. H. (1955). Increasing reliability in content analysis. *Journalism Quarterly, 32*, 449–455.

Taylor, R. S. (1968). Questions-negotiation and information seeking in libraries. *College and Research Libraries, 29*(3), 178–194.

Tenopir, C. (1994). The emotions of searching. *Library Journal, 119*, 134–135.

Tufte, E. R. (1997). *Visual explanations: Images and quantities, evidence and narrative.* Cheshire, CT: Graphics Press.

Turner, M. M., Rimal, R. N., Morrison, D., & Kim, H. (2006). The role of anxiety in seeking and retaining risk information: Testing the risk perception attitude framework in two studies. *Human Communication Research, 32*(2), 130–156.

Wang, P., & Tenopir, C. (1998). An exploratory study of users' interaction with World Wide Web resources: Information skills, cognitive styles, affective states, and searching behaviors. In M. E. Williams (Ed.), *19th National Online Meeting Proceedings* (pp. 445–454). Medford, NJ: Information Today, Inc.

Weiss, R. P. (2000). Emotion and learning. *Training and Development, 54*(11), 45–48.

Wilson, T. D. (1981). On user studies and information needs. *Journal of Documentation,* *37*(1), 3–15. Accessed December 5, 2006, from informationr.net/tdw/publ/papers/1981infoneeds.html.

Wilson, T. D. (1997). Information behaviour: An interdisciplinary perspective. *Information Processing & Management, 33*(4), 551–572.

Wilson, T. D., Ford, N., Ellis, D., Foster, A., & Spink, A. (2002). Information seeking and mediated searching. Part 2. Uncertainty and its correlates. *Journal of the American Society for Information Science and Technology, 53*(9), 704–715.

Yankelovich, D. (1996). A new direction for survey research. *International Journal of Public Opinion Research, 8*(1), 1–9.

Zillmann, D. (1988). Mood management: Using entertainment to full advantage. In L. Donohew, H. E. Sypher, & E. T. Higgins (Eds.), *Communication, social cognition, and affect* (pp. 147–171). Mahwah, NJ: Lawrence Erlbaum Associates.

Zorn, T. E. (1993). Motivation to communicate: A critical review with suggested alternatives. *Communication Yearbook, 16*, 515–549.

CHAPTER 4

The Role of Affect in Judging "What Is Enough?"

Nicola Parker and Jennifer Berryman
University of Technology, Sydney

INTRODUCTION

The concept of *enough* is central to productivity and success in an information-saturated world. In the face of information abundance, the continuous question of "What is enough?" moves beyond a series of quantitative judgments to complex negotiations, which are fluid, highly contextually and personally embedded, and intertwined with affect.

This chapter reports on an investigation that explored *enough* in information seeking—a concept described by Kuhlthau (2004) as fundamental but under-researched. The role of affect in this important judgment is highlighted. Empirical findings from the interpretive study indicate that practised information seekers experience *enough* in five qualitatively different ways, and show a picture of *enough* as generative and exploratory. The findings extend our understanding of the concept beyond its status as a barrier associated with difficulties, gaps, and stopping, and reveal the importance of affect in information interactions. The research is a useful step toward clarifying a key concept for information seeking in context and exploring the role of affect.

CONCEPTUAL BACKGROUND: RELATION BETWEEN AFFECT AND ENOUGH

Researchers into human information behavior have recognised the significance of affect as one of the three domains of cognition, emotion, and action. However, the field has approached the challenge of understanding the nature of affect from different perspectives. Kuhlthau (2004, p. 206), for example, emphasised the "interplay of thoughts, feelings and actions" throughout the information search process and reported on feelings of vagueness, frustration, and doubt in the early stages. These feelings move to more positive sensations of satisfaction, sureness, and relief in the closing stages of search. Nahl (2004, p. 192) took a different approach to conceptualising the relationship between cognition, affect, and behaviour, defining information seeking behaviour as a "form of goal-directed behaviour in which people are motivated (affective) to form a plan (cognitive) and perform it (sensorimotor)." The role played by the affective dimension in information seeking also continues to be the subject of conceptual debate. For example, one affective element frequently associated with information seeking is uncertainty (Kuhlthau, 2004; Nahl, 2004; Wilson, Ford, Ellis, Foster, & Spink, 2002). While often depicted as primarily a negative response (e.g., Kuhlthau, 2004; Nahl, 2004), uncertainty, although disruptive, may also play a more positive role in information seeking. For example, in the research context "working through uncertainty becomes a mediating strategy for knowledge generation/production" (Anderson, 2006), whereas in a context such as the workplace, uncertainty is a natural and unremarkable part of the working environment (Berryman, 2006). In this chapter, affect is conceptualized as a system that activates cognitive, physiological and behavioral components, or actions (Athenasou, 1999; Forgas, 2000; Nahl, 1998, 2001).

People face a series of choices throughout the information search process (Kuhlthau, 2004), suggesting the assessment of *enough* can be seen as a judgment, one element of a "multistage cognitive process" (Jungermann, 2000, p. 587), with the decision itself a commitment to action following ongoing evaluations such as *enough* (Harrison, 1999, p. 5). Understanding this relationship, the action of stopping or continuing can be differentiated from the evaluations that precede that action.

Particularly relevant to this investigation into *enough* and affect are Simon's (1997) theories of bounded rationality and the inter-related constructs of satisficing and levels of aspiration. Satisficing sees an individual accepting an alternative good enough to allow them to achieve the outcome they seek rather than seeking the optimal outcome. Importantly, satisficing occurs against pre-existing levels of aspiration, shaped by personal experience and contextual factors (Simon, 1997). Decision theorists have traditionally understood human judgment and decision making as primarily a cognitive behaviour and one limitation of the early judgment and decision-making theories was this focus on the cognitive limits of rationality (Browne, 1993; Gigerenzer & Goldstein, 2000). Recently, however, decision theorists have begun to explore the role of affect in all aspects of the judgment and decision-making process (e.g., Forgas & George, 2001; Hanoch, 2002; Tyszka, 1989), particularly asserting that affective priming often precedes cognition.

Affect is increasingly recognized as a fundamental component of information behaviour and part of all information interactions (Julien, McKechnie, & Hart, 2005; Kuhlthau, 2004; Nahl, 2004). Positioning *enough* as one of the judgments made during information seeking and acknowledging the role of affect in human judgment and decision making, it is timely to consider how affective factors influence this key concept in information contexts.

Early interest in the field of library and information science focused on the decision to stop searching for information, unsurprisingly, as this research occurred within the classical decision-making tradition. Nonetheless, affect showed up in these experimental studies in the form of how stopping rules, such as disgust (Kraft & Waller, 1981) or frustration (Morehead & Rouse, 1982), affected search length. More recently, two studies (Agosto, 2001; Zach, 2005) drew explicitly on Simon's theories of bounded rationality to understand the choices being made during information seeking. Other human information behaviour researchers have illuminated *enough* without explicitly drawing on judgment and decision-making theories. Time available, positioned as one of the major constraints by behavioural decision theorists, has been a recurrent theme (Kuhlthau, 2004; Limberg, 1999). However, also important were a range of affective factors such as boredom, frustration, and physical discomfort (Agosto, 2001). Positive affective factors were also reported, such as increasing certainty and confidence, especially when the puzzle was solved, or the answer was found (Kuhlthau, 2004; Wilson, et al., 2002; Zach, 2005).

METHOD

A small-scale qualitative study investigated postgraduate coursework students' experiences of the research and assessment processes of "doing an assignment" (Parker, 2005). The overall study was shaped by four research questions. The research question related to the findings discussed in this chapter was: How do postgraduates experience *enough* in the context of completing an assignment? The importance of affect in the participants' experiences emerged during the course of the study.

Participants

Participants were students with a graduate diploma or master's of arts in a joint class of an Information and Knowledge Management course at an Australian University. They were six mature female students (early 20s to mid-40s) of no discernible minority group with several years of prior professional work experience. As volunteer participants, all were highly engaged in the subject and could be described as "taking a deep approach" to the assignment (Ramsden, 2003, p. 43). Participants were all highly achieving students from an assessment viewpoint, both for the assignment and for the subject overall, with course grades of Distinction or High Distinction level.

Because participation was voluntary and the research context was held constant (one specific subject and the same assignment), participants were self-selected. Drawing participants from the same subject, taught in a similar way over three semesters, allowed the researcher to keep the assignment context stable. Students in classes taught by the researcher and one other lecturer were given a five-minute explanation of the study during which the voluntary nature of participation was emphasised. They were then provided with an information sheet and contact details. Interested full-time and part-time volunteers contacted the researcher to discuss potential participation. All but one of the students who expressed interest took part in all three phases of the study. Therefore, being enrolled in the selected subject and volunteering for the study were the only selection criteria.

Data Collection

A report-based assignment was the focus of in-depth conversational interviews with the students (Dortins, 2002; Kvale, 1996). The research task asked students to investigate a sector of the information industry of their choice, using the research and professional literature, and write a report of about 3,000 words. To avoid any misapprehensions about students' marks being affected by their participation or non-participation, those students who took part in the study had their assignments marked by the head of the department. These steps for ensuring objectivity in assessment and avoiding marking bias implications were clearly outlined to the participants.

The interviews took place at three different phases during each student's process of completing the assignment, which gave a total of 18 in-depth interviews, three from each of the six participants. The first interview took place before the student started working on the assignment; the second, in the middle; and the third, sometime after receiving feedback and marks. The timing of each of these phases was determined by each student. The interviews were unstructured and based on the question: "What is important to you at this stage of 'doing the assignment'?" During the interviews, the students shared control of the wide-ranging conversations, and throughout all three, each participant returned to *enough* (or not enough) again and again, both directly and indirectly.

Data Analysis

The interviews were recorded and fully transcribed, and inductive data analysis was carried out. Intensive "audio analysis" of the interviews began before the written transcripts were available. Listening to the audiotapes revealed important signals of affective responses embedded within students' experiences of *enough*. Listening to participants' voices and words allowed the researcher to identify important themes, which lost their impact when the written transcript was read by itself. Audio analysis remained the major analysis tool, and this facilitated the communication of the elusive affective elements of the judgment of *enough*. Two case studies were created, as well as a phenomenographic analysis of the ways in which students experienced *enough* (for more on phenomenography, see Limberg, 1999). Findings presented in this chapter draw on both of these analyses.

FINDINGS

Findings from the full analysis showed that postgraduates experience enough in five qualitatively different ways. These findings are presented in Table 4.1 in a hierarchy ranging from less complex (Category 1) to more complex (Category 5). It is important to emphasise that meanings of *enough* for the students in these varying experiences were not statically held by one individual student or another but were compiled from evidence across the entire set of transcripts. The illustrative quotes in the table are also taken from the pooled transcripts from all the participants.

Judgments of *enough* were made by the postgraduates on many different levels and the types of *enough* referred to also changed. In the conversations, these six different types were interwoven with what was important to the students when doing an assessed research paper (Parker, 2004). These different types of *enough* were associated with one or more of the varying experiences of *enough*, depicted in the five categories. The findings revealed *enough* as a judgment, which was balanced, negotiated, and returned to constantly throughout the entire assignment process. Therefore, when thinking about *enough*, we need to consider: "Enough for what?"

Instances of four of the categories of *enough*, outlined in Table 4.1, as well as the interweaving of affect can be seen in the extract captured in Table 4.2.

The extract in Table 4.2 came from a segment of a single transcript and takes us into the experience of one student, describing how she dedicated a day to spend in the library. The day started with the student, Caroline, browsing through the New Journal shelves close to the main entrance of the library. Caroline's experiences revealed many emotions in play. She talked about the atmosphere she created for herself when she started her search in the library and how she used this as a technique to manage her motivation and her mood, and to start her search. The following examples and explanation are taken from Caroline's case study and illustrate the affective dimension that emerged during the course of analysis.

First, Caroline described *enough* as Control and Getting Done (Enough 1). At this point, enough meant what was required to give her a feeling of control, avoid distraction and getting off track, and to get the assignment done. *Enough* also enabled Caroline to Optimize her assignment process and end product (Enough 2). This was present when she pointed out that what she wanted at this point was what would enhance her library visit and her searching and give her the most up-to-date information so she could fashion a good assignment. Caroline herself had set out to trigger an affective response of pleasure.

Enough for Caroline's Engagement and Understanding (Enough 3) was revealed when she was looking for something she liked and sat down to read journals out of sheer interest, indicating her interaction and engagement with the literature and professional identity of the field. How she arranged these interactions for herself triggered interest and pleasure. *Enough* as a

Table 4.1   Postgraduate Students' Experiences of *Enough* during
an Assessed Research Task

Categories of Enough[a]		Affective Elements[b]	Indicative Quotes[c]
No.	**Label (Category)**		
1	**CONTROL AND GETTING DONE** (*Enough* experienced as the right amount of essential elements of acceptable standard in place in order to keep or regain control, get the task done, and avoid disaster)	Strong physical emphasis, to make the task concrete ... avoiding personal embarrassment, helping cope with uncertainty and pressure, and produce on time and to requirements.	"But I say now 'Okay, you write a 1,000 today,' " ... "Yeah, I think—'Okay, I'll just stick to these, otherwise, I could get too out of control.' "
2	**OPTIMAL PRODUCTION** (*Enough* experienced as what enables optimal physical production in order to get it right and create a good "thing")	Not wasting time ... allowing them to feel organized and in control and pleased with the quality of the process and product of their work. With emphasis on quality, also often not enough (or negative enough).	"Okay—so looking at the academic report, yeah, I would want to know where I was going with it before I started doing any research because I can't stand just accumulating information."
3	**UNDERSTANDING AND ENGAGEMENT** (*Enough* experienced as what allows qualitative engagement with a process of discovery and "working out" in order to understand and successfully produce)	Seeking a good learning experience, about process ... helping keep boredom at bay. Passion for research and finding out. Flow.	"But I am very happy with the quality of the learning that's gone on in producing this thing." "I love researching ... I like finding out about things. It doesn't matter really what it is."
4	**COMPLETION AND SATISFACTION** (*Enough* experienced as an internalised qualitative sense of completeness and coverage to satisfy curiosity and make sense for oneself)	Being driven by curiosity— enough as a sense of no gaps, of closure ... a state or feeling, including a feeling of completion.	"And I'd written a section that I felt answered—the question, then I was, like, that feels complete ... that does feel as such ... yes!"
5	**GENERATION AND CREATION** (*Enough* experienced as a generative driver of the content vision and development process in order to engage in discovery and create a unique, ideal product of value)	Desiring creativity—taking risks ... stretching beyond what they already know and working to an ideal vision of something intrinsically aesthetic.	"... for me the biggest thing about the assignment was deciding to take the risk to use nontraditional sources. ... But I went through incredible angst and almost like a great sort of depression. Because that was what I wanted to do! I wanted to do it that way." "[an assignment] As artworks!"

Note: Represents synthesis of pooled phenomenographic analysis of data from all participants
a. Categories assigned by the researcher
b. Researcher's interpretive comments
c. Illustrative quotes taken from pool of transcripts from all participants

Table 4.2   An Extract: One Student's Experience of Seeking
Information in the Library

Transcript Segment[a]	Related Affective Indicators	
	Text Level Labels[b]	Audio Level Description and Interpretation[c]
A pattern is starting to develop now ... And I am realizing that it can't be done in a week. There's that kind of—there's the online search, the general questions, and then there's the set, I like to set a day aside, or at least a day (1)[d] *where there are no constraints either side of the search*[e] *where I just go and grab* ... **whatever**[f]! Guided by my initial search. But umm, there might be one or two key texts that I'm looking for but ... the rest of the process is browsing, umm. Also I find looking at the, just on walking **in** going straight to the journal shelf, scanning **that**, it's also (2) *a gentle way (laugh) of getting into the whole thing. Umm, yeah and,* and looking at the most up to date things **there**!	(1) Sense of Control and Freedom, Explanation, Pride (2) Exploratory mood. Enjoyment of browsing. Getting a "feel" for the area.	Student sounds rueful then businesslike as she enthusiastically outlines her developing approach to the process of searching. (1) Sounds relaxed and voice slows as she describes the structured freedom she builds into her searching. Then businesslike again. (2) Voice warms and softens. Sounds dreamy and then slightly embarrassed.
OK and when you are looking at that what are you actually looking for? It's a scan. It's umm ... Oh, to use a metaphor? Rather than ... going to Paris to look at the Eiffel Tower, or going to Paris and going straight to the Eiffel Tower. (3) *It's like going to Paris and going and have a coffee first. (Laughs)* So it's kind of umm ... it's (4) *getting **a feel** for the environment in which this topic sits. And you might find **a gem*** that will be a direct lead.	(3) Shaping Feelings, Enjoyment (4) Anticipation, Happiness	(3) Sounds happy, enthusiastic, and rather amused as she explains her desire to enjoy the task by easing into it with aesthetic immersion, soaking up the atmosphere, getting a feel for the area and acclimatising herself. (4) Voice slows and she sounds earnest and then enthusiastic.
And so how do you decide when you've got the feel that you want. What would be your criteria for saying "right I'll do the next thing now"? It's just scanning. Grab a couple of journals, or probably look through (5) *if there's something I like,* I'll photocopy it.	(5) Interest, Curiosity	(5) Sounds businesslike again. Hunts for something that she "'likes'" at this stage rather than specific things.
... It's a really useful metaphor that one of sitting down having a coffee—but what does that give you that if you didn't do it—if you walked out cold—you wouldn't get? Yeah ... well ... umm ... I wonder whether it's got something to do with kind of—well OK— oh (6) *an identification thing.* So I'm researching that thing but sat down and read some of the journals out of *(7) pure interest—* I am (Laugh) ... not I am an information professional but like this is the field which is what I am in. (8) *It's as much a feeling as information (laugh) collecting.*	(6) Explanation, Enthusiasm (7) Interest, Enjoyment (8) Happiness, Excitement	Sounds like she is smiling as she talks. Thoughtful and pondering as she (6) explains trying to adopt the identity of the profession she is learning about. (7) Sounds happy as she talks about reading for interest, then amused. (8) Sounds happy and laughs as she reiterates that for her, searching is "a feeling."
Is it a feeling of feeling comfortable? And also umm you get an idea of the range of people involved in, in the area. Sometimes going straight to books or articles on line it's umm, it all (9) *seems a bit distant—or it looks like mountains of words.* Whereas something in the journal has a kind of a social umm **a** (10) *social feel to it* as well ...	(9) Anxiety, Sense of being overwhelmed (10) Comfort, Confidence	Sounds keen to explain how she familiarises herself with the literature and imbues the information with a "social feel" (9) to make it less intimidating. (10) Sounds thoughtful as she thinks out loud.

a. Transcript extract is a single segment taken verbatim from audiotape
b. Labels assigned by researcher based on text only
c. Describes the overall affective tone audible in each part of the transcript on the audiotape recording
d. Bracketed numbers label each italicised fragment of the transcript and relate to text labels and audio description and interpretation
e. Italics indicate points at which participant's words demonstrate some of the affective dimensions found in the study
f. Bold text indicates the participant's strong vocal emphasis

sense of Completion and Satisfaction (Enough 4) can be seen in a fragmentary way when Caroline said she had a feeling that she had enough to capture a sense of what it means to be an information professional. This triggered a feeling of satisfaction and pleasure.

Although *enough* as Generation and Creation (Enough 5) was not explicitly focused on here, it was evident in the broad thrust of Caroline's manipulation of her early searching. *Enough* was what would creatively drive both her vision and the process for achieving that. This way of experiencing *enough* brought feelings of excitement and anticipation but also anxiety and disappointment because of the unattainable nature of her ideal. Looking in detail at a small part of this interview illuminated the interweaving of affect into all these elements of assignment experiences; affect infused everything.

DISCUSSION

The findings reported here demonstrate the complex and fluid nature of the judgment of enough information, highlighting the integral role of affect and showing that *enough* is a much more complex concept than has been recognized. These practised and successful information seekers experienced *enough* in five different ways and referred to six different types of *enough*. They used various strategies depending on the meaning enough had for them at that point in their information seeking process. The emotions described by postgraduates are complex, subjective experiences with many components, including physical, cognitive, organizational, expressive, and highly subjective personal meaning.

Although affect can be seen throughout the experience captured in Table 4.2, variations in the meaning of *enough* are also accompanied by shifts between the physical, cognitive, and affective domains. For example, there was a focus on physical production in Category 1 to make the task concrete and maintain a sense of control. This focus shifted in Category 2 toward the quality of the content. In Category 3, cognitive elements such as understanding, learning, and discovery emerged as priorities. Nonetheless, affective elements were linked to this, feeding a passion for discovery and keeping boredom at bay. A further shift was apparent in Category 4 with a move to a focus that was principally affective, a focus on internalised feelings of *enough*. This focus is reflective of Kuhlthau's (2004) findings of the importance of affective factors in the information search process. The strongest affective (or aesthetic) aspect was apparent in Category 5 where postgraduates went beyond internal feelings resulting from the assignment process itself. The focus expanded to creating the right atmosphere and, thus, the appropriate feelings for oneself, and included a shift to ideals of creativity, artistry, and the ideal of perfection in research.

Changing focus was also evident in other ways. In the less complex categories (1–2), there was a focus on closure of the task itself, a focus which evolved into a force for generation in the more complex categories (3–5). This aspect of *enough* seems similar to the indicative and invitational mood corollary that Kuhlthau (2004) found in her research.

It is important to remember that in this analysis the affective dimension of experience has been separated conceptually from a holistic experience of information seeking. However, the differing experiences of *enough* for these highly achieving students, as they managed their entire research and assessment process, are part of holistic, integrated information behaviour (Given, 2000) in their daily experiences during the assignment process.

CONCLUSION

The empirical work reported in this chapter is not only a useful step toward clarifying the key concept of *enough* but also demonstrates affect at work in human information behaviour. These insights into the different components and the affective experience of *enough* can inform sensitive, consumer-focused information systems design (Barr, Burns, & Sharp, 2005). Findings reveal many of these elements of *enough* are generative and exploratory as opposed to the difficulties, gaps, problems, and stops usually associated with the idea of enough, thus enhancing our understanding of *enough* in information seeking and use. Importantly, the components of *enough* all include affective elements, an indication of the complexity, diversity, and richness of postgraduates' experiences of the concept of enough that emerged from this research.

REFERENCES

Agosto, D. E. (2001). Bounded rationality and satisficing in young people's Web-based decision making. *Journal of the American Society for Information Science and Technology, 53*(1), 16–27.

Anderson, T. (2006). Uncertainty in action: Observing information seeking within the creative processes of scholarly research. *Information Research, 12*(1), Paper 283. Accessed July 8, 2007, from informationr.net/ir/12-1/paper283.html.

Athenasou, J. A. (Ed.). (1999). *Adult Educational Psychology*. Katoomba, NSW: Social Science Press.

Barr, T., Burns, A., & Sharp, D. (2005). *Smart Internet 2010*. Melbourne, Vic: Swinburne University of Technology, Faculty of Life and Social Sciences. Accessed November 28, 2006, from smartinternet.com.au/ArticleDocuments/123/Smart-Internet-2010.pdf.

Berryman, J. M. (2006). What defines 'enough' information? How policy workers make judgements and decisions during information seeking: Preliminary results from an exploratory study. *Information Research, 11*(4), Paper 266. Accessed November 28, 2006, from informationr.net/ir/11-4/paper266.html.

Browne, M. (1993). *Organizational decision making and information*. Norwood, NJ: Ablex.

Dortins, E. (2002). Reflections on phenomenographic process: Interview, transcription and analysis. In A. Goody, J. Herrington, & M. Northcote (Eds.), *Proceedings of the 2002 Annual International Conference of the Higher Education Research and Development Society of Australasia* (HERDSA) (pp. 207–213). Canberra, ACT: HERDSA.

Forgas, J. P. (Ed.). (2000). *Feeling and thinking: The role of affect in social cognition.* Cambridge: Maison des Science de l'Homme & Cambridge University Press.

Forgas, J. P., & George, J. M. (2001). Affective influences on judgments and behaviour in organisations: An information processing perspective. *Organizational Behavior and Human Decision Processes, 86*(1), 3–34.

Gigerenzer, G., & Goldstein, D. G. (2000). Reasoning the fast and frugal way: Models of bounded rationality. In T. Connolly, H. R. Arkes, & K. R. Hammond (Eds.), *Judgment and Decision Making: An interdisciplinary reader* (2nd ed., pp. 621–650). Cambridge: Cambridge University Press.

Given, L. M. (2000, August). *Student life on the margins: Mature students' information behaviours and the discursive search for a 'student' identity.* Paper presented at the Information Seeking in Context: The 3rd International Conference on Information Needs, Seeking and Use in Different Contexts, Gotheburg, Sweden.

Hanoch, Y. (2002). "Neither an angel nor an ant": Emotion as an aid to bounded rationality. *Journal of Economic Psychology, 23,* 1–25.

Harrison, E. F. (1999). *The managerial decision-making process* (5th ed.). Boston: Houghton Mifflin.

Julien, H., McKechnie, L. (E. F.), & Hart, S. (2005). Affective issues in library and information science systems work: A content analysis. *Library and Information Science Research, 27*(4), 453–466.

Jungermann, H. (2000). The two camps on rationality. In T. Connolly, H. R. Arkes, & K. R. Hammond (Eds.), *Judgment and decision making: An interdisciplinary reader* (2nd ed., pp. 575–591). Cambridge: Cambridge University Press.

Kraft, D. H., & Waller, W. G. (1981). A Bayesian approach to user stopping rules for information retrieval systems. *Information Processing and Management, 17*(6), 349–360.

Kuhlthau, C. C. (2004). *Seeking meaning: A process approach to library and information services* (2nd ed.). Westport, CT: Libraries Unlimited.

Kvale, S. (1996). *Interviews: An introduction to qualitative research interviewing.* Thousand Oaks, CA: Sage Publications.

Limberg, L. (1999). Experiencing information seeking and learning: A study of the interaction between two phenomena. *Information Research, 5*(1), paper 68. Accessed November 28, 2006, from informationr.net/ir/5-1/paper68.html.

Morehead, D. R., & Rouse, W. B. (1982). Models of human behavior in information seeking tasks. *Information Processing & Management, 18*(4), 193–205.

Nahl, D. (1998). Learning the Internet and the structure of information behavior. *Journal of the American Society for Information Science, 49*(11), 1017–1023.

Nahl, D. (2001). A conceptual framework for explaining information behavior. *Studies in Multimedia Information Literacy Education (SIMILE), 1*(2). Accessed November 28, 2006, from www.utpjournals.com/simile/issue2/nahl1.html.

Nahl, D. (2004). Measuring the affective information environment of Web searchers. *Proceedings of the 67th annual meeting of the American Society for Information Science & Technology, 41,* 191–197.

Parker, N. (2004). Assignment information processes: What's "enough" for high achievement? [Summary of a research note delivered at the Information Seeking In Context 2004 conference, Dublin, 1–3 September, 2004]. *Information Research, 10*(1), Summary 3. Accessed November 28, 2006, from InformationR.net/ir/10-1/abs3.

Parker, N. (2005). Diversity in high places: Variation in highly achieving students' experiences of course work assignments. In C. Rust (Ed.), *Improving student learning: Diversity and inclusivity.* Oxford: The Oxford Centre for Staff and Learning Development.

Ramsden, P. (2003). *Learning to teach in higher education.* New York: Routledge Falmer.

Simon, H. A. (1997). *Models of bounded rationality: Volume 3. Empirically grounded economic reason*. Cambridge, MA: MIT Press.

Tyszka, T. (1989). Information and evaluation processes in decision making. In N. Eisenberg, J. Reykowski, & E. Staub (Eds.), *Social and Moral Values* (pp. 175–193). Mahwah, NJ: Lawrence Erlbaum Associates.

Wilson, T. D., Ford, N., Ellis, D., Foster, A., & Spink, A. (2002). Information seeking and mediated searching: Part 2. Uncertainty and its correlates. *Journal of the American Society for Information Science and Technology, 53*(9), 704–715.

Zach, L. (2005). When is "enough" enough? Modeling the information-seeking and stopping behaviour of senior arts administrators. *Journal of the American Society for Information Science, 56*(1), 23–35.

PART II

Macro-Emotional Information Environment

CHAPTER 5

Developmental Social-Emotional Behavior and Information Literacy

Lesley S. J. Farmer
California State University, Long Beach

INTRODUCTION

K–12 library media programs are attempting to establish correlations between well-implemented library service and student achievement. In terms of curriculum, school library teachers (SLT) tend to focus on information literacy. In attempts to measure information literacy competency, professionals are examining student research processes and developing corresponding rubrics. SLTs are using those rubrics more specifically to assess student work, although such work is difficult to generalize and extrapolate or to perform on a large scale.

Most of these information literacy assessments tend to focus on cognitive skills with little regard to students' social-emotional competence (Cahoy, 2004). Kuhlthau's 1985 seminal work focused on students' feelings *during* their research processing, an approach that has been replicated and expanded over the years, particularly in the online environment. Nevertheless, Martzoukou asserted in her 2005 review of Web information seeking studies that "it is important that individual Web information seeking behavior is studied from all its multiple facets, such as experience, information need, *affective and cognitive characteristics, and social and culturally determined traits*" [author's emphasis].

Furthermore, measuring students' social and emotional *predispositions before* conducting research has not been widely studied, particularly from a developmental standpoint. When SLTs and classroom teachers identify prerequisite skills when designing learning activities, typically the main social-emotional skill noted is the global ability to work collaboratively if the ensuing activity requires group effort. This social task comprises several subtasks: active listening, sharing feelings, responding to ideas, mediating, etc. (Johnson, 1994). As Finnish researchers Jarvela, Lehtinen, and Salonen (2000) discovered, social and emotional skills also impact individual research processing as students seek and use information.

The study described in this chapter attempts to measure the possible correlation between social-emotional maturity and high school students' research processes and projects. If such social and emotional developmental characteristics *are* found to impact students' efforts, then SLTs and classroom teachers need to address those issues explicitly *before* students engage in research. In short, direct instruction in social and emotional behaviors would constitute a significant part of the information literacy "curriculum."

LITERATURE REVIEW

Nahl's (2001) conceptual framework for explaining information behavior provides a good starting point for examining the literature relative to social and emotional factors that impact information literacy. She reviews the psychodynamics of information behavior, which are largely driven by personality, and sense-making communication theory, which reflect individuals' social competence. Nahl's taxonomy includes the affective domain in terms of information adjustment problems, search process problems, and personal information problems.

One of the earlier researchers in the area of affective considerations in information behavior, Carol Kuhlthau (1985) focused on students' emotional status during their research process. Her recent studies (2003) note the importance of students' perspectives in building their own worlds of meaning and expanding their understanding of the learning process. She highlights the need for SLTs and classroom teachers to collaboratively intervene and guide youth throughout their research because skills and emotions vary at different stages in the process.

Tenopir's (2003) analysis of more than 200 research studies on users of electronic library resources demonstrates current interest in focusing on user information behaviors in an online environment; in the area of predispositions, the most relevant finding was that students who had positive attitudes about learning electronic searching skills performed better. Nahl and Harada (1996), for example, noted the correlation between levels of self-confidence and skills ratings as students used Web resources. In a related area of study, library anxiety, students who were anxious about the use of technology *even if they had some technical skill* fared less well than students who were less tech-savvy but more comfortable with libraries (Jiao & Onwuegbuzie, 2004).

Information literacy researchers have given some attention to personality and its impact on research skills, drawing from constructivist personality theory (e.g., Kelly, 1963). Kernan and Mojena (1973), Bellardo (1985), and Palmer (1991) were early researchers on personality as a determinant in information seeking behaviors. Heinstrom (2003) identified five personality dimensions—neuroticism, extraversion, openness to experience, competitiveness, and conscientiousness—that influenced information behavior. She concluded that "inner traits interact with contextual factors in their final impact on information behavior." Allen and Kim (2001) concluded in an earlier study that highly motivational tasks impact behavior, but routine tasks are more influenced by personal characteristics.

Social cognitive theory (e.g., Bandura, 1986) has provided another research lens: Information literacy, and deriving meaning from information, may be socially constructed. Dervin (1977), Savolainen (1993), and Solomon (1997) examined the tension between institutional or imposed informational tasks and individual adaptive behaviors. Personality, in this context, impacts the motivation toward information seeking and the mechanisms used in engaging with information. The question emerges: Are personality traits permanent, or do they grow and change developmentally?

The vast majority of information seeking behaviors focused on college age and adult populations. Examining elementary school students, Jarvela et al. (2000) noted that in "cognitive apprenticeship" learning environments, which are reflected in students' research project learning, individual students' social and emotional orientations lead to different and unanticipated interactions. Wanting to examine more nuanced information literacy skills, which tend to be used in middle and high school research projects, the current study under investigation focused on that age group's social and emotional maturity. Erikson's (1968) work forms one basis of those aspects of human development. He contended that preadolescents need to deal with competence: understanding the use of rules and becoming self-disciplined, both of which impact student research efforts. Likewise, adolescents need to deal with self-identify: exploring different roles, developing goals, and achieving them. These issues also lend themselves well to research as students take intellectual risks. Erikson also noted that boys tend to mature later socially than do girls, which impacts their information literacy research efforts. More recently, the Search Institute in Minneapolis (Benson, Scales, Leffert, & Roehlkepartain, 1999) focused on adolescents, developing a framework of 40 development assets. Half of these assets are internal psychological qualities that guide decisions, self-concept, and impact research information processing: commitment to learning, positive values, social competencies, and positive identity. Just as with reading readiness, there may be a developmental and psychological aspect that influences student success with information literacy. In that regard, Bilal and Kirby (2002) compared the success of information seeking behaviors of seventh grade science students and graduate library science students, and found the graduate students were significantly more effective; significant emotional differences were found in self-recovery from "breakdowns" and focus on task.

With the advent of the term "emotional intelligence," used first by Salovey and Mayer (1990), more attention has been paid to social-emotional learning, which enables learners to effectively "understand, process, manage, and express the social and emotional aspects of [their] lives" (Cohen, 2001, p. 3). Butler and Cartier (2005) examined how emotional stages reflect students' inquiry learning success; for instance, low self-esteem or low interest can result in poor achievement, and high stress during the inquiry process can also negatively impact results. Ellis and Bernard (1983) have led the research in social-emotional behavior therapy, which examines students' affective-motivational characteristics as contributing independently from students' cognitive characteristics to student achievement: organization, persistence, emotional resilience, and getting along. Similarly, Martin and Marsh (2006) developed a unidimensional academic resilience construct that identified five factors that predicted academic resilience: confidence, coordination, control, composure, and persistence. On a broader scale, the Collaborative to Advance Social and Emotional Learning (2003) has developed a research-validated, theoretical framework labeled "social decision making and problem solving" that integrates key social and emotional competencies with curriculum and instruction (Cohen, 1999, p. 76). Their list of competencies includes a number that align with information literacy, such as problem identification and solving, communication skills, and social skills of cooperation and help-seeking. Thus, as students exhibit positive social-emotional behavior, they may be more likely to achieve information literacy competency.

Todd and Kuhlthau's (2004) Ohio study of school library's impact on student achievement validates the role that SLTs can have on students' social-emotional behavior within this context:

> "The school library enables me to complete my work on time."

> "The school library helps me by providing a study environment for me to work."

> "The school library helps me take stress out of learning."

> "The school library helps me do my work more efficiently." (p. 13)

In other words, the SLT can help students develop social-emotional skills that will facilitate their information literacy efforts, and provide an environment for students to practice positive those skills. By identifying significant social-emotional behaviors as they correlate with informational task success, SLTs can craft targeted interventions that can facilitate information literacy learning.

RESEARCH QUESTIONS

Informed by the literature and their underlying premises, this exploratory study investigated the correlation of social-emotional behavior and information literacy competencies of sample high school students. The goal was to determine if affective domain factors needed to be considered when teaching information literacy skills to students. Based on the statement of the problem, the guiding research questions were:

1. To what degree does a correlation exist between students' social-emotional behavior status and students' research information literacy competence?

2. To what degree does a correlation exist between students' social-emotional behavior status and students' research project quality?

3. To what degree is gender a significant factor in students' social-emotional behavior status and students' research information literacy competence and research project quality?

This research builds on the effort by the American Association of School Librarians (AASL) to ensure that high-quality library media programs support the mission of assuring both students and staff are effective users of ideas and information (1998, 1999). It also builds on IFLA/UNESCO's 2002 publication *School Library Guidelines,* which provides a model for study skills and information literacy programs. The project also links to various research correlating information literacy standards and student achievement (Goodin, 1991; Harada & Yoshina, 1997; Lance, 2002; Todd & Kuhlthau, 2004). On a more personal note, this investigation links to Farmer's (2006) work on identifying correlations between the degree of library media program implementation and student achievement.

METHOD

The strategy for answering the research questions consisted of administering three assessment instruments to students and teachers, and analyzing the triangulated data.

Setting

The population consisted of students attending a high school in Orange County, California. The site was chosen for three reasons: (1) the demographics reflected a middle-class, diversified student body (25 percent Asian/Pacific Islander, 3 percent African American, 12 percent Latino, 60 percent Anglo), (2) the school was within driving distance of the researcher, and (3) the SLT agreed to facilitate the administration of the instruments.

Participants

The participants consisted of four classes, all taught by one teacher, for a total of 72 ninth graders, and two classes, taught by another teacher, for a total of 41 eleventh graders. The ninth grade classes were designated as gifted and talented, while the eleventh grade classes were not so designated. Two grades were chosen to explore the possible impact of age on social-emotional maturity and information literacy competency. The choice to target gifted ninth graders was an attempt to minimize the maturity and literacy competency gap between the two grades. The two English teachers were chosen because they routinely assigned research papers each semester and understood the basic concepts of information literacy. Their research paper assignments were similar in that both consisted of having students contextualizing a literary work within the period's social conditions; the assignments required students to locate, evaluate, comprehend, organize, and share relevant information.

Procedures

All students were assigned a research paper, which consisted of having students contextualizing a class-assigned literary work within the period's social conditions; the assignments required students to locate, evaluate, comprehend, organize, and share relevant information. The two grades used different texts, and the eleventh grade assignment focused on American historical significance.

At the beginning of their research project, four ninth grade classes (all with Teacher A) and two eleventh grade classes (both with Teacher B) self-completed the Students' Foundation for Achievement and Social-Emotional Well-Being Student Form (Bernard, 2003) and the Research Process Rubric (Redwood High School Research Study Group [RHSRSG], 2000). At the end of the research project, the teachers completed the Research Product Rubric (RHSRSG, 2000).

The researcher triangulated the data to determine possible correlations.

Instruments

The Students' Foundation for Achievement and Social-Emotional Well-Being Inventory (Bernard, 1990; Bernard 2003; Bernard & Cronan, 1999; Bernard & Laws, 1988) was used to measure students' self-reported *social-emotional* maturity. The instrument has been validated for use with 10- to 17-year-olds. Bernard's questionnaire groups 25 social-emotional factors into five attributes: confidence, persistence, organization, getting along, and emotional resilience. Participants self-rated the frequency that they exhibited the listed behaviors along a 10-point Likert scale (from 1 = never to 10 = always).

One instrument consisted of a research process rubric created by the Redwood High School Research Study Group (2000), based on the information literacy competency work of the Colorado State Library and Adult Education Office and Colorado Educational Media Association (1997) and Grover (1997). The Research Process rubric addresses: defining the task, developing search strategies, accessing information, comprehending information, organizing information, communicating the findings, and evaluating.

A parallel rubric, measuring the quality of a research product, was also adapted from these sources and the American Association of School Librarians (1998). The Research Product rubric measures how well students: adhere to the assignment, organize their product, justify their stances, communicate, and follow writing conventions. The research product instrument was used to analyze sample student research reports as a cross-validation of student self-assessment of research information literacy competency. The two research instruments were used and validated by the investigator and the rest of the Redwood High School Research Study Group for the Tamalpais Union High School District (2000).

Data Analysis

The instrument scores were coded and entered into a spreadsheet. The process rubric was coded from 1 (emerging) to 4 (exceptional), and the product rubric was coded from 1 (unsatisfactory) to 6 (exceptional); these scores were treated as ordinal numbers. Grade level and gender were also coded and entered. A code number was generated for each student to link the three instruments while ensuring confidentiality. The data were then imported into SPSS version 12 (2003).

A series of Kendall Tau tests were used to determine the degree of correlation between:

- Social-emotional well-being and research processes
- Social-emotional well-being and research product
- Research processes and research product

It was found that gender also made a significant difference in terms of self-perceptions and teachers' evaluations relative to these behaviors and products. An independent sample T-test on these five attributes confirmed that boys and girls represented the same population. Research process behavior self-assessment and teacher-assessed research products were also analyzed using independent sample T-tests.

If a significant correlation emerged, then the next step in social-emotional behavior therapy might be investigated. Specifically, SLTs could focus on critical affective and behavior competencies within the information literacy framework, and provide effective interventions so students would be given opportunities to learn and practice these behaviors during the research process. Likewise, the degree of correlation between research processes and research products should indicate if separate skill sets occur, which should be treated (taught and assessed) differently.

FINDINGS

Instrumental Inner-Correlations

Before looking at the correlations, it was useful to examine students' self-perceptions about their social-emotional well-being. When the data for the two grades were compared, it was found that ninth graders rated themselves significantly higher/more mature than eleventh graders for persistence (7.82 vs. 7.29 with .033 significance) and organization (8.16 vs. 7.51 with .026

significance), which was entirely accounted for by the ninth grade girls' responses. Initial data analysis of the five attributes did not reveal enough differentiation, so individual factors were analyzed, as detailed in Table 5.1.

Table 5.1   Significant Differences by Grade of Social-Emotional Behaviors

Factor	9th Graders' Mean	11th Graders' Mean	Significance
Complete difficult assignments	7.96	7.05	.002
Persistent	8.22	7.10	.010
Understand teacher instructions	7.76	6.59	.004
Follow rules	8.20	7.49	.000
Sensitive to others' feelings	8.42	8.20	.006
F24	6.72	6.34	.018

In Table 5.2, in terms of research processes, eleventh graders self-assessed their skills as significantly higher for the steps of determining information need, developing a search strategy, and interpreting/organizing information. Ninth graders thought that they did a better job of evaluating product and process. Gender did not seem to be a significant factor in self-reporting of research processes, but between ninth grade and eleventh grade girls, ninth grade girls thought they were more capable in determining an information need, strategizing, comprehension, and interpretation of information. Again, ninth grade self-perceptions could have been accounted for by their gifted/talented designation, or it could be due to perceptions shaped by experience in high school courses that were more difficult and nuanced than middle school work.

In Table 5.3, the ninth grade teacher assessed the students' research product significantly higher than the eleventh grader teacher relative to adherence to assignment, organization, and proof and justification.

Table 5.2   Significant Differences by Grade of Research Process Behaviors

Process	9th Graders' Mean	11th Graders' Mean	Significance
ID info need	3.29	3.90	.011
Develop search strategy	3.31	4.00	.008
Interpret/organize info	3.32	4.07	.012
Evaluation	3.31	2.95	.004

Table 5.3   Significant Differences by Grade of Research Product Indicators

Indicator	9th Graders' Mean	11th Graders' Mean	Significance
Adhere to assignment	4.31	3.32	.046
Organization	4.64	3.10	.000
Proof/justification	4.78	3.05	.001

Research Question 1

To what degree does a correlation exist between students' social-emotional behavior status and students' research information literacy competence?

Overall, getting along ($r = .247$) and emotional resilience ($r = .175$) were found to be significant at the .01 level of confidence, and persistence was found to be significant ($r = .141$) at the .05 level. Table 5.4 shows the two research process indicators that correlated most closely with social-emotional well-being were communicating findings and evaluating the process/product; for the population as a whole, all attributes but organization *as a whole* were found to be significantly correlated positively at the .01 level of confidence.

Persistently putting in the effort to complete difficult work was a significant factor to communicating the information, particularly for eleventh grade boys. For ninth graders, being organized in schoolwork was positively correlated with communicating ($r = .240$, $p<.01$). For eleventh graders, working cooperatively with classmates on projects was another somewhat significant factor ($r = .287$, $p<.05$), particularly for girls. Being able to calm down quickly and bounce back when upset was significantly correlated for all subgroups.

Table 5.4   Significant Positive Correlations Between Social-Emotional Behaviors and Research Processes

Attribute	Process 6: Communicate Correlation Coefficient/ Significance	Process 7: Evaluate Correlation Coefficient/ Significance
Self-confidence	.297/.001	.236/.002
Persistence	.345/.000	.273/.000
Organization	.013/.890	.225/.003
Getting Along	.389/.000	.231/.002
Emotional Resilience	.315/.001	.256/.001

Research Question 2

To what degree does a correlation exist between students' social-emotional behavior status and students' research project quality?

For these subjects, the most highly correlated research product indicator relative to social-emotional well-being was "proof and justification" ($r = .338$; $p<.01$).

For ninth graders, the behaviors that correlated negatively with research product indicators clustered around human relationships. Thus, those students who were more social tended to adhere less to the assignment, were less organized, had less substantial proof and justification, and exhibited less sophisticated language and search strategies.

Table 5.5 shows that for eleventh graders, persistence behaviors of checking over work correlated highly with adherence to assignments and putting in the needed effort to complete difficult assignments related to organization, proof and justification, and use of language and strategies. Interestingly, these behaviors were positively correlated with the evaluation step of

Table 5.5   Significant Positive Correlations Between Social-Emotional Behaviors and Research Product Indicators by Grade and by Gender

Behavior	9th Graders	11th Graders	Girls	Boys
Confident meeting new people	D1: -.226/.017 D3: -.242/.012 D4: -.249/.011	NS	NS	NS
Check work when finished to make sure it's correct	NS	D1: 304./.020 D2: .322/.014 D3: .297/.023	NS	D1: .292/.008 D2: .290/.008 D3: .250/.018 D4: .234/.034
Put in effort needed to complete difficult assignments	NS	D1: .344/.011	NS	D1: .423/.000 D2: .280/.012 D3: .352/.001 D4: .378/.001 D5: .270/.015
Work cooperatively on projects	D2: -.278/.004 D3: -.280/.004	D2: .278/.039 D3: .340/.011 D4: .274./043	NS	NS
Follow important rules for safety and have better world	NS	NS	NS	D1: .231/.037 D2: .239/.031 D3: .324/.003 D4. .313/.005 D5: .310/005
Get along well with others	D1: -.245/.012 D3: -.283/.004 D4: -.271/.007	D1: .300/.026 D3: .340/.010	D2: -275/.012 D3: -231/.029 D4: 251/.020 D5: .236/.029	NS

D1: Adherence to Assignment; D2: Organization; D3: Proof & Justification; D4: Language & Strategy Use; D5: Spelling & Grammar
(Correlation Coefficient/Significance in terms of level of confidence)

research processes for ninth graders, but they did not translate into significant correlations with research product indicators.

It was anticipated that students who were competent in research processes would produce high-quality research projects. Table 5.6 shows that for eleventh graders, strong positive correlations exist between the research processes of communication and evaluation and research products.

Table 5.6 Significant Positive Correlations Between Research Processes and Research Product Indicators

Process Indicators	Adherence to Assignment	Organization	Proof & Justification	Language & Strategy Use	Spelling & Grammar
Communicate	.418/.003	NS	.467/.001	.337/.020	.333/.019
Evaluate	.341/.018	.559/.000	.570/.000	.506/.001	.337/.019

However, significantly *negative* correlations between research processes and products tended to apply to ninth graders ($r = -.321$, $p < .01$).

For 11th graders, particularly girls, evaluating the research process and product correlated closely with risk-taking (willingness to participate in new activities and to try even when schoolwork is hard). Table 5.7 shows that checking work when finished to make sure it is correct appears to be more significant for ninth graders. Being able to "bounce back" when upset is another significant factor, particularly for ninth graders.

Table 5.7 Significant Positive Correlations Between Social-Emotional Behaviors and Research Processes by Grade and by Gender

Behavior	Overall	9th Grade	11th Grade	Girls	Boys
Volunteer to participate	C6: .187/.016 C7: .273/.000		C7: .399/.002	C6: .227/.033 C7: .292/.007	C7: .245/.032
Continue to try	C6: .201/.011 C7: 209/.009		C6: .304/.021 C7: .276/.007		C6: .284/.014
Check work	C6: .183/.017 C7: .269/.001	C6: .197/.042 C7: .264/.007		C7: 258/.019	C7: .272/.016
Complete difficult tasks	C6: .227/.004 C7: .264/.001	C7: .249/.013	C6: .442/.001 C7: .262/.047	C7: .350/.002	C6: .345/.003
Persistent	C6: .249/.002 C7: .239/.003		C6: .400/.002 C7: .285/.031	C7: .301/.007	C6: .316/.006
Organized	C6: .208/.008 C7: .273/.002	C6: .259/.009 C7: .272/.006		C7: .273/.015	C6: .233/.040 C7: .202/.023
Cooperate with peers	C6: .270/.001		C6: .438/.001	C6: .293/.009	C6: .242/.036
Calm down quickly	C6: .300/.000 C7: .265/.001	C6: .226/.021 C7: .241/.014	C6: .426/.001 C7: .306/.020	C6: .352/.001 C7: .283/.010	C6: .275/.017 C7: .290/.011
Bounce back	C6: .266/.001 C7: .252/.001	C6: .271/.006 C7: .244/.013	C6: .263/.045 C7: .272/.038	C6: 221/.040	C6: .307/.007 C7: .288/.011

C6=Process 6: Communicate; C7=Process 7: Evaluate
(Correlation Coefficient/Significance in terms of level of confidence)

Research Question 3

To what degree is gender a significant factor in students' social-emotional behavior status and students' research information literacy competence and research product quality?

For each gender as a whole, there was no significant difference in process and product assessments. Table 5.8 shows that gender did play a role in self-perceptions of social-emotional maturity. Ninth grade girls rated their behavior significantly higher than their male peers as well as their eleventh grade female counterparts in seven areas. By eleventh grade, boys' and girls' self-perceptions of behaviors did not differ significantly.

Table 5.8   Significant Differences of Social-Emotional Behaviors Between Ninth Grade Girls and Boys

Factor	9th Grade Girls' Mean	9th Grade Boys' Mean	Significance (two-tailed)
Continue to try	8.53	7.26	.045
Understand teacher instructions	8.50	6.94	.000
Write down assignments	8.39	5.53	.007
Organized work	8.37	6.76	.041
Sensitive to others' feelings	8.53	7.15	.015
Control temper	7.68	6 76	.003

In terms of research process behavior self-assessment, ninth grade girls self-assessed their research process skills as significantly higher ($p<.01$) than eleventh grade girls in terms of determining information need, developing search strategy, assessing and comprehending information, and interpreting and organizing information.

In terms of products, ninth grade girls performed significantly better ($p<.01$) for research product indicators overall. Eleventh grade girls out-performed boys in terms of adhering to the assignment (3.45 girls' mean vs. 3.16 boys' means with a .036 significance).

For eleventh grade girls, evaluating the research process and product correlated closely with risk-taking (willingness to participate in new activities and to try even when schoolwork is hard) ($r = .399$; $p<.01$).

Table 5.9 shows that there was one social-emotional behavior that boys exhibited that correlated significantly across all research product indicators: following rules. In contrast, when girls followed rules, their research product factors were not necessarily significantly better than if they did *not* follow rules.

Table 5.9   Significant Positive Correlations Between Boys' Research Product Factors and Following Rules

Research Product Factor	Correlation Coefficient	Significance (two-tailed)
Adhere to assignment	.231	.037
Organization	.239	.031
Proof and justification	.324	.003
Language/strategy use	.313	.005
Spelling/grammar	.310	.005

LIMITATIONS

This exploratory study examined students' social-emotional well-being and its possible correlation with research processes and products. Because the study was limited to one site, it could control to some extent school expectations, but the students studied in this investigation represent two different curricular "tracks," which limited comparisons. Additionally, having one teacher per grade optimized consistent assessment but limited the generalizability of the findings. Nevertheless, the investigation unearthed some interesting patterns, and suggests some directions to take.

DISCUSSION

The findings provided a rich dataset to analyze and underlined the complex developmental interactions among individuals, information, and social context. In that respect, the data mirror the findings of Heinstrom (2003) and Jarvela et al. (2000).

Research Question 1

To what degree does a correlation exist between students' social-emotional behavior status and students' research information literacy competence?

In terms of research processes, eleventh graders self-assessed their skills as significantly higher for the informational tasks of determining information need, developing a search strategy, and interpreting/organizing information. Ninth graders thought they did a better job of evaluating product and process. Again, ninth grade self-perceptions could have been accounted for by their gifted/talented designation, or it could be due to perceptions shaped by experience in high school courses that were more difficult and nuanced than middle school work.

A significant positive correlation was found between the social-emotional attributes of getting along and emotional resilience and students' self-perceptions about the ability to conduct research. Social cognitive theory would support the impact of getting along as students have to negotiate public/social encounters as they are assigned information tasks, and need to gather and communicate information. The complexity of the information task speaks to the Martin and Marsh (2006) academic resilience construct as it encompasses emotional resilience.

All five social-emotional attributes correlated significantly with communicating research findings and evaluating the research process/product. Since these two research tasks synthesize information behavior, it is not surprising that they would reflect a gestalt social-emotional repertoire. Ninth graders' organizational attributes correlated significantly with communicating information, while eleventh graders' self-reported collaborative ability was linked with communication skill. These grade-specific differences could indicate developmental or academic growth: Ninth graders might still be learning how to plan their homework schedule, and they might not have learned how to channel their social energy into constructive research communication.

Overall, though, the data seem to indicate that research can be a frustrating process, so being able to deal with obstacles emotionally and intellectually and to revise the work to a satisfactory conclusion are important social-emotional skills across grades and gender.

Research Question 2

To what degree does a correlation exist between students' social-emotional behavior status and students' research product quality?

The potential correlation between social-emotional well-being and research project is particularly interesting because it compares students' self-assessment of their personal information behaviors and the assessment of their ultimate research product. When the self-assessment data about information behaviors were examined in light of the students' research product as assessed by teachers, it appeared that the study's eleventh graders self-assessed their behaviors more accurately and realistically than the ninth graders. Since the ninth graders were designated as gifted and talented, they may have an elevated sense of well-being. In a follow-up communication, the SLT and ninth grade teacher asserted that the subject ninth graders tended to overestimate their abilities. Indeed, the more highly they rated their research process expertise, the more likely that their work would be considered lower quality by their teachers. This finding aligns with Competency Theory as researched by Dunning, Johnson, and Ehrlinger (2003). They posited that incompetent individuals do not self assess themselves accurately and do not improve by seeing models of competency. They need to be explicitly taught the skills that render them competent.

Alternatively, eleventh graders may find their studies more challenging than in freshman year and so self-assess themselves less optimistically. It would be useful to have parallel classes to test this hypothesis. Additionally, since the two assignments differed slightly, it is difficult to determine the relative complexity of each aspect of the product, let alone the teachers' differences in assessment. What *can* be examined, however, is the relative level of performance within each grade. A longitudinal study of the same subjects over time would provide more valid information about developmental growth.

For all subgroups (e.g., grade and gender) though, students who self-reported social-emotional maturity or well-being demonstrated the ability to build a case or stance and justify it with appropriate facts. This correlation recalls Nahl and Harada's (1996) findings about students' self-confidence and their Internet skills ratings.

The data showed that ninth grade students who exhibited more social behaviors did less well in their final project. It could well be that they were distracted by their peers or asked peers for advice rather than the teacher. Eleventh graders, on the other hand, leveraged their social skills to improve their research project, which matched the finding in the self-reported research processes. Again, follow-up interviews with the ninth grade subjects could provide more meaningful data. It appears that ninth graders might see social behavior as an end in itself rather than as a means to an academic goal. In their Seattle Social Development Project intervention study, Hawkins, Smith, and Catalano (2004) asserted that social competence by itself is not sufficient; it must be coupled with skills for successful participatory learning.

Dealing with fear and frustration seems to underlie other correlations between social-emotional well-being and the research product. Ninth graders who could "bounce back" when frustrated tended to create higher-quality research products; this is one case where self-confidence can overcome momentary obstacles. For eleventh grade girls, this self-confidence came into play when dealing with the unknown: Risk-takers were more apt to evaluate and revise their work. Nahl's (2001) information behavior taxonomy verifies this situation.

Research Question 3

To what degree is gender a significant factor in students' social-emotional behavior status and students' research information literacy competence and research product quality?

Students' self-perceptions about their social-emotional well-being provide a grounding for discussing possible gender correlations. Ninth grade girls rated their behavior higher than their male peers as well as their eleventh grade female counterparts. The factors that were found to be significant followed the expected behavior styles of females: waiting to understand teachers' instructions, not interrupting, and being sensitive to others' feelings. However, by eleventh grade, boys' and girls' self-perceptions of behaviors did not differ significantly. When comparing *all* girls and *all* boys, though, girls self-reported more mature social-emotional behaviors in terms of trying hard, being organized, and self-regulating emotions.

When these results are examined in light of the students' research product as assessed by teachers, it appears that the study's eleventh graders self-assessed their behaviors more accurately and realistically than did the ninth graders. Persistently putting in the effort to complete difficult work was a significant factor to communicating the information, particularly for eleventh grade boys. For eleventh graders, working cooperatively with classmates on projects was another highly significant factor, particularly for girls. Since girls in general are less likely to take risks (Moir & Jessel, 1991), helping them develop this willingness will "pay off" in the research process. For eleventh graders, particularly girls, evaluating the research process and product correlated closely with risk-taking (willingness to participate in new activities and to try even when schoolwork is hard).

CONCLUSION

One of the skills within information literacy is metacognition. It appears that self-reporting is a developmental skill in itself. Erikson (1968) posited that one of the tasks that adolescents need to address is self-identification and self-regulation. Ninth graders might have a less accurate self-picture of themselves, particularly in their first year of high school where they have had fewer opportunities to assess themselves relative to others in the same setting. The fact that the ninth grade subjects were labeled "gifted and talented" could also distort their sense of self by overestimating their "objective" information literacy competency.

This study also points to correlations between social-emotional well-being and information literacy, defined as research processes and products, which confirmed the findings of Jarvela et al. (2000). The current study's findings further refine the developmental differences of children and adults' information behaviors as examined by Bilal and Kirby (2002). Specifically, students who can negotiate their social environment and persist in their engagement (whether the motivation is inner- or outer-directed) with an informational task are more likely to be able to communicate their information efforts and exhibit metacognitive evaluative skills.

By eleventh grade, students' self-reporting of information behaviors also correlate significantly with the teachers' assessment of their research product; their self-expectations "calibrated" with the assignment expectations. In effect, they are more aware of self, others, and the information task—and they are more likely to act positively on their awareness.

This study offers new evidence about the role that gender plays in developmental, social-emotional well-being as it relates to information literacy. The study's ninth grade female subjects self-reported high social-emotional maturity and information literacy expertise; however, their performance belied their self-belief. Eleventh grade girls, on the other hand, seemed to have assessed their ability more accurately within their setting, and self-reported about the same way that boys did.

Nevertheless, girls in general reported a greater frequency of being organized, trying hard, and self-regulating emotions than boys did, behaviors that are echoed in Moir and Jessel's book *Brain Sex* (1991). On the other hand, when boys made a greater and more persistent effort, and followed directions, their research products tended to be rated better; and when girls took more intellectual risks, they tended to revise and improve their products. In short, males and females can learn valuable social-emotional skills from each other.

IMPLICATIONS

The study notes the impact that social-emotional well-being has on information literacy and suggests that students need to be explicitly taught relevant social-emotional skills before they conduct research, and they should have opportunities to practice these skills in personally meaningful information tasks.

Zins, Weissberg, Wang, and Walberg (2004) gathered research findings about the impact of social and emotional learning on academic success. Especially as schools make coordinated efforts to teach these dispositions, learning environments (such as the library) become better managed, and students become more engaged and committed to school and their own positive development. Of particular benefit is engaging students "actively and experientially in the learning process" (12), which speaks to inquiry-based research projects. In their review of social-emotional learning in school systems, Elias, Zins, Graczyk, and Weissberg (2003) asserted that focused attention and interventions need to be done on a schoolwide basis for efforts to be effective. Jarvela et al. (2000) recommended that teachers should have goal-oriented discussions with students to foster a sense of shared expertise; interaction should focus on solving the task at hand with the teacher (including the SLT) providing "process-relevant support in the student's zone of proximal development" (p. 304).

To this end, SLTs and classroom teachers should pay attention to the social and emotional skills of students. Elksnin and Elksnin (2003) provide a good set of teaching strategies to improve students' social and emotional problem-solving skills. Teachers need to address listening accuracy explicitly; one practice is to have students check their own work to see if it adheres to the teachers' directions. Both SLTs and classroom teachers should encourage students to persist in their research efforts; classroom teachers can emphasize the benefits of revising research questions, interpretation and manipulation of information, and communication of findings. School library teachers can help students rethink key words, broaden their research strategies, and recycle the research process to refine questions and answers. Both classroom and library media teachers can help students by telling them frankly that conducting research can be a frustrating experience for students as well as information professionals, and that students should try to think of different approaches when they "hit the wall" and to keep on refocusing to find satisfying solutions to research questions.

On the positive side, AASL included social skills (i.e., collaborative work) in their information literacy standards. What needs to be addressed, as revealed in this study, is the need for teachers to help students differentiate between social interaction and academically centric collaboration. While it appears that this issue is resolved by eleventh grade, teachers can recognize freshman developmental behaviors and facilitate their actions to align more closely to academic demands. In addition, ninth grade teachers can help students think about how their behaviors impact their academic performance by using metacognitive exercises that concretely illustrate the relationship between social-emotional behavior and research processes. This reality check can help students become more objective and accurate in their self-assessments. Peer review of these self-reflections can offer a socially acceptable and developmentally appropriate way to examine research efforts.

Particular attention should be made to gender-specific issues. For example, girls should be encouraged to take intellectual risks, and boys should be encouraged to follow directions, both with the goal of producing more accurate and substantive work. These issues can be expressed to the entire class since the ones who need that particular encouragement can apply that information, and those who already follow those ideas will be affirmed in their behavior.

In the final analysis, conducting research is an emotional and social process as much as it is an intellectual one. Therefore, library media and classroom teachers should pay attention to these dynamics in a pro-active way so that students will be more successful in each of these developmental domains.

REFERENCES

Allen, B., & Kim, K. (2001). Person and context in information seeking: Interaction between cognitive and task variables. *New Review of Information Behaviour Research, 2*, 1–16.

American Association of School Librarians. (1998). *Information power.* Chicago: American Library Association.

American Association of School Librarians. (1999). *A planning guide for information power.* Chicago: American Library Association.

Bandura, A. (1986). *Social foundations of thought and action: A social cognitive theory.* Englewood Cliffs, NJ: Prentice Hall.

Bellardo, T. (1985). An investigation of online searcher traits and their relationship to search outcome. *Journal of the American Society for Information Science, 36*(4), 241–250.

Benson, P., Scales, P., Leffert, N., & Roehlkepartain, E. (1999). *A fragile foundation: The state of developmental assets among American youth.* Minneapolis, MN: Search Institute.

Bernard, M. (1990). Rational-emotive therapy with children and adolescents. *School Psychology Review, 19*(3), 294–303.

Bernard, M. (2003). *You can do it!* New York: Time Warner.

Bernard, M., & Cronan, F. (1999). The child and adolescent scale of irrationality: Validation data and mental health correlates. *Journal of Cognitive Psychotherapy, 13*(2), 121–131.

Bernard, M., & Laws, W. (1988, August). *Childhood irrationality and mental health.* Paper presented at the 24th International Congress of Psychology, Sydney, Australia.

Bilal, D., & Kirby, J. (2002). Differences and similarities in information seeking: Children and adults as Web users. *Information Processing and Management, 38*(5), 649–670.

Butler, D., & Cartier, S. (2005, April). *Multiple complementary methods for understanding self-regulated learning as situated in context.* Paper presented at the American Educational Research Association conference, Montreal, Canada.

Cahoy, E. (2004). Put some feeling into it! *Knowledge Quest, 32*(4), 25–27.

Cohen, J. (Ed.). (1999). *Educating minds and hearts: Social emotional learning and the passage into adolescence.* New York: Teachers College Press.

Cohen, J. (Ed.). (2001). *Caring classrooms/intelligent schools: The social emotional education of young children.* New York: Teachers College Press.

Collaborative to Advance Social and Emotional Learning. (2003). *SEL competences.* Chicago: Collaborative to Advance Social and Emotional Learning. Accessed November 25, 2006, from www.casel.org/about_sel/SELskills.php.

Colorado State Library and Adult Education Office and Colorado Educational Media Association. (1997). Rubrics for the assessment of information literacy. In California Library Media Educators Association, *From library skills to information literacy* (2nd ed.). San Jose, CA: Hi Willow.

Dervin, B. (1977). Using theory for librarianship: Communication, not information. *Drexel Library Quarterly, 13,* 16–32.

Dunning, D., Johnson, K., & Ehrlinger, J. (2003). Why people fail to recognize their own incompetence. *Current Directions in Psychological Science, 12*(3), 53–57.

Elias, M., Zins, J., Graczyk, J., & Weissberg, R. (2003). Implementation, sustainability, and scaling up of social-emotional and academic innovations in public schools. *School Psychology Review, 32*(3), 303–319.

Elksnin, L., & Elksnin, N. (2003). Fostering social-emotional learning in the classroom. *Education, 124*(1), 63–76.

Ellis, A., & Bernard, M. (Eds.). (1983). *Clinical applications of rational-emotive therapy.* New York: Plenum Press.

Erikson, E. H. (1968). *Identify: Youth and crisis.* New York: Norton.

Farmer, L. (2006). Degree of implementation of library media programs and student achievement. *Journal of Librarianship and Information Science, 38*(1), 21–32.

Goodin, M. (1991). The transferability of library research skills from high school to college. *School Library Media Quarterly, 20,* 33–42.

Grover, R., Lakin, J., & Dickerson, J. (1997). An interdisciplinary model for assessing learning. In L. Lighthall & K. Haycock (Eds.), *Information rich but knowledge poor?* Seattle: International Association of School Librarianship.

Harada, V., & Yoshina, J. (1997). Improving information search process instruction and assessment through collaborative action research. *School Libraries Worldwide, 3,* 41–55.

Hawkins, J., Smith, B., & Catalano, R. (2004). Social development and social and emotional learning. In J. Zins, R. Weissberg, W. Wang, & H. Walberg. (Eds.), *Building academic success on social and emotional learning: What does the research say?* New York: Teachers College Press.

Heinstrom, J. (2003). Five personality dimensions and their influence on information behavior. *Information Research, 9*(1). Accessed November 25, 2006, from http://informationr.net/ir/9-1/paper165.html.

IFLA/UNESCO. (2002). *School library guidelines*. The Hague, Netherlands: IFLA.

Jiao, Q. G., & Onwuegbuzie, Λ. J. (2004). The impact of information technology on library anxiety: The role of computer attitudes. *Information Technology and Libraries, 23*, 138–144.

Jarvela, S., Lehtinen, E., & Salonen, P. (2000) Social-emotional orientation as a mediating variable in the teaching–learning interaction: Implications for instructional design. *Scandinavian Journal of Educational Research, 44*(3), 293–306.

Johnson, D. (1994). *Cooperative learning in the classroom*. Alexandria, VA: Association for Supervision and Curriculum Development.

Kelly, G. A. (1963). *A theory of personality: The psychology of personal constructs*. New York: W. W. Norton.

Kernan, J., & Mojena, R. (1973). Information utilization and personality. *Journal of Communication, 23*(3), 315–327.

Kuhlthau, C. C. (1985). *Teaching the library research process*. Englewood Cliffs, NJ: Prentice-Hall.

Kuhlthau, C. C. (2003). *Seeking meaning*. Westport, CT: Libraries Unlimited.

Lance, K. (2002). Proof of the power. *Teacher Librarian, 29*(2), 29–34.

Martin, A., & Marsh, H. (2006). Academic resilience and its psychological and educational correlates: A construct validity approach. *Psychology in the Schools, 43*(3), 267–281.

Martzoukou, K. (2005). A review of Web information seeking research: Considerations of method and foci of interest. *Information Research, 10*(2), paper 215.

Moir, A., & Jessel, D. (1991). *Brain sex*. New York: Dell.

Nahl, D. (2001). A conceptual framework for explaining information behavior. *Studies in Media & Information Literacy Education, 1*(2). Accessed November 25, 2006, from http://www.utpjournals.com/simile/issue2/nahl1.html.

Nahl, D., & Harada, V. (1996). Composing Boolean search statements: Self-confidence, concept analysis, search logic, and errors. *School Library Media Quarterly, 24*(4), 199–207.

Palmer, J. (1991). Scientists and information: II. Personal factors in information behaviour. *Journal of Documentation, 47*(3), 254–275.

Redwood High School Research Study Group. (2000). *Research handbook*. Larkspur, CA: Tamalpais Union High School District. Accessed November 25, 2006, from http://rhsweb.org/library/researchhandbook.htm.

Salovey, P., & Mayer, J. (1990). Emotional intelligence. *Imagination, Cognition, & Personality, 9*, 185–211.

Savolainen, R. (1993). The sense-making theory: Reviewing the interests of a user-centered approach to information seeking and use. *Information Processing & Management, 29*, 13–28.

Soloman, P. (1997). Discovering information behavior in sense-making: III. The person. *Journal of the American Society for Information Science, 48*, 1127–1138.

Tenopir, C. (2003). *Use and users of electronic library resources: An overview and analysis of recent research studies*. Washington, DC: Council on Library and Information Resources. Accessed November 25, 2006, from www.clir.org/pubs/reports/pub 120/pub120.pdf.

Todd, R., & Kuhlthau, C. C. (2004). *Student learning through Ohio school libraries.* Columbus, OH: Ohio Educational Library Media Association. Accessed November 25, 2006, from   www.oelma.org/StudentLearning/documents/OELMAReportof Findings.pdf.

Zins, J., Weissberg, R., Wang, M., & Walberg, H. (Eds.). (2004). *Building academic success on social and emotional learning: What does the research say?* New York: Teachers College Press.

CHAPTER 6

Affective Dimensions of Critical Care Nurses' Informative Interactions: Gentle Nurse Jekyll and Harried Nurse Hyde

Michelynn McKnight
Louisiana State University

INTRODUCTION

Critical care nurses spend most of their time gathering, using, storing, retrieving, and passing on information. They spend more time with individual patients than other healthcare workers in hospitals do, and they enter more data into patient specific medical records than any other healthcare providers. Without any help from nurses' aids, they care for the two to four patients to whom they are assigned on a given shift. They are responsible for the coordination of all care for the patients in their charge (Thelan, Lough, Urden, & Stacy, 1998). Their on-duty information behavior in this intense information ecology (Nardi & O'Day, 1999) can literally be a matter of life and death. The environment is stressful for patients, patients' family and visitors, as well as for the care providers. These professional nurses must pay close attention to everyone's affective behaviors, including their own.

RESEARCH QUESTION

Critical care nursing is a constantly repeated cycle of frequent informative interactions with, on one hand, a very sick patient, the patient's visitors, and the patient's real time physiologic monitors, and, on the other hand, a very important set of documents and patient specific record systems collectively and colloquially known as "the chart." This information seeking process has been described as "The Nurse's Patient-Chart Cycle" (McKnight, 2007). While on duty, the nurses do not have time to consult the kind of literature and knowledge-based information typically provided by healthcare library services (McKnight, 2004).

Increasingly complex chart systems require much more of the nurses' on-duty time than older systems did. Nurses often experience and express frustrations with the chart systems. This study addresses these research questions: What are the observable affective aspects of critical care nurses' on-duty information behavior as they cycle between the patient and the chart? Do critical care nurses express or hide those feelings from the patient?

RELEVANT LITERATURE

Roberts, While, and Fitzpatrick (1995), and Patterson, Blehm, Foster, Euglee, and Moore (1995) and many others have studied nurses' use of patient specific information (medical records) in the nursing process. Because nurses have more direct interaction with the patient record than any other healthcare providers, nurse researchers and others have studied analog patient records and the informatics of clinical information systems (digital patient records). A major challenge for nurses using these systems is that the driving forces in their development are not nursing but medical, legal, and financial (Corcoran-Perry & Graves, 1990). The interfaces that nurses use with these systems are designed for data security, not for ease of use.

In her recent study, Haghenbeck (2005) described nurses' anger, frustration, surprise, and shock. Some expressed doubts about their own competence or worries about their professional image when equipment failed.

There have been no studies observing and comparing the affective behavior of the same nurses during direct patient care and during other on-duty activities. Such evidence can inform our understanding of their on-duty information behavior and aid in the design of clinical information services and systems.

METHOD

This study used narrative data gathered from participant observation and in-context interviews to describe the information behavior, including affect, of on-duty critical care nurses.

The site selected for this study was a 20-bed critical care unit in a 275-bed community hospital. Fifty-eight RNs worked in this unit; each on-duty RN is responsible for the total care of two to four patients each shift. Conforming to Institutional Review Board (IRB)-approved procedure, volunteer participants were recruited through presentations at unit meetings and flyers. They were told that the researcher was not a nurse and would not be judging anyone's professional competence. The six RN participants in this study constituted a purposeful representative sample of the staff in gender, education, and experience.

The researcher (as participant observer) accompanied each RN participant for one shift (ranging from four to 13 hours) for a total of 50 hours of fieldwork. She made observations on weekdays (7 A.M.–7 P.M.), weekday nights (7 P.M.–7 A.M.), weekend days, and weekend nights. While in the field, the investigator interacted with the participants, took descriptive notes, and made some audio recordings of open-ended interviews with the participant nurses, observing their affective information behavior. EasyScript speedwriting method (Legend Co., Newton, Mass.) was used to record all observations that were not audio recorded.

Within 24 hours of each observation, all of the field notes and the recorded interview were transcribed. The member check technique (Glesne, 1999, p. 23) was used to verify the accuracy and validity of the data. Within two or three days of each observation, the nurse participants received and reviewed the transcript of data from their shifts. The data comprises 4,236 paragraphs of text. Fewer than 250 of these paragraphs described activities that were not information behavior.

The data were imported into a file in N6 qualitative research software (QSR International, Melbourne, Australia). All paragraphs in which the nurses' affective information behavior was recorded were coded. These paragraphs were further coded for instances in which the nurses displayed affect during an interaction with a human or automated information system not in a patient's room. Then the data were coded for display of affect when the nurses visited patients in the patients' rooms.

It was possible that the participant nurses could, of course, alter behavior because of the presence of the researcher. While the researcher occasionally detected some "performance" behavior at the beginning of a shift, the opinion of this researcher is that the nurses' work was so constant and intense that they could not continue that behavior for very long. The fact that the researcher in this study is not a nurse is both a limitation and a strength of the study. This study did not begin with a particular nursing theory or formal process, but rather with observation of nurses' actual information behavior.

Member checking (each participant's review of the researcher's transcript of her field notes and interview data for that participant) helped to verify the accuracy of the data. After reading the transcripts, the nurse participants often commented on how they had not realized how often they had some interactions. On duty, the nurses' concentration was clearly on the patients' care and recordkeeping; it was not on the classification of their own informative interactions. The use of thick description enriched the credibility of the data and the reliability of the findings. Several researchers with experience and expertise analyzing qualitative data reviewed the data coding for consistency and accuracy.

FINDINGS

This study examined the affective aspects of critical care nurses' on-duty information behavior. It addressed two research questions. The findings are reported in the context of these questions.

Affective Aspects of Critical Care Nurses' On-Duty Information Behavior

What are the observable affective aspects of critical care nurses' on-duty information behavior as they cycle between the patient and the chart? During data collection, parts of the patient record (the chart) were in computer systems and parts were on paper. A few functions moved from paper systems to online systems during the observation period. Most, but by no means all, of the paper and online documents the nurses used are part of the patients' permanent medical records. Most of the paper documents were in a binder kept at the nurses' station; most of the online record systems were accessible both at workstations at the nurses' station and also from wireless laptops on stands elsewhere in the unit. (The latter were rarely used. The nurses preferred to sit down at the nurses' station.)

The nurses frequently expressed frustration with a variety of human, paper, and automated information systems. They encountered difficulties with illegible handwriting, the unavailability of people who had needed information not recorded in the chart, difficult navigation of online systems, multitasking with several complex systems (personal, digital, and analog) and social protocol barriers, as well as obvious equipment malfunction.

Examples of Nurses' Expressed Affect

Participants included both male and female nurses. For confidentiality, female pronouns are used for nurses and male pronouns are used for patients and others in the examples that follow.

Example A

At the beginning of a shift, this nurse is less anxious when she has reviewed charts before the doctor arrives.

> **RN**: There. I feel better. My charts are all open. You try to get your charts open before you talk to the doc … It's not unusual for me to be at least an hour into the shift before I see a patient.

Example B

The same information is recorded in both computer and paper systems because of lack of confidence in the system.

RN at nurses' station retrieves a monitored vital signs printout from the printer.

RN copies the numbers from the printout into the paper chart. Researcher asks why.

> **RN**: The monitor system records vitals every 15 or 30 minutes. You can put the printout in the chart like this [points to a printout with

a patient bar code sticker attached], but it may be lost from the chart. Because I know it may disappear, I copy it here. I know this form will stay with the chart. If not, some day in court some lawyer may say "Did you take vital signs?" and if the record isn't there, I'm screwed.

Example C
The nurse is worried about making charting mistake.

RN: [entering data at workstation] Is this the right patient? Oh, yes, it is ... I've done that before.
Researcher: Done what?
RN: Charted on the wrong patient. I'm getting tired and my dyslexia is setting in.
Researcher: It doesn't matter if you catch it, but it does if you don't catch it.
RN: That's what's really weird with this [new computer] system. You can't see what you've written. I've come in and noticed that someone else has charted on the wrong patient the entire time. Ugh! That would be so bad if it went to court! Really terrible. It's so much easier to make that kind of mistake on the computer. On paper, it would be obvious that there's been a big change, but not so obvious ...

Example D
Multitasking stress.

RN: If I just stay calm and just plug away at it one thing at a time, eventually it all gets done. It's just a matter of ... and some nights are worse than others. You know there are nights whenever you got two or three codes [cardiac arrests] running at once. Those nights really get unnerving and that's when you kind of lose track of ... and just get flustered and everything. Once you're flustered, then everything just goes out the window.

Example E
Frustration with hard-to-read handwriting and redundant orders.

RN: [reading a paper document at the nurses' station] What does this say?
Unit secretary: [helping interpret the doctor's handwriting in a handwritten order] It looks to me like "other meds."
RN: "Other meds"? [Sighs heavily] We were already doing those meds.

Unit secretary: That's what he wants.

Example F

Frustration with equipment error.

RN looks at monitor printout with a big gap in the data.

RN: Look at these vitals [recordings of vital signs]. What do you do with this? Several hours it's there, then for several hours there are no readings ... then when it comes back on, it's all different. What to do? I don't know. [Sarcastically] I just work here.

Example G

Frustration with multitasking.

RN: [at nurses' station, to unit secretary] Will you please page {doctor's surname} again?

Unit secretary pages the doctor.

RN goes to the automated drug-dispensing system down the hall and returns to the nurses' station.

RN: [to unit secretary] They don't have that new person in the {drug-dispensing system name} computer yet.

RN returns to the drug-dispensing system, has a problem with it, and swears at it. Eventually RN gets medication from the system. RN takes medication to the drug preparation room and prepares medication for patient.

The phone rings.

Unit secretary: [to RN] Line {number} is for you.

RN puts down the filled syringes and rushes to the phone. She tells the doctor what is going on with the patient, describing the crisis episode and current condition. RN listens and looks for her personal note sheet on the clipboard. She can't find it. She puts the phone down and runs back and forth between the nurses' station and the medication preparation room before finding it with the medication administration record in the medication room. She tries to recall something from memory.

RN: [rushing and muttering to herself] I don't remember if it is him or the other gentleman ... or, here it is ... no, can't find that ... [to researcher] my paperwork is scattered all over here.

Eventually, the RN finds the notes in question and continues the conversation with the doctor on the phone, watching her patient's monitors while she talks. After the phone call ends, she retrieves the syringes and goes to the patient's room. She composes herself before entering the room.

Example H

This nurse is upset with mistakes she makes because of interruptions.
RN is at the nurses' station writing in the paper chart.
A soft alarm sounds.

> **RN:** [to researcher who is seated close to the remote patient monitors] What's the blood pressure?

Researcher tells her.

> **RN:** [growling] I need that checked q 15 [every fifteen minutes], not q 30!

RN goes to the patient's room and changes the settings on the monitor.
RN returns to nurses' station.

> **RN:** OK, I *have* to chart.

RN sits down at the computer, opens the {clinical information system program}, signs in with ID and password, pulls up the patient record, and goes through several screens to find an assessment page in the patient record.

RN reads from her personal note sheet and copies the numbers to small boxes on the screen. She chooses some selections available and clicks on several check boxes.

The phone rings. The unit secretary answers, tells RN that it's for her, and gives her the handset.

RN makes hand gestures at several people in the area who are talking so loudly that she cannot hear.

After the phone call, she goes back to the {clinical information system}. The same people are still talking.

> **RN:** [muttering to self while entering data] Wrong! Wrong! Wrong! Wrong!
> **Researcher**: What?
> **RN:** I thought that I was in my patient, but I wasn't ... grr ...

RN takes out what she has just entered, changes screens and reenters data.

Example I

A failure to communicate.

RN tries to call {patient's family member} who is to come to take the patient home. RN discovers that the phone number she has is wrong.

> **RN**: OK. I'll try another way.

RN finds in her personal notes the number for another family member. She calls that family member and asks that the message be relayed.

RN tries unsuccessfully to make some more calls.

> **RN**: [sighs] I feel like I'm having a bad dream.

Example J

Frustration with voicemail instead of a person who can help.

RN needs to have a medication sent from the pharmacy. She calls the pharmacy and gets voicemail instead of a real person. She leaves a message.

> **RN**: I *hate* that. I need that for him ASAP!

Much later … after no response from the pharmacy …

> **RN**: I'm hacked off at that voicemail in the pharmacy.

[Later]

> **RN**: [looking at the medication administration record] I don't know *what* we are going to do. He never called me back.

RN calls pharmacy again.

Do Critical Care Nurses Express or Hide Those Feelings from the Patient?

The nurses' demeanor markedly changed between interactions with the charts and interactions with the patients. No matter how stressed, rushed, frustrated, or overwhelmed they may have been, they dropped all outward signs of discomfort when they walked through a door into a patient's room. Often they were observed stopping before the door, taking a deep breath, and waiting a beat to compose themselves. The nurses consistently made this conscious change in their outward demeanor. The curtain drawn around the patient's bed was as a curtain for a stage. The nurses' body language, facial expression, and speech patterns were dramatically different in these two segments of the patient-chart cycle. They very rarely expressed any frustrations with the chart or other systems in the patient's room. No matter what urgent responsibilities were waiting for them back at the nurses' station, they always said before leaving the room "Is there anything else I can do for you? I have the time." (It was a unit policy that all nurses use that "script" before leaving the room.) This difference can be characterized allegorically as "Gentle Nurse Jekyll" and "Harried Nurse Hyde."

Gentle Nurse Jekyll always presents to the patient a relaxed, caring, and reassuring persona. There is no sign inside the patient's room of the Harried Nurse Hyde who may have been swearing at a paper chart, the computer, or a system malfunction just seconds before. Harried Nurse Hyde may be juggling several tasks, but when she rushes (sometimes runs) to a patient's room, she stops just outside the door and composes herself before walking calmly in as Gentle Nurse Jekyll. Following are three examples from the data.

Examples of the Nurse Presenting an Affect to the Patient Which Is Different from What She Is Expressing Away from the Patient
Example K
Many things are going wrong, but this nurse smiles and laughs with the patient.

RN has just dealt with a difficult family situation for one of her patients. She retrieves and prepares a fluid bolus for her other patient. In spite of her high level of stress, she changes her expression just before she enters the room to deliver it. She walks in looking cheerful and relaxed.

> **RN**: [to patient] You're not going anywhere until you get stable. [smiles]
> **Patient**: Am I acting out?
> **RN**: You're not acting out. This will help.

Patient tells an X-rated joke.

> **RN**: [smiling] *Now* you're acting out! [laughs]
> **RN**: I'm going to give you a fluid bolus. Right now, you're just a little bit dehydrated.

RN and patient laugh and chatter while she administers the bolus.

RN returns to automated secure medication dispensing system to retrieve and prepare an anti-nausea medication. The automated intravenous infusion system (malfunctioning) beeps loudly in the patient's room.

> **RN**: [frowning] I *hate* that thing!

RN goes to patient room. Again, her body language changes at the door. She lifts her head, drops her shoulders, and smiles as she enters the room.

> **RN**: [to patient] OK, I gave you some fluid, and I'm giving you some medicine for the nausea.

Patient coughs up something.

> **RN**: You're coughing up some pretty gross looking stuff here. I'm going to get you something for that …

RN goes to the nurses' station. She sits down at a terminal to chart. She sighs heavily.

> **RN**: [tense, with a set jaw, talking to herself while entering data] You are a positive, loving person. You are sweet and kind.

Another nurse asks RN where something is.

> **RN**: [grumbling] We don't have that. If it costs money, we don't get it!

Example L

I have to be good.

> **Researcher**: You're good when you go in the room. Very good.
> **RN**: I have to be good. One good thing about the computer is that I can growl at the computer.

Example M

Frown to smile to frown.

RN frowns at monitor printout.

> **RN**: This is so dumb!

RN copies numbers from monitor printout into a patient record system.

> **RN**: This one takes respiration first. The vitals [vital signs record entries] are in a different order in the printout from the [proprietary patient record system]. I think they should change my title to "Data Entry" … then I'd get paid more!

RN continues charting at nurses' station. She is having problems with multiple screens. An alarm on a patient monitor goes off.

RN: [to Researcher] What's his pressure?

Researcher reads numbers off of the remote monitor at the nurses' station.

RN growls.

RN goes to patient's room, putting on a smile as she enters. RN pulls up the covers over the patient, says soothing things, checks monitor, repositions oxygen and oxygen sensor. She checks the monitor one more time before returning to charting at the nurses' station. The frown returns as she leaves the patient's room.

Example N

Patient is scared. This nurse is worried about patient but does not show it to patient.

At the nurses' station, RN has been watching the display for the patient's heart monitor. RN goes to patient's room.

RN: You said you weren't doing so well. What's bothering you?
Patient: I get so out of breath.
RN: Yes. You're going to be pretty weak for a while …. You're going to be doing breathing exercises tonight. You need to do a lot of coughing and deep breathing. There's some congestion in your lungs.

Patient coughs. [Nurse glances at heart monitor.]

RN: Good cough! That's what I want you to do … a lot of coughing like that tonight. Any time you cough and you need to spit, just put this [suction tube] to your mouth and spit.
RN: I'll check back with you a lot tonight. [Looks at monitor] It looks like your heart's converted back to normal. Your heart had converted back with some {name of cardiac dysrhythmia}. We're going to give you a little medication for that. Are you having any pain?
Patient: A little bit.
RN: Your heart or your chest?
Patient: Chest
RN: I'm going to check your blood pressure. Is that all right? [RN watches monitor] All right, everything is working OK. Your heart just doesn't like to …

Patient's expression changes to fear.

RN: You're OK. Are you scared?

Patient: I'm scared.
RN: It's OK. You don't have to be scared. Just rest. I'll check on you frequently through the night.

After leaving the room, the RN rushes to get additional medication to administer through the patient's intravenous infusion system. He had had a temporary cardiac dysrhythmia, but it had converted back to a normal rhythm. RN asked the heart monitor technologist for a printout of the ECG during the episode.

RN: [frowning and shaking head while speaking to monitor technologist] I'll see if I can get you a lead with a P wave [ECG]. He's teetering back and forth. His heart rate jumped up to {number}. There's no more question about whether or not we're gong to wean him off {cardiac drug}. We're not going to wean him off {cardiac drug} tonight.

DISCUSSION

Harried Nurse Hyde appeared to be successful at hiding recently expressed emotions and presenting Gentle Nurse Jekyll to the patient. The nurses' intense information activities outside of the rooms are essentially hidden from patients, family members, and visitors. When the patient presses the nurse call button and expresses a request, for instance, for a pain medication, they expect the immediate appearance of the nurse for this seemingly simple task. Some may believe that a perceived delay is a result of the nurse's being inattentive or even lazy. They do not see the flurry of activity as the nurse must interact with three or more complex information systems before she can get the needed medication in her hand.

During interviews, the nurses all told the researcher that they had chosen the nursing profession because of a desire to care for sick people. Although they were computer and information literate (some had their own Web sites, searched bibliographic databases, or both during their off duty time), they believed that recordkeeping took too much (for some, perceived as the majority) of their on-duty time. Part of their Jekyll and Hyde change in affect might have been because of a preference for interacting with people rather than with systems.

This was a small pilot study, and it would be helpful to compare its findings with results of similar studies in different hospitals and different kinds of nursing care departments. It would be particularly interesting to study the nurses' affect in instances where interaction with the chart occurs in the patient room at the point of care.

CONCLUSION

On-duty critical care nurses spend most of their work shift, gathering, using, recording, and passing on various kinds of information in human, paper and online systems. They display a wide range of emotions while doing so. Outside of the patient room, one can easily observe nurses consciously changing the affect their demeanor communicates as they enter a patient's room. As Harried Nurse Hyde, they may furrow their brow, shout, swear, and growl while working at the Nurse's station one minute and just a few seconds later be a smiling Gentle Nurse Jekyll for the patient, the patient's family, and the patient's visitors.

REFERENCES

Corcoran-Perry, S. & Graves, J. (1990). Supplemental-information-seeking behavior of cardiovascular nurses. *Research in Nursing & Health, 13,* 119–127.

Glesne, C. (1999). *Becoming qualitative researchers: An introduction.* New York: Longman.

Haghenbeck, K. (2005). Critical care nurses' experiences when technology malfunctions. *Journal of the New York State Nurses Association, 36,* 13–19.

McKnight, M. (2004). Hospital nurses: No time to read on duty. *Journal of Electronic Medical Resources in Libraries, 1,* 13–23.

McKnight, M. (in press). A grounded theory model of on-duty critical care nurses' information behavior: The patient-chart cycle of informative interactions. *Journal of Documentation.*

Nardi, B. A., & O'Day, V. L. (1999*). Information ecologies: Using technology with heart.* Cambridge, MA: MIT Press.

Patterson, P. K., Blehm, R., Foster, J., Euglee, K., & Moore J. (1995). Nurse information needs for efficient care continuity across patient units. *Journal of Nursing Administration, 25,* 28–36.

Roberts, J., While, A., & Fitzpatrick, J. (1995). Information-seeking strategies and data utilization: Theory and practice. *International Journal of Nursing Studies, 32,* 601–611.

Thelan, L. A., Lough, M. E., Urden, L. D., & Stacy, K. M. (1998). *Critical care nursing Diagnosis and management* (3rd ed.). St. Louis, MO: Mosby.

CHAPTER 7

Emotion, Response, and Recommendation: The Role of Affect in Children's Book Reviews in a Digital Library

Sheri Anita Massey, Allison Druin, and Ann Carlson Weeks
University of Maryland College Park

INTRODUCTION

To effectively develop collections and programs that address and respond to children's interests, school and public librarians need to understand how children respond to the literature they read for school assignments, as well as for recreation. The challenge is further exacerbated by the need to develop library collections and programs that effectively meet the needs of increasingly international user communities from Emporia, Kansas, to Wellington, New Zealand. While many studies have looked at cross-national assessments of students' school achievement in various subject areas (Foshay, Thorndike, Hotyat, Pidgeon, & Walker, 1962; Heyneman, 2004; International Association for the Evaluation of Educational Achievement [IEA], n.d.; Morra & Lazzarini, 2002; Ogle et al., 2003; Purves, 1973), no studies have explored children's responses to books read recreationally across countries or cultures. Until recently, it has not been possible to provide identical collections of materials simultaneously in multiple locations.

Today, however, the Internet and related technologies make it possible for users all over the world to access the same collection of materials on demand through digital libraries. With the development of online digital collections, such as the International Children's Digital Library (ICDL), it is now possible to explore patterns in readers' responses to identical works in multiple international settings. By exploring patterns in readers' responses in different nations and over time, this research may begin to provide a greater understanding of children's interactions with books selected for recreational reading. This knowledge can then be applied to tailor collections and services that better meet children's various information needs. The work presented here offers a unique glimpse at international patterns in reader response when responses are made as children review and recommend books to other children. The work also addresses the paucity of reader-response research with children in the library and information studies field.

RELATED RESEARCH

Reader Response Theory

Reader response theory posits that every reader constructs meaning from an interaction with a literary work. A reader's constructed meaning is greatly influenced by factors such as feelings, beliefs, the structure and elements of the text, and the reader's context at the time of the interaction (Neuman, 2004; Probst, 2003; Rosenblatt, 1978). A reader's response may also change frequently and dramatically during an interaction with a text (Newton, Stegmeier, & Padak, 1999; Rosenblatt, 1991).

In a review of the reader-response literature, Martinez and Roser (2003) report that although adults and children process meaning in literature differently, young children are capable of making interpretations, thematic statements, and connections to their lives from what they read. Probst (2003) also reviewed the response literature but solely focuses on children's responses to literature. He found that as individuals, children bring different experiences, histories, beliefs, contexts, and purposes to the act of reading and, therefore, their responses and interpretations of what they read will differ. Probst adds that meaning is created from the interaction between the reader and the text. The one-to-one interaction between the reader and the text is known as "literary transaction" (Hepler & Hickman, 1982; Rosenblatt, 1978). Reader response research suggests that in order to understand a response, it is necessary to explore attributes of not only the text and the reader but also of the socio-cultural context in which the reading transaction occurs (Galda, 1982; Galda, 1983; Galda & Beach, 2001). Researchers explain that as children encounter the social practices, identities, and tools of their worlds, these experiences affect their responses to texts (Hynds, 1997; Sumara, 1996; Wilhelm, 1997).

Although the body of reader response research is extensive, few studies have examined response in international settings. What is available on international response has focused on adults, more specifically undergraduate college students (e.g., Brewer & Lichtenstein, 1982; Brewer & Ohtsuka, 1988; Halász, 1991; Larsen & László, 1990; László & Larsen, 1991; Martindale, 1988; Pritchard, 1990). The results of these largely quantitative studies vary significantly. Some studies found national differences in response to literature, others found slight differences within smaller groups, and others found no difference in response at all.

Investigations of children's response to literature in international contexts are also limited. Since Purves's (1973) nine-country study, little research has been done on the topic. In his study, Purves investigated the relationship between nationality and reading comprehension and found that the environment (i.e., home or school) had a stronger effect on comprehension than did the school curriculum.

In addition to studies on international differences in reader response, some studies explore cultural differences in response. Culture is a dynamic set of beliefs, values, and practices that shape and are shaped by a group of people (Hall, 1997). Anthropologists state that emotions are cultural artifacts and must be analyzed within the social and cultural contexts in which they are experienced (Geertz, 1973). Findings from studies that looked at the influence of culture on response (Altieri, 1995; Leung, 2003; Purves & Beach, 1972; Sims, 1983; Spears-Bunton, 1990; Spears-Bunton 1993; Tomlinson, 1995) suggest that readers prefer to read about people who share their backgrounds and experiences, and draw on various cultural perspectives, models, and tools to interpret and contextualize stories (Galda & Beach, 2001). However, this line of inquiry has also shown that it is difficult to separate the effects of culture from other factors, such as nationality, class, or socio-economic status, and expressed a need for additional international and cross-cultural research.

Researchers in library and information science (LIS) have also explored children's literary responses (Asselin, 2000; Steinfirst, 1986; Vandergrift, 1987). In an empirical study, Vandergrift (1990) analyzed 57 ninth- and tenth-graders' written and oral responses to a fantasy text to test her model of children's meaning-making processes. The model depicted readers moving from very personal (or "felt") responses to public (or "social") responses. She validated the model, finding that students were able find meaning in what they read and metacognitively track the development of their understanding. The young people identified elements from the text and from their personal experiences that influenced their perceptions, interpretations, and evaluations of the literature. While educators have explored students' responses to literature in the classroom, LIS research may add to this body of work by exploring children's responses to recreational reading.

Book Reviews

Book reviews—from sources such as *Booklist* and *Library Journal*—are important tools that librarians use to assist in readers' advisory, to assess the quality of a literary work, to make comparisons among literary works, and to place works within the larger literary context (Duda, 2005). Child-generated book reviews also have a place in readers' advisory. In a study of 66 primary school children in New Zealand, Irvine (2002) found that children responded best to peer recommendations to books compared to adult recommendations. Children who express justifications for accepting or rejecting and share those opinions with peers assume a readers' advisory role. Irvine also found that children are able to articulate their preferences with an emotional and narrative response. McGowen (2003) found that children who read and review books for their peers develop a sense of ownership about their reading and develop the skills to make their thoughts and feelings explicit and put them into concrete form to be shared.

With the development of the Internet, online recommendations of consumer products from large-scale networks like Amazon have become a mechanism for raising awareness about consumer experience with goods and services (Li & Hitt, 2004). Similar user-generated evaluative sites exist for reviewing and recommending products and services for children. Web sites with child-generated reviews, such as Stonesoup (www.stonesoup.com), the Spaghetti Book Club (www.spaghettibookclub.org), and BookHive (www.bookhive.org), are places where children can develop reviewing skills and practice sharing their emotional responses with others.

Building on the research in reader response and book reviewing, this chapter explores how children respond to books in a digital library when asked to review books for other children. With a better understanding of how children in different countries respond to recreational reading material, LIS professionals can more effectively develop policies, collections, and programs that complement the needs and interests young readers.

METHOD

This study employed qualitative inquiry methods because the research questions required in-depth information for answers rather than a one-time collection of statistical data (Neuman, 2003). These methods allowed researchers to study reader-response holistically, resulting in the identification of patterns that emerged from the data (Bunbury & Tabbert, (1988); Creswell, 1994; Creswell, 1998; Maxwell, 1996). A purposive sample was chosen for this study to "maximize the range of information collected" (Guba & Lincoln, 1982, p. 248). The 12 children from diverse settings contributed response data and, therefore, contributed 12 perspectives. These perspectives illustrated common characteristics within and across countries. Children's overlapping perspectives showed how they were able to respond to literature consistently.

Data were collected over a three-year period to investigate the relationship among reader response, digital libraries for children, and international contexts. The primary questions guiding this research were: (1) What role does emotion play when children are asked to read books in a digital collection, review them, and make recommendations to other children?, (2) In what ways are children's emotional responses similar or different in different countries?, and (3) How might emotional responses to literature and their role in readers' advisory inform the development of digital collections for children?

Research Study Participants and Locations

The International Children's Digital Library (ICDL; www.childrens library.org) is an ongoing research project to create a digitized collection of international children's books. A major focus of the research is to develop a deeper understanding of the relationship between children's access to a digital collection of multicultural materials and their attitudes toward books, libraries, reading, technology, and other countries and cultures (International Children's Digital Library Foundation, 2006).

As part of the ongoing research, the ICDL team is examining the longitudinal effects of the digital library on young users. The findings reported here represent a smaller piece of a more extensive ICDL development and implementation project. The full study, including aspects of the research being reported in this paper, is being implemented in four locations: Wellington, New Zealand; La Ceiba, Honduras; Munich, Germany; and Chicago, Illinois (see Table 7.1). Site selection was based on the ability to identify children from diverse ethnic and economic backgrounds, as well as the opportunity to take advantage of existing relationships with schools and libraries around the world.

The 12 children in the study were 8 years old when the study began and in the third grade. Research team members asked the librarian or a classroom teacher in each of the four sites to work with school administrators to identify the child participants. The site representatives were asked to identify children who were 8 years old and able to speak and understand English to enable communication with the research team, who were likely to continue at the school for the three years of the study, and whose parents were likely to support the research. In addition, the researchers asked that the child participants be of both genders in each setting. The children were not meant to be representative of the entire population of the country nor the demographics of the school. Using the above criteria, the school staff created a convenience sample of children for the study (Yin, 1989).

Germany

Gail, Manfred, and Skylar are all at the top of their class at the affluent international school they attend. All of the children in Germany read well-above grade level and have regular opportunities to read and discuss their reading experiences in school and at home. The children have access to diverse literary collections in multiple languages at both home and school. Gail is learning German as a second language. She reads chapter books in English and shorter, picture books in German for fun. Both Manfred and Skylar are bilingual and can read even the longest chapter book in both English and German.

The children are able to visit the school library before, during, and after school in addition to the biweekly visits they make to the library with their classmates. The large collection has materials in English, German, and numerous other languages exhibited in the school's international population. The children's parents are college educated and solidly middle and upper class. The parents have the time and resources available to supply Gail, Manfred, and Skylar with books to meet their changing reading preferences.

Table 7.1   Overview of Research Study Population, Participants, and Locations

Overview of Research Study Population, Participants, and Locations				
Country	**Germany**	**Honduras**	**New Zealand**	**U.S.**
City	Munich	Le Ceiba	Wellington	Chicago
Public/Private	Private International School	Private School	Public School	Public School
Student Ages	Pre–K (age 3) to 12th grade (age 18)	1st grade (age 6) to 12th grade (age 18)	Kinder (age 5) to 8th grade (age 14)	Infant (6 months) to 8th grade (age 14)
Student Population	• 600 students • 65 nationalities • Mid-high income • Majority intact families	• 300 students • Primarily Spanish • Middle income • Majority intact families	• 250 students • 22 cultures • Low-mid income • Majority divorced families	• 800 students • African American • Low income • Majority single-mother families
School Curriculum	• International baccalaureate program • Taught in English & German	• More traditional teacher-driven lessons • Taught in English & Spanish	• Child-centered constructivist pedagogy • Taught in English & Maori	• Teacher-centered with focus on discipline • Taught in English
Library	2 libraries with 10,000 books total	1 library with 10,000 books (50% outdated)	1 library with 6,000 books	1 library with 7,000 recently purchased books
Facilities	• Technology-rich • Expansive physical space	• Partial technology integration • Expansive physical space with security	• Lack of technology • Lack of physical space	• Technology-rich • Expansive physical space (new building)
Parental Involvement	Parent advisory group	Parent advisory group	Parent board of trustees who hire/fires school staff	Parent-Teacher Association (PTA)
Child Research Participants	• 1 German • 1 German/British • 1 British • 2 girls & 1 boy • All speak English & German • All age 8 at beginning of study	• All Spanish • 2 boys & 1 girl • All speak English & Spanish • All age 8 at beginning of study	• 1 Maori (indigenous tribal culture) • 1 British/Indian • 1 continental New Zealander • 2 girls & 1 boy • All speak English • All age 8 at beginning of study	• All African American • 2 girls & 1 boy • All speak English • All age 8 at beginning of study
Adult Research Participants	• 6 parents • 1 teacher • 2 media center staff • 1 principal	• 6 parents • 1 teacher • 1 media center staff • 1 principal	• 3 parents • 2 teachers • 2 media center staff • 1 principal	• 3 parents • 2 teachers • 1 media center staff • 1 principal

Honduras

In spite of rapid urban growth, the average standard of living in the mostly agrarian country of Honduras is the lowest of the countries in this study. The Honduran children's parents in this study, however, are college educated, solidly middle-class professionals. Most of the parents are employed by the fruit company that supports the school and thus receive discounted school tuition for their children. The parents stress the importance of academic achievement for their children as future leaders of their changing country. Honduras' family-oriented culture is evident in the children's interactions with their parents. The parents read with and to their children regularly at home. Because of their socio-economic status, the parents can supply their children with high-quality, multilingual texts. Antonio, Arcelia, and Juancarlos's families have been able to provide them with an exemplary private-school education without leaving their mother country.

The Honduran children in this study read above grade level in both Spanish and English and select chapter books to read recreationally. The school library collection includes book in multiple languages and the children have additional access to rich print collections in English and Spanish at home. Antonio, Arcelia, and Juancarlos visit the library as a class during the week and often spend time there before and after school.

New Zealand

Caroline, Maata, and Ojas attend public urban elementary school with an experimental curriculum and a diverse, welcoming school community. The children all read above grade level and enjoy chapter books when reading recreationally. Although the children come from middle- and lower-income homes where divorce is common, the children's parents are white-collar professionals, and both parents are in some way involved in the children's lives. The parents read to their children and, whenever possible, discuss the stories with them. The combination of a dependable home life and a nurturing school community are obvious in the children's academic and personal achievements.

The school has a newly renovated library with multicultural texts to meet the students' diverse literary and research needs. However, the library is not staffed with a certified library media specialist and access to the collection is facilitated by classroom teachers. While the children in the other sites reviewed books with their school library media specialist, Caroline, Maata, and Ojas worked with their classroom teachers throughout this study.

U.S.

Chalondra, Dinari, and Safara attend a public elementary school in the U.S. The school population is currently made up mostly of low-income, working-class African American families living in public housing. The children live with their mothers in single-family homes. Chalondra and Safara both read above grade level, while Dinari reads at grade level. Although he reads at grade level, Dinari is a reluctant reader. He is new to the school and to the research project. He is participating in the study in place of a child that left the school at end of the study's first year. When reading recreationally, the children usually select transitional chapter books and picture books related to programs they have seen on television or in the popular media.

For Chalondra, Dinari, and Safara, access to children's literature at home is limited and the children rely on the school library for quality reading materials. The school building is new, and the library collection is rich with multicultural materials at various reading levels. The children visit the library once a week with their classes, with flexible scheduling possible for additional visits as a class. The media specialist asks repeatedly for assistance from teachers in helping the children with their book reviews, but receives little, if any, response. The library is open before and after school, but the children rarely visit outside of the school day.

Digital Library Materials

The ICDL (www.childrenslibrary.org) is a collection of fully digitized children's books from around the world. The digital library includes books in multiple languages, including picture books and chapter books; fiction and nonfiction titles; and historic and contemporary materials. Materials in the collection are appropriate for children ages 3 to 13 years (International Children's Digital Library Foundation, 2006). The age range for the collection spans a wide spectrum of ability and interest levels, and not all materials are appropriate for all visitors to the library; however, the collection was sufficient for the purposes of this study (see Figure 7.1).

In addition to many traditional subject headings, books in the ICDL are indexed by *feeling*, or how the book makes the child feel. By enabling children to search by feeling, it becomes possible to investigate the role of emotion in the book selection and reviewing processes. Previous content analysis results of book reviews done by children in this study suggested that when the children freely selected books to read, they most often chose books that made them feel happy or books that were fun to read. When children chose sad books, they said they would recommend such books to their friends when the book allowed the child to feel multiple emotions in one reading transaction. Children were more likely to recommend books that evoked multiple feelings when the books started out sad and ended happily (Massey, Weeks, & Druin, 2005).

During the first year of the study, the children were provided with laptop computers containing a local version of the ICDL as it existed in the summer of 2003 with 261 books. The local version was made available in case of failures in Internet connectivity. For the following years of the study, the children were encouraged to access the online version of the ICDL whenever possible.

Figure 7.1   Picture of ICDL interface

Data Collection

The full data collected for this longitudinal study will include interviews, book-response forms, Web pages, drawings, and observations in each of the four sites over the course of three years. For the embedded analysis described in this chapter, the authors chose to analyze the book response forms as a cohesive, consistent data source, allowing for a structured entry point into the data collected over the course of the next few years. The book response forms analyzed in this paper were collected during the second year of the research study and will continue to be collected and analyzed throughout the longitudinal study.

The response form was available in both electronic and print formats. The children in Germany, Honduras, and New Zealand completed the forms electronically using a word processing program. Due to the U.S. children's need for significant guidance from the library media specialist, these children most often completed their response forms on paper. In all of the sites, children submitted their completed forms to the teacher or library media specialist each week. Once a month, the teacher or library media specialist compiled the book responses and sent them via email or postal mail to the team in Maryland.

The research team introduced the book review process and form to the children in all sites as a pleasurable recreational activity. The researchers asked the children to review ICDL books the same way a movie critic reviews movies and told them the reviews would be transferred to the "live" digital library to help other children select books to read.

The review form used in the first year of the study consisted of five short sections. The first section collected information about the reader and the book: name of respondent, date, book title and author, and how many times the child had read that particular book. The second section asked the child how the book made him or her feel by selecting one or more of five prespecified feelings: *happy, sad, scared, funny,* or *other.* The feelings listed on the form were previously identified by the group of children who work with ICDL design team at the university as the emotions that they most often felt when reading books. The *other* category was added for this study to enable the children to specify additional emotions that they may have experienced when reading. The third section asked the child what the book was about. The fourth section asked children to rate the quality of the book on a scale of three to five stars. The fifth section asked the child to identify a book that he or she would add to the collection.

After the first year, the book review form was revised. A preliminary analysis of the book review data suggested that the initial form fell short in collecting the richness and detail of the children's responses (Massey et al., 2005). As a result, for the study's second year, new prompts were developed to help clarify the reasons behind the children's feeling and rating selections.

After reading each book, the children responded to five prompts from the book review form:

1. What is the most important thing to you in this book? Why?

2. How does this book make you feel? This book made me feel this way because …

3. How would you rate this book (3, 4, or 5 stars)? I chose this rating because …

4. If I could add a book to the ICDL I would add … I would add this book because …

5. Draw a picture about something you read or how you felt after reading the story.

In this chapter, the children's responses to prompts 1, 2, 3, and 5 are analyzed because they relate directly to the reading transaction taking place at that moment. Responses to the fourth prompt will be analyzed in a separate paper (see Figure 7.2).

As is typically the case with international, longitudinal research, situations beyond the researchers' control prevented the children from reviewing the preselected books on the same schedule. For example, the students in New Zealand were on summer vacation while the children in Honduras were in the middle of their winter semester. Thus, the preselected books were introduced to the children in New Zealand after they were introduced at the other sites. In addition, some of the children were unable to review all seven of the

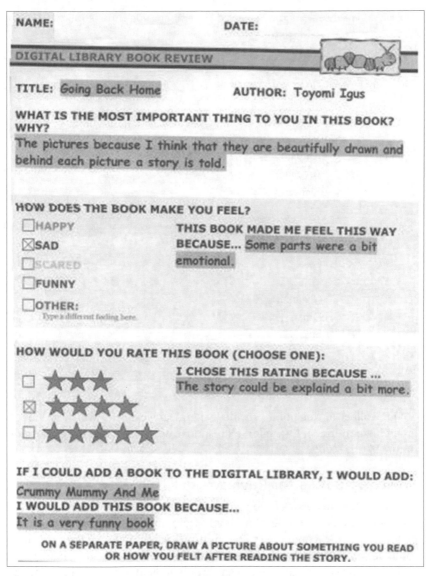

Figure 7.2 Picture of completed book review form

preselected books. In New Zealand, one child transferred schools and was unable to continue participation in the research study. In total, 68 of the anticipated 84 preselected books reviews were collected between November 2004 (the date the preselected books were introduced to the participants) and April 2006 (the time in which this chapter was written; see Table 7.2). We believe the number of book reviews and the kinds of information we were

Table 7.2 Preselected Books Reviewed November 2004–April 2006

Country	Child	No. of preselected books expected	No. of preselected books reviewed
Germany	Gail	7	7
	Skylar	7	7
	Manfred	7	7
		21	21
Honduras	Antonio	7	7
	Arcelia	7	7
	Juancarlos	7	7
		21	21
New Zealand	Caroline	7	4
	Maata	7	6
	Ojas	7	3
		21	13
U.S.	Chalondra	7	5
	Dinari	7	3
	Safara	7	5
		21	13
All		84	68

able to collect to this point provide a significant basis on which to identify emerging patterns in the children's response behavior given the exploratory nature of this study.

Selecting Books for Review

During the first year of the study, the children were asked to independently select, read, and review four books from the ICDL each month (Massey et al., 2005). They could read different books each month or the same book multiple times. The adult participants in the study reported challenges the children had keeping up with the study demands in addition to their school assignments, and we found that the children's responses were short and not adequately informative. Consequently, during the second year of the study, we reduced the number of books the children read from four books per month to two per month, allowing the children additional time to engage with the literature and to think, write, and draw in response to what they read. We expected each child to respond to 14 books over seven months. None of the books were used in conjunction with school assignments.

As previously noted, during the first year, the children self-selected all the books they reviewed. On the rare occasion that more than one child reviewed the same book, it was possible to compare responses to that book. To facilitate the comparison of multiple responses to the same book during the second year of the study, the research team selected seven books in advance. The children selected the remaining seven of the 14 books they would read throughout the year. The self-selected, or "reader's choice," books included any book from the ICDL collection that had been added after the first year of study. This chapter describes the results of the analysis of the preselected books.

The seven preselected books were chosen from the books added to the ICDL collection after 2003, the first year of study. The researchers wanted to explore the children's reactions to books that they were unlikely to read of their own accord, based on the data collected during the first year of the study. The findings showed that the children almost never chose to read nonfiction books, books with unfamiliar stories from an unfamiliar culture, books written in a language the child did not speak, books that made them feel sad or scared, or chapter books (Massey et al., 2005). Based upon these findings, books were chosen for the children to read that represented these under-represented areas (see Table 7.3).

Data Analysis

This study uses content analysis to analyze response forms to identify patterns in responses to literature from 12 children in four countries. According to Cruger Dale (1989), content analysis allows for the systematic examination and evaluation of text or media in order to ascertain its meaning or possible effects. In the content-analysis method, materials rather than people are examined so that the study is often replicable. This technique applies the quantitative technique of frequency analysis to summarize qualitative data that result in "quasi-statistics" from which inferences can then be drawn (Maxwell, 1996). Like theories from related forms of qualitative inquiry, findings from content analysis apply to a specific population. While the 12 child sample is too small to allow generalizations to be made regarding differences among cultures, it was possible to identify differences and similarities among the diverse children in the study.

Of the 68 preselected book reviews collected, eight responses were for the book *How To Make Peace* (Samuel, 1994). Although the story was selected to explore how children responded to a book with racism or classism in the central story, the book was written in Hebrew, a language none of the children speak. Consequently, separating the children's response to the story from their response to being unable to read the language confounds the nature of the reviewing task. As a result, responses to *How To Make Peace* have been removed from the data analysis.

Table 7.3   Preselected Books for Year Two of the International Longitudinal Study

Category	Book Title(s)	Book Summary
Nonfiction	*Going Back Home*	**English**; African American artist Michele Wood travels through the rural South to better understand her ancestors' experience.
Written in English about an unfamiliar culture	*A Dozen Brothers/ Sandosenang Kuya*	**Filipino/English**; A boy has 12 older brothers— all of whom look different from one another! He lives in an orphanage so his family may be unusual, but they are very happy.
Language none of the children in the study speak	*Uninvited Guests /* مهمامنهای خانواخدنه	**Persian/Farsi**; A retelling of a Persian folktale about an old woman whose hospitality extends to every animal passerby.
Language none of the children in the study speak	*The Adventure of Ahmad and the Clock /* ماجرای احمد و ساعت	**Farsi**; Ahmad, a preschool boy, loves to go out hiking with his father. When they try to go earlier than planned, they get into trouble.
Racism or classism [Removed from data analysis]	*How To Make Peace/* איא עושים שלום	**Hebrew**; The Red People and the Blue People cannot seem to get along. The adults are unable to understand one another and do not accept each others' differences. They prepare to go to war with one another, when the children step in and teach them about tolerance.
Evoke strong emotional response	*Ciconia, Ciconia White Store/Ciconia, Ciconia Bijela Roda*	**Croatian/English**; When the white stork's Croatian village is destroyed by war, he searches for a new place to live. However, he finds out that there's no place like home.
Chapter book	*The Survivors*	**English**; Philosophical tale about a war of words and claws between safari ants and termites in eastern Kenya. The terrible things the ants and the termites say as they shout at each other are very funny. Human beings enter the story on the side.

Note: Book summaries are from the ICDL book preview page and were written by ICDL contributors.

FINDINGS

Responses to a Nonfiction Book

The 12 children participating in this study responded to the book *Going Back Home* (Igus & Wood, 1996), the story of an African American artist who travels through the rural South learning about her ancestors' experiences.

The children's reluctance to self-select nonfiction texts from the first year of the study prompted the researchers to add this book to the preselected list for the second year.

The children identified the author's connection to her ancestors and her desire to share that connection as the most important element to them in this book. Maata responded, "Well, I think the most important thing to me was the pictures and their meanings. To me they weren't just pictures they had meaning and if you looked you could see lots of things that were hidden" (Maata, 2/22/2006). The story is told through vibrant paintings that echo the rich fabrics and textures of African art, which appealed to children in all of the locations. Gail wrote, "The pictures ... are beautifully drawn and behind each picture a story is told" (Gail, 11/29/2005).

Most of the children in this study said this book made them feel *sad*, focusing on the hardships of slavery in the Deep South. Antonio wrote, "It is sad to know how the slave(s) were treated in the past" (Antonio, 3/13/2005). Manfred also felt sad when reading this book and wrote, "[This book made me feel sad because] you experience in the book everything the slaves had to do" (Manfred, 12/15/2004). Gail reflected, "Some parts were a bit emotional" (Gail, 11/29/2005). Five of the children focused on the connections the author maintained with her family. When the connection to family was strong, the children classified the book as *happy*. Ojas explains, "[The most important part of this book to me is] how the illustrations strongly represent the woman's family by blending in colours, objects, etc. that are important parts of her and her family's past, present, and future" (Ojas, n.d.). The connection to family was also expressed as a feeling of *interesting* by Chalondra. She wrote how important it was that "the girl knew about her family because some people really need to know about their family. I want people to know about their family" (Chalondra, 12/07/2006). Dinari was the only child to classify this as a *funny* book. However, to support his emotional response he wrote, "No one died or got hurt. I don't know some people in my family. It was a good book" (Dinari, 12/07/2004).

Responses to a Book in English About an Unfamiliar Culture

A Dozen Brothers (Molina, Fucio, & Popa, 2003) is the Filipino story of a boy who has 12 older brothers. The boys live in an orphanage, look very different from one another, and are not related by blood. Siblings in this family come and go, but together they are a happy family. Findings from the first year of the study revealed that the children seldom self-selected books that depicted cultures unfamiliar to them. Therefore, the researchers preselected this book written in English, but depicting the Filipino culture, which is unfamiliar to the study participants.

Four children were not able to respond to this book. Dinari's participation in the study at the school in Chicago became sporadic, while the three children from New Zealand were unable to access this book due to a problem with their Adobe book reader. These technical and contextual factors kept the children from responding to this and other books during the study.

Eight children responded to *A Dozen Brothers*. All of the children from Honduras and Germany reviewed this book, as well as two children from the U.S. After reading *A Dozen Brothers*, five children focused on the loss of a sibling and, for that reason, classified the book as being *sad*. Even when the child wrote about the positive experience related to the older brother's departure, the focus was on how sad the main character must have been. Antonio wrote, "[This book made me feel sad because] the older brother left and they are sure that he remembers their happy memories. … The family is there for each other because that's what family is for" (Antonio, 3/31/2005). Three of the children felt the book was *happy*. In these cases, the children focused on the support members of a family give to one another. "[The most important part of this book is] the young boy who lived in an orphanage … it is touching how the others cared for him. The boy had a lot of people that would help him when he was sad or hungry," explained Skylar (1/31/2005). The universal theme of family and familiar support resonated with all of the children who were able to relate on some level to the main character.

Responses to a Book in an Unfamiliar Language

Scholars suggest that pictures in books can communicate more readily and universally than text, and the diverse ICDL collection presents an opportunity for children to explore other cultures through images (Nodelman, 1988). The children in this study speak one or more of the following languages: Spanish, German, Rarotongan/Maori, and/or English. However, regardless of the diverse mother-tongues represented in this group, the first year of the study showed that the child participants were unlikely to self-select books in languages they could not read, even with adult encouragement (Massey et al., 2005). In order to explore the lack of interest for books in unfamiliar languages, the researchers preselected two picture books with text in a language that none of the children in the study speak.

Twelve children responded to *Uninvited Guests* (Farmaanfarmaaeeian & Farjaam, 1984), a retelling of a Persian folktale about an old woman who offers shelter to animals that pass by her home on a rainy night. The animals clean and cook for the old woman to repay her kindness. The children's responses displayed overwhelming consensus, with 10 of the 12 children classifying the book as one that made them feel *happy*. The children seemed to classify the book based on their personal feelings about animals. For example, Arcelia wrote, "[The most important thing in this book] is that the lady helps a lot of animals because you have to protect the animals. I like to help animals" (Arcelia, 12/10/2005).

When the children could not read the story, they relied on the pictures for not only the story, but to convey the mood. "Happy. This book made me feel this way because of the pictures. They were happy pictures and everybody was smiling and everything worked out well. Even from the start it was happy" (Maata, 2/23/2006). Ojas focused on the responsibility the animals and the old woman had for one another: "The message, if someone is nice to you, you should repay them in some way ... The animals repay the woman, they don't just go away" (Ojas, 10/31/2005). The round lines, jubilant facial expressions, and lively colors in the pictures conveyed a message of warmth and happiness that the children recognized regardless of their location.

The second book in an unfamiliar language that the children read was *The Adventure of Ahmad and the Clock* (Ta'erpoor, 1986), the story of an impatient boy who tricks his family into waking up early by moving the hands on their clock ahead. Eight children responded to this book. At this point in the study, none of the children in the U.S. was participating regularly. Due to the loss of staff at the school and no parental participation at home, the children from the U.S. did not have the adult support necessary for continued involvement. In New Zealand, Maata did not review this book.

Of the eight respondents, five said *The Adventure of Ahmad and the Clock* made them feel *happy* or *funny*. Antonio felt happy after reading the book and wrote, "The baby moves the clock forward he wakes everyone and they start changing and eating breakfast ... the book is funny because Ahmad wakes his family up before the right time" (Antonio, 5/22/2005). Other feelings the book evoked were written in and included *strange* (Juancarlos, n.d.), *confused* (Skylar, n.d), and *bored* (Ojas, n.d.). Caroline also said she felt *annoyed* that "Ahmad had to wwwwaaaiiiittt" (Caroline, 10/31/2005). Overall, responses to books in unfamiliar languages were directly tied to the amount of story information conveyed in the images. In *Uninvited Guests*, the children were able to look beyond the unfamiliar language and enjoy the story told in the illustrations. However, more negative feelings were attributed to *The Adventure of Ahmad and the Clock* because the children experienced difficulty using the images to interpret the story.

Response to a Book with a Strong Emotional Message

Results from the first year of the study showed that the children were unlikely to converge on a single book with a strong emotional message. Therefore, the research team selected one book with a strong emotional message to compare children's responses. *Ciconia, Ciconia* (Huseinovic, 2003) is the story of a stork whose Croatian village is destroyed by war and his quest for a place to call home. Nine children responded to *Ciconia, Ciconia*, listing multiple feelings. Dinari, Caroline, and Maata did not respond.

Of the nine responses to this book, five children classified that book as one that made them feel *happy*, four children felt *sad* after reading the book, and one was *confused*. Two children listed more than one emotion. Children who felt *happy* after reading this book focused on how they felt at the end of the reading experiences when the stork was able to return to his home. Children who felt *sad* focused on the overall mood of the book and the feeling at the beginning of the reading transaction. For example, Antonio felt *sad* after reading *Ciconia, Ciconia* and wrote, "[The most important thing in this story was] that the stork wanted to find a home to live. Because in his old house there was a war" (Antonio, 4/29/2005).

Stronger readers expressed mixed emotional responses to *Ciconia, Ciconia*. Manfred and Gail noted two feelings they felt after reading the book. Manfred felt *sad* and *happy*. He wrote, "I find the story *sad* because war breaks out and the storks must go away. At the end I was *glad* because the storks could go home again" (Manfred, 4/5/2005). Skylar felt *sad* and *confused*. She felt *sad* because "It was rather sad that his home was destroyed, but then, he did not die so it was not too bad" and *confused* because "the stork was very dim" (Skylar, 5/9/2005).

Apart from the feeling, in some instances, the children identified with the main character and put themselves in the fictional situation. This was especially true for the children in the U.S. "It makes me feel *happy* because if that was me trying to get back home I would have been scared trying to find it" (Chalondra, 3/1/2006). Safara expressed, "The bird couldn't find its way home. But if it was me I know that if my friends lived around me I would follow them home." (Safara, 3/1/2006). This ability to empathize with the main character possibly played a role in the feelings the children ascribed to the book.

Response to a Chapter Book

Exploration during the first year of the study revealed that when the children self-selected books, they were unlikely to select a chapter book to read on the computer (Massey et al., 2005). To explore the children's responses to a chapter book, the researchers preselected the 72-page story *The Survivors* (Maillu, 2002), a philosophical tale about a war between safari ants and termites in eastern Kenya. Of the 12 children participating in the study, only seven responded to this book. None of the children in the U.S. read the book because their time with the media specialist was limited; although they were capable of reading the text, they could not complete a chapter book in the short sessions available. In addition, family issues and absences from school prevented Caroline and Maata from New Zealand from responding to the chapter book.

Of the seven remaining children who read *The Survivors*, there was little consensus among the group about the emotions they felt after reading. Antonio and Arcelia felt *sad* after reading the book. Antonio wrote, "One colony of termites killed the king and queen from the other colony. The other colony fights for revenge. Many termites died" (Antonio, 4/22/2005). Arcelia explained, "The most important thing is that the ants and termites learn a lesson because that's how you learn. I think that telling bad stuff about other people might hurt their feelings" (Arcelia, 12/20/2005). These children focused on the negative aspects of war in the book. On the other hand, Juancarlos focused on the reconciliation between the ants and termites at the end of the book and felt *happy* after reading it. He wrote, "The termites and the safari ants chose not to fight and get along. They did not kill each other" (Juancarlos, 5/29/2005). Gail and Manfred worked on their book reviews together, and both wrote that they felt *bored* after reading the story. They both noted being *confused* and found the book "hard to get into" (Gail, 6/12/2005). Ojas felt *involved* while reading the book: "I got myself involved in the story. It's involved, captivating, and interesting. I got behind a particular group of characters" (Ojas, n.d.).

DISCUSSION

The following three questions guided this study:

1. What role does emotion play when children are asked to read books in a digital collection, review them, and make recommendations to other children?

2. In what ways are children's emotional responses similar or different in different countries?

3. How might emotional responses to literature and their role in readers' advisory inform the development of digital collections for children?

Each of these questions is addressed in the following section along with implications for future research and digital library design.

Emotion and Response

What role does emotion play when children are asked to read books in a digital collection, review them, and make recommendations to other children? Through a content analysis of the children's book reviews, we learned that children's emotional experiences change frequently during the reading transaction. Their emotional responses varied based on the attributes of the reader, the structure of the text, and the universality or strength of the book's emotional message. Literature on reader's response is consistent with the findings here in that the children identified the multiple emotions they felt during the reading transaction (Newton, Stegmeier, & Padak, 1999; Rosenblatt, 1991). The children enjoyed having multiple emotional experiences when reading a single book and expressed their changing emotions using the options and write-in section of the review form.

Characteristics of the child affected the children's emotional responses to the preselected books. Dinari's response to *Going Back Home* is a startling example of how response lies at the intersection of text/reader and context/reader. Dinari is a jovial child and prefers humor in literature he reads. His focus on no one dying or getting hurt in *Going Back Home* could be a reflection of the hardships he faces in his environment. Dinari's response suggests that it might be quite easy in his world to be funny, as long as there is no death or violence.

The structure of text influenced the children's response to the preselected books. Happy endings were the salient indicator of children's decisions to recommend books to friends. Children preferred to leave a reading transaction feeling happy. If they felt *sad*, they indicated this in their reviews and often gave that book a low rating. This behavior suggests that when the children in this study felt mixed emotions when reading, they were more likely to recommend that book to a friend if it had a happy ending.

The strength of a book's message affected the children's emotional responses to the preselected books. We found that the children's emotions converged on similar feelings when the book they read had a strong message. In many cases, the children were able to identify familiar messages or morals in the books they read. When children believed the importance of friendship or helping was the moral of the story, as in the book *Uninvited Guests*, they would classify that book using *happy* or *funny*, even if they did not personally enjoy the story. As a result, in books with strong morals or messages, the children's emotional responses were remarkably similar across study sites.

Culture and Response

In what ways are children's emotional responses similar or different in different countries? Language capabilities were a stronger factor in the children's emotional responses to the preselected books than culture or nationality. The children in this study spoke English, Spanish, German, and Maori. Despite these diverse language skills, the children were not likely to choose books in languages they did not speak. In all four sites, being unfamiliar with a culture was less of a deterrent to reading a book than being unable to read the printed text, and the children often requested that books be available in multiple languages. Reading the same book in multiple languages might motivate children to discover unique aspects of an unfamiliar culture with the potential for further linguistic exploration.

In books in unfamiliar languages such as *The Adventure of Ahmad and the Clock*, being able to not only explore the images but also read the text emerged as an important factor in how children evaluated books. Despite the use of rich, vibrant images to tell the story, the children in all of the sites agreed that text in unfamiliar languages was a distraction. When the children could not read the story, they often used the colors and characters' facial expressions in the illustrations to interpret the story and to gauge how the book made them feel. In this case, the emotional classifications were often varied based on the child's interpretation of the images. In response to being unable to read the text, however, the children were clear in expressing their frustrations.

Digital Libraries and Response

How might emotional responses to literature and their role in readers' advisory inform the development of digital collections for children? Digital libraries such as the ICDL can present rich cultural texts in their original languages, but they also have the potential to offer translated versions of powerful stories from other countries. The children were able to interpret the strong meanings and messages when looking at a book's pictures, but they strongly expressed the desire to have the accompanying text in a language they could read. One possible area for further research might be to provide translated versions of books in the ICDL and investigate whether children's responses to those translated books differ.

At the moment, the ICDL's online tools for searching and reading are most appropriate for colorful, short, picture books. The children commented on the vibrant images they found especially pleasing and helpful when interpreting stories. Along with an expressed preference for reading picture books in the ICDL came strong resistance to reading chapter books on the computer. These reactions could be because the children were accustomed to reading shorter books for this study. Another possible explanation would be the nature of associated technologies that facilitate reading online. Perhaps better tools are necessary for reading the small type and numerous pages of chapter books on the computer.

The children in this study took the task of reviewing books seriously and approached the task with care. When asked to review books for others, they separated their emotional experiences from their personal decisions to recommend a book to a friend. They made clear distinctions between their emotional book classifications and their quality ratings when quality was related to the willingness to recommend that book to others. After reading a *happy* story, a child might write that the book made him feel *happy* but would not always indicate that he/she would recommend the book to a friend. The personal recommendations often were related to the child's abilities or preferences at the time of the reading transaction. For instance, a book would not be recommended if the story were too short for the child, or if it were too easy, or if the child could not read the text. Thus, classifying books by feeling was considered one part of the reviewing task, and recommending a book to a friend was considered a separate task.

Book reviews are essential to the way librarians perform readers' advisory and collection development tasks (Duda, 2005). By combining emotional and evaluative responses with narrative responses, children provide rich book information not typically collected. Information that allows children to search for books by how it might make them feel is a novel addition to traditional summaries and ratings usually available. Book review data suggest that children can and are willing to share how they feel at different stages of the reading transaction. The digital library allows for the incorporation of information such as "how the book makes you feel" into the larger metadata scheme. Information professionals can now refer to affective assessments by other young readers to assist in readers' advisory and in helping children find a book that meets their emotional needs.

Literature on readers' advisory suggests that children respond strongly to reading recommendations from their peers (Irvine, 2002). Allowing children to participate in the review process in some way not only offers practice in expressing thoughts and opinions, but it provides an opportunity to help others find books to read for fun. Additional research might also explore how digital environments such as online communities might provide a space for readers to share their thoughts and feelings about books with other children around the world.

There are a number of limitations related to this research. First, study participation was limited to 12 students, thus results from this research cannot be generalized from this small group. Second, because the book reviews were done electronically, technical and contextual constraints such as slow Internet connections and power failure influenced how and when the children submitted their reviews. Finally, due to the international, long-distance nature of the study, the children's responses to the books they read were captured solely on paper. Consequently, information on the children's physical and verbal responses at the time of the reading transaction was not collected. Future research could address some of these limitations.

Although there is a long history of reader response research in education, the library and information studies field is just beginning to investigate children's responses to literature in the digital context. Overall, little research has explored recreational reading or the factors that influence children's reading responses. This line of research has implications for library services and digital library design that respond to the interests of children.

ACKNOWLEDGMENTS

The authors would like to acknowledge and thank their partners on the ICDL team in the U.S, and around the world for their many contributions to this research. This project is supported by the National Science Foundation and the Institute of Museum and Library Services.

REFERENCES

Altieri, J. L. (1995). Multicultural literature and multiethnic readers: Examining aesthetic involvement and preferences for text. *Reading Psychology: An International Quarterly, 16*, 43–70.

Asselin, M. (2000). Reader response in literature and reading instruction. *Teacher Librarian, 27*(4), 62–63.

Brewer, W. F., & Lichtenstein, E. H. (1982). Stories are to entertain: A structural-affect theory of stories. *Journal of Pragmatics, 6*, 473–486.

Brewer, W. F., & Ohtsuka, K. (1988). Story structure and reader affect in American and Hungarian short stories. In C. Martindale (Ed.), *Psychological approaches to the study of literary narratives* (pp. 133–158). Hamburg: Buske.

Bunbury, R., & Tabbert, R. (1988). "Midnite" and other bushrangers: Heroes for children or adults? A bi-cultural study of identification: Readers' responses to the ironic treatment of a national hero. *International Review of Children's Literature and Librarianship, 3*, 74–83.

Creswell, J. W. (1994). *Research design: Qualitative and quantitative approaches.* Thousand Oaks, CA: Sage Publications.

Creswell, J. W. (1998). *Qualitative inquiry and research design: Choosing among five traditions.* Thousand Oaks, CA: Sage Publications.

Dale, D. C. (1989). Content Analysis: A research methodology for school library media specialists. *School Library Media Quarterly, 18*(1), 45–48.

Duda, A. E. (2005). *A content analysis of book reviews from a readers' advisory perspective.* Unpublished master's dissertation, University of North Carolina at Chapel Hill. Accessed November 28 2006, from, etd.ils.unc.edu/dspace/bitstream/1901/143/1/Paper.pdf.

Foshay, A. W., Thorndike, R. L., Hotyat, F., Pidgeon, D. A., & Walker, D. A. (1962). *Educational achievements of thirteen-year-olds in twelve countries.* Hamburg: UNESCO Institute for Education. Accessed November 28, 2006 from unesdoc.unesco.org/images/0013/001314/131437eo.pdf.

Galda, L. (1982). Assuming the spectator stance: An examination of the responses of three young readers. *Research in the Teaching of English, 16*, 1–20.

Galda, L. (1983). Research in response to literature. *Journal of Research and Development in Education, 16*(3), 1–7.

Galda, L., & Beach, R. (2001). Response to literature as a cultural activity. *Reading Research Quarterly, 36*(1), 64–73. Accessed November 28, 2006, from www.reading-halloffame.org/Library/Retrieve.cfm?D=10.1598/RRQ.36.1.4&F=RRQ-36-1-Galda.pdf.

Geertz, C. (1973). *The interpretation of cultures.* London: Fontana Press.

Guba, E. G., & Lincoln, Y. S. (1982). Epistemological and methodological bases of naturalistic inquiry. *Educational Communications and Technology Journal, 30*(4), 233–252.

Halász, L. (1991). Understanding short stories: An American-Hungarian cross-cultural study. *Empirical Studies of the Arts, 9*, 143–163.

Hall, S. (1997). *Representation: Cultural representations and signifying practices.* London: Sage.

Happy Medium Productions, Inc. (2006). *Spaghetti Book Club: Book reviews by kids for kids!* Accessed November 28, 2006, from www.spaghettibookclub.org.

Hepler, S. I., & Hickman, J. (1982). "The book was okay. I love you": Social aspects of response to literature. *Theory into Practice, 21*(4), 278–283.

Heyneman, S. P. (2004). The use of cross-national comparisons for local education policy. *Curriculum Inquiry, 34*(3), 345–352.

Hynds, S. (1997). *On the brink: Negotiating literature and life with adolescents.* New York: Teachers College Press.

International Association for the Evaluation of Educational Achievement. (n.d.). *Current studies.* Accessed November 28, from www.iea.nl/current_studies.html.

International Children's Digital Library Foundation. (2006). *International Children's Digital Library.* Accessed November 28, 2006, from www.childrenslibrary.org.

Irvine, J. R. (2002). *Ask them! Children's fiction book choices and the implications for libraries.* Working paper. Accessed November 28, 2006, from www.openpolytechnic. ac.nz/research/wp/res_wp302irvinej.pdf.

Larsen, S. F., & László, J. (1990). Cultural-historical knowledge and personal experience in appreciation of literature. *European Journal of Social Psychology, 20,* 425–440.

László, J., & Larsen, S. F. (1991). Cultural and text variables in processing personal experiences while reading literature. *Empirical Studies of the Arts, 9,* 23–34.

Leung, C. (2003). Bicultural perspectives and reader response: Four American readers respond to Jean Fritz's Homesick. *Canadian Modern Language Review, 60*(1). Accessed November 28, 2006, from www.utpjournals.com/product/cmlr/601/601_leung.html.

Li, X., & Hitt, L. M. (2004). *Self selection and information role of online product reviews.* Working Paper. University of Pennsylvania, Wharton School. Accessed November 28, 2006, from opim-sky.wharton.upenn.edu/wise2004/sat321.pdf.

Martindale, C. (Ed.). (1988). *Psychological approaches to the study of literary narratives.* Hamburg: Buske.

Martinez, M., & Roser, N. L. (2003). Children's responses to literature. In J. Flood, D. Lapp, J. Squire, & J. Jensen (Eds.), *Handbook of Research on Teaching the English Language Arts* (2nd ed.). Mahwah, NJ: Lawrence Erlbaum Associates.

Massey, S. A., Weeks, A. C., & Druin, A. (2005). Initial findings from a three-year international case study exploring children's responses to literature in a digital library. *Library Trends, 54*(3), 245–265.

Maxwell, J. A. (1996). *Qualitative research design: An interactive approach* (Applied Social Research Methods Series No. 41). Thousand Oaks, CA: Sage Publications, Inc.

McGowen, K. (2003). Student choice: Empowering students with tools for reading. *Houston Teachers Institute, 7.* Accessed November 28, 2006, from www.uh.edu/hti/cu/2003/7/09.pdf.

Morra, S., & Lazzarini, S. (2002). A cross-cultural study of response to Icelandic and Italian folktales. *Empirical Studies of the Arts, 20*(1), 61–82.

Neuman, D. (2003). Learning in an information-rich environment: Preliminary results. In D. Callison (Ed.), *Measuring student achievement and diversity in learning: Papers of the Treasure Mountain Research Retreat #10* (pp. 39–50). San Jose, CA: Hi Willow Research & Publishing.

Neuman, D. (2004). The library media center: Touchstone for instructional design and technology in the schools. In D. H. Jonassen (Ed.), *Handbook of Research on Educational Communications and Technology* (2nd ed., pp. 499–522). Mahwah, NJ: Lawrence Erlbaum Associates.

Newton, E., Stegmeier, G., & Padak, N. (1999). Young children's written response to text. *Reading Horizons, 39*(3), 191–208.

Nodelman, P. (1988). *Words about pictures: The narrative art of children's picture books.* Athens, GA: University of Georgia Press.

Ogle, L. T., Sen, A., Pahlke, E., Jocelyn, L., Kastberg, D., Roey, S. et al. (2003). *International comparisons in fourth-grade reading literacy: Findings from the Progress in International Reading Literacy Study (PIRLS) of 2001.* Washington, D.C.: National Center for Education Statistics. Accessed November 28, 2006, from nces.ed.gov/pubs2003/2003073.pdf.

Pritchard, R. (1990). The effects of cultural schemata on reading processing strategies. *Reading Research Quarterly, 25,* 273–295.

Probst, R. E. (2003). Response to literature. In J. Flood, D. Lapp, J. R. Squire, & J. M. Jensen (Eds.), *Handbook of Research on Teaching the English Language Arts* (2nd ed., pp. 814–824). Mahwah, NJ: Lawrence Erlbaum Associates.

Public Library of Charlotte & Mecklenburg County. (2006). *The BookHive.* Accessed November 28, 2006, from www.bookhive.org.

Purves, A. C. (1973). *Literature education in ten countries*. Stockholm: Almqvist and Wiskell.

Purves, A. C., & Beach, R. (1972). *Literature and the reader: Research in response to literature, reading interests and the teaching of literature*. Urbana, IL: National Council of Teachers of English.

Rosenblatt, L. M. (1978). *The reader, the text, the poem: The transactional theory of the literary work*. Carbondale, IL: Southern Illinois University Press.

Rosenblatt, L. M. (1991). Literature-S.O.S.! *Language Arts, 68*, 444–448.

Sims, R. (1983). Strong black girls: A ten year old responds to fiction about Afro-Americans. *Journal of Research and Development in Education, 16*(3), 21–28.

Spears-Bunton, L. A. (1990). Welcome to my house: African American and European American students' responses to Virginia Hamilton's House of Dies Drear. *Journal of Negro Education, 59*, 566–576.

Spears-Bunton, L. A. (1993). *Cultural consciousness and response to literary texts among African-American and European-American high school junior*s. Unpublished doctoral dissertation, University of Kentucky, Lexington.

Steinfirst, S. (1986). Reader-response criticism. *School Library Journal, 33*(2), 114–116.

StoneSoup.(2006). *StoneSoup.com: For young writers and artists*. Accessed November 28, 2006, from www.stonesoup.com.

Sumara, D. J. (1996). *Private readings in public: Schooling in the literary imagination*. New York: Peter Lang.

Tomlinson, L. M. (1995). *The effects of instructional interaction guided by a typology of ethnic identity development: Phase one. Reading Research Report No. 44*. Athens, GA & College Park, MD: National Reading Research Center.

University of Maryland & Internet Archive. (2002). *International Children's Digital Library: International research*. Accessed November 28, 2006, from www.icdlbooks. org/about/research/international.shtml.

Vandergrift, K. E. (1987). Using reader response theories to influence collection development and programs for children and youth. In J. Varlejs (Ed.), *Information Seeking: Basing Services on Users' Behaviors* (pp. 52–66). Jefferson, MD: McFarland.

Vandergrift, K. E. (1990). The child's meaning-making in response to a literary text. *English Quarterly, 33*(3/4), 125–140.

Wilhelm, J. D. (1997). *"You gotta BE the book": Teaching engaged and reflective reading with adolescents*. New York: Teachers College Press.

Yin, R. K. (1989). *Case study research: Design and methods* (Applied Social Research Methods Series No. 5). Newbury Park, CA: Sage Publications.

REFERENCED CHILDREN'S BOOKS

Farmaanfarmaaeeian, J., & Farjaam, F. (1984).[1] *Uninvited guests*. Iran: The Children's Book Council. Accessed November 28, 2006, from www.childrenslibrary.org/icdl/SaveBook?bookid=uninvit_00390064&lang=English.

Huseinovic, A. P. (2003). *Ciconia, Ciconia*. Croatia: Kašmir Promet. Accessed November 28, 2006, from www.childrenslibrary.org/icdl/SaveBook?bookid=baucico_0004 0009&lang=English.

Igus, T., & Wood, M. (1996). *Going back home*. San Francisco, CA: Children's Book Press. Accessed November 28, 2006, from www.childrenslibrary.org/icdl/SaveBook? bookid=woogoin_00030021&lang=English.

Maillu, D. G. (2002). *The survivors*. Kenya: Sasa Sema Publications. Accessed November 28, 2006, from www.childrenslibrary.org/icdl/SaveBook?bookid=thesurv_004600 10&lang=English.

Molina, R., Fucio, H., & Popa, A. (2003). *Sandosenang kuya*/A dozen brothers. Philippines: Adarna House, Inc. Accessed November 28, 2006, from www.childrens library.org/icdl/SaveBook?bookid=molsand_00370010&lang=English.

Samuel, N. (1994). *How to make peace*. Israel: Lilach. Accessed November 28, 2006, from www.childrenslibrary.org/icdl/SaveBook?bookid=smlhwtm_00190001&lang=English.

Ta'erpoor, F. (1986).[2] *The adventure of Ahmad and the clock*. Iran: Children's Book Council. Accessed November 28, 2006, from www.childrenslibrary.org/icdl/SaveBook?bookid=ahmadan_00390073&lang=English.

ENDNOTES

1. 1363 by the Iranian calendar.
2. 1365 by the Iranian calendar.

CHAPTER 8

Emotional Entanglements on the University Campus: The Role of Affect in Undergraduates' Information Behaviors

Lisa M. Given
University of Alberta

INTRODUCTION

Undergraduate students' informational activities are dynamic and reflect a range of needs related to academic work. Students use many sources to complete assignments and rely on different media to support their work. However, little attention has been paid to the role of affect in shaping students' informational activities. Although researchers such as Carol Kuhlthau (2004) lay the groundwork for exploring emotion in educational settings, few studies examine affect in higher education. Indeed, emotional responses to information resources, to people, and to the physical campus are important in determining the information behaviors of undergraduate students. Exploring the emotional underpinnings of students' information behaviors offers an important contextual framework for understanding the holistic experiences of undergraduates and for developing information services that can best support students' academic activities.

AFFECT: A REVIEW OF CURRENT RESEARCH

The role of affect—or emotional states of being—remains an area of information behavior research that is under-studied but holds great promise for understanding individuals' holistic and contextually grounded information experiences. In education, researchers examine the affective elements of students' activities, including motivation and anxiety (e.g., Blimling, 1999; Schlosser & Sedlacek, 2001). Hanna Järvenoja and Sanna Järvelä (2005), for example, found that while teenagers' sense of self and personal context were important in determining emotional and motivational responses to learning, these were also driven by the nature of the task, performance, and broader social markers (p. 477).

In library and information science, numerous studies examine undergraduate students' information behaviors including their experiences with information technology and the research process. Ethelene Whitmire (2004) has explored epistemological differences in students' informational activities. Lisa M. Given (2002) examined the overlap between students' academic and everyday information behaviors. Kristie Saumure and Lisa M. Given (2004) have explored the informational activities of visually impaired undergraduates. However, few studies have examined affect in shaping and determining students' informational activities. Jannica Heinström (2005) found that where students' psychological energy is consumed by negative feelings, little is left for information seeking (p. 240). Similarly, Wendy Holliday and Qin Li (2004) explored the ways that the information behaviors of the "millennial generation" are shaped by their comfort with new technologies.

These current studies have their roots in earlier landmark projects. Mellon (1986) examined how library anxiety (and its attendant feelings of shame and inadequacy) shaped undergraduates' use of library resources. Kuhlthau's (2004) Information Search Process model was the first to consider high school students' affective responses alongside information activities. Over the past decade, other scholars have examined affective responses to information technologies, including implications for individuals' searching processes. Diane Nahl (1998) explored such affective elements as enthusiasm and stress on novices' experiences with the Internet. Onwuegbuzie and Jiao (2000) examined the relationship between graduate student procrastination and library anxiety. Despite these initial forays into affective elements of information seeking, a content analysis by Julien, McKechnie, and Hart (2005) found that affective issues "continue to receive minimal attention from authors of systems-related work in LIS" (p. 461). Those studies that have examined emotion focus on individuals' responses to computer-related searching in isolation from other informational and library-related activities and environments (e.g., Bilal, 2000; Dimitroff, Wolfram, & Volz, 1996).

HOLISTIC EXPLORATIONS OF THE INFORMATION CONTEXT—A CENTRAL PLACE FOR EMOTION

Recently, scholars have turned to holistic examinations of emotion and information seeking. Jette Hyldegård (2006) examined Kuhlthau's (2004) Information Search Process model in the context of group-based learning and found that contextual, social, and emotional factors affected students' behaviors. Jacqueline Kracker (2002) explored Kuhlthau's model as a teaching tool and found that a "30-minute presentation of Kuhlthau's model appears to reduce [student] anxiety associated with research paper assignments" (p. 289). Kracker and Pollio (2003) examined students' emotional responses to libraries and found that while college students felt "lost" or "overwhelmed" by the physical size of the library, their early memories of the library were of "a positive place of fun, of play" (p. 1113). Emotions in these studies are deeply embedded in individuals' information behaviors, shaping both physical searching activities and the cognitive sense of personal place.

This recent trend also reflects a shift toward the development of ecological models of information behavior. Kirsty Williamson (1989) designed a model that focuses on the individual "in a particular physical, social and cultural environment" where information behavior must be understood in context, or not at all (p. 25). Bonnie Nardi and Vicki O'Day (1999) extend this idea in *Information Ecologies: Using Technology with Heart*. They describe the library as an information ecology, or an ever-evolving setting in which "individuals have an active role, a unique and valuable local perspective, and a say in what happens" (p. ix). In conducting research in libraries, they note:

> In a healthy information ecology [people and tools] work together in a complementary way. In a library information ecology … librarians fill niches such as handling rare books, telling stories to children, answering reference questions, and publishing World Wide Web materials. All of these different roles of librarians help make the library work well for its community, providing different resources for varied audiences and their needs. (pp. 51–52)

Although technology-related issues form the core of Nardi and O'Day's (1999) text, their comments on the "human" element in successful information ecologies serve as a theoretical framework for understanding undergraduates' emotions in the context of their academic information behaviors. They note that as individuals engage with information ecologies (such as classrooms), the "human touch" embodied in the actors in those spaces (e.g., professors) shapes emotive and behavioral responses to events (p. 92).

Examining the tools of the student trade, such as the use of online databases, is insufficient in this type of ecological model of the information space. By focusing on approaches that explore the acts of searching for relevant articles, constructing appropriate bibliographies, or selecting interesting essay topics (to name only a few activities) in isolation from students' internal, emotional lives, researchers (and practitioners) in library and information science risk understanding (and serving) only a few, small elements of students' information needs. It is vital that the whole human experience, including the role of affect in shaping information behaviors, inform this work. When a student's frustration with one essay topic leads him/her to choose another, or when a student's comfort level with books leads him/her to ignore other potentially useful resources, researchers and practitioners must respond to these emotive practices. Studies that embed questions concerning affect into the design and analysis of individuals' information behaviors allow for a better understanding of these individuals' holistic needs and offer insights that can shape future information practices and areas for new research.

METHOD

This chapter examines data from two related studies gathered at two large Canadian universities: (1) 25 in-depth, qualitative interviews with mature undergraduate students, and (2) 18 in-depth, qualitative interviews and walks around campus with younger undergraduates. The goals of the projects were to:

1. Examine the influence of institutional markers of academic success on students' learning goals.

2. Examine the ways that undergraduate students' identities were socially constructed on campus, and how these constructions match or conflict with students' personal identity formations.

3. Explore the role of campus-based information resources and informational spaces in fostering (or hindering) students' academic achievements.

4. Advance the understanding of the personal and institutional complexities of students' academic information behaviors, and the implications for academic success within the university context.

In examining these issues, the place of affect in shaping students' identities, in their interactions with the campus environment (including interpersonal relationships), and in the context of their academic information behaviors was a concrete and powerful emergent theme. This paper reports on some of the emotional entanglements that directed and shaped many of the students' campus experiences, with implications for the ways they located and used information for their academic work.

Each interview lasted approximately 90 minutes, with the second set also including walking tours of campus to discuss students' information behaviors in the context of the physical spaces they inhabited. The combined results extend current research on affective information behaviors by including younger (i.e., enrolling directly from high school) and mature undergraduates' (i.e., at least 21 years old and returning to formal study after an absence of three years or more) experiences. Including data from within and outside of the library, the findings examine students' information behaviors (and emotional responses) in various informing spaces on campus (e.g., computer labs, classrooms).

The university contexts studied here share a number of common characteristics. They are both research-intensive institutions that offer doctoral-level and advanced professional degrees, and they are currently ranked in the top 10 of medical-doctoral institutions in Canada by *Maclean's* magazine, an annual publication that critiques Canada's universities (Keller, 2006, p. 18). Each university has an undergraduate student body of more than 30,000, with another few thousand graduate students, and large faculty and support staff complements. Located in different parts of the country (i.e., one in Central Canada and one in Western Canada), both institutions have diverse populations and attract students from their local regions, across Canada, and around the world (Keller, 2006, pp. 60–61 and 146–147).

Participants

Interviewees were recruited using posters (e.g., posted in student unions and academic units) and snowball sampling techniques, then selected using maximum variation to achieve a broad representation of gender, age, academic discipline, family status, employment, and previous education. Participants ranged in age from 18 to 55, with 15 men and 28 women. Thirteen students were registered in social sciences disciplines (e.g., sociology), 20 were studying in the arts and humanities (e.g., philosophy), and 10 students were registered in the sciences (e.g., chemistry). The interviews used semi-structured interview guides designed to facilitate conversations with the participants that examined their perceptions of academic success, undergraduate life, information behaviors, and the design and availability of campus spaces. Questions covered demographics (e.g., program and year of study), student identity issues (e.g., "Has returning to school as a mature student affected your perception of yourself as a mother?"), the types of assignments typically completed, and the students' information seeking processes (e.g., "Describe a typical assignment in your discipline and how you would start locating information to do that work."). It is important to note that, in keeping with a qualitative approach, the exact wording and inclusion or exclusion of particular questions depended on each individual's personal circumstances (e.g., questions about the role of family members in shaping the students' information seeking processes changed depending on each participant's particular family structure). Students shared thoughts, feelings, and examples that illustrated their experiences and perceptions. The data were analyzed using a grounded theory approach, with themes and patterns coded and categorized as they emerged from the data. This type of thematic coding (particularly when used across such a large set of interviews) allows the analysis to cut across individuals' personal circumstances and the individual questions discussed during each interview, resulting in theme-based findings that are transferable to other undergraduate populations at similar universities.

FINDINGS AND DISCUSSION

Mature and younger undergraduates certainly have many unique experiences and specific academic information needs. Where younger undergraduates grapple with moving from home and being separated from high school friends, mature students may need to re-learn essay writing and other academic skills (Given, 2002). However, in investigating the role of affect in shaping students' academic and informational experiences, these groups have much in common. Although students' financial, family, and academic situations vary, the emotional impact of everyday concerns and academic demands were remarkably similar across age, gender, and disciplinary lines in these two studies. The findings presented here point to complex perceptions and experiences that inform students' information behaviors, and that are shaped by the full range of human emotions. They also extend Nardi and O'Day's (1999) description of the library as an information ecology by providing a more detailed account of the human element that defines the library (and campus) context.

Figure 8.1, the Affective Information Behavior Ecology, documents these experiences in a model of students' macro- and micro-emotional spheres. This model was developed in response to the themes that emerged during the analysis of the interview data from the younger and mature undergraduate students, and in considering the exploration of affect in the current research literature. As the range of students' emotive responses was quite vast—and as language and labels, in part, shape the way that individuals think about affect—the model condenses the diversities and subtleties of human emotion into six broad categories (inspired, in part, by the work of Shaver, Schwartz, Kirson, and O'Connor (1987)). These six categories—love (or feelings of connectedness), joy (representing happiness, relief, and hope),

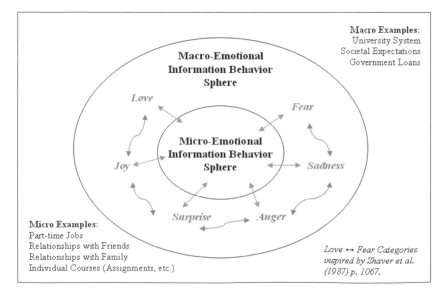

Figure 8.1 Model of the Affective Information Behavior Ecology

surprise (including amazement and shock), anger (including frustration and envy), sadness (including guilt, disappointment, and alienation), and fear (including anxiety and intimidation)—are reflected in much of the research and practical literature that explores human emotion (e.g., in the field of psychology), and are intended to encapsulate the complexity of human emotion, within a single, visual representation of affective response. In the discussion of findings presented here, many of the subtleties of human emotion (e.g., where "fear" or "anger" are manifested as anxiety or frustration) are also explored.

At the macro level, external influences (e.g., government funding; university regulations; societal expectations related to academic success) have an impact on students' academic (and affective) experiences. Under-funding of libraries (for example) results in fewer materials and librarians, while increases in government aid can free students from working outside of school, providing more time to seek information and to complete assignments. At the micro level, a student's home or work situation, relationships with family, friends, and professors, as well as individual course requirements, all shape the student's ability to seek academic information and their emotional responses to these situations. Although peer support can result in sharing textbooks or study techniques (for example), being intimidated by a professor can cause students to avoid asking questions. When the macro and micro spheres collide (e.g., when a student cannot afford interlibrary loan fees, but the institution has implemented these in response to cuts to government funding), the adverse effect on students' information behaviors can be powerful, and often manifests itself in feelings of frustration, anger, and resignation. Students may choose not to access relevant materials to save money, resulting in incomplete or otherwise inadequate assignments being submitted for assessment; the resulting (often, poor) grade can influence students' future informational activities, but it also has an emotional impact on those students, which may adversely affect their future academic successes.

In both the macro and micro contexts, students' emotions mesh with daily activities and shape students' information behaviors. Although all of these emotions (from love to fear) were reflected in the students' descriptions of their academic work, it is also important to note that it is not easy to mark particular emotions as inherently positive or negative. Where anxiety or disappointment appear to be negative emotions, many students described these feelings in positive ways (i.e., forcing them to rise to the academic and informational challenges they faced). Similarly, feelings of ease and satisfaction were not always positive; students described instances where their work was going "too well," leading them to wonder what they had missed. For this reason, the model was purposefully designed *not* to present students' affective responses on a negative-positive continuum or to otherwise divide human emotion along these lines. The findings of this study point to a far more complex relationship between information behaviors and students' affective states, where feelings of frustration with a challenging text can feed a student's positive drive to succeed, or where feelings of ease with the location of course materials can lead to anxieties that important information has been missed. The sections that follow provide examples of these students' complex affective experiences and the implications for their academic information behaviors.

Macro-Emotional Context—Shaping Students' Information Behaviors

One core, defining element that shapes students' campus (and informational) experiences is the university system. Program design, interactions between academic units, the value placed on undergraduate teaching, and other systemwide elements have a dramatic impact on students' lives. In addition, government funding to institutions, provincial student loan systems, the availability of specialized funding (e.g., scholarships, awards, bursaries), program requirements set by accrediting bodies, and other macro-level influences affect students' information behaviors. All of the students—regardless of age, gender, academic discipline, and other individual factors—described interactions with external agencies and/or the impact of imposed academic requirements as shaping their informational activities. Time spent applying for scholarships, for example, often took time away from students' academic work—resulting in feelings of indignation, frustration, anxiety, and other emotions represented in Figure 8.1 by such affective descriptors as "fear," "sadness," and "anger." From the moment students enroll in academic programs, they come to the university with preconceived notions of learning, student life, and career prospects, and they are filled with hopes, dreams, and fears that inform their academic work. Although students are excited about starting their educational careers, the size of the campus, the design of library buildings, and other external factors influence students' informational activities.

Fear, Sadness, Anger—Challenging Affective Responses to the Academic Context

Zoe, a 42-year-old, philosophy student in her fourth year of study, for example, noted her frustration with the design of course assignments:

> I think that rather than do three short essays for a course and one exam … I would just like to take something that I'm really interested in, and do a good job on that one thing … In a sense I feel indignant …because [these assignments are] designed for people who don't do their work. Who don't do their reading. I mean, I've been in courses where you had to hand in a paper once a week … you know, condense a five- or 10-page article into one page … I

mean, all I'm really doing is proving to the professor that I've actually read it. You know, there's nothing more meaningful in it for me. And I feel very indignant and very frustrated and I think, 'Well, give me some credit here. Let me do my thing.'

For Zoe, this concern represented systemic problems in the university that discouraged independent thinking requiring advanced informational skills. Such indignant frustration caused some interviewees to fight against the system by gathering additional information for course projects and submitting advanced work. Others retreated, completing baseline assignments despite personal desires to do more. In many cases, resigning oneself to university expectations was exacerbated by problems with technology, reflecting an environment that privileges technological developments over users' needs. Emma was 18 years old and a third year education student at the time of the interview. She had constructed her academic program on a "fast-track" model, taking spring and summer courses to complete her program in fewer terms (and, having skipped some earlier grades, she was one of the youngest students in her program cohort). She noted that efforts to provide remote access to information resources were unsuccessful and frustrating:

> I have my own computer, but I use the labs on campus ...because when I'm at home it's kind of slow. Like, when I log onto WebCT [for course materials or to post comments] it takes about 20 minutes to get in, whereas when I'm [on campus] it takes three minutes. And I don't know why that is ...but most of my [course] information is on WebCT. And it's just so slow ... it gets frustrating.

All of these types of feelings—frustration, resignation, uncertainty—were manifested in the students' fears of academic failure, sadness that their academic careers were often controlled by external forces, and anger over the perceived injustices and misunderstandings that frequently defined their interactions with university administrators, faculty, and peers. These affective responses are illustrated in Figure 8.1 in the macro-emotional sphere of students' information behaviors; however, individuals' micro-level emotional responses (discussed later in this chapter) also interact with the macro level, depending on each student's personal experiences.

Love, Joy, Surprise—Pleasing Affective Responses to the Academic Context

It is, however, important to note that the macro-level sphere also instilled very positive emotions; for example, many interviewees chose to study in older libraries on campus, as the architecture inspired a "deep reverence" for those successful students who had already graduated. Jonathan, a 22-year-old fourth year computing science student, described feelings of "awe" at being surrounded by world-class researchers; he noted that listening to lectures and watching professors debate ideas inspired his own academic pursuits. Other students described the large university context, and their resulting feelings of anonymity or "smallness," as leading them to build stronger relationships with family, friends, and professors. Jessica, a 22-year-old fourth year kinesiology student, described relying on friends to locate available computers or useful resources (and thereby providing relief in stressful times). Other students described regular meetings with friends to socialize or play cards and to take a break from the pressures of school. Using campus spaces for these many purposes—all of which fulfilled particular emotional needs—was a core theme in the interviews. Feelings of pleasant surprise, joy, and love for the campus environment, for the individuals they interacted with during their time on campus, and for the support of family, friends, and others outside of the university environment were reflected in all of the interviewee's experiences—regardless of age, gender, academic discipline, or personal situation. Even where students struggled to succeed in their academic work or described their frustrations with government student loan policies, the interviewees also described very positive emotions relating to their experiences with the university and with broader, social structures, as they strove to complete and succeed in their academic work.

Micro-Emotional Context—Shaping Students' Information Behaviors

At the micro level, students' personal situations also shaped their academic (and informational) experiences. Family commitments (such as childcare), the number of hours required for employment, and the support (or lack of support) of family and friends in completing academic work all affected the interviewees' abilities to seek information for their academic work and to complete assignments to suit their personal needs and academic expectations. All of the students—regardless of age, gender, academic discipline, and other individual factors—described interpersonal and intrapersonal situations as influencing their informational activities. Time spent caring for a child or an aging parent, for example, often took time away from students' academic work—resulting in feelings of indignation, frustration, anxiety, and other emotions represented in Figure 8.1 by such affective descriptors as "fear," "sadness," and "anger." In addition, supportive family members (e.g., children who helped with the interviewee's photocopying at the library) often resulted in feelings encapsulated by the terms "love," "joy," and "surprise," and could be powerful motivators for students struggling to complete their academic work. As with the macro-level experience, students' micro-level affective responses were complex and interwoven with their academic information behaviors.

Fear, Sadness, Anger—Shaping Students' Micro-Level Information Behaviors

At the micro level, students' personal situations (e.g., family commitments; assignment deadlines) often resulted in negative emotions that adversely affected their information behaviors. Lynn, a 30-year old, mature first-year science student, described the frustration she felt in balancing personal and academic needs. Here, she describes anxieties that were taking time away from looking for library resources and meeting with professors:

> The course load that I have ... with my financial situation ... in some ways, I feel like I've bitten off more than I can chew ... I wonder about instead of taking a full course load, maybe taking a half course load, maybe taking a half course load in the spring and working. I don't know whether I can work and take a full course load ... If I had a job, I don't know how I would be able to cope with it.

Technology-related issues were also problematic, causing frustrations with completion of informational and educational tasks. For students like Zoe, personal, micro-level problems also demonstrated broader, macro-level concerns; but here, her anger actually served a positive end, as she forced her professor to shift his own view of students' behaviors:

> I had an essay ... I had to get printed out at school because there was a virus on my disk. So I go into class, I show [the professor] the disk and I say that I just haven't got it printed out yet. And he said some snide comment about 'Oh, all sorts of excuses you students give me.' ... And I got really mad with him, and I just said straight out, 'Oh, don't give me that. I've been working on this for three days and I don't need to stand here and justify this to you' [laughs]. And he was awfully embarrassed, and I was too ... but it was just always that sense that 'a student will say anything to get out of anything.' And I think that's the mentality professors have.

Social isolation and feelings of alienation also had a profound effect on students' self-esteem and ability to gather information for their work. As many students relied on their peers to borrow class notes, arrange study groups, or discuss relevant readings, students who lacked strong social networks were intimidated and frustrated in their attempts to complete their work. As Lynn noted:

> There's a problem of isolation as well, that interferes ... with my ability to do my work. And that's why I decided to see a counselor ... I don't have many friends. I have only limited contacts. The

contacts I've had here have only been on campus … This first half of [my first] year has been pretty difficult. I don't think it's going to stay this way. I think, once I get into the swing of things … I'll be able to do better.

This ability—to turn isolation and personal despair into a fervent belief that things will get better—often meant the difference between a student who would, ultimately, succeed and one who dropped out of school. For educators, librarians, and other individuals on campus to provide emotional (as well as information and academic) support to students like Lynn is vital to these students' successes.

Love, Joy, Surprise—Supporting Students' Micro-Level Information Behaviors

For other students, being isolated from peers offered a positive respite: a chance to read and think without distractions. However, these students therefore wanted comfortable chairs, natural lighting, and other environmental elements conducive to long periods of reading, computer work, or quiet reflection. Many students carved out spaces for themselves on campus, such as a favorite chair or computer. Jonathan noted the following path in describing how he located an ideal study space: "First … I'll try and get a comfy seat. And then … I'll look for plug-ins [for my laptop]. Then I'll go for the brightest place. And then, somewhere I can see other people, but not get distracted by them." As Maggie, a 27-year-old third year history student, noted during her walking tour, "that couch is mine. And if I want to lay down and read with my feet dangling over the edge, then that's fine. I'm not disturbing anybody … And, you know most people … that go to these spaces are looking for the same thing. They want their own little space." Other students described instances of including children in the act of retrieving books from the library shelves or photocopying articles to take home with them. These students saw their academic work as offering important family time and the opportunity to demonstrate the value of lifelong learning to their children, while providing activities that would keep the children busy while mom or dad located information for their schoolwork. Finding the small joys where home life and academic work could neatly coincide was reflected in all of the participants' experiences—across age, gender, and academic discipline. Often, it was the ability to bridge home and school in positive ways that motivated these students to continue with their studies and to invest the time and effort needed to locate relevant information for their work.

CONCLUSION

Although much research in library and information science includes elements of affect (e.g., where individuals discuss their frustrations with computers—often without prompting—in studies of information retrieval strategies), more work is needed where emotion is explicitly examined as a core component of information behavior. Often, researchers discuss the mechanics of searching for information resources in isolation from individuals' affective responses, or they discuss affect as an interesting side effect of information policies without fully attending to the substantive impact that emotional responses to technologies or library services can have on individuals' information behavior. As research results lead to alterations in practice (e.g., where librarians redesign Web sites to meet usability standards or implement instructional programs as a result of research on information literacy needs), the role of emotion may be easily dismissed or sidelined when addressing changes that may be more concrete and therefore easier to implement (e.g., revising opening hours based on patron feedback). As researchers enhance their work by more fully discussing the role of emotion in information seeking practices, librarians will need to find ways to address these elements in their daily information services and in the design of information systems. In guiding library patrons in the use of new online systems, for example, librarians need to consciously address computer anxiety or many of the other (often, unspoken) emotional impacts of information seeking. This demands more time and skill on the part of librarians—to ask questions about patrons' feelings, to open spaces for dialogue about affective consequences of information behavior, and to develop strategies that can enhance patrons' comfort levels with the various resources on offer in the library and on its Web site. As libraries move to 24-hour access across areas of service and as patrons physically remove themselves from libraries in favor of remote access to resources, librarians face even greater challenges in attempting to meet patrons' affective needs.

The interviews reported here provide some guidance on immediate steps that librarians and researchers can take to best address undergraduate students' emotionally bound information needs. First, researchers must be open to discussing the emotional aspects of individuals' information behaviors and to recognizing how deeply embedded affective elements are in individuals' daily informational activities. Qualitative approaches, in particular, are easily aligned with this type of inquiry, as they typically allow room for participants to explore the emotional consequences of the phenomena under study; however, researchers may need to consciously prompt study participants to discuss their feelings in this context. When using more quantitative research methods with individuals (e.g., questionnaires), researchers should include questions that invite respondents to examine affective elements of information seeking. Even in projects not expressly designed to address emotion, it would be useful for researchers to reflect on (and publish) findings related to individuals' affective responses and to build a larger body of work—across populations and settings—that can inform our research approaches in the future.

From a practice standpoint, the interview results point to a number of areas for reflection and possible change. Designing library services or educational programs to eliminate "negative" experiences and bolster the "positive," for example, is too simplistic for this type of information ecology. Instead, library and information professionals must identify students' needs, guide them as they interact with information resources, and push students to challenge their emotionally laden assumptions. Further, librarians should acknowledge that library policies not only have real consequences for students' activities, but that these consequences can become deeply embedded in students' responses and may shape future informational activities. Where students are not allowed to borrow certain materials or are restricted by brief loan periods, for example, students may feel that the library is working against their interests and may see the library in an adversarial relationship to the university's mission to promote student learning—even though such restrictions may be the result of funding limitations or other external forces beyond the librarian's control. By conducting user surveys prior to policy implementation, by openly discussing the reasons for implementing policies, and by examining the impact of those policies at regular intervals, students may feel that the library cares about their opinions and about their academic successes. By working to promote students' feelings of joy and affection for their campus, for their academic work, and for the library itself, while lessening the fear and sadness that will shape many students' academic experiences (at some point in their academic careers), librarians can reshape the library as a hopeful space that acknowledges students' affective needs alongside the informational ones. By adopting holistic views of users' informational interactions, researchers and librarians can best decide what kinds of services users require and examine the potential emotional effects of library and campus environments on students' lives.

ACKNOWLEDGMENTS

The author thanks the Social Sciences and Humanities Research Council of Canada for funding this work, as well as the research assistants who devoted time and energy to these projects.

REFERENCES

Bilal, D. (2000). Children's use of the Yahooligans! Web search engine: I. Cognitive, physical, and affective behaviors on fact-based search tasks. *Journal of the American Society for Information Science and Technology, 51*(7), 646–655.

Blimling, G. S. (1999). A meta-analysis of the influence of college residence halls on academic performance. *Journal of College Student Development, 40*(5), 551–561.

Dimitroff, A., Wolfram, D., & Volz, A. (1996). Affective response and retrieval perform-ance: Analysis of contributing factors. *Library and Information Science Research, 18*(2), 121–132.

Given, L. M. (2002). The academic and the everyday: Investigating the overlap in mature undergraduates' information-seeking behaviour. *Library & Information Science Research, 24*(1), 17–29.

Heinstrom, J. (2005). Fast surfing, broad scanning and deep diving: The influence of personality and study approach on students' information-seeking behavior. *Journal of Documentation, 61*(2), 228–247.

Holliday, W., & Li, Q. (2004). Understanding the millennials: Updating our knowledge about students. *Reference Services Review, 32*(4), 356–366.

Hyldegård, J. (2006). Collaborative information behaviour: Exploring Kuhlthau's Information Search Process model in a group-based educational setting. *Information Processing and Management, 42*(1), 276–298.

Järvenoja, H., & Järvelä, S. (2005). How students describe the sources of their emotional and motivational experiences during the learning process: A qualitative approach. *Learning and Instruction, 15*(5), 465–480.

Julien, H., McKechnie, L. (E. F.), & Hart, S. (2005). Affective issues in library and infor-mation science systems work: A content analysis. *Library and Information Science Research, 27*(4), 453–466.

Kracker, J. (2002). Research anxiety and students' perceptions of research: An experi-ment. Part I. Effect of teaching Kuhlthau's ISP model. *Journal of the American Society for Information Science and Technology, 53*(4), 282–294.

Kracker, J., & Pollio, H. R. (2003). The experiences of libraries across time: Thematic analysis of undergraduate recollections of library experiences. *Journal of the American Society for Information Science and Technology, 54*(12), 1104–1116.

Kuhlthau, C. C. (2004). *Seeking meaning: A process approach to library and information services* (2nd ed.). Westport, CT: Libraries Unlimited.

Mellon, C. A. (1986). Library anxiety: A grounded theory and its development. *College & Research Libraries, 47*(2), 160–165.

Nahl, D. (1998). Learning the Internet and the structure of information behavior. *Journal of the American Society for Information Science, 49*(11), 1017–1023.

Nardi, B. A., & O'Day, V. L. (1999). *Information ecologies: Using technology with heart.* Cambridge, MA: MIT Press.

Onwuegbuzie, A. J., & Jiao, Q. G. (2000). I'll go to the library later: The relationship between academic procrastination and library anxiety. *College and Research Libraries, 61*(1), 45–54.

Saumure, K. & Given, L. M. (2004). Digitally enhanced? An examination of the infor-mation behaviors of visually impaired post-secondary students. *The Canadian Journal of Information and Library Science, 28*(2), 25–42.

Schlosser, L. Z., & Sedlacek, W. E. (2001). The relationship between undergraduate stu-dents' perceived past academic success and perceived academic self-concept. *Journal of the Freshman Year Experience, 13*, 95–105.

Shaver, P., Schwartz, J., Kirson, D., & O'Connor, C. (1987). Emotion knowledge: Further exploration of a prototype approach. *Journal of Personality and Social Psychology, 52*, 1061–1086.

Whitmire, E. (2004). The relationship between undergraduates' epistemological beliefs, reflective judgment, and their information-seeking behavior. *Information Processing and Management, 40*, 97–111.

Williamson, K. (1989). Discovered by chance: The role of incidental information acqui-sition in an ecological model of information use. *Library and Information Science Research, 20*, 23–40.

CHAPTER 9

Understanding the Rogue User

Rich Gazan
University of Hawaii

INTRODUCTION

Visions of a harmonious online community are usually crushed quite quickly once humans start to participate. A totem of user-centered design is that people use technologies in ways never intended by their designers (see, for example, Nielsen, 1993), sometimes emotionally, but distinguishing destructive and creative interactions with an information system is often difficult. This distinction is addressed in this chapter via the concept of a rogue user, an active participant in an online community who violates the community's rules or spirit. Evidence of rogue behaviors in the Answerbag (www.answerbag.com) online question answering community was obtained through user postings and site logs, and analyzed through the lens of the American Psychiatric Association's Diagnostic and Statistical Manual of Mental Disorders (DSM-IV-TR 2000) to suggest ways in which rogue behaviors can be understood and mitigated in the design of future online communities.

BACKGROUND AND THEORETICAL FRAMEWORK

While the majority of affective information behavior research relies on direct observation of users or the design of tools that are responsive to affective input, the emotional aspects of interaction within online communities have been comparatively understudied. Though evidence of affective interaction is usually restricted to text on a screen and transaction log data, it can indicate patterns of emotional behavior. Since online question-answering communities are relatively recent phenomena and access to data that does exist is usually tightly controlled by the owning organization, this study fills a gap in the literature by analyzing transcripts of online interactions in a naturalistic environment.

Increasingly, a person's online life is one of their many contexts (Turkle, 1995), and an online community can serve as a "small world" within which standards of behavior are defined and shaped (Chatman, 1999). Solomon (2005) extends Chatman's work and conceptualizes a kind of exchange: An individual accepts the norms of a small world in exchange for making life manageable. Since a person's online identity is often a vehicle for forms of expression and interaction that aren't possible elsewhere, some individuals become emotionally invested in both the online community and their identity within it. In an analysis of deviant behavior in cyberspace, Suler and Phillips (1998) challenge the concept of online disinhibition; they argue that though anonymity might remove some behavioral inhibitions, online community participants also seek the reward of recognition.

Baym (1997), studying Usenet, writes that online interactions allow participants to "co-construct the values, identities and conventions that make a group feel like community." Burnetta and Bonnici (2003) make a distinction between an online community's explicit norms and its implicit norms, such as who is entitled to post, what constitutes appropriate content, and community etiquette. Rogue users bend or break the rules in order to challenge or even attempt to control the implicit norms of a community.

The term "rogue user" has been used somewhat loosely in the computer science literature to describe individuals who are not full-fledged hackers, but who have gained access to files or functions beyond their permission level. However, McNee et al. (2002, p. 118) specifically employ the term to describe users who undermine the rating system in a collaborative filtering environment. This chapter extends this definition to include any violation of an online community's rules or spirit by an active participant.

SITE AND METHOD

Answerbag is an online question-answering community that supports both anonymity and recognition. Users submit frequently asked questions (FAQs) in a nearly limitless variety of categories, submit answers under a screen name, and also rate answers as useful (100 percent), somewhat useful (75 percent), or incorrect/not useful (50 percent). Multiple answers to a question are permitted, and the highest-rated answers are listed first, providing collaborative filtering while still allowing users to see the range of different answers. Participants with the highest percentage of useful answers gain status in the community; their screen name and statistics are displayed on the site, viewed by thousands of people per day. While this competitive aspect of recognition increases site traffic, it also motivates some users to bend the rules.

Answerbag is both a public Web site and a research testbed, and administrator-level access to all site data was readily available. Initial research questions included:

- Why do some frequent online community participants engage in rogue behaviors?

- How can rogue behaviors be mitigated?

While some rogue behaviors can be measured statistically, many were initially reported by site moderators who edit and categorize user submissions, monitor categories for inappropriate content, and interact with users via feedback forms. Data collection took place throughout 2005 and is ongoing. Instances of inappropriate activity collected by moderators were aggregated and analyzed to develop a list of common rogue behaviors including:

- *Vindictive rating* – e.g., downgrading all answers submitted by a given user to advance a person's own position.

- *Abusive language* – In answers or rating comments.

- *Flooding* – Submitting multiple questions or answers in an attempt to dominate a category with a single point of view or to increase submission statistics.

- *Excessive contact with administrators* – Lobbying to get an offensive question, answer, or rating removed, or to make self-serving design or policy suggestions. More than 10 contacts is deemed excessive.

- *Creating "sock puppets"* – Separately registered identities under which rogue behavior is undertaken to shield the user from identification or retaliation.

- *Requesting special privileges* – Asking to be exempt from certain site rules and policies.

While this list was compiled to train moderators, these behaviors were observed so often that a more structured analysis was undertaken. Instances of rating irregularities, flooding, and excessive contact were obtained from usage statistics. Moderators flagged examples of abusive language. Though "sock puppets" are not always obvious, they were triangulated from login times, content analysis, unusual submission patterns, and reports from other users.

Of roughly 40,000 registered users, only 46 were identified as having engaged in one or more rogue behaviors. However, of these 46 individuals, six ranked among the top-50 site contributors in terms of questions submitted, answers submitted, and useful rating percentage. Three ranked among the top 10. Understanding why such high participators in an online community would engage—often repeatedly—in behaviors that undermine the community's integrity motivated a deeper affective analysis.

DATA ANALYSIS AND NARCISSISTIC PERSONALITY DISORDER

The field of psychology has institutionalized personality diagnosis in DSM-IV-TR (2000). While DSM-IV-TR has been critiqued for taking an over-categorical approach to symptoms of mental illness, it does provide common dimensions of personality that can be compared and aggregated to form a diagnosis with more or less confidence depending on how many criteria are observed. According to DSM-IV-TR, Narcissistic Personality Disorder (NPD) is an Axis II (diagnosed in adulthood), Cluster B (dramatic, emotional, or erratic behavior) personality disorder, defined as a "pervasive pattern of grandiosity (in fantasy or behavior), need for admiration, and lack of empathy, beginning by early adulthood and present in a variety of contexts." Five of following nine criteria must be met to diagnose NPD, which is estimated to occur in 0.7 percent to 1 percent of the population:

1. Self-importance

2. Fantasies of unlimited success, power, etc.

3. Belief that he or she is special and unique

4. Requires excessive admiration

5. Unreasonable sense of entitlement

6. Interpersonally exploitative

7. Lacks empathy

8. Envious of others or believes that others are envious of him or her

9. Arrogance

Since indicators overlap, it is difficult and potentially misleading to categorize rogue behaviors as instances of one NPD dimension and not another, so a numerical breakdown of frequency data is not included here. Also, evidence of online interaction is certainly not sufficient for a clinical diagnosis. However, Table 9.1 demonstrates that many rogue behaviors observed in Answerbag users could be coded as positive dimensions of NPD.

When a rogue behavior was identified, the transaction data surrounding the question, answers, answer ratings, users, and the category in which the rogue behavior appeared were flagged for closer content and traffic analysis. When users elsewhere in the site referenced a rogue user, question or answer (such as in the "Answerblog," a bulletin board for free-form discussion about the site), any positive or negative comments were also factored into the analysis to get a sense of the wider effects of the rogue behaviors.

RESULTS AND CONCLUSION

Though rogue users tend to be high participators themselves, overall participation is reduced when their roguish behaviors are apparent to other users. There may be an initial flood of negative ratings and complaints in a category in which rogue behavior has taken place, but subsequently the number of participants tends to fall. The following plea from one non-rogue user, responding to abusive language in a religion subcategory, indicates the chilling effect of rogue behavior on community participation:

Table 9.1 Examples of Rogue Behaviors and Corresponding NPD Dimensions

NPD Dimension	Rogue Behavior	Example [Comment]
Self-importance	Excessive contact with administrators	*"I cannot sit idly by and let them ruin my ratings ... It takes courage to stand alone and defend against this kind. When a person gives truthful responses and are rated so low, then the site itself is failing ... I wonder if they are being allowed to personally attack me because it boosts interest in Answerbag?"* [To date, this user has made more than 200 contacts with administrators, usually over "unfair" ratings.]
Fantasies of unlimited success, power, etc.	Requesting special privileges	*"I think you guys have the greatest site in the world, but you need someone to get the word out better. I would be happy to discuss a consulting arrangement ...[that would] make us all rich."* [If this user's profile information and question submissions are any indication, he is a recent college graduate who is seeking employment.]
Belief that he or she is special and unique	Requesting special privileges	*"I'm probably your best contributor, I given [sic] my heart and soul to AB, I think I deserve not to have my questions edited anymore."* [Neither the quality nor the quantity of this user's submissions was remarkable, save for a one-week submission binge immediately prior to this message.]
Requires excessive admiration	Excessive contact with administrators	*"Can AB give acclaim to users whose question submissions appeared on the front page by having their user profile show a medal?"* [This user's 80+ site suggestions usually include a "look at me" element, and his aggressive defense of his submissions recalls a quote by Napoleon Bonaparte, circa 1807: "I have made the most wonderful discovery. I have discovered men will risk their lives, even die, for ribbons!"]

Table 9.1   (cont.)

Unreasonable sense of entitlement	Flooding	*"I hope to have asked the most questions so whenever Answerbag launches a tangible rewards program that awards those who have the "bests" and "mosts" of anything, that I get rewarded dearly for having asked the most questions."* [In the Name Origins category, this user had recently submitted more than 400 variants of the question "What is the origin of the name X?," to reach the coveted "Most Inquisitive" title.]
Interpersonally exploitative	Creating "sock puppets"	*"If you cannot stop [user] from calling me a liar and a satan, I'll have to call in my own troops."* [Soon after this communiqué, two new "members" registered on Answerbag, whose sole purpose seemed to be giving 100 percent ratings to every one of the above user's answers, and 50 percent to those of the alleged name-caller. Whether "sock puppets" or not, this can be interpreted as exploiting another online identity to serve one's own ends.]
Lacks empathy	Abusive language	*"Who is monitoring your home, [username], to make sure you're not abusing children? Have you stopped molesting children yet?"* [This was posted in response to a question regarding secrecy in the practices of a certain religion, and how accusations of child abuse are handled.]
Envious of others, or believes that others are envious of him or her	Vindictive rating	*"I think it's wise to react to paranoia and stop the actions of anyone when they are destructive in a personal way. Do you agree? Does the crime of stalking carry the same penalty for the perpetrator if he or she were stalking someone online rather than doing so in person?"* [This user insisted that another user was envious of her position as a category expert, and was "stalking" her across Answerbag by down-rating her answers. This message was her explanation for why she had vindictively rated the answers of the user in question.]

Table 9.1   (cont.)

Arrogance	Abusive language	*"This has to rank as the most ignorant answer on Answerbag, maybe on the entire Internet ..."* [This now-deleted rating comment was made by a frequent contributor of quality content, who nonetheless seems to go on jags of belittling others via insulting rating comments.]

> ... curb the ongoing negativity ... some of us haven't ventured onto the killing fields and don't plan to.

The results suggest that using DSM-IV-TR (2000) to interpret rogue behavior through the lens of NPD yielded both greater understanding of why the behavior occurred and several mitigation strategies. Attempting to reason with rogue users by first expressing appreciation for their contributions (appealing to their sense of self-importance), then requesting that they curb rogue behaviors for the good of the site, were usually met with resistance, defensiveness or defiance (NPD dimensions: lacks empathy, arrogance), and no change in rogue behaviors. However, in a parallel development, Answerbag began to allow users to construct enhanced personal profile pages on the site. Along with detailed usage statistics, users now had an "About me" section where they could post personal information, links, quotes, or anything else. Profiles are linked from the user's screen name, and accessible from any page on which the user has contributed content. Of those users who have visited the site since the upgrade, less than 10 percent have created enhanced profiles, while 77 percent of rogue users have. In the first four months after enhanced personal profiles were made available, instances of rogue behavior fell from an average of 12 per month to five. Providing an area of the community where one is by definition "special and unique" and where no one can edit or rate their content seems to have served as an outlet for emotional expression, and less rogue behavior now occurs on the site.

CONCLUSION

Virtual identities can exhibit the same range of emotions as the people behind them. Rogue users in online communities can be viewed not simply as destructive miscreants, but as individuals with emotional needs that information systems might be better designed to address. Though this is a small initial study, the results suggest that diagnostic personality tools such as DSM-IV-TR (2000) can provide one avenue to understanding rogue behaviors, and suggest productive ways to channel the emotional needs behind them, to keep online communities useful and sustainable for all.

REFERENCES

American Psychiatric Association. (2000). *Diagnostic and statistical manual of mental disorders* (4th ed., text revision). Washington, DC: American Psychiatric Association.

Baym, N. (1997). Interpreting soap operas and creating community: Inside an electronic fan culture. In S. Keisler (Ed.), *Culture of the Internet*. Mahwah, NJ: Lawrence Erlbaum Associates.

Burnetta, G., & Bonnici, L. (2003). Beyond the FAQ: Explicit and implicit norms in Usenet newsgroups. *Library & Information Science Research, 25*(3), 333–351.

Chatman, E. A. (1999). A theory of life in the round. *Journal of the American Society for Information Science, 50*(3), 207–217.

McNee, S. M., Albert, I., Cosley, D., Gopalkrishnan, P., Lam, S. K., Rashid, A. M., et al. (2002). On the recommending of citations for research papers. In *Proceedings of the 2002 ACM Conference on Computer Supported Cooperative Work* (pp. 116–125). New York: ACM Press.

Nielsen, J. (1993). *Usability engineering*. San Francisco: Morgan Kaufmann.

Solomon, P. (2005). Rounding and dissonant grounds. In K. E. Fisher, S. Erdelez, & L. E. F. McKechnie (Eds.), *Theories of information behavior* (pp. 308–312). Medford, NJ: Information Today, Inc.

Suler, J. R., & Phillips, W. (1998). The bad boys of cyberspace: Deviant behavior in multimedia chat communities. *CyberPsychology and Behavior, 1*, 275–294.

Turkle, S. (1995). *Life on the screen: Identity in the age of the Internet*. New York: Simon & Schuster.

PART III

Micro-Emotional Information Environment

CHAPTER 10

Affective Dimensions of Information Seeking in the Context of Reading

Lynne (E. F.) McKechnie and Catherine Sheldrick Ross
University of Western Ontario

Paulette Rothbauer
University of Toronto

INTRODUCTION

A growing body of research in Library and Information Science (LIS) points to the importance of affective variables in both information seeking and information retrieval. Wilson (1981) was one of the first to acknowledge the role of affect, incorporating it in an early version of his model of information seeking behavior where it was presented as one of the personal contexts giving rise to information seeking. Kuhlthau's (2004) Information Search Process (ISP) postulates that feeling, or affect, plays a role in each of the six steps associated with the information search process. Savolainen's (1995) framework of everyday life information seeking is inclusive of affect in its four ideal types of mastery of life. The work of Diane Nahl is particularly notable. Starting from the position that positive affect influences cognition and learning, Nahl (2004) identifies self-efficacy, optimism, uncertainty, time pressure, expected effort, task completion motivation, and expected difficulty as important affective dimensions. A number of individual studies have also explored affect including Mellon's (1986) examination of library anxiety in college students, Metoyer-Duran's (1991) investigation of affective dimensions in her study of the information-seeking behavior of gatekeepers in ethnolinguistic communities, Bilal's (2000, 2002) consideration of affective states in children searching with Yahooligans, and Massey, Weeks, and Druin's (2005) study of children's responses to literature in digital libraries.

The importance of reading to LIS is clear (see Ross, McKechnie, & Rothbauer, 2006; Wiegand, 1997). Yet, as Davis and Scott (2002) so concisely tell us, "Reading is not adequately taken into account in its own right as a legitimate step in information seeking (IS) models. ..." Outside of work that has looked at the impact of reading levels on information seeking (for example, Baker, Wilson, & Kars, 1997) and recognized that information seeking occurs during reading (Ross, 1999), very little work has been done in this area. As researchers of reading and readers working within an LIS framework, we agree with Davis and Scott, and we begin with the motivation to take reading out of its metaphorical "Black Box." This chapter reports on the results of a study undertaken to explore the following research questions: Do the affective dimensions of reading play a role in information behavior practices and, if so, how?

METHOD

To answer this question, we conducted a meta-analysis of more than 375 in-depth qualitative interviews with readers, collected in four separate studies. These interviews include more than 220 with adults (Ross, 1991, 1995, 1999), about 25 with young adults (Rothbauer, 2004a, 2004b, 2004c), and more than 130 with children and young adults (McKechnie, 1996, 2000, 2004).

Interested in finding out about the experience of pleasure-reading, Ross and the students in successive classes of her graduate MLIS course on Genres of Fiction and Reading have conducted open-ended, qualitative interviews with avid readers who read a lot and read by choice. In these interviews, which were recorded and transcribed, avid readers were invited to talk about a variety of reading-related themes including: factors that fostered or discouraged reading in childhood; the value and role of reading in their lives; what it would be like if for one reason or another they *couldn't* read; books that helped them; rereading; how they choose books to read; and feelings associated with reading particular books.

In her dissertation research, Rothbauer (2004a, 2004b, 2004c) examined the voluntary reading practices among young women who were negotiating non-mainstream identities. She conducted in-depth, flexibly structured, qualitative interviews with 20 young women between 18 and 23 years of age. The interviews captured information about the role of reading in their lives: what reading meant to them and what it offered to them as they sought to make sense of the changes in their lives. There was also data on how and why they chose certain kinds of reading materials, on the role of trusted reading mentors, and on the paramount importance of how reading made them feel about themselves and their place in the world. Other sources of data included personal writing exercises conducted by participants and researcher field notes. Following guidelines for interpretivist human inquiry, data analysis was largely a matter of textual reflection. Interpretation was guided by open-coding techniques developed by Strauss and Corbin (1998) and involved hermeneutic procedures such as active listening, immersion in the data, data reduction, structuring meaning through narratives, and thematic analysis (Cohen, Kahn, & Steeves, 2000; Kvale, 1996; Watson, 2001). Interview transcripts were also interpreted using modified techniques of phenomenological writing (van Manen, 1990), including analytical, exemplificative, and exegetical arrangement of texts.

McKechnie (1996, 2000) completed an observation and interview study with 30 girls (4 years old) and their mothers to determine what took place during an ordinary visit to each girl's local public library. Participants were recruited through convenience and snowball sampling. Library visits were audio-recorded (the children wore a small recorder housed in a special pocket in a shirt) and observed. In addition, during the week following the library visit, mothers maintained a diary where they made notes of incidents related to the library visit, which formed the basis for a follow-up interview. Data included transcripts and observation field notes from the library visit and diary/diary interview. In a second study, McKechnie (2004) and MLIS students enrolled in LIS 566 (Literature for Children and Young adults) completed book ownership case studies (interviews and inventories of personal collections) with child and young adult readers. Participants were largely recruited through convenience sampling. To date, 133 case studies have been completed, 100 with children (4 to 12 years) and 33 with teens (13 to 19 years). Girls (n=79) outnumber boys (n=54) in the sample.

Using a grounded theory approach (Strauss & Corbin, 1998), we analyzed the transcripts of our interviews to identify themes related to affective dimensions of reading as an information behavior practice. A surprising and unexpected finding across all four studies was that emotions or affective dimensions have much to bear on the reading choices and reading practices among our research participants.

AFFECTIVE DIMENSIONS OF READING

In an article that explores information encounters in the context of voluntary reading, Ross (1999) classifies into six categories the claims that readers make about the power of reading: an awakening or new perspectives; models for identity; reassurance, comfort, confirmation of self-worth, strength; a connection with others and an awareness of not being alone; courage to make a change; and acceptance. Ross's more general claim—that for avid readers, reading is an important way of finding out about the world—is one that underpins the research reported here. The readers' claims reported by Ross rely on affective dimensions of information seeking and of reading itself. What counts as information is filtered through emotional responses and memories of how reading certain kinds of texts at certain times made readers *feel*. The value of information, the measure of how useful information found through voluntary reading practices can be, is assessed using affective variables that emerge from what readers themselves have to say about the role of reading in their lives.

Lynne Pearce's (1997) concept of the relationship between the reader and what she calls the "textual other" (found both inside and outside of the text itself) is another way to explicitly articulate the affective dimensions of reading. Her theory allows us to move an analysis of what readers say about the books they read beyond interpretative processes to focus on the intensity of the emotional experiences of reading—experiences that we emphasize in the remainder of this section.

Several themes emerged from our data that illustrate the emotional density and that extend the affective dimensions of Ross's typology of information found in the process of avid engagement with texts. While space does not permit a nuanced presentation of these additional themes as articulated by our readers, we do offer some exemplary excerpts from the transcripts.

Shared Reading as an Act of Love

A dominant theme is the close and loving relationships often associated with the sharing of texts. For example, in the data collected in McKechnie's studies (1996, 2000, 2004) of young children and reading, those books identified by young people as having special significance are often those in their personal libraries that have been inscribed by beloved family members. Sometimes the intensity of this loving relationship forged by a shared engagement with texts is communicated as a simple expression of love, as in the case of 4-year-old Fatima whose mother made a point of bringing home a copy of *Mike Mulligan and His Steam Shovel* (Burton, 1939) from the public library. When her mother gave her the book, Fatima said, "Mom, thanks for *Mike Mulligan*, I love you." When asked what she likes best about *Stuart Little* (White, 1945), Sarah (4 years old) replies, "It's best that we read it together. With Mommy and …with Mommy and that's all." Another reader, a 10-year-old girl, identified as her special book the one she is only reading with her dad when he comes for a visit.

Similar themes are evident in interviews with much older readers. For example, an avid 18-year-old reader, Nicky, had this to say about one of her all-time favorite books that was received as a gift from her best friend: "… it's our book, it's us. We *are* this book. She read it and she gave it to me for Christmas and now we've both read it." Nicky takes this powerful connection through textual engagement further when she describes the communication between readers as a being possible because "you speak the same language," or "we speak the same writers/readers language."

Emotional Connections to Textual Worlds

Sometimes the most powerful relationships emerge from memorable connections that readers make with fictional or textual characters. The author is a special kind of textual persona especially, but not exclusively, among readers of nonfiction. For example, Truus (40 years old), said that after her daughter was born with Down Syndrome, she looked for books written by parents of children with chronic conditions: "Sometimes … you think that you're the only person in the world who ever felt this way. And then you can go out, pick up a book, start to read it and go, 'That's me!' That is some-body else who is doing the same thing and felt the same way and maybe I'm not so ... alone. It's a way of reconnecting."

Laurie (24 years old) describes this feeling of connection through reading using Nicky's metaphor of communicating through a shared understanding of language: "[Finding yourself in the text] means a *lot* because when you're looking for somebody to speak back to you and you can say, 'Oh! That's me.' Like you can find [it] through writing, that this text in particular speaks to you. And you feel a connection to it ... Then, you can explore that feeling more in depth because somebody has written it down."

This connection with the text is not always a pleasurable experience, how-ever, as some readers strongly resist this close identification. But at the same time, they describe the powerful sense of recognition. For example, it is a gradual process of acceptance for Madeline (20 years old): "The character, the girl, was very much [as] I saw myself, especially going through her child-hood and the kind of experiences she had and how she dealt with them. Like it was just kind of slap in the face, you know, that's me ... It is shocking to see yourself on the page and have it leap out at you. The first instinct is 'that's not me. I would never do that.' But when you think back and you realize it is you, it's kind of a more gradual thing where you come to accept it."

Reading for Coping Information

Over and over, the readers in our studies have told us that they read because it is an activity that gives them comfort in their lives. Even 4½-year-old Shrek (a self-chosen pseudonym) pointed to a book titled *First Experiences: My First Day at Preschool* (Riddell, 1992), explaining that it was a good book for reading when you are scared about starting school. Similarly, Emma (20 years old) looked for books to help her understand her emergent homosexuality: "I was searching for something that I needed to know ... I looked for books to help me. And the same, it's an experience, when you're reading something and you can relate to it, and you're like, 'yes, yes, go on. Tell me what I'm going to do next!'" Joanne (27 years old) takes a different approach, illustrating that an affinity with the textual characters is not always necessary to learn from their fictional experiences: "I think just see-ing other people's lives is helpful, so that if that experience ever comes up ... I know what kind of reaction would be appropriate or expected. This is how this person coped with it; it didn't work for them, so maybe I should try something else."

Mastery and Control of Emotions

An emotional engagement with texts means that for some readers some books are "too much to handle" at certain times in their lives. One reader lit-erally put books that were too upsetting into deep freeze: "I've re-read it a couple of times. Sometimes, because it is a really intense, emotional book, you just have to not read it. And in our house, when books are too much we literally put them in the freezer ... where you can't read them. It goes in the freezer usually maybe once a year and I don't take it out until I'm ready."

Another reader describes a similar process of reading that allows her to manage negative or overwhelming emotions: "Sometimes I think books are more important to me than people and I don't think that's very good ... I think sometimes that reading is my way out of relationships or interactions. Books are lovely companions. They don't talk back. They're very accessible. They give you what you want out of it. And if you don't want it, you can close it and hand it back. If it's uncomfortable, you don't have to read it; you can stop."

The Book as an Emotional Touchstone

The object of the book itself plays an important role in the reading accounts of real readers. Earlier we cited Nicky's emphatic statement that *Summer Sisters* by Judy Blume (1998) came to be a kind of holding place for her relationship with her best friend (i.e., "We *are* this book"). A young reader, Gillian (6 years old), looked forward to a special book at home, waiting for her like a best friend, "Mum, *The Cake That Mac Ate* is waiting in the house for me" (*The Cake That Mac Ate*: Robart, 1986). Ross (1994) has explored the role of L. M. Montgomery's books as childhood favorites, especially at times when readers are seeking reassurance, comfort, or courage. At least one reader in Rothbauer's study (Rothbauer 2004a) found familiar comfort in her *Anne of Green Gables* (Montgomery, 1908) collection: "... I'll see [them] and I'll remember, 'Oh yeah; when I was 10, you know and that happened.' There's comfort just to have them." Not all of our readers referred to Anne and Emily, but many of them did describe books that were freighted with personal significance and emotions, books that they regard as friends, books that they carried with them whenever they moved, books that provided continuity and security when other things in their lives were changing or books that changed with you. Books become touchstone artifacts through their association with special people, special moments and situations in life, or special places. Joyce (19 years old) describes how this works for her with her favorite book, *Charlie and the Chocolate Factory* (Dahl, 1964): "... [It] has different meanings ... so that it changes according to what's going on in your life, so it's not like the same book; [it] helps me to figure out things ... to get back on track." Laurie's articulation of the same theme illustrates just how powerful these kinds of books are to their readers: "... I was attached to that book; my life was in this cover. Even though it's exactly the same book, I put myself in it."

DISCUSSION AND CONCLUSION

We have presented some representative claims from readers about the affective significance of reading. Our empirical studies of what real readers said about the role of reading in their lives lend support to the idea that elicitation of emotions can yield transformative insights. Our readers chose to read a range of texts: fiction, easy readers, picture books, comic books and graphic novels, Webzines, magazines, memoirs, biographies, armchair travel and science books, histories and gaming manuals, and more. And in case after case, they made sense of their reading choices and reading practices by speaking of their emotions and by describing *how they felt* when they read specific texts or kinds of texts. The effects of this kind of reading should be taken seriously by those designing information systems to aid readers and those who help readers.

The affective dimensions of reading also have implications for LIS professionals seeking to serve readers. For example, it is apparent that human relationships (with family, friends, and librarians) influence what an individual may read and how they experience the reading process and therefore the information seeking process. Affective variables play a strong role in reading-related information behavior especially in the domain of everyday life. This is also consistent with the principles of information seeking as articulated by Harris and Dewdney (1994) in the early 1990s that indicate that individuals prefer interpersonal sources of information given with empathy or affective support. The readers' advisory interview and readers' advisory tools need to be revised to take into consideration and to provide access to materials according to affective as well as content characteristics.

Our findings suggest that it should be imperative for electronic readers' advisory tools that aim to match reading interests and reading materials to incorporate the affective dimensions of relational aspects of reading into interface design and navigational strategies. New interactive, participatory digital technologies can play a role in the design of information access systems: Readers can be given the option of creating and articulating relationships that rise up around reading practices through use of social computing tools that invite multiple levels of interpretation, many modes of expression, and flexible query structures to enable readers to tailor their reading practices in relation to the affective dimensions of their reading preference. The desire to make connections with other readers, with authors, and even to express an affinity with textual characters is a serious factor in the reading choices and reading practices of all the readers in our studies from those who are very young to those who are expert, avid lifelong readers.

Our research gives credence to the view that reading constitutes a memorable *event* in the lives of those who do it. This notion disrupts the pervasive conception of reading as a process of finding (or being directed) to a book whose contents can then be assimilated to a reader's existing state of knowledge. Reading is more than just a process of making sense, of interpretation, of decoding. It is an experience of overlapping worlds that is made meaningful to readers through affective responses and processes as they engage with textual materials.

REFERENCES

Baker, L. M., Wilson, F. L., & Kars, M. (1997). The readability of medical information on Info Trac: Does it meet the needs of people with low literacy skills? *Reference and User Services Quarterly, 37*(2), 155–160.

Bilal, D. (2000). Children's use of the Yahooligans! Web search engine: I. Cognitive, physical, and affective behaviors on fact-based search tasks. *Journal of the American Society for Information Science and Technology, 51*(7), 646–655.

Bilal, D. (2002). Perspectives on children's navigation of the World Wide Web: Does the type of search task make a difference? *Online Information Review, 26*(2),108–117.

Cohen, M. Z., Kahn, D. L., & Steeves, R. H. (2000). *Hermeneutic phenomenological research: A practical guide for nurse practitioners.* Thousand Oaks, CA: Sage Publications.

Davis, M., & Scott, C. (2002). Where does reading fit in citation theory and information seeking? Operalisation of reading: The "black box" of information use. In H. Bruce, R. Fidel, P. Ingwersen, & P. Vakkari, (Eds.), *Emerging frameworks and methods: Proceedings of the Fourth International Conference on Conceptions of Library and Information Science (CoLIS4),* (pp. 301–304). Greenwood Village, CO: Libraries Unlimited.

Harris, R. M., & Dewdney, P. (1994). *Barriers to information: How formal help systems fail battered women.* Westport, CT: Greenwood.

Kuhlthau, C. C. (2004). *Seeking meaning: A process approach to library and information services* (2nd ed.). Westport, CT: Libraries Unlimited.

Kvale, S. (1996). *Interviews: An introduction to qualitative research interviewing.* Thousand Oaks, CA: Sage Publications.

Massey, S. A., Weeks, A. C., & Druin, A. (2005). Initial findings from a three-year international case study exploring children's responses to literature in a digital library. *Library Trends, 54*(3), 245–265.

McKechnie, L. (1996). *Opening the "preschoolers' door to learning": An ethnographic study of the use of public libraries by preschool girls.* Unpublished doctoral dissertation, University of Western Ontario, London, Ontario, Canada.

McKechnie, L. (2000). The ethnographic observation of preschool children. *Library and Information Science Research, 22*(1), 61–76.

McKechnie, L. (2004). "I'll keep them for my children" (Kevin, nine years): Children's personal collections of books and other media. *Canadian Journal of Library and Information Science, 27*(4), 75–90.

Mellon, C. A. (1986). Library anxiety: A grounded theory and its development. *College & Research Libraries, 47*(2), 160–165.

Metoyer-Duran, C. (1991). Information-seeking behavior of gatekeepers in ethnolinguistic communities: Overview of taxonomy. *Library and Information Science Research, 13*(4), 319–346.

Nahl, D. (2004). Measuring the affective information environment of Web searchers. *Proceedings of the 67th annual meeting of the American Society for Information Science & Technology, 41,* 191–197.

Pearce, L. (1997). *Feminism and the politics of reading.* New York: Arnold.

Ross, C. S. (1991). Readers' advisory service: New directions. *RQ, 30*(4), 503–518.

Ross, C. S. (1994). Readers reading L. M. Montgomery. In M. H. Rubio (Ed.), *Harvesting thistles: The textual garden of L. M. Montgomery* (pp. 23–35). Guelph, Ontario: Canadian Children's Literature.

Ross, C. S. (1995). "If they read Nancy Drew, so what?": Series book readers talk back. *Library and Information Science Research, 17*(3), 201–236.

Ross, C. S. (1999). Finding without seeking: The information encounter in the context of reading for pleasure. *Information Processing and Management, 35*(6), 783–799.

Ross, C. S., McKechnie, L., & Rothbauer, P. M. (2006). *Reading matters: What the research reveals about reading, libraries and community.* Westport, CT: Libraries Unlimited.

Rothbauer, P. M. (2004a). *Finding and creating possibility: Reading in the lives of lesbian, bisexual and queer young women.* Unpublished doctoral dissertation, University of Western Ontario, London, Ontario, Canada.

Rothbauer, P. M. (2004b). The Internet in the reading accounts of lesbian and queer young women: Failed searches and unsanctioned reading. *Canadian Journal of Library and Information Science, 27*(3), 89–112.

Rothbauer, P. M. (2004c). "People aren't afraid anymore but it's hard to find books": Reading practices that inform the personal and social identities of self-identified queer and lesbian young women. *Canadian Journal of Library and Information Science, 27*(4), 53–74.

Savolainen, R. (1995). Everyday life information seeking: Approaching information seeking in the context of 'way of life'. *Library and Information Science Research, 17*(3), 259–294.

Strauss, A., & Corbin, J. (1998). *Basics of qualitative research: Techniques and procedures for developing grounded theory* (2nd ed.). Thousand Oaks, CA: Sage Publications.

Van Manen, M. (1990). *Researching lived experience: Human science for an action sensitive pedagogy.* London, Ontario: Althouse Press.

Watson, J. S. (2001). Making sense of the stories of experience: A methodology for research and teaching. *Journal of Education for Library and Information Science, 42*(2), 137–148.

Wiegand, W. (1997). Out of sight, out of mind: Why don't we have schools of library and reading studies? *Journal of Education in Library and Information Science, 38,* 314–326.

Wilson, T. D. (1981). On user studies and information needs. *Journal of Documentation, 37*(1), 3–15. Accessed December 5, 2006, from informationr.net/tdw/publ/papers/1981infoneeds.html.

REFERENCED CHILDREN'S BOOKS

Blume, J. (1998). *Summer sisters: A novel.* New York: Delacorte.

Burton, V. L. (1939). *Mike Mulligan and his steam shovel.* Boston: Houghton Mifflin.

Dahl, R. (1964). *Charlie and the chocolate factory.* New York: Knopf.

Montgomery, L. M. (1908). *Anne of Green Gables.* Toronto: Ryerson Press.

Riddell, E. (1992). *My first day at preschool.* Hauppauge, NY: Barron's.

Robart, R. (1986). *The cake that Mac ate.* Toronto: Kids Can Press.

White, E. B. (1945). *Stuart Little.* New York: Harper Collins.

CHAPTER 11

Memory of Frustrating Experiences

Helena M. Mentis
Pennsylvania State University

INTRODUCTION

As ubiquitous computing grows, computers are migrating from the task-driven workplace into our everyday lives. Information system interaction can occur while watching television, walking down the street with an MP3 player, or sitting in a Wi-Fi café sipping a cappuccino. We can no longer consider efficiency to be the primary concern in all situations. Sometimes—perhaps even most of the time—the user's overall perception of the experience matters more.

Affective research in library science, human–computer interaction, and information science have spent a great deal discussing emotional responses to lost efficiency and the impact on the end goal—whether or not the goal was achieved and how much time was lost due to problems. However, intense emotions can arise throughout a task and not always as a response to a failure. Study of frustration, in particular, has been led by psychological literature, which defines frustration loosely as the thwarting of a goal (Freud, 1921). However all usability incidents thwart goals in some sense, and yet not all of them elicit strong frustration. Clearly, we require a more detailed description of frustration so we can design better information systems for a multitude of domains and experiences.

In order to consider emotion in the design of interactive systems, we need a better understanding of the occurrence of particular emotions with technology. This chapter illustrates a method for gathering evidence of a user's frustrating experiences and a method for categorizing frustrating experiences to better understand what leads to frustration. From these two methods, we learn where frustration can most affect the user experience and thus generalize design guidelines.

Frustration in Psychology

The concept of frustration has its roots with Sigmund Freud. He first postulated the idea of a specific emotion arising in reaction as an obstacle to satisfaction (Freud, 1921). Many psychologists over the years have agreed that frustration is a product of goal attainment being thwarted. Lawson (1965) defined frustration as "the occurrence of an obstacle that prevented the satisfaction of a need." Amsel (1992) classified frustration as the emotion that occurs from a delay of reinforcement. Some theories have stated that the thwarting itself of an action is not the frustrating incident; rather, it is the expectation or anticipation of attainment of the goal that frustrates the actor (Berkowitz, 1978).

The blocking of goals can be internal or external (Shorkey & Crocker, 1981). First posited by Freud, an internal block is a product of the participant not knowing how to complete the goal, whereas an external block is an outside force thwarting the goal (Freud, 1921).

A number of factors influence the level of frustration experienced. The theory of goal commitment states that the importance of a task is related to the belief that it can be attained (Dollard, Doob, Miller, Mowrer, & Sears, 1939). The level of frustration is then linked to the degree of interference with goal attainment, which is based on the severity and unexpectedness of the block (Dollard, et al., 1939). This frustration level could be lower, though, if the user believes the interruption to goal attainment was socially acceptable (Baron, 1977).

Numerous studies have shown that emotionally rich events in one's life are remembered more often and with more clarity and detail (Rapaport, 1950; Revelle & Loftus, 1990; Rubin & Kozin, 1984; Schacter, 1996; White, 1989). Vivid memories have been shown to have attributes of consequentiality and surprise; these attributes seem to induce a greater emotional change than those of non-vivid memories (Rubin & Kozin, 1984). Other studies have supported these findings and assert that the type of emotion is not as important as the level of arousal when the memory is formed (Reisberg, Heuer, McLean, & O'Shaughnessy, 1988).

In addition, emotionally tagged memories seem to be forgotten more slowly than those formed at a time of less intense affect. This slowing of forgetting is thought to be a product of three factors: physiological arousal itself, the distinctiveness of emotional events, and the extra attention and rehearsal that one devotes to emotional events (Heuer & Reisberg, 1990). It is thought that one reflects on emotional events more often than others primarily because they are more "personal" and more closely connected to one's thoughts and feelings (Burke, Heuer, & Reisberg, 1992; Christianson & Loftus, 1991).

Frustration in Information Science

There have been attempts in library and information science and human–computer interaction to quantify where frustration occurs and how it affects efficiency. Before home computers and the Internet, Saracevic, Shaw, and Kantor (1977) observed the causes of user frustration in book acquisition at the library at Case Western University in 1972 and 1974. The researchers identified failures leading to frustration in retrieving library books: acquisition failure, circulation failure, library operations failure, and user error. These failures were categorized by the cause of the failure in which three were a failure of the library, and the fourth was a failure of the patron. Murfin (1980) followed up the Saracevic, et al., study by focusing on periodical accessibility as opposed to book acquisition. Again, the researchers found the same causes of failure and thus frustration. A different type of library study focusing on library card catalog searches discovered that there was a slight interaction between expectations and frustration (Dalrymple, 1990). The study indicates that frustration occurs more often when expectations are heightened.

In a study interested in information behavior, Nahl (2004) introduced a new concept, affective load, which is defined as uncertainty multiplied by time pressure. To work under increasing affective load, a user needs more adequate coping skills, which are a combination of self-efficacy and optimism. If affective load becomes too high, then users will terminate their task. Thus, the more users can manage uncertainty (or perhaps have it managed for them), the more they can reduce their affective load.

In a recent study, Lazar, Jones, Hackley, and Schneiderman (2006) recorded frustrating incidents of 107 student and 50 workplace computer users during their daily computing. The researchers had participants record frustrating incidents in a time diary. The researchers sought to minimize the amount of information lost to underreporting and to maximize the possibility of recording all types of frustration. Their study found that error messages; timed out, dropped, or refused connections; freezes; long download times; and missing or hard-to-find features were the most common frustrating incidents. These incidents were also found to have a large impact on efficiency—users lost one-third to one-fifth of work time to these incidents. The researchers concluded that frustration correlates positively with the amount of time it takes to fix the incident, the amount of time or work lost due to the incident, and the importance of the task.

MOTIVATION AND DESIGN

Since frustration has traditionally been conceptualized as occurring from the thwarting of a goal or from impairing efficiency, one might assume that any computer usability incident would be equally frustrating since all usability incidents thwart a goal. In addition, one might assume that the more critical the usability problem and the longer the time delay, the more intense the frustration. This study sought to challenge these assumptions and determine the types of interactions that most lead to frustration in interactive systems. In addition, the aim was to determine why these interactions cause frustration and how we can design better information systems. In summary, this study addressed the following research questions:

Research Qs

1. What interactions with information systems lead to significant frustration?

    2. Why do these interactions cause frustration?

To this end, four goals in the study design were devised. The primary goal was to not focus on frustration as a result of inefficiency or thwarted goals. The second goal was to gather real-world examples of frustration as opposed to experiments, which focused on contrived goals. The third was to gather those frustrating experiences that had a significant impact on the user. Finally, the fourth goal was to specifically determine at what point during task completion frustration occurs. The following methodology was the result of these four goals.

METHOD

Like much of the work in frustration, the level of analysis for this study was at the individual level. However, unlike most individual level studies, a qualitative methodology was used for both data generation (open-ended questionnaire) and coding. After data generation and coding, the data was quantitatively analyzed through both descriptive and inferential statistics. A grounded theory approach was taken since we wanted to be open to incidents of frustration that other studies have not addressed. However, a positivist epistemological stance was taken in that a causal relationship was expected to emerge from the data.

The research questions were the primary motivation for employing a qualitative inquiry method in this study. There was still uncertainty as to what leads to frustration with technology and how those experiences relate to one another. Qualitative data generation could lead to richer stories behind the statistics and figures since it is more flexible and sensitive to social contexts.

Data Generation

Understanding the occurrence of frustration in this study was best achieved by analyzing what users deem most important in their personal experiences with the technology—what types of incidents are most prominent in their minds. The method of collection was aimed at finding which frustrating experiences from the set of all frustrating experiences significantly affect the user experience. Toward this end, memory of emotional events was chosen to generate data for analysis.

To determine what types of incidents significantly frustrated users, an open-ended questionnaire was used to collect memories of frustrating experiences. The underlying theory is that remembered events are those that are subjectively significant to the individual. Because emotionally laden incidents are the most salient to the user's experience, they will be most clearly remembered.

To collect frustrating experiences, participants were asked to reflect upon their own experiences of frustration while using a variety of applications.

Participants were allowed to decide for themselves what constituted frustration. Since this study primarily concerns a user's memory and perception of incidents, it was felt that the most important definition of frustration came from the user. Negative valence, medium- to high-arousal incidents were sought, which include the emotional states of being annoyed, upset, stressed, nervous, and tense.

Instrument

The instrument used for this study needed to address the following issues: to have the participants remember as many frustrating experiences as possible, to be able to describe them as fully as possible, and to remember incidents using a variety of applications and contexts. To address the first and second issues, participants were given as much time as they needed to recall their experiences with various applications. It was also important to let the users return to using the application in question to better describe the incident. To address the third issue, it was decided that prompting the users to remember using various applications was not going to contaminate the results in an undesirable way. Having the questionnaire online was deemed necessary in order to allow the participants an ample amount of time to recall frustrating experiences in addition to being able to reenact the incident in question for a better description.

A survey was used to determine user demographics and computer experience. The online survey began by asking the participants for their most often used operating system, browser, text editor, and email client, along with their sex and age. Each subsequent page prompted the participant to think back to the use of one of the following: operating systems, browsers, Web sites, text editors, email clients, PDAs, digital video recorders, and any other technology. For each of these categories, the participants were asked to relate any frustrating experiences they remember as descriptively as possible. Participants were allowed to write multiple incidents for each category, or if they had no experience with a particular technology or had no incidents to report, they could skip that category.

Participants

Seventy participants ($n = 70$, 32 men, 38 women) were recruited from two undergraduate communication classes, one undergraduate psychology class, and one graduate psychology class at a large university in the northeastern U.S. The median age of students was 20, with a minimum of 18 and maximum of 45.

Coding the Incidents

Three coding schemes were used to address the research questions: the user's cognitive or physical interaction with the system at the point of frustration, technological cause of remembered incident, and usability severity.

The first coding schema was the User Action Framework (UAF), which categorizes incidents by when it affects the user's cognitive and physical interaction with a system (Hartson, Andre, Williges, & van Rens, 1999). The UAF builds upon Norman's seven stages of actions toward goal attainment (1990). It is based on the user's cognitive and physical interactions with the computer. The Interaction Cycle UAF has five high-level phases: Planning, Translation, Physical Action, Outcome, and Assessment. Table 11.1 shows the issue each phase of the UAF addresses. Success in Planning, Translation, and Assessment relies on the user's cognitive processing of the problem. Physical Action relies on the user's motor systems. Outcome is the system's internal reaction to the user's commands; it is also the only phase not associated with the user's abilities.

Table 11.1   UAF Phases and Issues They Address

Phase of the UAF	Issue It Addresses
Planning	Establishing goals, tasks, and/or intentions
Translation	Translating intentions into plans for physical actions
Physical Action	Making physical input actions
Outcome	System internal response to a user's actions
Assessment	Perceiving, understanding, and evaluating outcome

The designers of the UAF never intended for it to be used in categorizing affective incidents, nor did they address the associated emotions at each one of these stages. However, research shows that the connection between cognitive and affective processes is tightly intertwined. Each cognitive phase of the user in the UAF has an intrinsic emotional connotation. For instance, Planning entails intentions and goal striving, Translation entails prioritizing and assessing actions, and Assessment entails evaluating and qualifying results (Nahl, 2007a). Physical Action is not a cognitive phase and thus has no emotional component, although there could be a physical action that is a result of a prior affective state. Likewise, Outcome has no related emotional component because it is the one phase of the UAF that is not an action of the user. However, this does not mean that there cannot be an emotional reaction to a problem in any one of these phases, since a user constantly evaluates his or her success and each stage of goal attainment.

The second coding schema categorized the incidents by what type of technical issue caused the frustration. This was an open-coding process based on what the participants cited as the reason for their frustration. Some examples of this are pop-up windows and hidden menu items.

The third coding schema rated the incidents' usability severity with a scale based on Nielsen (1994) (1 = mild problem, 2 = moderate problem, 3 = big problem, 4 = showstopper). Nielsen's severity rating scale was a 5-point scale (0 = not a usability problem, 1 = cosmetic problem, 2 = minor problem, 3 = major problem, 4 = catastrophe). These two rating scales are primarily an indication of how long it takes to recover from the incident.

Data Analysis

Each participant gave an average of 5.77 frustrating experiences (ranging from 1 to 11), which yielded a total of 404 incidents to categorize. All of the reported incidents were first coded into one of the five top-level categories of the UAF by two coders (Table 11.2 provides examples of coded incidents in each UAF phase). For this study, a test for intercoder reliability was performed to ensure the validity of the coding. Using 10 percent of the data, two coders had a reliability rating of 90 percent using an approach illustrated in Holsti (1969).

Both descriptive and inferential statistics were used in analyzing the data. Descriptive statistics were first used to summarize the demographic information and results of coding the remembered frustrating experiences in the

Table 11.2   Examples of UAF Frustrating Incident Categorization

Frustrating Incident	UAF Category
It can be hard to locate information on some Web sites because they are not well organized.	Translation
When I'm trying to draw a line, it gets messed up very easily.	Physical Action
I hate making lists in Word because it automatically starts continuing to number your list for you, and I never want to use the format it uses. I then have to fiddle with the format for a while until I get it the way I want it.	Outcome
When I receive an "error" message for some reason, the message is often in computer jargon that I don't understand.	Assessment

three coding schemes. Inferential statistics were used to allow us to draw significant conclusions from the data and generalize the findings to a larger population. The nature of the data generated and coding scheme provided only categorical data to analyze and thus a chi-squared test was used.

FINDINGS

Demographic information from the survey showed that the majority of the respondents used one of the Windows operating systems (n = 66, 94.3 percent). It also showed that the majority of participants used Internet Explorer as a browser (n = 59, 84.3 percent), Microsoft Word as a text editor (n = 66, 94.3 percent), and Eudora (n = 37, 52.9 percent) or Outlook (n = 15, 21.4 percent) as an email client. Thus, this was not a comprehensive sample of all possible issues that arise in every application context that is available to users.

Frustrating Experiences in the UAF Phases

First, the frustrating experiences (n = 404) were categorized into one of the five high-level UAF categories. Figure 11.1 illustrates how the majority of the incidents were in the Outcome phase ($X^2(3, N = 404) = 598.356, p< .001$). This was in sharp contrast to previous work with the UAF, which showed that most usability incidents occur in the Translation phase (Hartson et al., 1999). The difference in UAF categories remained significant for both men and women. No difference was found between the sexes ($X^2(3, N = 404) = 4.167, p = .244$), and both sexes remember more incidents in the Outcome phase.

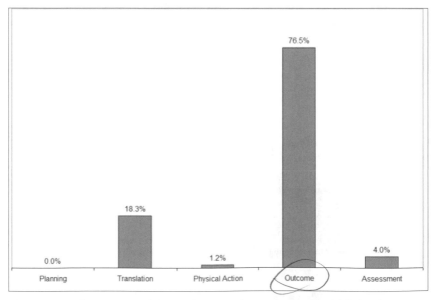

Figure 11.1   Percentage of frustrating experiences in the five high-level UAF categories

An analysis of remembered incidents in each application category was then performed. As can be seen in Figure 11.2, Outcome incidents were significantly more frustrating in operating systems, browsers, Web sites, text editors, and email.

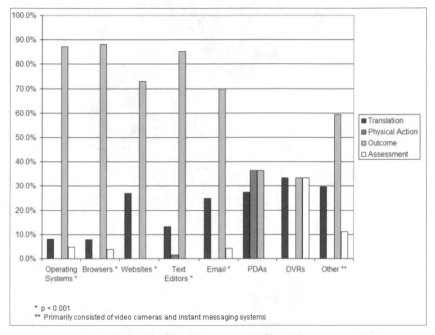

Figure 11.2   Analysis of remembered frustrating incidents in each application category

Cause of Outcome Frustrating Experiences

Next, the Outcome incidents were categorized by type of technical issue that caused the frustration. Figure 11.3 shows that 26.2 percent ($n = 81$) were attributed to specific bugs in the software, 17.2 percent ($n = 53$) were attributed to systems freezing or crashing, 21.7 percent ($n = 67$) were attributed to autoformatting, 13.9 percent ($n = 43$) were attributed to pop-up windows, 12.3 percent ($n = 38$) were attributed to a slow system response, and 8.7 percent ($n = 27$) were attributed to other issues. By virtue of the definition of an Outcome incident, all of these incidents were associated with something outside of the user's locus of control. However, these issues also suggest that many of the remembered Outcome incidents require the users to stop what they are attempting to do in order to address the issue. In other words, they interrupt the users' cognitive flow while trying to achieve a task.

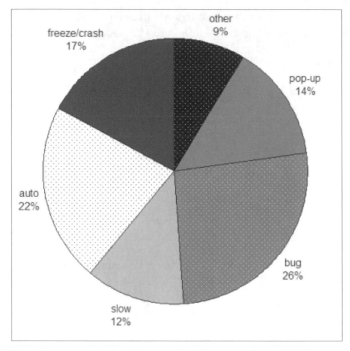

Figure 11.3 Outcome incidents categorized by type of technical issue
that caused the frustration

Frustrating Experiences and Usability Severity

More than a quarter of the reported incidents in Outcome were quite insubstantial. Primarily, they were issues such as pop-up windows or auto-formatting. In addition, 35 percent ($n = 26$) of the Translation issues dealt with wanting a certain feature that was not provided. This type of frustrating incident is also not considered a large usability issue. This highlights that frustrating experiences are not always those that are the largest usability issues and are not simply those that thwart goal attainment the most.

It was found that almost half (47.9 percent, $n = 148$) of the reported incidents in Outcome were categorized as mild usability problems ($X^2(3, N = 309) = 93.913, p < .001$), whereas in Translation, 29.7 percent ($n = 22$) were deemed mild usability problems ($X^2(3, N = 74) = 4.162, p = .244$) and 63.6 percent of these were due to missing features (see Figure 11.4). Thus, it was found that the severity of the usability problem is not a factor in how frustrating the incident is; rather, it is when the usability breakdown occurs.

DISCUSSION

The studies of emotion in information behavior have focused on efficiency and goal-related problems, and thus, they have failed to properly

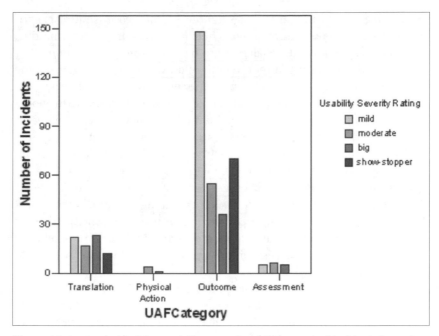

Figure 11.4   Analysis of the usability severity of the reported incidents in each
UAF category

identify emotional design criteria for information systems other than stress-
ing the importance of usability. For instance, all of the studies cited in this
study's literature review conclude that inefficiency or failing to achieve goal
completion are the primary causes of frustration.

In this study, the first coding scheme used to analyze the recalled frustrating experiences, the UAF, has historically shown that the majority of usability
incidents occur in Translation. If usability incidents were the primary cause
of frustration, then we would have seen the same trend when categorizing
the remembered frustrating incidents. However, in this study, frustrating
experiences were recalled more often in Outcome than in the other four
phases. This was found to be true for both sexes, and the same trend was
found across technology types. Even though the recall methodology does not
capture all occurrences of frustration, it does capture those experiences that
are arousing enough to be remembered and related by the user. Thus, there
must be something particularly arousing about frustrating experiences that
occur in the Outcome phase for them to be encoded in the user's memory so
vividly.

The second coding scheme used to analyze the recalled experiences, technical issues that caused the frustrating experience in Outcome, led to an
answer as to why there were so many more remembered frustrating incidents

in Outcome. It showed that the majority of remembered frustrating experiences were attributed to bugs, systems freezing or crashing, autoformatting, and pop-ups. These incidents all seem to have one thing in common: They are unrelated to the user's current cognitive flow, and thus, they interrupt the user's task. These external, frustrating experiences take control away from the user. When users decide on which goal they want to achieve, they plan the steps that are needed to complete that goal. However, when there is an unanticipated interruption, the user has to compensate for that interruption.

The third coding scheme used to analyze the recalled experiences, usability severity, showed that, for Outcome incidents, it is not the severity of the usability incident that determines the level of frustration. For instance, although an autoformatting incident such as bolding a section of text is easily recoverable for a moderately experienced user, it accounts for 21.7 percent of remembered frustrating Outcome incidents. In addition, almost half (47.9 percent) of remembered frustrating experiences in Outcome were mild usability incidents.

When one considers these findings, it is clear that, for the user, interruption may be more important than efficiency. In addition, not immediately knowing how to do something is not always a cause of intense frustration. For instance, most examples of frustrating incidents in Translation were caused by big usability problems or showstoppers. Thus, most Translation incidents are only remembered when they cause big, drawn-out problems, not problems that took a little time to figure out. In contrast, Outcome problems are remembered no matter how big or small a usability problem it was. Thus, external interruptions are shown to detract from the user experience in the user's eyes, no matter how little time it takes away from the task at hand.

Interaction Design and Information Behavior Implications

These findings suggest that in order to mitigate frustration, one should concentrate on preventing problems in the Outcome phase. Interruption's effect on frustration seems to be an important finding, especially for intelligent and responsive systems. Responses of a system should not interrupt the user's cognitive flow and should not take control away from the user. If a system response could possibly be intrusive, then allow the user to regain control easily since these interruptions are remembered by the users and color their perception of the experience of using the system.

Another guideline from these findings is not to interrupt the experience in which the technology is being used. The experience of writing a letter is about expressing oneself and creating meaningful sentences, as opposed to using the text editing software. Thus, designers should strive to create technology that enhances and does not interrupt already enjoyable experiences.

There is one possible exception to the rule of decreasing interruption. An instance where interruption might be useful could be when a user is experiencing such a high level of frustration that they are stuck in a negative cognitive loop. For example, if a user continues to choose the same menu item to format their text document, then they are most likely stuck in a continuous loop facilitated by the negative affect, and thus, they would need to be interrupted or broken out of that cycle to be able to rethink their approach to the task at hand.

A number of studies could be done to support or invalidate these research findings. One would be to conduct a more expansive collection of recalled frustrating experiences across a variety of operating systems, applications, and technological experiences. In addition, an analysis of frustration incidents gathered by the Lazar, et al. (2006) method should be done to determine if all frustrating experiences are found to be in Outcome—not only those which are significant enough to be remembered. This would also allow for determining if frequency of occurrence is more to blame for these remembered incidents. In addition, since the majority of incidents were in the Outcome phase, it would be beneficial to categorize them in the subsequent levels of the UAF to get a more finite understanding.

To design for emotion, we need a better understanding of the occurrence of particular emotions in an information systems environment. From this study, we have learned that we cannot just assume that bad usability leads to frustration or that the psychological literature provides adequate guidelines for interaction design. From results such as those provided in this chapter, we have ascertained a deeper understanding of users' emotional interactions with technology and can begin to design emotional interfaces.

REFERENCES

Amsel, A. (1992). *Frustration theory*. Cambridge: Cambridge University Press.

Berkowitz, L. (1978). Whatever happened to the frustration-aggression hypothesis? *American Behavioral Scientist, 32*, 691–708.

Baron, R. A. (1977). *Human aggression*. New York: Plenum.

Burke, A., Heuer, F., & Reisberg, D. (1992). Remembering emotional events. *Memory & Cognition, 20*, 277–290.

Christianson, S. A., & Loftus, E. (1991). Remembering emotional events: The fate of detailed information. *Cognition & Emotion, 5*, 81–108.

Dalrymple, P. W. (1990). Retrieval by reformulation in two library catalogs: Toward a cognitive model of searching behavior. *Journal of the American Society for Information Science, 41*(4), 272–281.

Dollard, J., Doob, L. W., Miller, N. E., Mowrer, O. H., & Sears, R. R. (1939). *Frustration and aggression*. New Haven, CT: Yale University Press.

Freud, S. (1921). Types of onset and neurosis. In J. Strachey (Ed. & Trans.), *The standard edition of the complete psychological works of Sigmund Freud: Vol. 12. Case history of Schreber, papers on technique and other works (1911–1913)* (pp. 227–230). London: Hogarth Press.

Hartson, H. R., Andre, T. S., Williges, R. C., & van Rens, L. (1999). The user action framework: A theory-based foundation for inspection and classification of usability problems. In H. J. Bullinger & J. Ziegler (Eds.), *Proceedings of the Eighth International Conference on Human–Computer Interaction. September 24–29, 1999, Munich, Germany* (pp. 1058–1062). Mahwah, NJ: Lawrence Erlbaum Associates.

Heuer, F., & Reisberg, D. (1990). Vivid memories of emotional events: The accuracy of remembered minutiae. *Memory & Cognition, 18,* 496–506.

Holsti, O. R. (1969). *Content analysis for the social sciences and humanities.* Reading, MA: Addison-Wesley Publishing Co.

Lawson, R. (1965). *Frustration: The development of a scientific concept.* New York: MacMillan.

Lazar, J., Jones, A., Hackley, M., & Schneiderman, B. (2006). Severity and impact of computer user frustration: A comparison of student and workplace. *Interacting with Computers, 18*(2), 187–207.

Murfin, M. E. (1980). The myth of accessibility: Frustration and failure in retrieving periodicals. *Journal of Academic Librarianship, 6*(1), 16–19.

Nahl, D. (2004). Measuring the affective information environment of Web searchers. *Proceedings of the 67th annual meeting of the American Society for Information Science & Technology, 41,* 191–197.

Nahl, D. (2007a). A discourse analysis technique for charting the flow of micro-information behavior. *Journal of Documentation, 63*(3): 323–339.

Nielsen, J. (1994). *Usability inspection methods.* New York: John Wiley & Sons.

Norman, D. A. (1990). *Design of everyday things.* New York: Doubleday.

Rapaport, D. (1950). *Emotions and memory.* New York: International Universities Press.

Reisberg, D., Heuer, G., McLean, J., & O'Shaughnessy, M. (1988). The quantity, not the quality, of affect predicts memory vividness. *Bulletin of the Psychonomic Society, 26,* 100–103.

Revelle, W., & Loftus, D. A. (1990). Individual differences and arousal: Implications for the study of mood and memory. *Cognition and Emotion, 4,* 209–237.

Rubin, D. C., & Kozin, M. (1984). Vivid memories. *Cognition, 16,* 81–95.

Saracevic, T., Shaw, W. M., & Kantor, P. B. (1977). Causes and dynamics of user frustration in an academic library. *College and Research Libraries, 38,* 7–18.

Schacter, D. L. (1996). *Searching for memory.* New York: Basic Books.

Shorkey, C. T., & Crocker, S. B. (1981). Frustration theory: A source of unifying concepts for generalist practice. *Social Work, 26,* 374–379.

White, R. T. (1989). Recall of autobiographical events. *Applied Cognitive Psychology, 3,* 127–136.

CHAPTER 12

Understanding the Information Behavior of Stay-at-Home Mothers Through Affect

Karen E. Fisher and Carol F. Landry
University of Washington

INTRODUCTION

In her February 21, 2005 *Newsweek* article "Mommy Madness," Judith Warner explained that women who stay at home with their babies can "live in a state of virtual, crazy-making isolation because [they] can't afford a nanny, there is no such thing as part-time day care, and husband[s] [don't] come home until 8:30 at night." According to a 2004 U.S. Census Bureau press release, an estimated 5.4 million women were stay-at-home mothers (SAHMs) in 2003. However, virtually no basic research has examined their information behavior (IB), i.e., how people need, seek, give, manage, and use information (Pettigrew, Fidel, & Bruce, 2001) for everyday situations. Little is known about the role information plays in their everyday lives and, specifically, how affect—or the more emotive right brain manner of thinking—influences their information seeking and giving. In this chapter, following an overview of conceptual developments in the field regarding affect, we share findings from a recent field study of 20 SAHMs with emphasis on how their information worlds are founded upon and spin around aspects of affect.

AFFECT AS A LENS FOR UNDERSTANDING INFORMATION BEHAVIOR

Affect as a lens for understanding information behavior has always lurked predominantly in the field's theoretical shadows. As discussed by Fisher (2006) and Pettigrew et al. (2001), while the 1980s bore a paradigm shift from a system-centered to a user-centered approach, the theories and models of the day focused primarily upon cognition. This banner ironically included Dervin's Sense-Making, Kuhlthau's information search process, and Wilson's information need and seeking model (Wilson, 1999)—three frameworks were instrumental in the identification and development of "affect" as a concept for understanding IB but were known at the time for their emphasis on users' cognitive stages. Dervin and Fraser (1985) identified 16 "helps" or ways that people benefited from libraries that were largely entwined with affect, including obtaining feelings of confirmation, hopefulness, happiness, and pleasure, or simply feeling connected. Through her research with students, Kuhlthau (1991, 2004) delineated affect—along with thoughts (cognition) and action—as one of three types of stages that information seekers experience. Wilson (1981) was a forerunner in identifying a person's affective needs as a key component in understanding his or her overall information seeking behavior.

The context-based or social frameworks of the 1990s, as discussed by Pettigrew et al. (2001), moved the field forward by asserting that information behavior occurs in social contexts and involves multiple people, thus illustrating that individuals do not seek information in a vacuum. This social constructionist lens was advocated by Tuominen and Savolainen (1997) and naturally complemented the growing interest in affect. One of the field's foremost investigators, Chatman (2000) proposed three different frameworks: information poverty, life in the round, and normative behavior—all of which were heavily conceptualized around affect and grew from her everyday life fieldwork with varied populations, including the working poor, janitors, female prison inmates, and elderly women. Regarding the last, for example, Chatman reported that fear of exposure of needing outside assistance prevented elderly women from openly expressing their situations and seeking information. The cumulative effect of these and other IB studies led Harris and Dewdney (1994, p. 26) to identify as their fifth principle of everyday life information seeking that "information-seekers expect emotional support" from information systems. They further elaborated that sympathy and support are valued as much by people as the information needed to resolve a situation, and that people gain greater satisfaction when information providers/systems consider affective aspects. In confirmation, Pettigrew (2000) concluded from her use of Granovetter's (1982) strength of weak ties (SWT) framework that seniors were drawn to nurses at Canadian foot clinics because they possessed both strong and weak tie attributes. For example, they provided access to everyday information that seniors could not obtain from other sources in ways that seniors associated with close family and friends. This characteristic enabled nurses to meet seniors' affective and social needs as well as their information needs. Thus, Pettigrew's findings supported the claims that affect is a major factor in information behavior and that multiple people are involved emotionally. She also proposed the information grounds (1999; c.f., Fisher & Naumer, 2006) framework for understanding interpersonal IB, and hence, emotive interactions in social settings. From her extensive studies since the late 1990s, Nahl (2005) analyzed concurrent self-reports and quantitative ratings of learners engaged in searching and problem-solving to develop the theory of affective load, which proposes "that all information behavior involves affective states that provide specific goal-directionality and motivation to support cognitive activity" (p. 41). Regarding professional practice in library and information science (LIS), Radford (1999) addressed nonverbal communication in reference transactions and confirmed Harris and Dewdney's (1994) earlier conclusion that how information is provided can be as important as the information itself.

Further confirmation of growing interest in affect is evident in Julien and Duggan's (2000) analysis of the 1984–1989 and 1995–1998 needs and uses literature, wherein one-third of articles addressed the affective dimension of information behavior. However, a subsequent review revealed that researchers paid scant attention to affective variables, which is noteworthy given the increased attention demonstrated by such wide-ranging disciplines as medicine, psychology, communication, marketing, and gender studies (Julien, McKechnie, & Hart, 2005). Despite this finding, Julien and colleagues acknowledged that LIS researchers have a "long standing recognition of the ways in which affect influences human information behavior" (p. 456) and cite many contributions to this area of study. Drawing on the grounded research of various disciplines and her investigation of children's information seeking, Bilal (2005) discusses the emergence of the "affective paradigm" and justifies the need for such a model in LIS research and specifically in information behavior.

STUDIES OF STAY-AT-HOME MOTHERS

Studies of stay-at-home mothers have been conducted by social scientists largely interested in the issues, attitudes, and the merits of staying at home against those of mothers who work outside (e.g., Boyd, 2002; Etaugh & Moss, 2001; Forgays, Ottaway, Guarino, & D'Alessio, 2001; Gorman & Fritzsche, 2002; Johnston & Swanson, 2004; Riday, 2003). In other studies, Johnston and Swanson (2003) focused on how popular magazines represent mothers; Rashley (2005) studied how questions of gender equity are expressed by parents at the Web site BabyCenter; Zimmerman (2000) examined feelings of marital equality and satisfaction of SAHMs and stay-at-home fathers; and Maatita (2003) explored how motherhood is manifested in the social setting of playgroups. In Library and Information Science (LIS), Guillaume and Bath (2004), and Helliwell (2003) concentrated on the health information needs of parents, while Nicholas and Marden (1998) explored the general information needs of parents. Through interviews and focus groups with 58 individuals in the U.K., Nicholas and Marden found the most requested topics concerned health, child development, school, children's behavior and careers, training, and education; while significant differences existed among the needs of single mothers, older women, fathers, and ethnic minority parents. Parents cited information currency and authority as important, and they used a range of sources; however, oral sources (professionals, friends, family) were valued most, while public libraries were not viewed as a source for parental information. Nicholas and Marden thus concluded that parents' information needs about schools, finance, and child behavior go largely unmet.

Non-LIS studies that come closest to examining SAHMs' information behavior are Tardy (2000), Tardy and Hale (1998), and Walsh (2002). Tardy used Goffman's (1959) work on regional behaviors to conduct participant observation, interviews, and surveys with 24 mothers at a mother-toddler playgroup. Consistent with Goffman, she found that boundaries existed between public and private presentation of self, and that the regions of front stage, backstage, and back-backstage could be used to explain participants' discussion of health issues, engagement in inappropriate or taboo talk, and how they define and exemplify the role of the "good" mother. Using the same data set and Roger's diffusion theory as a lens, Tardy and Hale focused on how mothers seek health information, and argued that there has been a research bias toward groups that have been marked by illness such that the more mundane interactions of individuals who are not facing critical problems have been ignored. In addition, Tardy and Hale commented on "a bias against informational support" versus emotional support (p. 337). For example, medical self-help groups concentrate on supporting the psychosocial needs of members in preference to their informational needs. Consequently, participants who currently have strong emotional networks but also seek information from the groups feel their specific needs go unmet. To understand how mothers seek information around the topic of spanking, Walsh conducted telephone interviews with 998 mothers and found that one-third of them rated information from workshops, pediatricians, newspapers and magazines, and books as "very important," while family and friends were rated less than 15 percent. Of note, mothers were more likely to spank when they perceived more intense messages to spank, less intense messages opposing spanking, had younger children, and were of lower socioeconomic status.

Two other non-LIS studies of particular interest are Drentea and Moren-Cross (2005) and Blackford (2004). Interested in whether virtual communities in cyberspace foster social capital and social support, Drentea and Moren-Cross used participant observation and discourse analysis to study a mothering discussion board on a parents' Web site. They found three main types of communication: emotional support, instrumental support (formal and informal), and community building and protection—all of which they claimed contributed to the creation and maintenance of social capital. A key finding here is that mothers gave and received emotional support as part of information sharing. Blackford's (2004) use of Foucault's concept of panopticism to understand the enactment of mothering in suburban and commercial playgrounds also provides interesting fodder for understanding SAHMs' information behavior. Blackford asserts that the mothers sitting in the ring of park benches symbolize the suggestion of surveillance (described by Foucault as the technology of disciplinary power under liberal ideals of governance).

According to Blackford, however, the mothers' panoptic force is a community that "gazes at the children only to ultimately gaze at one another, seeing reflected in the children the parenting abilities of one another" (p. 227). Blackford also analyzed the elaborate rules of playground etiquette and social competition that occupied the mothers, linking their social discourses to the public neighborhood playground as a symbol for child-centered (suburban) ideology.

In sum, little research has addressed the information worlds of SAHMs—at least from an LIS perspective. The scant, unsystematic research to date suggests that SAHMs have substantial information needs though little is known about the range of these needs, how they emerge, how they are (or are not) met, and how SAHMs share information with others—all against a backdrop of largely social isolation and constantly emerging new situations.

THE PRESENT STUDY

The current study was part of a larger investigation funded by the National Science Foundation (NSF) about interpersonal information seeking, specifically, why people turn to other people when seeking everyday information. SAHMs were selected as one of two populations for study (the other was tweens, kids ages 9–13) as it was hypothesized that they have continuous but wide-ranging information needs due to their manifold roles as mothers, and yet have access to few resources due to their social isolation (including severed ties with co-workers, and the tendency of living far apart from family ties) as a result of being at home. Constant interruptions, long hours, and other factors also propelled the notion of SAHMs occupying an information world characterized by information poverty.

Chatman's theories of information poverty (1996, 2000) and normative behavior (2000), along with Fisher's information grounds (c.f., Fisher & Naumer, 2006) and Harris and Dewdney's (1994) principles of everyday information behavior, were used to guide data collection and analysis. Wilson's revised general model of information behavior (1981, 1997) was also employed during the analytic stage to help make sense of the data. (While information ground theory and our respective findings are shared later due to their focus on affect and social interactions, our use of the other frameworks are discussed in-depth elsewhere.)

Research Questions

Research questions guiding our study are as follows:

- What roles do SAHMs assume on a given day?

- What types of everyday information do SAHMs seek in their everyday lives?

- How do SAHMs seek everyday information?

- What criteria do SAHMs use in assessing and sharing information and information sources?

- How do SAHMs feel when seeking or giving information?

- What are SAHMs' information grounds?

Data were collected over two stages. Stage one involved unobtrusive and participant observation by three observers (recruited from the Information in Everyday Context (IBEC) team) at a weekly mother-baby class and a parent support group. An observation checklist was used to facilitate the reporting of information sharing. For each incident, observers noted such issues as who was involved, who said what to whom, how people reacted to the exchange, whether another sharing incident followed as a result, what types of emotions were attached to the exchange of information, etc. To further understand participants' seeking and sharing of information, observers recorded how well participants knew one another, if they arrived early or stayed late, and whether or not amenities such as food influenced the information process.

In stage two, SAHMs participated in three audio-recorded interviews. To qualify, a woman must have been a full-time SAHM for at least six months. SAHMs were recruited from the mom-baby classes and through announcements posted on a community listserv. Interviews, consisting primarily of open-ended questions, were carried out at the SAHMs' homes, mom-baby classes, a hotel, the university, or by telephone. Interviews lasted about 60 minutes and were scheduled one to two weeks apart. Toys were provided for young children, and participants were compensated $30 for their involvement with the study. Audio recordings were transcribed and coded using Atlas.ti, a qualitative data-analysis program.

To determine which sources SAHMs turned to for everyday information, participants were asked to identify the types of roles or the different hats they wear daily, such as nurse, disciplinarian, or educator. Of these, one or two roles were selected as the focus for discussion of associated information needs. SAHMs were prompted to reveal what they needed to know in relation to a specific role, what prompted the need, where they turned to for information and why, whether the source was helpful and why or why not, and if not helpful, what did SAHM do next? Furthermore, participants were asked to indicate if they had used the source before, would they use it again, and whether or not they shared the information with another. According to Leckie and Pettigrew (1997) and supported by Wicks (1999), roles exhibit significant influence over sources chosen in the information seeking process.

To learn how information seeking was influenced by "place," moms were asked about their information grounds (IG) or places that they go where people are present and information is shared. This step afforded the opportunity to ascertain how SAHMs encountered information at their information grounds, the types of information learned, how frequently they visited their information grounds, what they liked about the place, and how useful the obtained information was for participants. As discussed by Fisher and Naumer (2006), most everyone can report having at least one IG.

SAHMs' everyday information giving and seeking was further explored during the second and third interviews as participants were provided with a diary in which to record information incidents. Diaries enabled SAHMs to document what they needed to know, what prompted the need, and how they felt about their information while seeking or sharing information independent of their daily roles or information grounds. (As a methodological note, the information diary was less effective as a data collection tool than was anticipated. Some mothers did not follow through with the diary since it was misplaced or forgotten about. Other mothers did not always know what to write down because they did not see information in terms of everyday needs, while others endeavored to record their scores of daily minutia. However, the diaries did serve their purpose of recording discussion points and prompts.)

Data Trustworthiness

Data trustworthiness (reliability and validity) was ensured by several measures (c.f., Chatman, 1992; Lincoln & Guba, 1985). Dependability (or reliability) was ensured through: (1) consistent note-taking, (2) exposure to multiple and different situations using triangulated methods, (3) comparing emerging themes with findings from related studies, (4) audio-recording interviews, (5) employing intracoder checks, and (6) analyzing the data for incidents of observer effect. Validity was tracked as follows:

- Face validity: asked whether observations fit an expected or plausible frame of reference

- Criterion/internal validity (or credibility): (1) pre-tested instruments, (2) prolonged engagement in field, (3) rigorous note-taking, (4) triangulated methods, (5) peer debriefing, (6) negative case analysis, and (7) member checks or participant verification

- External validity: provided "thick description" and comprehensive description of our methods and theory so that others can determine if our findings can be compared with theirs

- Construct validity: examined data with respect to information behavior principles and theories of information poverty and information grounds

Learning and adopting participants' "language" (e.g., play dates, meltdowns) greatly improved the efficiency of the study and increased the trustworthiness of the data. By employing interview and observational methods, we listened for and adopted the participants' languages, thus allowing for subsequent interpretation from the participants' perspectives. In the remainder of this paper, we share our findings regarding the role of affect in the mothers' information behavior.

SAHMS AND THE AFFECTIVE ASPECTS OF INFORMATION AND EVERYDAY LIFE

SAHMs and the affective aspects of information and everyday life were investigated by recruiting 20 stay-at-home mothers from Washington State, Iowa, and New Jersey. Of these, 18 were married and their average age was 37.6 years (ranging from 30 to 45 years). Children ranged in age from newborn to 18 years, and families included between one and four children (with an average of two children per family). SAHMs were typically well-educated: 11 held bachelor of arts or science degrees, four held master's degrees, and one attained a PhD. Previous occupations reflected their education level, with 37 percent working in management and real estate, 32 percent employed in such fields as teaching, social work, or writing, and 32 percent were clerical, technician, or student. Income varied from low to high, and only two mothers were single parents.

The basic roles that the mothers identified themselves as playing included housekeeper and laundress, planner and social organizer, cook, nurse, disciplinarian, entertainer, gardener, shopper, bookkeeper, chauffer, teacher, etc. Subsequent routine daily tasks included cooking, cleaning, playing with or reading to their children, running errands, exercising, and taking children to and from school (their children's daily activities entailed playing, napping, eating, reading, and school). As the participants reported, each role and its inherent tasks were associated with particular information needs. As further revealed through data analysis, each role and its related tasks, and hence, information behavior, were also embodied by affect (Table 12.1).

Throughout our daily lives, emotions influence how we communicate with others to how we view the world around us. Towne and Adler (1996) identified 132 emotions, whereas Petress and Harrington (n.d.) compiled 152 on their list. Our analysis of field notes, interview, and diary data determined that SAHMs communicated 25 emotions associated with their information behavior, however, specific affect presented more frequently than others (Figure 12.1). Affect was inferred from the data based on the words, tone of voice, and body language of the moms as they spoke of their information seeking and sharing. Similar forms of affect were collapsed into a single category to minimize the list but not the nuance of the affective experience. An example of this coding strategy is represented by the unhappy/sad/sorrow category.

Table 12.1 Overview of Participants' Demographics and Information Seeking and Giving Topics

SAHM	Age	No. of Kids	Previous Job	Example of Info Seeking and Sharing	Affect Examples
Judy	41	2	Apartment Manager	Organic blueberries	Frustrated that no local, organic u-pick blueberry farms exist in the area
				House painting	"Creeped-out" that painter was more interested in her 3-year-old twin boys than painting job
Lisa	38	2	PR Director	Laughing gas	Worried that young daughter may be overexposed to nitrous oxide or laughing gas at dental appointment
				Child's independence	Relieved to learn child was old enough that SAHM did not need to accompany her to restroom now
Cadence	40	4	Commercial Underwriter	Anorexia nervosa	Angry husband did not tell his parents about daughter's anorexia nervosa, making SAHM do it
				Bulimia	Trust friend's advice since she has had to cope with bulimia most of her life
Sheila	41	1	Payroll	Lesbianism	Disagreed with sister-in-law's views on lesbianism, particularly as an influence on SAHM's daughter
				Welt on baby's bottom	Fearful that baby's welt was serious, going to get worse, possibly cause anaphylactic shock
Ginny	42	2	Social Worker	YMCA camp	Happy that "Adventurers" camp was something that daughter and husband could do together
				Handbag	Disappointed that "totally cute" handbag was out-of-stock one week after SAHM had seen it
Laura	37	2	Database Designer	Sale of parents' home	Resented that brothers did not listen when SAHM identified a problem with parents' allocation of funds
				Baby's urinary reflux	Confused by medical jargon presented in PubMed compared to lay language presented by Google
Trista	45	4	Secretary	Death of young boy	Surprised to learn of boy's sudden death from cancer when SAHM was previously told he was recovering
				Autism	Empowered to provide info to woman responding to SAHM's letter to the editor about autism
Renee	38	2	Hearing and Speech	Biracial children	Reassured talking with biracial friend that positive life experience was possible for SAHM's biracial children

Table 12.1   (cont.)

				Child's speech problems	Felt social cost of son's speech problems as info would likely stigmatize child
Isabella	39	2	Freelance writer	Attention deficit disorder (ADD)	Irritated that doctor told SAHM she was diagnosing husband's ADD when it was diagnosed 5 years earlier
				Italian lessons	Empowered to find a native-speaking Italian willing to teach language to both SAHM's children
Alonsa	34	2	Teacher	Child's preschool	Optimistic about chosen preschool because teachers have been there a long time
				Playgroup	Disappointed mom-baby class was not conducive to helping form a playgroup with other moms
Avery	45	3	Geologist	Provisional license	Doubts son is driving to a place while friend takes bus, provisional license allows no passengers
				Psychogenic mushrooms	Angry that teenager obtained illegal drugs without thinking about consequences that it engenders
Bonnie	35	2	Office Manager	World religions	Curious about world religions so SAHM reads library book brought home for her children
				Starting a business	Stressed about learning to budget money for new business teaching improvisation
Marilee	41	2	Real Estate	Providing job info	Happy to be able to offer friend better job options than was available with his existing position
				Wood finish for porch	Anticipated carpenter will give good information on outdoor wood finish to protect new porch
Melissa	40	1	Software Designer	Challenges of motherhood	Grateful to hear other moms reveal that it is normal to not have everything be perfect as a mother
				Tiny baby	Reassured to learn that preeclampsia will not have a long-term effect on baby's overall growth
Sonya	31	1	Registrar	Testimonials on Internet	Doubts the veracity of testimonials presented by people on the Internet
				Wine	Appreciated the infectious enthusiasm for the subject by a knowledgeable employee in the wine department
Laureen	36	2	Bank Manager	House-hunting	Excited to look for and learn if family could afford home in a desirable new town
				Immunizations	Empowered to investigate child's immunization schedule

Table 12.1 (cont.)

					rather than submitting to doctor's order
Jackee	34	2	Graphic Designer	Gymnastic class	Happy to learn that her daughter can attend gymnastic class at age 4 rather than the customary age 5
				Croup	Confused why information found on the Internet did not work well for her daughter's croup
Eva	31	1	Software Test Manager	Childrearing experiences	Felt safe sharing child-rearing experiences with moms as they understand, they have been there
				Safety locks	Worried baby will hurt self by smashing fingers in cabinet doors
Kaylene	30	1	Graduate Student	Strollercize class	Irritated that staff at the YMCA didn't even know about the strollercize class being offered by the Y
				Car burglary	Angry to find SAHM's car had been burgled sometime in night
Naya	34	1	Teacher	Alternative medicine	Disappointed that daughter's pediatrician discounted the value of alternative medicine
				Breastfeeding	Empowered to affect a mom's decision to stop nursing by sharing that SAHM just discontinued it

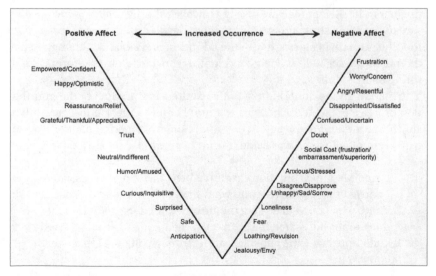

Figure 12.1   Affect Experience by SAHMs

As indicated in Figure 12.1, empowerment was a significant affective aspect of the information process and encompassed such facets as having the ability to affect decision-making, the confidence to find something out for oneself, and the ability to provide information to others. Demonstrating the importance of this affective dimension was Marilee,[1] a 41-year-old mother of two boys (ages 4 and 6 years), who left her job as a real estate agent following the birth of her first child. Marilee acknowledged a feeling of empowerment as she "countered some of that tendency to be a shrinking violet" following an informative conversation with her neighbor concerning different personalities and confrontational relationships. Avery's 16-year-old son rethought his decision to make a 3 AM trip to the airport with fellow teenagers after she "asked the questions to help him make the right decision." As a mother of three teenage boys, 45-year-old Avery found communicating with the middle son difficult. She asserted that he did not listen to her, while he claimed that Avery was unreasonable when she expressed concerns regarding his decisions. Following the son's announcement that he and four friends intended to take a buddy to the airport early one morning, Avery felt empowered to affect her son's decision making by asking him about such issues as sleep, driving with provisional licenses, speeding on wide-open highways, and "doing things that probably aren't the smartest thing in the world" when nothing is open at 5 AM. Renee, on the other hand, felt emboldened to provide information concerning an adoption attorney to an acquaintance. As a recent newcomer to Washington State, 38-year-old Renee did not know many people as her two small children keep her busy and her current pregnancy had left her feeling poorly. However, she had met a few women by way of her Bible study group. Through conversations, one woman revealed that she was moving forward with the adoption process and, although Renee did not know her well, she felt confident to provide relevant information to this woman.

Irritation and frustration frequently resulted as a product of the information process for SAHMs. Choosing to forgo her low wage, clerical-type job to stay home with her baby boy, 31-year-old Sonya claimed to neither like nor trust technology, which was evident from her efforts to locate a nearby park:

> I used Mapquest but didn't get anywhere. I was highly frustrated, annoyed that I wasn't getting what I needed from the Internet ... That's why I don't like using the Internet. If I don't get it right, if I don't input the search info correctly, then I don't get what I need and I don't have the patience to sort through all the garbage that comes up.

Similarly, 40-year-old Melissa considered herself an intelligent woman who had previously worked in the field of information technology. She relied on scientific and verifiable data to meet most of her information needs.

Consequently, Melissa experienced both anger and resentment when she and her 9-month-old daughter took their cat to the vet because of its urination problems. Melissa cared for her cat for seven years and believed she knew it well, so it outraged her when the vet "talk[ed] to me as if I just fell off the turnip truck or like I had never seen a cat before." Social cost also presented as a product of the information process. For example, Trista is an information monitor (c.f., Baker, 2005), a widow and mother of four living in a rural community of 350 people. This 45-year-old SAHM enjoyed staying informed by spending hours on her computer reading newsletters, visiting nontraditional news sites, receiving email, and participating in an assortment of listservs. Trista considered herself an activist for a variety of causes. She also recognized that her interests and causes cost her socially since others had labeled her as "opinionated" and "superior." Trista used to participate in online discussion boards until one too many members responded that "Well, you know, not everyone is as perfect as you are." She defends herself, stating, "I like people to be informed. I can't stand being around ignorant people," but in the end, she felt penalized as a result of her information seeking and sharing.

Worry and concern motivated many SAHMs to seek information. Marilee was highly concerned with the avian flu pandemic since "my kids are exposed to a lot at school." Judy, a 41 year old, found it disconcerting to witness one of her 3-year-old twin boys jump into the lake and take "in a mouthful of water and start flailing around," while the family was at a local beach. Worry triggered the former manager to seek information on children's flotation devices. Confusion also resulted from information seeking. Sheila, a 41-year-old SAHM who was pregnant with her second child, found she could not put her baby in daycare and return to doing payroll once her maternity leave ended. During Sheila's mother-baby class, she conveyed confusion over the administration of alcohol to a fussy baby. A friend had promoted the use of crème de menthe for just such a situation, while the class facilitator opposed such a prescription. Sheila acknowledged that she did not know crème de menthe was alcohol but was now uncertain how to handle her fussy baby.

Positive affect was found in abundance among SAHMs as well. Ginny elected to become a SAHM when her work situation as a medical social worker deteriorated due to staff reductions and daycare costs for two children consumed most of her paycheck. At age 42, Ginny has been caring for her children full time for four years. Recently, her 7-year-old son reminded her that she had promised to buy an invisible ink pen. Not knowing where to look for this item, Ginny asked a woman and her young son at the mall if they knew where to find an invisible ink pen. She was delighted that the boy could tell her where to buy one. Similarly, Jackee, a 34-year-old mother of two little girls, was excited to learn that Amazon.com offered a child's "plasma car" for half the price of that found on eBay. Her daughter had become quite fond of this toy at a friend's house and wanted one of her own. Many SAHMs also sought confirmation over children's behavioral, attitudinal, or developmental issues. Lisa, who left her public relations job "to be there for her children," felt reassured about her 8-year-old daughter's behavior after talking to a friend regarding her "kid doing something weird." She learned from this mom that "my kid ate dog food, too, and lived to tell about it." Humor, too, results from information. Naya, a 34-year-old former schoolteacher and mother of a toddler, found her sister-in-law's comment concerning the arrival of a second child as being "not just twice as hard but ten times as hard," an amusing anecdote for her *not* to have an additional child.

SAHMs indicated that affect is an integral part of their everyday information behavior. It can drive the information process, as was the case for 40-year-old Cadence, whose concern over her teenage daughter's anorexia nervosa/bulimia motivated her to seek nutritional and counseling information. Cadence gave up her commercial underwriting career to become a stay-at-home mother for her husband's two kids and, subsequently, her own two children. She describes her 15-year-old stepdaughter as "having issues" since her mother died when the girl was age 2. The daughter does not like the two younger kids and simply grunts rather than talk to her parents. Although not diagnosed, Cadence believes this girl also suffers from obsessive-compulsive disorder (OCD), which may be associated with her anorexia nervosa/bulimia. The anorexia, or simply not eating, presented two years ago, but it is now accompanied with the "throwing up" symptom of bulimia. Cadence's concern is notable in the following:

> I need to go find information about nutrition. Not that she's going to listen to me, or anybody, because this is what teenagers are like. But like, what kind of damage does this do to your body, what is this going to mean for you down the road … It's a lifetime thing. So I want to help her get control over it.

Affect was also found to be a product of information process. For Ginny, it was revulsion when her 7-year-old son wanted a pet snake. Ginny went online to research milk snakes. After learning that they grow to 6 feet in length and eat live mice, she said to her son, "Honey, I can't do that. I can't have a snake that's going to—that we have to feed mice. I can't do it." Lisa, however, has been a member in her women's group for about seven years. Over the years, the women have discussed many issues and shared personal information about themselves and their families. At their last meeting, the subject of birth control came up, and Lisa was saddened to learn just how many of these women had chosen abortion as a means of birth control. The information affected her to the extent that she claimed, "I wish I didn't know that [about them]."

Finally, information can encompass an affective range. For example, 30-year-old Kaylene experienced a multitude of emotion concerning her 18-month-old daughter's lack of growth. Kaylene became a full-time, stay-at-home mother after completing her PhD in genetics. Concern for her daughter's well-being prompted Kaylene to stay home as the little girl was frequently sick at daycare. Prior to Kaylene's graduation, she observed that her daughter was not growing. Worry motivated her to take the baby to the doctor, where she became angry when the doctor was neither helpful nor concerned about her lack of growth. Furthermore, Kaylene felt stressed that her child's health issue arose at the same time she was preparing to defend her doctoral dissertation, frustrated that she was not able to get answers, and finally relieved when she learned that the problem was partially associated with illness and partially due to the little girl adopting her own growth curve.

SAHMS' INFORMATION GROUNDS

SAHMs sought everyday information from a variety of sources such as books, the Internet, magazines, experts or friends, and family. However, "place" frequently played an important function in their information seeking and sharing. To understand the role of affect via place in SAHMs' lives, we used Pettigrew's (1999, p. 811) information ground framework, which was derived from her research at community foot clinics. Information grounds are synergistic "environment[s] temporarily created when people come together for a singular purpose but from whose behavior emerges a social atmosphere that fosters the spontaneous and serendipitous sharing of information." This framework holds strong implications for the design and delivery of information systems because it identifies people's natural gathering places for sharing information. Fisher, Durrance, and Hinton (2004) derived the following information ground propositions based on their study of new immigrants in Queens, New York:

1. Information grounds can occur anywhere, in any type of temporal setting, and are predicated on the presence of individuals.

2. People gather at information grounds for a primary, instrumental purpose other than information sharing.

3. Information grounds are attended by different social types, most, if not all, of whom play expected and important, albeit different roles in information flow.

4. Social interaction is a primary activity at information grounds such that information flow is a byproduct.

5. People engage in formal and informal information sharing, and information flow occurs in many directions.

6. People use information obtained at information grounds in alternative ways and benefit along physical, social, affective, and cognitive dimensions.

7. Many subcontexts exist within an information ground and are based on people's perspectives and physical factors; together, these subcontexts form a grand context.

Beyond health clinics, Fisher proposed that information grounds occur in such settings as barber shops and hair salons, knitting circles, playgrounds, coffee shops, metro buses, food banks, waiting rooms, etc. Fisher et al. (2004) hypothesized that information grounds "hold likely regional and global impact in that they occur across all levels of all societies, especially as people create and utilize information grounds as they perform tasks in the course of daily life." Indeed, the two most popular information grounds, as learned via a telephone survey with residents of King County, Washington, were places of worship and informal subspaces within the workplace, e.g., lunchroom, water fountain, mailroom, etc. (Fisher & Naumer, 2006). The premise behind a deep understanding of information grounds, from a systems design perspective, is that it suggests ways of effectively delivering or facilitating different types of information, especially through utilizing social types (e.g., opinion leaders and gatekeepers). By identifying people's information grounds, one can design systems that provide information on needed topics in ways that complement people's everyday lifestyles. Additionally, one can use research findings on the public's preferred "people, place and information" attributes—a tripartite scheme developed for analyzing information ground (IG) data (Fisher, Landry, & Naumer, 2006)—to create information grounds in public spaces around specific topics such as government services and information.

When asked about their information grounds, SAHMs indicated that they attended more than one. The most common information grounds were places with structured children's activities (13 percent), stores (12.2 percent), and community centers and parks/playgrounds at 9.8 percent (Table 12.2).

Having identified their information grounds, SAHMs were then asked which information ground represented the "best" place for encountering information. Nearly 28 percent stated that their children's school was the best place, while parenting groups and classes were favored by 22.2 percent. Playgroups (16.7 percent), social activities (11.1 percent), and neighborhoods (11.1 percent) were also of consequence to many SAHMs, whereas fewer preferred stores and adult athletic activities (5.6 percent each). When asked why their information grounds were important for information, SAHMs offered a range of responses that were coded using the people-information-place trichotomy. Roughly 54 percent of responses revealed SAHMs appreciated the "people" aspect of their information grounds for its trustworthiness, diversity, similar beliefs, common interests,

Table 12.2   SAHMs' Information Grounds

Information Grounds	No. of SAHMs	Percentage
Structured children's activities (dance, swimming, soccer, etc.)	16	13.0%
Shopping/store	15	12.2%
Community center/community gatherings	12	9.8%
Park/playground	12	9.8%
Parenting groups or classes	9	7.3%
Social activities (book club, wine making, orchestra, bunko, etc.)	9	7.3%
Adult athletic activity—gym, pool	8	6.5%
Neighborhood	8	6.5%
Children's school	8	6.5%
Library	7	5.7%
Playgroup	7	5.7%
Other	4	3.3%
Online/Listserv	4	3.3%
Hair salon	2	1.6%
Church/place of worship	1	0.8%
School bus stop	1	0.8%
Total	**123**	**100.0%**

and common experiences with trustworthiness comprising the most significant factor followed by common experiences. "Information" was favored 23 percent of the time for authority, guidance and feedback, relevance, reliability, accessibility, and comprehensiveness, and that information was simply interesting. Reflecting the importance of "place," SAHMs found that comfort, convenience, and the fact that they frequently attend an information ground was similarly significant.

To augment our understanding about SAHMs' information grounds, it was essential to learn what they liked about their information grounds. When asked, the trichotomy of people, information, and place presented once again. Representing almost 51 percent of responses, "people" was the foremost category. SAHMs liked making connections with people, the diversity of people and ideas, shared beliefs, common interests, and common experiences. Of these, SAHMs found that making connections with people at their information grounds was the most significant. Illustrating this point, Judy typifies the sentiments of many SAHMs, "[I]t's of course the social aspect. It's nice to have an adult conversation now and then." Similarly, Cadence has this to say about The Body Shop party that she attended, "[I]t was just a chance to meet and talk to people that you know or don't know." However, shared experiences often made the information flow more meaningful as Naya reveals, "[Y]ou just feel like you're part of the sisterhood and you're all in the same boat. You're part of the camaraderie." This is consistent with Zimmerman's (2000) finding that SAHMs are inclined to socialize with other SAHMs. Diversity can be equally important. Eva enjoyed her book club since "we are all from totally different backgrounds and have totally different perspectives on things and so it's a good information source because we all just approach the same thing, you know, a billion different ways."

SAHMs enjoyed the "information" component of their information grounds slightly more than 27 percent of the time for getting questions answered, learning new things, and finding their available resources. Referring to her electronic discussion group, Trista was pleased that she could use the group's resources to get questions answered, while Melissa was happy to learn that "if you drop something in a puddle, it gets more germs than if you drop it in a dry place." However, 22 percent of SAHMs' responses revealed that the "place" aspect was liked for its atmosphere, amenities, or convenience. Alonsa explains that she enjoyed Trader Joe's because "for some reason [it] is more of an inviting place for that type of conversation than, say, a bigger store."

Regarding the SAHMs' social networks and information grounds, we found that mothers of very young children tended to be more isolated than mothers of older children. The all-consuming nature of early child rearing appears to contribute to this phenomenon as Judy indicated when describing a typical day for her 3-year-old twin boys: "The schedule is all centered around meals, nap time, and then in-between, we just try to figure out ways to entertain them and teach them." Sonya portrays life with her 9-month-old son as "all-encompassing, there isn't much outside of life besides the baby. The world revolves around the baby." Conversely, mothers of older children typically had more information grounds as a result of their children's activities. Drop-off and pick-up times at their children's schools were common places for SAHMs to seek information, as were places for children's organized activities such as swimming lessons or dance classes. Furthermore, as children grew more independent, mothers pursued their own activities such as going to the gym, participating in a winemaking club, bunko night, or returning to school.

THE RIGHT BRAIN APPROACH

"Experimentation has shown that the two different sides, or hemispheres, of the brain are responsible for different manners of thinking" ("Right brain/left brain thinking," 2001), which is commonly referred to as left brain and right brain. Left brain thinking is known for being logical, sequential, analytical, objective, rational, and looking at parts. The more emotive right brain mode of thinking is random, intuitive, holistic, synthesizing, subjective, and looks at wholes. Aside from the work of Dervin (e.g., 1992), Harris and Dewdney (1994), Chatman (e.g., 1992), Kuhlthau (e.g., 1991), Nahl (e.g., 2004) and Wilson (1981, 1997), researchers have by and large taken a left brain approach to studying information behavior. This is evident by the volume of studies devoted to the examination of sources and systems, how easy they are to use along with their physicality, and the expense of systems. Models focusing on this practicality reflect this left brain thinking.

As explained by Case (2002) and Fisher, Erdelez, and McKechnie (2005), information behavior as a field of study has received enormous attention over the years and has reached critical mass. The 1960s and 1970s saw the dissemination of studies focusing on system-centered designs. A paradigm shift was noted in the 1980s as the user-centered approach to information behavior (IB) came to the fore. However, as important as user-centeredness was to IB, the 1990s ushered in a new, context-centered focus. We suggest that the new century raise research to a higher level by continuing to concentrate on context but add to it an emboldened emphasis on affect. As indicated earlier, affect is central to information behavior. This motivating factor is tied to human relationships and emotion, and it is key to taking a right brain approach to information science.

FUTURE RESEARCH AND IMPLICATIONS FOR SYSTEM DESIGN

Our study represents one of the few explorations into the everyday information worlds of women and SAHMs particularly. Research is needed to learn if our findings represent women in other geographic locales and with different sociodemographic characteristics, especially younger ages and those with less education, as our participants were largely in their late 30s, well educated, and with incomes well above the poverty line. Research also is needed on mothers who work outside the home to determine how their daily roles and, hence, tasks and information needs may differ, and how affect figures throughout. To this end, co-spouses—both those who stay at home and those who work outside—also need to be drawn into the picture, while a deeper holistic view could be gained by including children and other stakeholders using a case study approach.

Forthcoming reports of the current data set include analyses of the data regarding Chatman's (2000) theories of normative behavior and information poverty, as well as Wilson's revised general model of information behavior (1981, 1997) and Harris and Dewdney's (1994) principles of everyday information seeking. Future analysis, however, will be guided by Belenky, Clinchy, Goldberger, and Tarule's (1986; c.f., Julien, 2005) women's ways of knowing (WWK), a feminist framework comprising five epistemological views of how women gain information (as defined by family and school as social institutions): silence, received knowing, subjective learning, procedural knowing, and constructed knowing. As Julien (1999) used the WWK theory for her dissertation on adolescents' career decision-making processes, thus, introducing WWK to researchers in library and information science, its past importation across the social sciences, humanities, and nursing suggests it may be an additional viable method for understanding our SAHM data.

For system design, our findings reveal through all aspects of information behavior—information need development and identification, information seeking, sharing, managing, and using—are fraught with emotive dimensions. Thus system designers are challenged to develop systems that encourage positive affect while diminishing and not causing negative ones. Systems must further reflect the information behaviors inherent in SAHMs' myriad daily roles and tasks, particularly via multitasking capabilities in how communications and facts are instigated, retrieved, stored, and shared. To be effective, systems need be portable, yet inexpensive, accessible to all family members, and also self-prompting. For example, a smart phone may send notice of an upcoming soccer practice while simultaneously triggering questions concerning transportation, children's uniforms, and snack requirements, and even provide directions via an electronic mapping system. By taking these factors into account, systems designers can greatly assist SAHMs with problem solving and planning throughout their busy days. Moreover, by taking SAHMs' multiroles into account by providing features that help to support information seeking and management as well as supporting the emotive aspect of the information process, information systems can enable SAHMs to cope with and master their domains.

CONCLUSION

The inherent roles embedded in the lives of SAHMs create many disparate information needs. Affect is an important component of the information worlds of these women for it impacts how their information needs are formed as well as how they seek and share everyday information. Furthermore, SAHMs' information grounds were valued as much for their affective attributes as for the information gathered at them. By excluding affect from the information process, an incomplete representation of this population's information behavior is presented. Information systems and services designers can use these findings to assist SAHMs in coping with the multifarious demands placed on their hectic lives.

ACKNOWLEDGMENTS

This material is based upon work supported by the National Science Foundation under Grant No. 0414447. Any opinions, findings, and conclusions or recommendations expressed in this material are those of the author(s) and do not necessarily reflect the views of the National Science Foundation.

ENDNOTE

1. Participants were assigned aliases to protect their privacy.

REFERENCES

Baker, L. M. (2005). Monitoring and blunting. In K. E. Fisher, S. Erdelez, & L. E. F. McKechnie (Eds.), *Theories of information behavior* (pp. 239–241). Medford, NJ: Information Today, Inc.

Belenky, M. F., Clinchy, B. M., Goldberger, N. R., & Tarule, J. M. (1986). *Women's ways of knowing: The development of self, voice, and mind.* New York: Basic Books.

Bilal, D. (2005). Children's information seeking and the design of digital interfaces in the affective paradigm. *Library Trends, 54*(2), 197–208.

Blackford, H. (2004). Playground panopticism: Ring-around-the-children, a pocketful of women. *Childhood: A Global Journal of Child Research, 11*(2), 227–249.

Boyd, E. R. (2002). "Being there": Mothers who stay-at-home, gender and time. *Women's Studies International Forum, 25*(4), 463–470.

Case, D. (2002). *Looking for information: A survey of research on information seeking, needs, and behavior.* New York: Academic Press/Elsevier Science.

Chatman, E. A. (1992). *The information world of retired women.* Westport, CT: Greenwood Press.

Chatman, E. A. (1996). The impoverished life-world of outsiders. *Journal of the American Society for Information Science, 47*(3), 193–206.

Chatman, E. A. (2000). Framing social life in theory and research. *The New Review of Information Behavior Research, 1,* 3–17.

Dervin, B. (1992). From the mind's eye of the user: The sense-making qualitative-quantitative methodology. In J. D. Glazier & R. R. Powell (Eds.), *Qualitative research in information management* (pp. 61–84). Englewood, CO: Libraries Unlimited.

Dervin, B., & Fraser, B. (1985). *How libraries help.* Sacramento, CA: California State Library (ERIC Document Reproduction Service N. 264857).

Drentea P., & Moren-Cross, J. L. (2005). Social capital and social support on the Web: The case of an Internet mother site. *Sociology of Health & Illness, 27*(7), 920–943.

Etaugh, C., & Moss, C. (2001). Attitudes of employed women toward parents who choose full-time or part-time employment following their child's birth. *Sex Roles: A Journal of Research, 44*(9/10), 611–619.

Forgays, D. K., Ottaway, S. A., Guarino, A., & D'Alessio, M. (2001). Parenting stress in employed and at-home mothers in Italy. *Journal of Family and Economic Issues, 22*(4), 327–351.

Fisher, K. E. (2006, May). *The death of the user and other ruminations on information behavior research.* Paper presented at the School of Library and Information Studies, Oslo University College, Norway.

Fisher, K. E., Durrance, J. C., & Hinton, M. B. (2004). Information grounds and the use of need-based services by immigrants in Queens, NY: A context-based, outcome evaluation approach. *Journal of the American Society for Information Science & Technology, 55*(8), 754–766.

Fisher, K. E., Erdelez, S., & McKechnie, L. (Eds.). (2005). *Theories of information behavior.* Medford, NJ: Information Today, Inc.

Fisher, K. E., Landry, C. F., & Naumer, C. M. (2006, July). *Social spaces, casual interactions, meaningful exchanges: An information ground typology based on the college student experience.* Paper presented at the *Information Seeking in Context VI* (ISIC) conference, Sydney, Australia. Submitted for publication.

Fisher, K. E., & Naumer, C. M. (2006). Information grounds: Theoretical basis and empirical findings on information flow in social settings. In A. Spink & C. Cole (Eds.), *New directions in human information behavior* (pp. 93–111). Amsterdam: Kluwer.

Goffman, E. (1959). *The presentation of self in everyday life.* Garden City, NY: Doubleday.

Gorman, K. A., & Fritzsche, B. A. (2002). The good-mother stereotype: Stay-at-home (or wish that you did!). *Journal of Applied Social Psychology, 32*(10), 2190–2201.

Granovetter, M. S. (1982). The strength of weak ties: A network theory revisited. In P. V. Marsden & N. Lin (Eds.), *Social structure and network analysis* (pp. 105–130). Beverly Hills, CA: Sage Publications.

Guillaume, L. R., & Bath, P. A. (2004). The impact of health scares on parents' information needs and preferred information sources: A case study of the MMR vaccine scare. *Health Informatics Journal, 10*(1), 5–22.

Harris, R. M., & Dewdney, P. (1994). *Barriers to information: How formal help systems fail battered women.* Westport, CT: Greenwood.

Helliwell, M. (2003). Building information bridges between parents and health care providers in the neonatal intensive care unit. In W. C. Peekhaus & L. Spiteri (Eds.), *Bridging the Digital Divide: Equalizing Access to Information and Communication Technologies. Proceedings of the 31st Annual Conference of the Canadian Association for Information Science, May, 2003, Halifax, Canada.* Halifax, Nova Scotia: Canadian Association for Information Science. Accessed November 25, 2006, from www.cais-acsi.ca/proceedings/2003/Helliwell_2003.pdf.

Johnston, D. D., & Swanson, D. H. (2003). Invisible mothers: A content analysis of motherhood ideologies and myths in magazines. *Sex Roles: A Journal of Research, 49*(1/2), 21–33.

Johnston, D. D., & Swanson, D. H. (2004). Moms hating moms: The internalization of Mother War rhetoric. *Sex Roles: A Journal of Research, 51,* 497–509.

Julien, H. (1999). Barriers to adolescents' information seeking for career decision making. *Journal of the American Society for Information Science, 50*(1), 38–48.

Julien, H. (2005). Women's ways of knowing. In K. E. Fisher, S. Erdelez & L. E. F. McKechnie (Eds.), *Theories of information behavior* (pp. 387–391). Medford, NJ: Information Today, Inc.

Julien, H., & Duggan, L. J. (2000). A longitudinal analysis of information needs and uses literature. *Library & Information Research, 22*(3), 291–309.

Julien, H., McKechnie, L. (E. F.), & Hart, S. (2005). Affective issues in library and information science systems work: A content analysis. *Library and Information Science Research, 27*(4), 453–466.

Kuhlthau, C. C. (1991). Inside the search process: Information seeking from the user's perspective. *Journal of the American Society for Information Science, 42*(5), 361–371.

Kuhlthau, C. C. (2004). *Seeking meaning: A process approach to library and information services* (2nd ed.). Westport, CT: Libraries Unlimited.

Leckie, G. J., & Pettigrew, K. E. (1997). A general model of the information seeking of professionals: Role theory through the back door? In P. Vakkari, R. Savolainen, & B. Dervin (Eds.), *Information seeking in context: Proceedings of an International Conference on Research in Information Needs, Seeking, and Use in Different Contexts (Aug. 14–16, 1996, Tampere, Finland)* (pp. 99–110). London: Graham Taylor. Accessed November 25, 2006, from projects.ischool.washington.edu/fisher/pubs/ISIC.1997.pdf.

Lincoln, Y. S., & Guba, E. G. (1985). *Naturalistic inquiry.* Beverly Hills, CA: Sage Publications.

Maatita, F. C. (2003). Mothers and playgroups: "Doing" motherhood in the social sphere. *Dissertation Abstracts International, A: The Humanities and Social Sciences, 64*(5), 1853-A. (UMI No. DA3089750.)

Nahl, D. (2004). Measuring the affective information environment of Web searchers. *Proceedings of the 67th annual meeting of the American Society for Information Science & Technology, 41,* 191–197.

Nahl, D. (2005). Affective load theory (ALT). In K. E. Fisher, S. Erdelez, & L. E. F. McKechnie, (Eds.), *Theories of information behavior* (pp. 39–43). Medford, NJ: Information Today, Inc.

Nicholas, D., & Marden, M. (1998). Parents and their information needs. A case study: Parents of children under the age of five. *Journal of Librarianship and Information Science, 30*(1), 35–47.

Petress, K., & Harrington, J. (n.d.). *List of emotions* [Internet document]. Accessed November 25, 2006, from www.umpi.maine.edu/~petress/feelinga.pdf.

Pettigrew, K. E. (1999). Waiting for chiropody: Contextual results from an ethnographic study of the information behavior among attendees at community clinics. *Information Processing & Management, 35*(6), 801–817.

Pettigrew, K. E. (2000). Lay information provision in community settings: How community health nurses disseminate human services information to the elderly. *Library Quarterly, 70*(1), 47–85.

Pettigrew, K. E., Fidel, R., & Bruce, H. (2001). Conceptual frameworks in information behavior. In M. E. Williams (Ed.), *Annual Review of Information Science & Technology: Vol. 35* (pp. 43–78). Medford, NJ: ASIST and Information Today, Inc.

Radford, L. (1999). *The reference encounter: Interpersonal communication in the academic library*. Chicago: American Library Association and the Association of College and Research Libraries.

Rashley, L. H. (2005). "Work it out with your wife": Gendered expectations in parenting rhetoric online. *NWSA Journal, 17*(1), 58–92.

Riday, J. D. (2003). "First and foremost, I'm a mom!": The experience of full-time and part-time stay-at-home mothering. (Doctoral Dissertation, Iowa State University, 2003). *Dissertation Abstracts International, A: The Humanities and Social Sciences, 64*(3), 1095-A.

Right brain/left brain thinking. (2001). From *Funderstanding.com* (Home–Engaging kids Theories–About learning). Accessed November 25, 2006, from www.funder standing.com/right_left_brain.cfm.

"Stay-at-home" parents top 5 million, Census Bureau reports. (2004, November 30). *U.S. Census Bureau News*. Accessed November 25, 2006, from www.census.gov/ Press-Release/www/releases/archives/families_households/003118.html.

Tardy, R. W. (2000). "But I am a good mom": The social construction of motherhood through health-care conversations. *Journal of Contemporary Ethnography, 29*(4), 433–473.

Tardy, R. W., & Hale, C. (1998). Getting 'plugged in': A network analysis of health-information seeking among 'stay at home moms'. *Communication Monographs, 65*(4), 336–357.

Towne, N., & Adler, R. B. (1996). *Looking Out Looking In* (8th ed.). Forth Worth, TX: Harcourt Brace.

Tuominen, K., & Savolainen, R. (1997). A social constructionist approach to the study of information use as discursive action. In P. Vakkari, R. Savolainen & B. Dervin (Eds.), *Information seeking in context: Proceedings of an International Conference on Research in Information Needs, Seeking, and Use in Different Contexts (Aug. 14–16, 1996, Tampere, Finland)* (pp. 81–96). London: Graham Taylor.

Walsh, W. (2002). Spankers and nonspankers: Where they get information on spanking. *Family Relations, 51*(1), 81–88.

Warner, J. (2005, February 21). Mommy madness. *Newsweek, 145*(8), 42. Accessed November 25, 2006, from www.msnbc.msn.com/id/6959880/site/newsweek.

Wicks, D. A. (1999). The information-seeking behavior of pastoral clergy: A study of the interaction of their work worlds and work roles. *Library and Information Research, 21*(2), 205–206.

Wilson, T. D. (1981). On user studies and information needs. *Journal of Documentation, 37*(1), 3–15. Accessed December 5, 2006, from informationr.net/tdw/publ/papers/ 1981infoneeds.html.

Wilson, T. D. (1997). Information behaviour: An interdisciplinary perspective. *Information Processing & Management, 33*(4), 551–572.

Wilson, T. D. (1999). Models of information behaviour research. *Journal of Documentation, 55*(3), 249–270.

Zimmerman, T. S. (2000). Marital equality and satisfaction in stay-at-home mother and stay-at-home father families. *Contemporary Family Therapy, 22*(3), 337–354.

CHAPTER 13

Critical Thinking Disposition and Library Anxiety: A Mixed Methods Investigation

Nahyun Kwon
University of South Florida

INTRODUCTION

For college students to meet their research needs, critical thinking is crucial throughout the information search process (Association of College and Research Libraries, 2000; Kuhlthau, 2004; Marchionini, 1995). Because of the importance of analytical and systematic thinking skills in using academic libraries, critical thinking has been examined either as an important component of information literacy education or as an outcome of library use (Bodi, 1992; Whitmire, 1998, 2002). While cognitions tend to have accompanying affective components (Isen, Daubman, & Gorgoglione, 1987), it appears that most research on critical thinking to date has been mainly on its cognitive aspect with much less attention given to its affective aspect.

Nonetheless, the ideal critical thinker has been characterized not merely by the individual's cognitive skills, but also by how she or he approaches life and living in general (Facione, Facione, & Giancarlo, 2000). As affective and attitudinal domains of critical thinking, the disposition toward critical thinking is defined as the consistent internal motivation to use critical thinking skills to decide what to believe and what to do when one approaches problems, ideas, decisions, or issues. Because affective behavior initiates, maintains, and terminates cognitive behavior (Isen et al., 1987), students' negative attitudes and mistrust about their own thinking abilities and skills could cause illogical fear and inadequacy in a library where they are supposed to be engaged in intellectual activities.

Indeed, the library and information science literature reports the prevalence of students' feelings of inadequacy toward using the academic library; these feelings are known as library anxiety (Bostick, 1992; Mellon, 1986). Researchers have demonstrated empirically that library anxiety debilitates effective use of libraries and information resources (Onwuegbuzie, Jiao, & Bostick, 2004). Subsequently, library anxiety may impede cognitive processes during the information search process in the library.

As such, both critical thinking (Facione, Facione, Blohm, Howard, & Giancarlo, 1998) and library anxiety (Onwuegbuzie et al., 2004) have been found to play an integral role in the learning process among college students. Since this link has not been examined empirically, the purpose of the present study was to explore a potential association between critical thinking dispositions and library anxiety among college students. It was hypothesized that college students with low critical thinking dispositions will have greater library anxiety when compared to students with high critical thinking dispositions.

METHOD

Participants

Participants were undergraduate students enrolled in six sections of a three credit-hour Library and Internet Research Skills course during spring 2006 at a southern research university. A total of 180 students were enrolled in this course either as a requirement or as an elective, and 137 students voluntarily participated in the study during the first two weeks of the semester. Sixty-nine percent were female and the ages of the participants ranged from 18 to 60 years (Mean = 22.9, SD = 6.9). The majority of the participants were white (78 percent), followed by African American (13 percent), Hispanic (5 percent), and Asian/Pacific Islanders (3 percent). Percentages for class standing were 6 percent freshmen, 28 percent sophomore, 42 percent junior, and 22 percent senior.

Data Collection

Both quantitative and qualitative data collection methods were employed for the current study. First, a quantitative survey method was used to measure the levels of critical thinking dispositions and library anxiety of each participant. Concurrently, students' narratives of their experience of using the library were analyzed by taking a qualitative approach. The use of this mixed methods approach was expected to allow for rigorous explorations of any relationships between the two affective variables (Tashakkori & Teddie, 2002).

For the quantitative investigation, participants were administered Facione and Facione's (1992) California Critical Thinking Disposition Inventory (CCTDI) and Bostick's (1992) Library Anxiety Scale (LAS). The CCTDI measures seven dimensions of critical thinking dispositions: (a) truth-seeking, (b) open-mindedness, (c) analyticity, (d) systematicity, (e) critical thinking self-confidence, (f) inquisitiveness, and (g) maturity. The 75 items on the CCTDI use a six-point Likert-type scale anchored by 1 = agree strongly and 6 = disagree strongly. A higher score on this scale represents more positive critical thinking dispositions.

Using a 5-point Likert-type scale, Bostick's (1992) 43-item LAS includes the following five dimensions regarding library anxiety: (a) barriers with staff, (b) affective barriers, (c) comfort with the library, (d) knowledge of the library, and (e) mechanical barriers. A high score on this scale represents high levels of anxiety. The subscales of both CCTDI and LAS are defined in Table 13.1 with their reliability coefficient scores generated for the sample under study. These survey data were used to test the research hypothesis that examined the relationship between critical thinking dispositions and library anxiety by undertaking correlation statistical analysis using SPSS+ version 14.0.

For the qualitative investigation, the participants were asked to write a take-home essay to report a critical incident of library use from their past experience by giving the following written instructions:

Table 13.1   Dimensions of Critical Thinking Dispositions and Library Anxiety with Reliability Scores

Dimension	Definition	Reliability ($\propto$)
CCTDI 7 Dimensions		.91
Truth-seeking	Eager to seek the truth, audacious about asking questions, and honest and objective in asking questions	.78
Open-mindedness	Open-minded and tolerant of divergent opinions and aware of one's own bias	.65
Analyticity	Attentive to the potential for problematic situations, values reason and the use of evidence when facing challenging situations	.71
Systematicity	Inclined toward organized, logical, focused, and attentive inquiry	.62
CT Self-confidence	Self-assured regarding one's own reasoning processes, very comfortable with own level of cognitive ability	.84
Inquisitiveness	Intellectually curious, values being well-informed and knowing how things work, values learning even without immediate rewards	.81
Maturity	Understands some problems to be ill-structured, therefore, multiple ways to solve any given problem	.69
LAS 5 Dimensions		.93
Barriers with Staff	Believes that librarians are threatening, unapproachable, inaccessible, too busy with duties to help students	.91
Affective Barriers	Feels inadequate or inept in attempting library tasks, which are exacerbated by assuming that other people are more proficient	.86
Comfort with the Library	Perceives the library as a comfortable, welcoming, secure, safe, and non-threatening place	.75
Knowledge of the Library	Degree to which students believe they are familiar with the library	.60
Mechanical Barriers	Discomfort stemming from using library equipment, including computers, printers, and photocopiers	.72

Recall your most recent or most memorable experience of using the library and its resources to write a research a paper. Write an essay in 500 to 1,000 words describing your thoughts and feelings as you worked from the beginning of the assignment to its conclusion. What were you thinking and how did you feel when you used the library and its resources to find information for the research paper?

A content analysis of student essays was undertaken as the major analytic technique for the qualitative data.

RESULTS
Quantitative Investigation

The critical disposition scores among the study sample ranged from 229 to 357 (Mean = 282.2; SD = 30.5). The library anxiety scores among the study sample ranged from 44 to 149 (Mean = 102.4; SD = 19.2). The correlation analysis was conducted to test the research hypothesis. As predicted, a statistically significant negative correlation was found between critical thinking dispositions and library anxiety, r = -.359; p < .001 (two-tailed). Therefore, the quantitative phase of the study revealed that students with less positive critical thinking dispositions tended to have greater library anxiety. While the fact that 13 percent of the explained variance (r squared = .128) indicated a highly systematic association between the two variables, the remaining 87 percent of the variance was unaccounted for and suggested that there were other factors influencing library anxiety besides weak critical thinking dispositions.

Qualitative Investigation

Following the quantitative data analysis, contents of student essays were analyzed to further understand the findings from the survey data. A certain pattern was observed repeatedly in students' reports of their critical incidents of library use. First, both library anxiety and research writing anxiety appeared to be common phenomena experienced by both high and low critical thinking disposition (CTD) students in the beginning of their library use. This phenomenon can be explained by Kuhlthau's (2004) principle of uncertainty, denoting that cognitive uncertainty about information tasks generally causes such affective symptoms as anxiety, confusion, frustration, and lack of confidence in the early stages of the information search process. More interestingly, this initial anxiety, a negative affect, appeared to hamper critical thinking skills and abilities:

When I first started my research, I felt like I was lost in a sea. I didn't know where to start from. For a few minutes I felt like my thinking abilities were gone. (Matt, 19, sophomore)

> When I went into the library I was immediately confused about
> which floor to go to, and the confusion quickly led to frustration.
> I do feel that I possess a very high level of thinking and logic skills
> but my patience with 'where do I even start' is what makes me
> most uneasy at the library. (Sarah, 19, sophomore)

Facing this problematic stage, students sooner or later activated their critical thinking dispositions to make sense out of their situations. In particular, some of Facione and Facione's (1992) CCTDI dimensions were observed more often than others. In Jen's case, for example, her critical thinking self-confidence (i.e., one's trust in one's own cognitive ability) helped to reinstate her thinking skills, which helped to reduce anxiety and finally helped her to find information:

> When I first walked in the library I was intimidated … It was a lit-
> tle bigger than what I was used to. Once I took a couple of deep
> breaths I realized that it was still a library and I have been using
> them since elementary school. When I finally calmed my nerves,
> I had no problem finding the information that I was looking for
> … I knew I could find plenty of resource material to research.
> (Jen, 22, senior)

Similarly, inquisitiveness (i.e., one's inclination to be inquisitive and well-informed) played positive roles in putting students back on the right track and enabled them to approach the problem adequately. Evidently, these positive dispositions helped in reducing library anxiety and restoring hampered critical thinking skills. This finding clearly demonstrates how affective states interact with cognition in the library information search process. While positive dispositions were observed among most students, certain thinking dispositions appeared more often among high CTD students. For example, Janet, a student with high CTD scores, reports positive critical thinking self-confidence and open-mindedness (i.e., one's tolerance to different opinions and viewpoints) quickly dispelled a glimpse of her initial anxiety:

> I am less secure in my ability to locate high quality sources. This
> doubt does not carry over into how I feel about the library or my
> ability to use it. Generally, I feel adequate to the task of utilizing a
> library to search out the information I need. I have some under-
> standing of the relative value of various sources and I factor that
> into my search … I was open to many viewpoints … I felt that I had
> made good decisions about my selection of sources. (Janet, 52)

This finding reveals a mechanism that shows how positive CTDs can help one to carry out the information search process effectively. In contrast, the positive CTDs that handled the anxious feeling were not activated among some students with lower CTD scores. For example, Michelle's initial confidence in research was weakened over time, and her anxiety and frustrations increased throughout the process:

> I was lost in the library. While some of my classmates had no trouble finding resources or asking for help … I was too shy and embarrassed to ask a librarian … When I first chose the story, I was confident that I could write a satisfactory essay … After three exhausting days of worrying and pretending my search was going well, I gave up. My search had not yielded any useful information. I had no good notes to refer to when I sat down to write the essay the night before the first draft was due. The resulting work was poor. (Michelle, 20, sophomore)

Apparently, because positive CTDs were not activated, negative feelings were not handled properly and students with lower CTD scores remained clueless and hopeless. Indeed, the content analysis of essays substantiated the findings of the quantitative approach, showing how library anxiety and critical thinking dispositions interact during information seeking. More importantly, positive CTDs played a crucial role in carrying out the cognitive information search task successfully by regulating the negative anxiety state.

DISCUSSION AND IMPLICATIONS

This exploratory, mixed methods study examined possible associations between critical thinking dispositions and library anxiety among college students. The triangulation of the results from the mixed methods investigation showed a negative association between the two affects. This study also revealed that critical thinking abilities, a crucial quality for successful information searches, could be hampered by library anxiety but may be reinstated by positive critical thinking dispositions.

The findings of this study have implications for research on affect in information behavior. Researchers in this area have attempted to reveal dynamic interactions between affect and cognition in the information context, and to understand the critical role of affect in creating effective coping mechanisms for information searchers suffering from uncertainty (Kuhlthau, 2004; Nahl, 2005a). Specifically, these findings further confirm Nahl's (2005b) affective load theory in which negative affective states disrupt cognitive strategies, interrupt the search, and often bring about a premature termination, while positive affective states, such as self-efficacy, command persistence and integration to cognitive strategies by handling ambiguity and cognitive load properly. By revealing the interactions between the critical thinking dispositions and library anxiety over the course of information searching in the library among college students, the present study augments current knowledge in the study of affect.

The findings of this study will provide practical implications for issues relevant to information literacy. Specifically, by revealing that affective states influence the cognitive process, information literacy instruction should be designed in such a way to ensure that any negative emotion is reduced while positive emotions are promoted to create a more effective learning environment.

REFERENCES

Association of College and Research Libraries. (2000). *Information literacy competency standards for higher education.* Chicago: American Library Association. Accessed December 3, 2006, from www.ala.org/ala/acrl/acrlstandards/standards.pdf.

Bodi, S. (1992). Collaborating with faculty in teaching critical thinking: The role of librarians. *Research Strategies, 10*(2), 69–76.

Bostick, S. L. (1992). *The development and validation of the library anxiety scale.* Unpublished doctoral dissertation, Wayne State University, Detroit, Michigan.

Facione, P. A., & Facione, N. C. (1992). *The California critical thinking dispositions inventory.* Millbrae, CA: California Academic Press.

Facione, P. A., Facione, N. C., Blohm, S. W., Howard, K., & Giancarlo, C. A. (1998). *The California critical thinking skills test. Form A and Form B test manual.* Millbrae, CA: California Academic Press.

Facione, P. A., Facione, N. C., & Giancarlo, C. A. (2000). The disposition toward critical thinking: Its character, measurement, and relationship to critical thinking skill. *Informal Logic, 20*(1), 61–84.

Isen, A. M., Daubman, K. A., & Gorgoglione, J. M. (1987). The influence of positive affect on cognitive organization: Implications for education. In R. E. Snow & M. J. Farr (Eds.), *Aptitude, learning, and instruction. Volume 3: Conative and affective process analyses* (pp. 143–164). Mahwah, NJ: Lawrence Erlbaum Associates.

Kuhlthau, C. C. (2004). *Seeking meaning: A process approach to library and information services* (2nd ed.). Westport, CT: Libraries Unlimited.

Marchionini, G. (1995). *Information seeking in electronic environment.* Cambridge: Cambridge University Press.

Mellon, C. A. (1986). Library anxiety: A grounded theory and its development. *College & Research Libraries, 47*(2), 160–165.

Nahl, D. (2005a). Affective and cognitive information behavior: Interaction effects in Internet use. *Proceedings of the 67th annual meeting of the American Society for Information Science & Technology, 41.*

Nahl, D. (2005b). Affective load theory (ALT). In K. E. Fisher, S. Erdelez, & L. E. F. McKechnie, (Eds.), *Theories of information behavior* (pp. 39–43). Medford, NJ: Information Today, Inc.

Onwuegbuzie, A. J., Jiao, Q. G., & Bostick, S. L. (2004). *Research methods in library and information studies: No. 1. Library anxiety: Theory, research, and applications.* Lanham, MD: Scarecrow.

Tashakkori, A., & Teddie, C. (Eds.). (2002). *Handbook of mixed methods in social and behavioral research.* Thousand Oaks, CA: Sage Publications.

Whitmire, E. (1998). Development of critical thinking skills: An analysis of academic library experiences and other measures. *College & Research Libraries, 59*(3), 266–273.

Whitmire, E. (2002). Academic library performance measures and undergraduates' library use and educational outcomes. *Library & Information Science Research, 24,* 107–128.

CHAPTER 14

Experiencing Information Literacy Affectively

Heidi Julien

School of Library and Information Studies, University of Alberta

INTRODUCTION

The study of information literacy is central to information behavior scholarship. Information literate individuals have the skills and attitudes required to effectively and efficiently access and use information. These skills are central to "literacy" in general, particularly in the 21st century, and are critical to ameliorating the "digital divide" that continues to characterize information access, a divide that includes a differential in information literacy skills. Many people believe that their skill level is significantly higher than they can demonstrate, which suggests that their access to information is compromised (Fallows, 2005). Thus, information literacy education remains very much needed and has long been an important service offered by school and academic libraries. Public libraries are only more recently participating in education for information skills; this is the context for the research reported here.

Affective issues such as confidence are primary variables in people's use of online information sources. Indeed, self-perceptions about one's information literacy are often expressed in affective terms. This study identifies the ways in which people's self-perceptions of being information literate relate to how online information is approached in everyday use in the public library setting. Within a larger examination of the role of public libraries in developing people's information literacy skills, 25 public library users were interviewed about their Internet use, the role of the public library in developing skills required to access online information, and how they experience being information literate. Affect was found to be fundamental to their experiences of information literacy.

Much research in human information behavior, including that related to affective issues, has focused on the experiences of students or other academic library users rather than ordinary people in daily life situations. A deeper understanding of information behavior is only possible when we examine people's experiences outside of academic or work contexts.

243

In addition, this study demonstrates that "affect" is a fundamental variable in information behavior. This variable has been ignored or marginalized in information science research for too long.

LITERATURE REVIEW

In the psychology literature up to the 1960s, emotion was considered either a barrier to rationality, a curiosity, or, at best, a significant challenge to measure (Mayer, 2002). More recently (Schwarz, 2002), the value of emotional intelligence in affecting task performance and the effects of moods and emotions on information processing style have been recognized. However, within the field of library and information studies (LIS), attention to affect has been minimal, especially compared with analysis of cognitive variables in information seeking, for example. The interest that has been focused on affect has significantly enriched understanding of information behavior and of information literacy. Early work by Jakobovits and Nahl-Jakobovits (1987), for example, demonstrated clearly that affect was one of three primary domains of user behavior. Kuhlthau (1988) also provided clear evidence of the role of affect in library use situations, and the affective aspects of her information seeking process (ISP) model have been closely examined by others (e.g., Kracker, 2002; Kracker & Wang, 2002). Savolainen (1995) incorporated affect as a significant variable in his everyday life information seeking (ELIS) model, and Solomon's work in sense-making behavior (Solomon, 1997) is also infused with concepts related to affect. Bilal (1998, 2002) includes affect in the design of her study of children's searching of Yahooligans! She reports both positive (self-confidence, satisfaction, and comfort) and negative (confusion and frustration) emotions associated with information searching. The work of Nahl is worthy of particular mention. Nahl starts from the position that affect influences cognition and learning (Nahl, 2004), and she emphasizes the importance of motivation. Nahl found predictable affective states associated with the reduction of uncertainty in information searching, including "uncertainty, pessimism, dissatisfaction, confusion, frustration, self-doubt and disappointment" (p. 192). Affective issues of particular importance to Nahl include self-efficacy, optimism, uncertainty, time pressure, expected effort, task completion motivation, and expected difficulty. For example, optimism will motivate a searcher to consider a greater range of problem-solving strategies, whereas pessimism leads to inflexibility. She also has found that "affective differences in behavior are associated with certain cognitive behaviors of searchers. People who attribute success to their own search skills experience significantly less uncertainty and affective load [the totality of affective issues influencing the task at hand] than those who attribute success to uncontrollable factors outside of themselves" (p. 196).

The role of affective variables in information literacy more specifically also has been the subject of recent research. Shoemaker (2005) noted that affect was an important aspect of skill development. Beile (2002) reported that self-efficacy with respect to information skills could be increased by providing information literacy instruction. Collins and Veal (2004) found that students' perceptions about their information skills affected their overall anxiety toward Internet use, and Kurbanoglu (2003) reported a clear association between information literacy self-efficacy and computer use. Similar results were reported by Ren (1999) in her study of small-business executives searching for government information on the Internet. Complementary research suggests that Internet self-efficacy affects consumers' use of e-commerce and e-services (Hsu & Chiu, 2004).

Thus, despite a relative deficit of attention to affect (Julien, McKechnie, & Hart, 2005), LIS research into the role of emotion in information behavior, and information literacy more specifically, appears to be gaining momentum. It is within this research context that analysis of findings related to affect was included in this study.

METHOD

This study focuses on the following research question: How do customers experience information literacy? Five public libraries in Canada were visited in order to interview customers. Customers were approached as they left Internet access stations and asked to participate in face-to-face interviews. Information letters outlining the study and the nature of participation were provided, and written consent was obtained for interview participants, who were guaranteed anonymity. The study received institutional ethics approval. Interviews were conducted immediately, except in one instance when an interview was scheduled at another convenient time during the on-site visit; interviews lasted between 15 minutes and 1 hour. The interview questions are found in Appendix A. Similar questions were used in a previous study conducted by the author (Julien & Boon, 2004) and were found to be useful starting points for eliciting participants' views about their information literacy. Interviews were conducted by the author and an assistant. The interviews were semi-structured, asking participants to comment on their Internet use in the library and on any information literacy training they had received.

Participants

The 25 study participants included men and women ranging in age from their 20s to their 70s, from a variety of backgrounds. Some participants were regular users of the library where they were interviewed; others were visitors. Several participants had Internet access at home or at their workplace, while others did not. What all participants had in common, however, was that they were using the Internet public access stations in a public library, they were approached during that use to request an interview, and they consented to participating in the study.

Settings

The public libraries where the participants were interviewed are in different regions of Canada (the west, central Canada, and the east coast), and included a large main branch of an urban public library in a city of about 2,000,000 persons (library A), a second large main branch of an urban public library in a city of about 1,000,000 persons (library B), a library in a smaller city of 75,000 persons (library C), a library in a small town of less than 1,000 persons (library D), and a public library housed within a community centre on a small Native reserve (library E) that serves a community of less than 100 persons. Each library provided typical services, including circulating materials and information/reference services, as well as Internet access for the public, including community residents and non-residents. Libraries D and E employed only non-professional library staff (i.e., without master's degrees or professional certification as librarians).

Data Analysis

Interviews were tape recorded and transcribed in full. Analyses were conducted qualitatively using a grounded-theory approach (Glaser & Strauss, 1967) with the assistance of NVivo software. These analyses revealed the central role of affect in participants' experiences of information literacy; thus, affect became a focus of analysis.

RESULTS AND DISCUSSION

All interview responses are not reported here; rather the results focus on the ways in which participants experienced being "information literate." In the main, participants used the Internet access in the public libraries for the following purposes (in rank order from most frequent to least frequent): email, reading online newspapers, online gaming, word processing (where that use was allowed in the library), online shopping, and conducting Google searches. Since quality of life has been associated with the use of the Internet for social purposes (Leu & Lee, 2005) and email is the primary use identified in this study, the ways the Internet was used in the public library provide valuable evidence for the positive role the library may play in enhancing quality of life for community members. All participants had developed some level of skill in accessing and using the Internet; those skills were reportedly developed through experience, the help of friends, family or colleagues, and some formal training (including training opportunities provided by the public library).

In addition, all participants provided insights into the role that various emotions played in their Internet use. When specifically asked about how it "feels" to be information literate, a question suggested by the research of Bruce (1997), some study participants described feeling superior to people who lack information literacy skills. Other participants revealed feelings of empowerment, personal control or mastery, independence, confidence, and pleasure. One male participant from library A said, "It feels good to the extent that it's exclusive … I like the idea that … I can get to the information and no one else can …" A woman at library A noted, "It's a sense of empowerment …" Also at library A, another male said, "I feel really pleased that I'm able to access the Internet … I feel pleased that I'm not completely isolated from … my family and friends … I'm not on the outside looking in." For that participant, the public Internet access at this library was clearly an emotional lifeline during a time of personal crisis (simultaneous job loss and marriage breakdown). A male at library C expressed satisfaction at being independent: "I don't have to be bothering people." A woman at library C noted, "I think I'm in control, actually I think being in the library doing it I felt more skilled than I did at home. And I don't know if that's because I think my husband's going to walk in or my child is going to walk in and say, 'Oh, that's not the way to do it!' And here nobody's watching me … no pressure." For this person, the relative privacy offered by the library provided some emotional security by ensuring that her information literacy skill level would not be ridiculed.

A second group of respondents suggested that possessing information literacy skills imparts no particular affective response, since these are simply second nature, like "tying shoes." One young woman at library B noted with respect to possessing information literacy skills, "… probably for my age group it's probably pretty normal … it probably just feels normal to have those skills but to another age group that's really got to work at it would feel … like an accomplishment, maybe." Another male (library D) said of his skills, "… [it] doesn't boost my self-esteem. It doesn't make me feel like a better person." A male at library B said, "I don't feel very proud or anything like that … it's a necessity." A woman at library C noted that being information literate is "part of everyday life; [like] brushing your teeth …" Also at library C, a male respondent said, "it's just another tool used around the home." The images of domesticity for this set of respondents provide a clear indication of the way in which applying information skills to Internet use is simply part of everyday life, evoking no particular affective response.

However, participants who did not believe themselves to be information literate reported feelings of frustration. One male customer at library C reported that his lack of skills is "frustrating … very frustrating." This participant also noted that his self-reported "lack of patience" is a barrier to successful Internet use. He noted, "… after five minutes if I haven't found it I just get frustrated and bored and leave." A male at library A noted that "[W]hen I'm standing next to somebody who's just banging away there at 120 words a minute and I'm barely able to put out 30, I get a little annoyed with myself or with my inadequacies." He later said, "perhaps if I had better Internet skills … I think I would not be where I am right now [i.e., unemployed]."

Because interviews with public library staff suggested that some customers feel anxious about their lack of information literacy skills, the interview transcripts of those participants who expressed negative affect such as frustration were scrutinized for evidence of anxiety, but such evidence was not found. This absence of expressed anxiety may be an artifact of the self-selection by participants; it may be that customers using the public Internet access stations who did feel anxious about their skill levels did not choose to participate in the interviews. The discrepancy about feelings of anxiety between reports by participants and suggestions by public library staff requires further examination. The relationship between existing anxiety with respect to information literacy levels and library anxiety overall (Mellon, 1986) is another avenue to be explored; recent research points to some complexity in this relationship (Jiao & Onwuegbuzie, 2004; Kracker & Wang, 2002).

CONCEPTUAL FRAMEWORK ARISING FROM THE DATA

The grounded theory approach used to analyze the data in this study proved fruitful in establishing a conceptual framework that invites further research. Study results revealed three principal participant experiences of information literacy, from an affective perspective: 1) a sense of empowerment, personal mastery, and control; 2) a sense of normal, everyday experience, with no particular affective element; and 3) a sense of frustration by those who do not believe themselves to be information literate. Since this study is qualitative and included a relatively small number of participants, further research would be required to test this framework on a larger sample of people. Most respondents who fell into the second group (no particular affective response) were relatively young, which suggests another avenue to explore: Are those people who have entered adulthood with significant Internet familiarity experiencing their information literacy as having no particular affective component? If so, what are the implications of that experience for their information behavior? And are those in the first group who feel positive and confident about their information literacy primarily adults who have made special efforts to develop their information literacy skills and feel a sense of accomplishment at having done so? Future study might also explore the relative skill level of these different groups of people to determine from an objective standpoint whether there exists an actual difference in the abilities of people who experience information literacy differently. For instance, do the feelings of empowerment experienced by the first participant group motivate these people to more active information seeking? These are some of the potential research questions arising from this study.

IMPLICATIONS

This study adds to the growing body of research addressing information behavior in a holistic way, especially scholarship showing how emotion shapes information behavior. The findings relating to the interplay between information literacy and emotion that are reported here demonstrate that a purely instrumental understanding of the value of public Internet access in public libraries is insufficient to fully appreciate the ways in which this service adds to customers' daily life experiences. That is, public library customers do not approach their information seeking from a cognitive perspective only. Whether or not customers are able to demonstrate effective search strategies is only part of the picture. At least as critical are the self-perceptions that facilitate or challenge their information seeking; these self-perceptions are clearly well grounded in emotions, both positive and negative.

With an increased awareness of the role of emotion in information behavior generally and in information literacy more specifically, public library staff could more effectively provide assistance to their customers. When providing training in information literacy skills, for instance, trainers could comment directly on the potential positive affective outcomes of that instruction. Additionally, since self-efficacy and success are related, developing learners' positive feelings about their information literacy skills could become a standard objective of training efforts. Those negative emotions such as frustration and anxiety, which may pose barriers for information seekers, should also be fully recognized by library staff charged with assisting customers. Nahl (1997) argues for this acknowledgment in what she terms "information counseling" activities. Finally, proactive offers of help by library staff, which were not observed during the course of the study, might help customers overcome negative feelings that are interfering with successful information seeking.

In addition, these findings complement calls for greater attention to affect in information design (Julien & McKechnie, 2005). There are myriad ways in which information systems may be designed to accommodate users' emotional needs (Kalbach, 2004; Norman, 2004); this study merely adds weight to the case for doing so.

ACKNOWLEDGMENTS

The author is grateful for the financial support of the Social Sciences and Humanities Research Council of Canada (Standard Research Grant 410-2003-0004). Sincere thanks are also due to the participants in this study who shared their time, experiences, and opinions so generously. Finally, I truly appreciate the diligent work of research assistants Ina Smith, Cameron Hoffman, and Michelle Whitehead.

REFERENCES

Beile, P. (2002, February). *The effect of library instruction learning environments on self-efficacy levels and learning outcomes of graduate students in education.* Paper presented at the Annual Meeting of the American Educational Research Association, New Orleans, LA.

Bilal, D. (1998). Children's search processes in using World Wide Web search engines: An exploratory study. *Journal of the American Society for Information Science, 35,* 45–53.

Bilal, D. (2002). Perspectives on children's navigation of the World Wide Web: Does the type of search task make a difference? *Online Information Review, 26*(2), 108–117.

Bruce, C. (1997). *The seven faces of information literacy.* Adelaide: Auslib Press.

Collins, K. M. T., & Veal, R. E. (2004). Off-campus adult learners' levels of library anxiety as a predictor of attitudes toward the Internet. *Library and Information Science Research, 26*(1), 5–14.

Fallows, D. (2005). *Search engine users: Internet searchers are confident, satisfied and trusting, but they are also unaware and naïve.* Washington, D.C.: Pew Internet & American Life Project. Accessed December 3, 2006, from www.pewinternet.org/pdfs/PIP_Searchengine_users.pdf.

Glaser, B. G., & Strauss, A. L. (1967). *The discovery of grounded theory: Strategies for qualitative research.* New York: Aldine de Gruyter.

Hsu, M.-H., & Chiu, C.-M. (2004). Internet self-efficacy and electronic service acceptance. *Decision Support Systems, 38,* 369–381.

Jakobovits, L. A., & Nahl-Jakobovits, D. (1987). Learning the library: Taxonomy of skills and errors. *College and Research Libraries, 48,* 203–214.

Jiao, Q. G., & Onwuegbuzie, A. J. (2004). The impact of information technology on library anxiety: The role of computer attitudes. *Information Technology and Libraries, 23,* 138–144.

Julien, H., & Boon, S. (2004). Assessing instructional outcomes in Canadian academic libraries. *Library & Information Science Research, 26*(2), 121–139.

Julien, H., & McKechnie, L. E. F. (2005). What we've learned about the role of affect in information behaviour/information retrieval. In J. Gascón, F. Bruguillos, & A. Pons, (Eds.), *Proceedings of the 7th ISKO (International Society for Knowledge Organization)-Spain Conference. The Human Dimension of Knowledge Organization* (pp. 342–356). Barcelona, July 6–8, 2005.

Julien, H., McKechnie, L. E. F., & Hart, S. (2005). Affective issues in library and information science systems work: A content analysis. *Library and Information Science Research, 27*(4), 453–466.

Kalbach, J. (2004). Feeling lucky? Emotions and information seeking. *Interactions, 11*(5), 66–67.

Kracker, J. (2002). Research anxiety and students' perceptions of research: An experiment. Part I. Effect of teaching Kuhlthau's ISP model. *Journal of the American Society for Information Science and Technology, 53*(4), 282–294.

Kracker, J., & Wang, P. (2002). Research anxiety and students' perceptions of research: An experiment. Part II. Content analysis of their writings on two experiences. *Journal of the American Society for Information Science and Technology, 53*(4), 295–307.

Kuhlthau, C. C. (1988). Developing a model of the library search process: Cognitive and affective aspects. *RQ, 28*(2), 232–242.

Kurbanoglu, S. S. (2003). Self-efficacy: A concept closely linked to information literacy and lifelong learning. *Journal of Documentation, 59*(6), 635–646.

Leu, L., & Lee, P. S. N. (2005). Multiple determinants of life quality: The roles of Internet activities, use of new media, social support, and leisure activities. *Telematics and Informatics, 22*(3), 161–180.

Mayer, J. D. (2002). Forward. In L. F. Barrett & P. Salovey (Eds.), *The wisdom in meaning: Psychological processes in emotional intelligence* (pp. x–xvi). New York: Guilford Press.

Mellon, C. A. (1986). Library anxiety: A grounded theory and its development. *College & Research Libraries, 47*(2), 160–165.

Nahl, D. (1997). Information counseling inventory of affective and cognitive reactions while learning the Internet. In L. E. M. Martin (Ed.), *The challenge of Internet literacy: The instruction-Web convergence* (pp. 11–33). New York: Haworth Press.

Nahl, D. (2004). Measuring the affective information environment of Web searchers. *Proceedings of the 67th annual meeting of the American Society for Information Science & Technology, 41*, 191–197.

Norman, D. A. (2004). *Emotional design: Why we love (or hate) everyday things.* New York: Basic Books.

Ren, W. (1999). Self-efficacy and the search for government information: A study of small-business executives. *Reference and User Services Quarterly, 38*(3), 283–291.

Savolainen, R. (1995). Everyday life information seeking: Approaching information seeking in the context of 'way of life'. *Library and Information Science Research, 17*(3), 259–294.

Schwarz, N. (2002). Situated cognition and the wisdom in feelings. In L. F. Barrett, & P. Salovey (Eds.), *The wisdom in meaning: Psychological processes in emotional intelligence* (pp. 144–166). New York: Guilford Press.

Shoemaker, S. (2005). Acquisition of computer skills by older users: A mixed methods study. *Research Strategies, 19*, 165–180.

Solomon, P. (1997). Discovering information behavior in sense making. III. The person. *Journal of the American Society for Information Science, 48*, 1127–1138.

APPENDIX A

Interview Questions

1. Why do you use Internet access stations in public libraries?
   a. Do you have Internet access at home, work, and/or school settings?

2. For what purposes are you using these stations?

3. Do you believe that you are "information literate"?
   a. Which specific skills do you believe that you have mastered?
   b. Which specific skills do you believe that you have yet to master?

4. To what degree are you confident about your ability to make effective use of the Internet?

5. How do you feel about being information literate?

6. Do you perceive that a lack of information literacy skills has been a barrier to effective/efficient access to information on the Internet?

7. Are there other barriers that get in your way of effective/efficient access?

8. What sorts of informal or formal training in information literacy skills have you received?
   a. To what degree have these training opportunities benefited you?
   b. How have these opportunities benefited you?

9. Would you like to receive more training?
   a. What form would you like this training to take?
   b. Where would you like to take this training?
   c. What skills would you like to develop further?

10. Do you have any other comments about your Internet use?

11. What is your household income level (0–$20,000/year, $20,001–$40,000, $40,001–$60,000, $60,001–$80,000, $80,001–$100,000, >$100,000)?

12. How long have you been using the Internet?

PART IV

Special Information Environments

CHAPTER 15

The Affective Dimensions of Information Behaviour: A Small World Perspective

Susan Hayter
University of Western Ontario

INTRODUCTION

Information access and social exclusion have for several years been major political buzzwords and are issues that have received considerable political attention. Many governments believe that more effective access to information is one factor that will contribute toward eradicating social exclusion. This chapter explores information behaviour (IB), including issues of access, from the perspective of people living in a socially excluded community, and emphasizes the key role of affective aspects, particularly trust. The literature review and theoretical framework of the project follow, along with methodological issues, the major findings, and associated implications for practice.

LITERATURE REVIEW

Although various cognitive issues associated with IB have emerged from previous research (Childers, 1975; Greenberg & Dervin, 1970; Ingwersen, 1984; Weigts, Widdershoven, Kok, & Tomlow, 1993), relatively few studies have focused on the accompanying affective dimensions (Chatman, 1996; Harris et al., 2001). The affective aspects relate to the emotions and feelings that accompany IB and "include(s) emotion, mood, preference and evaluation" (Julien, McKechnie, & Hart, 2005, p. 454). Among early studies noting the role of affect is the work of Wilson (1981), whose first model of information seeking behaviour includes the dimension of "personal, inter-personal and environmental barriers" (p. 8). Nahl-Jakobovits and Jakobovits (1985) moreover noted the importance of affective elements in motivating users to use library information services. Around the same time, Mellon's (1986) research noted college students' feelings of "library anxiety." Similarly, Kuhlthau (1991) recognized the role of "uncertainty" in information behaviour, noting that students searching for information often experienced "anxiety and lack of confidence" (p. 347) when looking for information. Kuhlthau also points out that students' confidence may increase during the search process, demonstrating the positive side of the affective dimension. The role of affect in the context of health information seeking has also been documented (e.g., Johnson, 1997) as well as in the context of everyday life (Pettigrew, 1999; Savolainen, 1995; Williamson, 1996).

Among affective elements associated with information behaviour, researchers have recorded participants' feelings of disappointment (Harris et al., 2001), reactions of "confusion, frustration (and) self-doubt" (Nahl, 2004, p. 191), "a feeling of lacking confidence" (Heinström, 2002), the need for emotional support (Fisher, Naumer, Durrance, Stromski, & Christiansen, 2005; Hersberger, 2001), and the importance of "friendly, caring sources that leave the information seeker feeling respected" (Julien & Michels, 2000, p. 7). The significance of these affective aspects of IB is considered in the present study.

THEORETICAL FRAMEWORK

The theoretical framework of this study was guided principally by Chatman's studies of the small world lives of disenfranchised populations. Affective and emotional issues of IB were a distinguishing aspect of Chatman's (1992, 1996) work. Her research explored information behaviour in various marginalized groups and settings in society including the working poor (1985), a retirement community (1992), and female prisoners (1999). She recognized the crucial roles of trust and a safe environment in IB, suggesting that "a social support system must exist before persons will engage in an interpersonal process of sharing information" (1992, p. 1), and these strands weave consistently through her findings. By seeking to understand social norms and social realities in order to reach an understanding of IB, Chatman contributed enormously to our theoretical and empirical understanding of information poverty and small world lives. Although the concept of small worlds was previously explored by Schutz and Luckmann (1974) and Kochen (1989), Chatman was the first to use the term within LIS and used the term to describe shared "physical and/or conceptual space within a common landscape of cultural meaning" (2000, p. 3). This conceptualization of a social space where common attitudes, behaviours, and norms construct a collective worldview informed the focus and direction of my study: I was interested in how everyday life within a disadvantaged community shaped information behaviour.

METHOD

As the intent of this study was to explore IB within the context of people's everyday lives, a qualitative, holistic, human-centered approach based on the naturalistic paradigm was adopted. The research questions were as follows:

- Learn about life in a poor community and how it affects information behaviour

- Explore participants' conceptualisations of the term "information"

- Discover the barriers to acquiring information and suggest ways for information providers to improve access to information for people living disadvantaged lives

Sampling

A setting was chosen that met the criterion of "being disadvantaged," according to Indices of Multiple Deprivation scores (Department of Environment, Transport and the Regions [DETR], 2000): a subsidized housing project built in the 1950s to house residents of a slum clearance programme, which was one of the 10 percent most disadvantaged in the U.K. Just over 2,000 people lived in the community, which was on the outskirts of a small but relatively wealthy town in northeastern England. The research participants were visitors to the local community centre, a resource space providing childcare, basic skills programmes, computer training, and interest courses, as well as a gathering spot for locals to chat and eat meals. Twenty-one residents formed the purposive sample along with 13 professional key support workers, including the children's worker, the local police officer, a number of social workers, and others.

Finding willing research participants within the community was difficult as people were wary of a stranger in their midst. Initially, three key community residents agreed to participate in the interviews; they were selected with the advice of the community centre manager and the community support worker. The three participants were key figures within the community; they were respected locally and had lived on the project for many years. All three advised me to delay interviewing other residents until they knew me better, since gaining trust was a key concern. This resulted in almost two years of participant observation although interviews began after six months of observation. This time period was crucial to gaining the research participants' trust and acceptance and to establishing rapport.

Data Collection Methods

Ethnographic data collection methods were appropriate to this investigation and included extended participant observation and semistructured narrative interviews with residents, as well as semistructured interviews with key support workers on the housing project.

Observation occurred for three to five hours at a time on two to four days a week within the community centre. I was interested in finding out what people's everyday lives were like, which cultural issues were important to them, how they communicated and interacted, what their everyday experiences and issues were, and what role information played in their lives.

Observational notes were transcribed immediately following each session. I spent many hours "actively participating" in the centre (Spradley, 1979, p. 60): chatting with respondents, listening to their stories, playing bingo, helping in the computer room and at coffee mornings, and joining in with community events. Listening to people talk about issues, problems, dilemmas they faced, and how, if at all, they resolved them, provided an illuminating picture of everyday lives and of information behaviour. Crucially, this time period allowed the essential development of trust between the participants and the researcher and revealed issues that might never have been discovered by direct questioning.

Interviews were resumed after six months of observation at a point when residents felt comfortable enough with me to agree to talk one-on-one. Furthermore, because of the observation phase, the researcher had sufficient knowledge of their everyday lives to feel confident that they could contribute useful, relevant data to the study. Eighteen further participants were recruited and narrative interviews took place over four months at the participants' convenience; each interview lasted between 20 and 90 minutes. The number of participants was not predetermined, and interviewing stopped when saturation was reached in terms of emerging themes and new ideas.

A narrative approach to interviewing was used as it encourages people to tell stories about their experiences (Flick, 1998) and is an informal method that helps the participants feel comfortable. The interviews opened with an explanation of the research that led to the opening question:

> Can you think of a time recently when you've needed to or wanted to find out about something for yourself or somebody else? [Can you tell me about it? Could you tell me what it was you were trying to find out? Where did you go to find out? Why did you choose that place to find it? Did you get what you needed?]

The questions in brackets were prompts. If the response was not clear, then a second question was asked: "What things concern you most in your life?" And sometimes a third: "If you had a problem you needed or wanted to sort out, where would you normally go?" Or even a fourth: "How do you find out about things that are important to you?" In this manner, the researcher hoped to discover the kinds of information and help needs the participants experienced. Further questions explored participants' interpretations of the word "information," their preferred information sources, and any barriers and enablers they encountered trying to find help. The questions asked were shaped by the participants' responses, and therefore, they were not exactly the same in each interview.

Semistructured interviews simultaneously took place with 13 key workers. The purpose was to supplement observational and narrative data and to explore the residents' lives from a different perspective via key people in their everyday lives, their support workers. For example, the community support worker was a well-known and well-regarded figure on the housing project who had daily interaction with residents. He was able to provide additional tangential information about the kinds of everyday problems and life issues people faced.

Data Analysis

During data collection, a framework for data analysis was developed using the constant-comparative method described by Glaser and Strauss (1967). All interviews were tape recorded and transcribed. Observational data were typed up immediately following each period of observation, resulting in 330 pages of data. Data analysis was inductive, and themes and codes were developed from the data and from the research questions. Although NVivo was initially considered as a data analysis tool, it was discarded in favour of the constant-comparative method, which allowed hands-on contact with the data sets. Because of the unwieldy amount of data, however, Excel was subsequently used to search the data more easily and thoroughly. Overall, four main categories emerged: small world lives, information needs, information sources, and information barriers. Small world categories consisted of three main levels, insularity, cultural issues, and everyday problems, within which were 30 subordinate categories. Twelve main categories of information needs plus an overarching category of "help and support" since affective support was needed to help participants through many information problems. The result of data analysis was a rich, illuminating picture of a unique information world.

FINDINGS
Life in the Community and Its Effects on Information Behaviour

People in this community lived complex and difficult small world lives. This was a community where, according to one resident, "We don't like strangers," and where, according to another, "I had confidence with my own people, my own class, but going to people I didn't know, professionals ... terrified," and also where poor health and financial problems were facts of life, and debt was seen as, "the only way you can cope, you know." Numerous interlinked problems including poverty, unemployment, and crime led to stressful lifestyles, which were compounded by narrow social networks and distrust of outsiders. People recognized their problems but did not always know that help was available or how to get it, and many lacked the energy and the self-confidence to find help or information, particularly outside the comfort zone of the community. People preferred to trust a local familiar information source that was potentially unreliable over an unfamiliar external expert, reaffirming previous studies including Harris et al. (2001), Chatman (1996, 1999), and Fisher et al. (2005), and affective elements determined many aspects of the participants' information behaviour.

Participants' Perceptions of the Term "Information"

One of the research aims was to explore what the term "information" meant to the participants. Participants were asked, "When you hear that word 'information,' what do you think?" For many, the term related to local situations in the community—gossip and local news, rather than to the wider world. This discovery reflected the insularity of the community where a "doorstep culture" predominated, and where people were reluctant to look for help or information in an outside world where people were seen as "foreigners" and not like them.

Other participants associated the term with feelings of unease and trepidation, and some found the term a "scary" and intrusive concept associated with formal institutions. People worried about official intrusions into their personal lives, equating "information" with a possible loss of confidentiality and with revelations about personal, private matters. The word itself formed a semantic barrier, which prevented people from accessing information. Lillian (pseudonym) explained her worries about complex language:

> The big word is: what do they want to know about me? What do they want to know about my life? Information is that big long word; it scares a lot of people … it frightens me; information is a big word. It still frightens us when you said information. That's— what do they want to know about me.

Barriers and Enablers to Accessing Information

Because of fears of others knowing their "business," participants sought help from those whom they trusted: someone friendly, helpful and approachable who would keep personal information private, usually friends and family, or trusted expert workers in the community centre. However, for some, even this step was impossible; Sharon (pseudonym) described how she coped with her depression and other personal problems, "I wouldn't have asked anybody. No, I don't trust anybody. I'd just have to sort it out myself." It was not until she attempted suicide that she reached out for help by phoning the Samaritans, a charity organisation providing confidential support.

The insularity of the community contributed to personal and cultural barriers to seeking information. People tended to look for information within the community where everyone was "helping each other" and where, according to Krissy (pseudonym), "I don't think people will have gone for outside help unless it's really serious." Many also lacked the self-confidence to resolve their problems. The community support worker described how residents needed support for "everyday issues, which might be writing to a gas company to say my bill's too high … make the call, write an appropriate letter, get a result from that. They're like, god, god, oh no, how do I get help with this?" Information that many of us would access easily was very difficult for the residents of this community because of affective issues of fear and anxiety.

In order to consider factors that would *enable* people to access help, participants were asked to think about the type of person or place they would prefer to ask for help or information. They identified many enablers, which focused principally on "soft skills" such as trust and friendliness. Regarding the type of person, participants had strong specific opinions: The person needed to be a good communicator who would "have time," "be approachable," "speak our language … use small understandable words," "be able to listen well," and "build up relationships with people. Trust, yeah." Trust, listening skills, rapport, and confidentiality were vital.

The preferred place would need to be "on the estate where there's people I know, where you know who you're talking to and that, [cause] you don't always know who you're talking to sometimes, do you?" For some, the community centre was such a place: It was a place where they felt comfortable and it was local. Residents had access to help and information from expert workers and, as Jim described:

> I come to the centre because they're really helpful, and if I don't know who to contact, there's always someone here who does … we all build our trust in each other.

The community centre contained various spaces where people shared information. It was an example of a thriving information ground (Pettigrew, 1999)—an informal place where people come together for a specific reason and serendipitously end up sharing information. Within the centre, a group of basic skills learners supported and helped each other in a trusting environment where they felt comfortable to ask for and share information. Within this setting, the residents researched local history, chatted, learned computer skills, and created a calendar for which they won a national award. The presence of this information ground enabled access to information: It was local, friendly, informal, helpful, and because of this, it was also successful.

Eileen's Story

The various affective aspects of information behaviour including the barriers and enablers to information access discussed previously are synthesized and illustrated in Eileen's search for help and information (see Figure 15.1). Although Eileen's help needs were unique to her, the ways she responded to them and the barriers she faced demonstrate the typical complexity and iterative nature of acquiring information in this specific context.

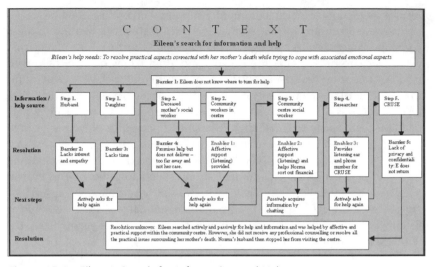

Figure 15.1   Eileen's Search for Information and Help

Her attempts to find help were broadly similar to other research participants' in that it was difficult for her to articulate the help she needed, she did not know where to start, she relied on trusted workers within the community to help her, and she did not want to go outside the community for help.

Eileen was in her early 40s, and married with two daughters and three grandchildren. She needed help sorting out her late mother's estate and resolving the emotional stress caused by her grief. Her problems had affective and cognitive dimensions. Eileen was desperately unhappy about her mother's death, beyond what appeared to be the norm. She was emotionally fragile owing to enduring constant verbal abuse from her husband and trying to help one of her daughters deal with the aftermath of rape. The daughter and grandson lived with Eileen and, in fact, the three of them slept in the same room as Eileen refused to sleep with her husband.

Eileen needed and wanted help, but she did not know how to find it. This was the first barrier she faced (Barrier 1). In Step 1 of help-seeking, she tried to talk to her husband, but he could not understand, had his own problems—he was a diabetic, had suffered a debilitating stroke, and had anger management problems—and he became angry with Eileen (Barrier 2). Her daughter was also unable to help as she was consumed with her own emotional problems (Barrier 3). Eileen had a brother, but they were estranged, and she did not intend telling him that their mother had died, so she could gain no emotional or practical support from him. Eileen's next step (Step 2) was to turn to two trusted community workers she knew in the community centre. For reasons that were unclear, Eileen did not progress with resolving her problem this way, although she said that sharing it lessened the burden (Enabler 1). Simultaneously (Step 2), Eileen contacted her mother's social worker to sort out her mother's effects. The social worker explained that since Eileen had no bank account, there might be problems with inheritance (this, in fact, was not true, but it worried Eileen as she did not want a bank account). The social worker also told her that she would find her the telephone number for a bereavement service. Eileen did not hear from her mother's social worker again. At this point in her search for resolution of her problems, she felt stuck (Barrier 4). Eileen's third step (Step 3) was to talk to a trusted social worker in the community centre about sorting out her mother's estate, and he did help (Enabler 2), but she still felt unable to resolve her emotional problems. At that point, I got to know her story (Step 4) when we were chatting in the community centre. She said she did not know how to get help and was feeling desperate: Her hair was falling out, and she was clearly emotionally anguished. I gave her the local bereavement service's telephone number and also asked Eileen's daughter to phone them (Step 5). Eileen said that chatting with me helped her feel better (Enabler 3). However, when she discovered that the bereavement session was in the town centre and that it was an open session, Eileen could not cope (Barrier 5), so her search for help floundered. Her husband then stopped her from visiting the centre when he was banned for threatening behaviour.

Several affective barriers hindered Eileen's search for help and information: her family's lack of interest and time, her own lack of self-confidence, her desire for privacy, her fear of being away from the community, her lack of knowledge about how she could resolve her problems, the unexplained inability of certain community centre workers to help her, and her lack of trust in outsiders. However, the emotional support she received did enable Eileen to resolve some of her problems and illustrates the ways in which emotional support can be crucial in help seeking.

IMPLICATIONS FOR PRACTICE

If people like Eileen are to access the help and information they so desperately need, then it is crucial to develop and maintain trusting relationships between information providers and this type of population. Several ideas can be extrapolated from this study and may directly improve practice:

1. *Value and develop interpersonal skills* – The role of trust in nurturing relationships that encourage those who are in some way disadvantaged to access information is huge. Interpersonal skills such as listening, caring, and sharing are essential to establishing and maintaining trust. People living in disadvantaged circumstances often need emotional support when looking for and accessing information. Staff training and attitudes are key.

2. *Use the term "information" with care* – For this particular group of people, the term was often a frightening one; it may be better

to talk in terms of "help" or "problem solving" when dealing with people who are insecure or lacking in confidence.

3. *Start where people are* – Information providers need to value and build upon local information sources within small worlds rather than expecting disadvantaged people to conform to systems and people that are unfamiliar and uncomfortable. People living in disadvantaged communities face difficult barriers in accessing appropriate information and information providers need to build bridges to access.

4. *Work in partnership* – It is imperative that help, advice, and information providers focus on working in sustained partnership with other help agencies such as social workers, health and education professionals, and financial institutions. If information providers want to be truly accessible to all, they need to be part of all community partnerships working with socially excluded people and focus on developing trusting relationships with people within their communities.

5. *Provide continuity* – Funding for initiatives to improve the lives of socially excluded people is often short-term, which means a lack of continuity and support. Gaining trust takes time and effort, often years of work. Better still, ensure that socially inclusive practices start at policy level so that they become part of the working culture.

CONCLUSION

The affective aspects of information behaviour, particularly trust and interpersonal skills, were vital to successful information and help seeking for this particular community. Their everyday lives were insular and difficult, and many of their help needs were complex and interlinked. Without access to relevant information from supportive, accessible, trusted information providers, it is possible that people living in these types of communities will remain locked out of help and information sources that could help them gain more control of their lives.

REFERENCES

Chatman, E. A. (1985). Information, mass media use, and the working poor. *Library and Information Science Research, 7*(2), 97–113.

Chatman, E. A. (1992). *The information world of retired women*. Westport, CT: Greenwood Press.

Chatman, E. A. (1996). The impoverished life-world of outsiders. *Journal of the American Society for Information Science, 47*(3), 193–206.

Chatman, E. A. (1999). A theory of life in the round. *Journal of the American Society for Information Science, 50*(3), 207–217.

Chatman, E. A. (2000). Framing social life in theory and research. *The New Review of Information Behavior Research, 1,* 3–17.

Childers, T. (1975). *The information poor in America.* Metuchen, NJ: Scarecrow Press.

Department of Environment, Transport and the Regions. (2000). *Indices of multiple deprivation.* London: Department of Environment, Transport and the Regions. Accessed December 5, 2006, from www.odpm.gov.uk/index.asp?id=1128626.

Fisher, K., Naumer, C., Durrance, J., Stromski, L., & Christiansen, T. (2005). Something old, something new: Preliminary findings from an exploratory study about people's information habits and information grounds. *Information Research, 10*(2), paper 223. Accessed December 5, 2006, from informationr.net/ir/10-2/paper223.html.

Flick, U. (1998). *An introduction to narrative research.* London: Sage Publications.

Glaser, B. G., & Strauss, A. L. (1967). *The discovery of grounded theory: Strategies for qualitative research.* New York: Aldine de Gruyter.

Greenberg, B. S., & Dervin, B. (1970). *Use of the mass media by the urban poor: Findings of three research projects with an annotated bibliography.* New York: Praeger.

Harris R., Stickney J., Grasley C., Hutchinson G., Greaves L., & Boyd T. (2001). Searching for help and information: Abused women speak out. *Library and Information Science Research, 23*(2), 123–141.

Heinström, J. (2002). *Fast surfers, broad scanners and deep divers: Personality and information seeking behaviour.* Åbo, Finland: Åbo Akademi University Press. Accessed December 5, 2006, from www.abo.fi/~jheinstr/thesis.htm.

Hersberger, J. (2001). Everyday life information needs and information sources of homeless parents. In P. Vakkari (Ed.), *The new review of information behaviour research: Studies of information seeking in context* (pp.119–134). Cambridge: Taylor Graham.

Ingwersen, P. (1984). Psychological aspects of information retrieval. *Social Science Information Studies, 4*(2/3), 83–89.

Johnson, J. D. (1997). *Cancer-related information seeking.* Cresskill, NJ: Hampton Press.

Julien, H., McKechnie, L. (E. F.), & Hart, S. (2005). Affective issues in library and information science systems work: A content analysis. *Library and Information Science Research, 27*(4), 453–466.

Julien, H., & Michels, D. (2000). Source selection among information seekers: Ideals and realities. *Canadian Journal of Information and Library Science, 25*(1), 1–18.

Kochen, M. (1989). *The Small World.* Norwood, NJ: Ablex.

Kuhlthau, C. C. (1991). Inside the search process: Information seeking from the user's perspective. *Journal of the American Society for Information Science, 42*(5), 361–371.

Mellon, C. A. (1986). Library anxiety: A grounded theory and its development. *College & Research Libraries, 47*(2), 160–165.

Nahl, D. (2004). Measuring the affective information environment of Web searchers. *Proceedings of the 67th annual meeting of the American Society for Information Science & Technology, 41,* 191–197.

Nahl-Jakobovits, D., & Jakobovits L. A. (1985). Managing the affective micro-information environment. *Research Strategies, 3*(1), 17–28.

Pettigrew, K. E. (1999). Waiting for chiropody: Contextual results from an ethnographic study of the information behaviour among attendees at community clinics. *Information Processing and Management, 35*(6), 801–817.

Savolainen, R. (1995). Everyday life information seeking: Approaching information seeking in the context of 'way of life'. *Library and Information Science Research, 17*(3), 259–294.

Schutz, A., & Luckmann, T. (1974). *The structures of the life-world.* London: Heinemann.

Spradley, J. P. (1979). *The ethnographic interview.* New York: Holt, Rhinehart and Winston.

Weigts, W., Widdershoven, G., Kok, G., & Tomlow, P. (1993). Patients' information seeking actions and physicians' responses in gynaecological consultations. *Qualitative Health Research, 3,* 398–429.

Williamson, K. (1996). The information needs and information seeking behaviour of older adults: An Australian study. In P. Vakkari, R. Savolainen & B. Dervin (Eds.), *Information seeking in context: Proceedings of an International Conference on Research in Information Needs, Seeking, and Use in Different Contexts (Aug. 14–16, 1996, Tampere, Finland)* (pp. 337–350). London: Graham Taylor.

Wilson, T. D. (1981). On user studies and information needs. *Journal of Documentation, 37*(1), 3–15. Accessed December 5, 2006, from informationr.net/tdw/publ/papers/1981infoneeds.html.

CHAPTER 16

Emotions in Information Seeking of Blind People

Wooseob Jeong
University of Wisconsin, Milwaukee

INTRODUCTION

Visual impairment includes a wide range of vision loss, from legal blindness with limited sight to complete blindness. For the visually impaired, routine tasks can be difficult and living independently a challenge. The American Disability Act, signed in 1990, has increased awareness of these challenges and improved public services to the visually impaired. There are also many national and local organizations that provide valuable information and administer programs that help the visually impaired meet challenges more easily and conveniently. These organizations and public service providers must continue to provide up-to-date information, services, and adaptive devices for the visually impaired.

Visual impairment of any degree complicates the way people access information. With technology playing a central role in information provision, developing computing solutions is necessary. Numerous accessibility studies in the computer related area have been completed. In order to develop information and communication technologies and services for the visually impaired, it is important to consider their information seeking behavior and their emotional frustration with the challenges of everyday life.

While studying the use of an alternative interface for the blind, data was collected about the blind participants' information seeking behavior with a focus on their emotions. A more complete understanding of information seeking behavior and of the emotional fluctuations inherent in accessing information will provide a valuable starting point for providing better information services to the visually impaired.

LITERATURE REVIEW

Preparation for this study included a review of research literature covering the study of the information seeking behavior of visually impaired people, the "small world" of blind people, and the differences and similarities between the totally blind and partially sighted people.

Research on Information Seeking Behavior of Visually Impaired People

Williamson, Schauder, and Bow (2000) deplored the paucity of studies on the information seeking behavior of groups with disabilities, but some research on the visually impaired has been completed. The Canadian National Institute for the Blind (CNIB) conducted a comprehensive survey on the everyday lives of visually impaired young people in 2005. Three hundred and thirty visually impaired youth participated in the survey. The results of the study were focused on three areas: the vocational and social domains, and the activities of daily life. While most of the findings were quantitative, some were qualitative (CNIB, 2005). The report covers some of the emotional and affective aspects living with visual impairment, including frustration in personal relationships, dating or marriage, and the difficulties of job seeking leading the seekers to "give up."

Another increasing area of research is vision loss among elderly people. People are living longer but often have trouble with their vision. Later vision loss results from diseases such as diabetes and combines with other circumstances such as a slowing of motion ability to complicate the lives of the elderly.

The incidence of emotional instability in blind people has also been studied. For example, Koenes and Karshmer (2000) conducted a study with 22 blind and 29 sighted adolescents and found that the blind adolescents were significantly more likely to suffer from depression than the sighted adolescents. Horowitz, Reinhardt, and Kennedy (2005) studied 584 adults, age 65 and older, and found that 7 percent were currently dealing with major depression and 26.9 percent met the criteria for a sub-threshold depression.

The provision of library services for the visually impaired is an active area of research, and there are hopes to improve access for them via digital libraries. Kavanagh (1999) noted that even in developed countries, services to blind patrons do not meet library service benchmarks set for the general population. However, with the advent of digital libraries, there is optimism that virtual libraries can make audio and video materials available to visually impaired people in their homes, overcoming the physical barriers in traditional libraries (Gunn 2002). Kautzman (1998) praised the availability of adaptive technology for digital libraries such as refreshable Braille displays, screen readers with a synthesized voice output, and large buttons on keyboards.

The role of the Internet in information seeking is no less important for the visually impaired than for the sighted. Williamson et al. (2000) conducted focus groups and individual interviews with 31 participants to find a wide range of usage of the Internet by the visually impaired and suggested more efforts to provide equitable access to the Internet, emphasizing independence in information seeking and the freedom to choose in information access strategies. However, the Internet forces the user to use nonlinear information provision, which is a tremendous challenge without vision especially on the World Wide Web (Craven, 2004). The hypertext mode, which gives sighted people the capability of jumping back and forth between search results and information sources, does not serve the visually impaired whose mode of information seeking is more linear. The linear mode is easily found in currently popular synthesized voice outputs.

Saumure and Given (2004) interviewed six visually impaired undergraduate students about their academic information seeking behavior and suggested possible improvements to library services, including interlibrary sharing of adapted resources such as Braille materials and the creation of services to facilitate visually impaired students' information behaviors while allowing them to maintain personal independence.

A number of studies have investigated the topic of adventure program outcomes for people with disabilities, particularly in relation to positive emotional attitude changes. Eagan's research (2004) uncovered the excitement and increased motivation of eight visually impaired students during a one-day sea-kayaking event.

"Small World" Concept

Among various information seeking behavior theories, Chatman's "life in the round" theory best explains blind people's information seeking behavior. The visually impaired live a "life in the round," which is generally routine and predictable and under the close examination of others, making information seeking outside of this small world unnecessary and undesirable (Chatman, 1991). Her "small world" concept helps increase the understanding of the indifference, rudeness, and independence of blind people, which are discussed in the following sections.

Totally Blind vs. Partially Sighted People

In visually impaired research, it is necessary to separate studies on totally blind people from those on partially sighted people. They are different groups, especially if the "legally" blind or those with low vision are included in the definition of visually impaired. Those partially sighted people have very close to normal lives, while the totally blind people cannot do anything without special assistance or consideration. In fact, the totally blind represent a very small portion of the visually impaired population. According to a DVR (Division of Vocational Rehabilitation) advisor in a Midwest state, less than 5 percent of her advisees are totally blind, and they need special attention quite different from partially sighted people.

Many studies combine both totally blind and partially visually impaired subjects in their data collection and analysis. This may lead to inappropriate generalizations being made. This may be partially caused by the lack of totally blind people to be included in their research.

In addition, few studies include blind people with multiple physical or mental disabilities. As discussed later, it is quite challenging to have multi-disability participants in experiments or interviews. Most studies dealt with people whose only disability is vision loss.

Literature on the visually impaired usually does not separate the totally blind people from the partially sighted even though the groups are quite different. While reference to the emotional aspects of the blind can be found sporadically in the literature, very few studies revealed them explicitly. This study will explore the emotional information seeking behavior of the totally blind in an explicit manner.

RESEARCH QUESTIONS

This study addressed how totally blind people personally cope with their emotions in various information seeking situations. In addition, it describes how they react to technology and society emotionally, and how those who assist them perceive their emotional behavior.

METHOD

This study employed a qualitative inquiry method. Nineteen totally blind people with Braille reading ability participated in data collection. The study took place in a city in the Midwest of the U.S. with a total population of about 1 million. Interviews were held in a community center for the blind, in a hotel lobby at a regional meeting of a national association for the blind, and at the participants' own homes.

The age of the participants was varied, including: teens (4), 20s (5), 30s (2), 50s (4), and 60s (4). There were nine females and 10 males. All participants were totally blind and 17 out of 19 were born blind. All were able to read Braille.

Interviews with open-ended questions were employed to gain qualitative data. Data were coded and analyzed based on a grounded theory to identify recurring themes and generate categories of affect that blind people experience in everyday life. Analyzed data included the participants' comments, the researcher's observational notes, the comments of two advisors who worked for the State Department of Vocational Rehabilitation (DVR), feedback from one former librarian who worked at the department for the visually impaired in a big city's public library, as well as parents or spouses involved in blind people's lives. Advisors were asked to describe their experiences with blind people's emotional information seeking behavior either in applying for a job or in using the library.

FINDINGS

Data analysis yielded affective dimensions that blind people experienced in everyday life and revealed salient characteristics about their lives. These are described in the following sections.

Denial of Blindness

It is extremely emotional for blind people to accept their blindness. However, the types of denial differ depending on when they became blind. One type of denial is more common for those who were born blind and have never seen anything, and the other type of denial is common for those who become blind later in life. Those who are born blind typically struggled as adolescents. As one participant, a married blind woman with three children, noted:

> I was a typical teenager and I did not want to be different from my friends at school. I really hated using my cane and I went to school without it. Well, I soon realized I need that cane not only for me but also for other students.

Most blind teenagers believe or are encouraged to believe they have as many career opportunities as sighted teenagers. That often hinders them from thinking realistically about their near future. A DVR teacher explained their enormous resistance to changing this way of thinking:

> They keep insisting they can do anything and keep asking me why now. I try to explain the reality to them as much as I can. Finally they cry, really cry loud. The moment is so important. The earlier that moment of crying, the better for their real start of life! From that moment, they can start a real life including their job. Before that, it is really just a denial of reality.

The lack of courtesy and understanding from sighted adolescents creates many issues for blind students. The following happened to a 14-year-old blind boy when he was waiting for his father after school. A vision teacher told this story:

> The blind boy, excited, told a sighted boy, 'You know what, I did wrestling this afternoon in my gym class. It was so fun.' And the sighted boy replied with denial, 'You're kidding. You can't do wrestling. You are blind!' The blind boy got emotionally disturbed. 'Yes, I did and I can.' 'No, you cannot!' the sighted boy disagreed. Then, the boy jumped on the sighted boy. They really wrestled.

According to the DVR advisors, people who became blind later in life had a hard time gaining new skills for information gathering, such as Braille reading and using voice synthesizer software. Some eventually realize and accept that they are blind and start to work on those skills, but others continue denying their blindness and become depressed.

Emotional Family Support

All of the parents watching their blind child's performance during the experiments provided extraordinary encouragement. In many cases, their supporting actions were carefully generated not to hurt their children's feelings. A 13-year-old boy's mother took great pride in his ability to play computer audio games, saying: "I'm so proud of my son. His brother cannot win the game because he is so good at the game." This kind of emotional family support, particularly from parents, leads to the controversial issue of mainstreaming blind students.

Mainstream Society: Separation vs. Integration

There were four blind teenagers in my experiments, and each attended a "mainstream" school, although there is a state-funded school designated for blind students two hours away. One of the participants had recently moved from that school to a mainstream school. The issue of whether separate schools or mainstream schools are better for blind students is controversial. According to the DVR advisors, parents believe it is better to put their blind children in schools with sighted students to help prepare them for integration into mainstream society. However, this might be wishful thinking on the parents' part. A 29-year-old male participant went to mainstream schools until his sophomore year in high school and then moved to the school for the blind. His mom believed the mainstream schools were better for him, but numerous incidents at school made him quite frustrated and isolated from other students. After he moved to the school for the blind, his life totally changed. He commented:

> The naughty kids were putting me in a girl's room instead of a boy's room. I did not see anything, but those girls screamed and I got really embarrassed. One time they left me at the boiler room instead of the cafeteria at lunchtime. It was so dangerous, you know. The kids had no idea and no attitude for the blind. The kids just did those things for fun, but they hurt really my feelings. My mom was wrong. When I moved to the school for the blind, I felt it was like heaven. The facilities were well laid out so that I did not have to bump a lot. I knew everybody in the school. We had really good time together.

Frustrations from Everyday Things

There are many things that can frustrate blind people in the course of everyday life. Some of these difficulties stem from the mere ignorance of sighted people. Blind people do not think ignorance is intentional, but they desire a little bit more attention and carefulness by sighted people when they develop technology that is used in everyday life. For example, most glucose meters have a fancy LED that visually displays a number, which has no value for the blind. As one participant said:

> I have diabetes. Currently only one talking glucose meter is available and it's pricy. I wish there were more alternative glucose meters with reasonable prices. Hearing about many cheaper glucose meters makes me frustrated often.

Washing machines and dryers are another example. One participant mentioned:

> Not long ago, those machines had geared knobs, which even blind people can figure out options and times. However, now many new wash machines and driers have only the fancy digital displays. I don't understand what the sighted people think of our blind folks.

The visual cues that accompany directions are also an area of frustration for the blind, especially for those born blind. Since they have never seen anything, they do not have any images in their minds. Even though they learn basic shapes by touching later in their lives, visual cues absolutely frustrate them. One subject commented:

> You sighted guys never understand that we don't have those visual cues. Everyday we come up with all the directions such as 'bend like J shape.' It doesn't make sense to us at all.

This problem was confirmed during the force feedback study. When they were presented with force feedback of the "L" shape, all of them identified it as "a triangle." In their minds, there is no "L" shape, but they have learned about a triangle, which approximates the "L" shape from their perspective.

Walled-Off, Indifference, and Lack of Motivation

During my recruiting efforts for participants in the Braille research, I felt distant from groups of blind people. This is a common feeling, confirmed by a former librarian for the blind. He explained:

> Until several contacts to the blind people, even with good
> intent such as outreach of library services, blind people do not
> open their minds easily. However, once they open their minds,
> they are really communicating with you. Accessibility research
> does not conduct enough experiments with blind people,
> which can be explained by blind people's lack of motivation to
> participate.

This walled-off phenomenon, especially the indifferent attitude, can be
further explained by Chatman's "small world" concept (1991). There is a designated apartment complex for blind people in town with 75 units. I expected
many of the residents to participate in this research, which offered a $20 an
hour incentive. However, only five people did so. I reminded the community
of the study several times, but no additional participants volunteered.

Many studies on visually impaired people's lives deal with both totally
blind people and partially sighted people. One speculated explanation is that
it is not easy to locate active and motivated people that are completely blind,
which can be quite frustrating for the researchers' point of view.

I visited the apartments of four blind people and was surprised to see the
high level of organization in their residences. They were as organized as
sighted people's apartments. As one participant noted, "Well, I have to be
organized to make my daily life easy. Everything should be at the same location." However, according to DVR advisors:

> There are some well-organized blind people, but there are other
> blind people who are totally unorganized and do not clean their
> houses appropriately. I have several clients whose houses I really
> do not visit. You cannot believe how filthy their houses are. The
> well-organized blind people got trained well and usually are
> older. Those who do not organize still depend on sighted family
> members help and they do not realize the benefit of organization
> yet. They don't have motivation.

Rudeness

During data collection, I often felt the participants were a bit rude. Several
appointments were cancelled abruptly, and some participants never showed
up for their scheduled appointments. It could be because blind people easily
forget things or can focus only on limited items at a time.

A DVR advisor concurred, saying,

> Yes, you are right. They are rude. You don't believe what the sit-
> uation looked like when blind people gathered at an annual

> meeting in a crowded hotel and literally swung their canes. It was
> absolutely horrible.

Emotions were also expressed in the form of rudeness in the course of
library service for the blind people. A main library in the city sends audio-
books requested by visually impaired people to their homes. Very often, if the
delivery is late one or two days, they call immediately and speak with anger
to library staff. As one former librarian said, "You have no idea how angry
they are when the delivery is delayed."

Independence on Their Own Terms

One of the most important aspects of blind people's everyday life is independence. However, it seems that they define independence in their own
ways, which may be viewed as "independent" independence. It leads to mil-
itarism in some organizations of the blind. Some blind associations are modest; others are more military-like. For example, in one national association
training facility, everybody—whether blind or sighted—is blindfolded from
the gate, thereby addressing the importance of everybody's independence.
One DVR advisor explained:

> It's a horrible experience for a sighted person in the facility.
> Even blind people feel uncomfortable with their strict rules and
> harsh training. However, they claim once they get through
> those courses, blind participants will get more confidence and
> motivation.

Feeling Good at Outdoor Activities

Some of the participants were not interested in outdoor activities due to
their limited mobility and fear-of being hurt. However, others enjoyed various outdoor activities and even encouraged their blind friends to participate in them. The active participants connected their motivation to
participate in those activities and their positive feelings after participating
to their independence.

When asked about their leisure time, the blind participants were quite
excited to discuss their outdoor activities, which included hobbies such as
horseback riding, milking cows, skiing, and shark fishing, as well as traveling
to Mardi Gras and taking cruise tours. This excitement was echoed in these
statements:

> It was really fun to ski although somebody holds you behind.
> You know what, I made the cruise. I could feel the whole
> bunch of water.

The shark was so strong, wow! I still can feel the power, so another guy helped and we got it. The more exciting thing happened then. Sashimi the shark! The feeling of sashimi knife's blade on the shark's flesh was unforgettable.

When we went cow milking, everybody got scared if the cow might hit us with her back legs. Nothing happened fortunately. The interesting texture of cow's teats is always reminded when I drink a cup of milk.

You never know what it looks like when you are in the middle of ONE million people passing you at Mardi Gras! They keep shoving you and you feel like floating to somewhere else.

Satisfaction with Current Technology

The blind participants are using computers and the Internet actively and extensively. Email and Web surfing are already a part of their daily life. About half of the participants contacted me via email showing their interest in my research. Several of them printed out the informed consent form ahead of their experiment session to save significant time for me. A high school senior turned on her instant messenger constantly so that she could chat with her friends. A 29-year-old male participant proudly told me about his active participation in an Internet community devoted to finding missing children. He receives hundreds of email messages everyday and spends most of his time replying to them. He also broadcasts his own radio talk show over the Internet with a free account from a personal Internet broadcasting company.

One interesting way computing has been integrated into blind people's everyday life is through the playing of audio-based computer games. These games have no screen display, but provide audio cues. They are totally linear and depend on the players' memory. Like sighted teenagers, a 13-year-old blind participant loves to play such games. He even showed how well he could play during the interview, getting completely immersed in the game and ignoring the interview itself. Another teenager showed me her driving and shooting game, which I could not follow entirely due to the linear mode of the design.

To my surprise, all the participants were happy with the current level of technology they can use for information seeking. Several of them tried to show off their refreshable Braille pads with great excitement, emphasizing that they could do many things with the expensive (several thousand dollars apiece) devices. They also expressed great satisfaction in voice synthesizing output software, even though it requires a linear retrieval with unusually fast speeds of mechanical reading voices. Over the phone, a participant tried to make an appointment using his email calendar program. It took a while to find a free slot on his schedule, but he was still excited that he could make it. When I asked him about the learning curve for the program, he said, "Yes, it took long for me to get used to this program, but I like it now. Technology we should learn anyway." An older female participant bragged that she has used computers for such a long time that she remembers the Apple II.

The participants' technology was often not up-to-date, which is surprising because it is either state and/or federally funded. One of the participants was using a Windows 95 notebook computer that was provided by the state in late 2005. At that time, sighted people were talking about Windows Vista, the newly available operating system. Yet, the participant appreciated the "gift" from the state and was satisfied with its functionality. One other participant showed off, saying he just got Windows XP, although it had been around for more than five years. It is possible that their need for new technology is suppressed. One participant commented:

> I would like to test like beta test with many new software programs if they provide. Now I'm excited to get used to the new operating system, XP. So far I used Windows 98.

CONCLUSION

This study investigated the emotional aspects of totally blind people's information seeking behavior, excluding partially sighted people. The findings revealed the various emotional aspects of blind people's information seeking behavior from the frustrations inherent in everyday life to the suppression of their technology needs. This implies that we may have to change the way we view the information needs of the completely blind instead of considering them to be the same as those of partially sighted people.

More research with the completely blind is necessary to draw a holistic picture of their everyday information seeking behavior. That will help us to better fulfill blind users' information needs while helping them maintain their independence.

REFERENCES

Canadian National Institute for the Blind (2005). *The status of Canadian youth who are blind or visually impaired*. Toronto, Canada.

Chatman, E. A. (1991). Life in a small world: Application of gratification theory to information-seeking behavior. *Journal of the American Society for Information Science*, *42*(6), 438–449.

Craven, J. (2004). Linear searching in a non-linear environment: The information seeking behavior of visually impaired people on the World Wide Web. *Lecture Notes in Computer Science*, *3118*, 530–537.

Eagan, N. (2004). The meaning associated with the experience of a sea kayaking adventure among adults with visual impairment. In P. Tierney & D. Chavez (Eds.), *The Fourth Social Aspects and Recreation Research Symposium, 2004 February 4–6*. San Francisco, CA: San Francisco State University. Accessed November 25, 2006, from www.fs.fed.us/psw/programs/recreation/pdf/2004_sarr_proceedings_session_08.pdf.

Gunn, H. (2002) Virtual libraries supporting student learning. *School Libraries Worldwide, 8*(2): 27–37.

Horowitz, A., Reinhardt, J. P., & Kennedy, G. J. (2005). Major and subthreshold depression among older adults seeking vision rehabilitation services. *The American Journal of Geriatric Psychiatry, 13*, 180–187.

Kautzman, A. M. (1998). Virtuous, virtual access: Making Web pages accessible to people with disabilities. *Searcher, 6*(6): 42–49.

Kavanagh, R. (1999). The virtual library for blind and visually impaired Canadians. *Feliciter, 45*(5), 296–299.

Koenes, S. G., & Karshmer, J. (2000). Depression: A comparison study between blind and sighted adolescents. *Issues in Mental Health Nursing, 21*(3): 269–279.

Saumure, K., & Given, L. M. (2004). Digitally enhanced? An examination of the information behaviors of visually impaired post-secondary students. *The Canadian Journal of Information and Library Science, 28*(2), 25–42.

Williamson, K., Schauder, D., & Bow, A. (2000). Information seeking by blind and sight impaired citizens: An ecological study. *Information Research, 5*(4). Accessed November 25, 2006, from informationr.net/ir/5-4/paper79.html.

CHAPTER 17

Affective Factors in Information Seeking During the Cross-Cultural Learning Process of International Doctoral Students in Library and Information Science Education

Bharat Mehra
University of Tennessee

INTRODUCTION

The role of affect as a control process that determines cognitive and sensory-motor behavior and provides directionality to cognition and action (Bilal, 2005; Nahl, 1998a, 1998b) in constructivist learning and information search processes (Kulhthau, 2004) is central to the idea of learning as a process of construction involving the complete individual and all dimensions of her or his experience (Bruner, 1973; Dewey, 1933). However, learning in cross-cultural experiences has not been directly addressed in past research on constructivist learning. This chapter attempts to fill the gap by documenting intersections between emotions and information seeking activities in cross-cultural learning of international doctoral students in library and information science (LIS) education.

The cross-cultural learning process is a holistic learning experience in which affective states are integral to actions and intellect. These connections must be recognized and understood within the cross-cultural learning process in order for LIS programs, and American academy as a whole, to make improvements for effectiveness in student learning, as well as extend internationalization via improvements in their own knowledge domains, programs and policies, curriculum planning and content, and instructional practices, among other areas, based on learning from international students' experiences (Mehra & Bishop, in press).

The focus of this research is on the cross-cultural learning process from the international doctoral student point of view. An operational definition of the "cross-cultural learning process" for this research is that it is a complex learning process, taking place across two or more cultural settings (based on the international doctoral student's nation, country of origin, and/or past resident country) and involving international doctoral students' thoughts, feelings, and actions over a prolonged period of time. The cross-cultural learning process represents intertwining of experiential elements shaped by both academic learning and cross-cultural adaptation. Often, the goal of academic learning in doctoral programs in the U.S. is clearly identified as teaching students to recognize the broad dimensions of the specific discipline, as well as establishing their own focused area of research, in the time they start and complete the program. On the other hand, the goal of cross-cultural adaptation is not clear since different individuals perceive and adapt in different ways. Both academic learning and cross-cultural adaptation processes are reflected in LIS international doctoral students' emotional-physical responses during their cross-cultural learning process. Cross-cultural learning is marked by a temporal beginning and an end to reflect the structural clarity in the goal of academic learning, while at the same end, the intermediate phases in the cross-cultural learning process represent non-sequential emotional, psychological, and/or symbolic markers in individual experiences that represent the ambiguities in the goal of cross-cultural adaptation.

THEORETICAL INTERSECTIONS

The theoretical basis for this research draws on intersections between emotions, actions, and learning as a process of construction during "sense-making" in a *culturally alien information environment.* When international students join educational institutions in the U.S., they encounter all-encompassing culturally alien information environments that are marked by uncertain situations resulting from cultural differences compared to what they are familiar with in their countries of origin and/or past resident country. The newness experienced in these everyday situations is a result of unfamiliarity with American norms and values, practices and behaviors, procedures and policies, and forms of social interaction, that together lead to a perception of *alienness* in the new cultural and educational environment (Mehra & Papajohn, in press). The alienness is accentuated and coupled with new socio-technical processes in LIS learning and information seeking environments; international students "make sense" of the newness in learning styles and teaching expectations in LIS education, as well as cope in response to the encountered new information-related processes in areas such as information processing and management, organization and representation of information, information retrieval and dissemination, among others.

This research recognizes the intersections between international doctoral students' feelings and actions in a cross-cultural learning process, and the information behavior changes in each phase along with the affective states, as important signifiers during "sense-making" experiences in the LIS culturally alien information environment. This awareness extends beyond "sense-making" research by better understanding the processes of "doing" and their relationship to emotions in "sense-making" (Dervin, 1993), instead of focusing on elusive, ever-changing and constantly challenged nouns as previously studied (Dervin, 1999).

Learning is viewed as a process of construction in which knowledge is constructed as an active process that learners are personally engaged in as a result of socialization with others, and in which learners construct knowledge and make their own symbolic representations of action (Gagnon & Collay, 2001). Only recently, scholars have realized the complex interplay between emotions and learning in the process of construction (Kort, Reilly, & Picard, 2001). For example, affect plays a critical role in decision making, performance, and cognitive processes in constructivist learning (Goldman, 1995; Picard et al., 2004). These assumptions are also applicable in any cross-cultural learning process—emotions drive actions to help cross-cultural learners navigate their experiences and construct knowledge to explain phenomena, behavior, and actions not immediately understandable to them— these ways may differ from person to person, based on individual and cultural factors and how associated individual and cultural variables shape perception of those experiences (Mehra, 2005).

Kelly's (1963) Personal Construct Theory extends Piaget's (1990) and Dewey's (1933) philosophical ideas to provide a psychological perspective to the process of learning in terms of five phases: confusion and doubt, mounting confusion and possible threat, tentative hypothesis, testing and assessing, and reconstructing. Like Dewey's ideas on reflective thinking, Kelly's sequence of phases also recognize affective states as integral to constructs or "patterns that one formulates to make sense of the world" that are highly personalized and based on one's past experiences (Kuhlthau, 2004, p. 17). Kelly's emphasis on the disruption of personal constructs based on new information and the resulting increase in confusion and doubt, especially during the early phases in the process of constructed learning, aptly applies to the cross-cultural learning experiences of LIS international doctoral students who face much apprehension owing to the newness of experiences that they encounter during the early phases of their cross-cultural learning process.

RESEARCH ON LIS INTERNATIONAL STUDENTS

International students have attended American library schools almost from the beginning of library education in the U.S. in 1887 (Marques de Oliveira, 1990). For example, 596 international students were reported to have attended American library schools during the period 1890 to 1940 (Danton, 1957). Moreover, a recent report published by the Association of Library and Information Science Educators [ALISE] (2003) shows significant augmentation in international student enrollment in LIS programs during the past few years. For example, 1,335 international students seeking any of the six LIS degrees (bachelor, master-LS: ALA-accredited, master-IS, master-other, post-master, doctorate) in fall 2002 represented a 4 percent increase over the 1,284 reported for fall 2001. In addition, increasing numbers of international students are reported specifically in LIS doctorate programs: Out of the 810 doctoral students seeking a PhD degree from 28 schools that reported doctoral enrollment during fall 2002, 279 (34.44 percent) students were international students (Saye & Wisser, 2003). In spite of the long history and the rising trends in numbers of international students in American LIS education, past research to document their experiences and perspectives have been sporadic and few (Cveljo, 1996; Rochester, 1986), and primarily based on sketchy and survey-based evidence that has provided a narrow and shallow representation of the experiences of LIS international students (Carnovsky, 1971; Sarkodie-Mensah, 1988).

Making international doctoral students a focus in this research develops a critical outlook in LIS education by providing voice to an under-represented group. One of the main distinctions in critical theory is acknowledgment of perspectives of all stakeholders in different situations, including the perspectives of the under-represented in order to "do justice to a diversity of socially defined perspectives while providing a grounding for the evaluation of controversial problems" (Endres, 1996, p. 24). Critical thinking calls for simultaneous immersion in a reflective process to challenge conservative conceptions and dissect prevalent principles, procedures, ideological frameworks, and processes (Froomkin, 2003; Habermas, 1993; Kellner, 1989). Application of critical thinking in this research recognizes value and significance of international doctoral students' realities and seeks holistic interventions based on those realities, initiatives that have been missing in prior work.

Representing a semistructured, open-ended, and qualitative data-collecting tool to document feedback gathered from international doctoral students, the use of narrative interviews in this research extends prior methodological strategies (Tallman, 1990) in that it provides a fuller and more systematic appreciation of case-participants' cross-cultural learning experiences and points of view. This chapter provides a comprehensive model of understanding the experiences of LIS international doctoral students in terms of their cross-cultural learning process, a domain of knowledge that is missing in current research. Mapping the intimate connections between affective factors and physical action in international doctoral students' cross-cultural learning process deepens our knowledge of their experiences, and subsequently, may help develop shared understanding, sensitivity, and inclusiveness toward global diversity in the discipline.

RESEARCH CONTEXT AND CASE PARTICIPANTS

The LIS graduate school (and its doctoral program) chosen as the context of research in this case study provided an appropriate authentic instance of a learning community reasonably representative of LIS education in the U.S. It has a long history of substantial numbers of international students in the doctoral program who come from various parts of the world and represent diverse cross-cultural experiences in the discipline. Focus in the doctoral program is on research and providing students' prospective interdisciplinary links to dispersed departments and divisions across the non-urban campus in order to support them while pursuing multidisciplinary vocations in academic, public, corporate, or community-based settings. The doctoral program has a reputation in American LIS education to serve as an active learning community owing to its strength, the quality of students to achieve successful careers and prestigious positions, and the social and technological opportunities the program provides for potential student involvement in teaching, research, and service-oriented activities, based on each student's interest and inclination, goals and objectives, and skills and abilities.

In terms of basic demographic data of case participants, all the international students from a total of 48 doctoral students in the program participated in this research. From the 15 female and six male international doctoral students interviewed, China was represented by 10 case participants, the maximum for any non-U.S. country, followed by Korea (3), India (2), Azerbaijan (1), Canada (1), France (1), Georgia (1), Russia (1) and the U.K. (1). The duration of study of case participants in the program (until the time of interview) ranged from the shortest time of less than a year (more than a semester) for three case participants to the longest time of seven years for two case participants. Ages of case participants fell between the ranges 20 to 29 and 40 to 49 years, with the largest number of international doctoral students in the 30- to 39-year range. Case participants reported completing their masters program from their country of origin, resident country, or in the U.S., in disciplines as diverse as engineering, computer applications, business, cognitive science, management of agricultural information, history of science, and LIS.

Though there was much variation among the case participants (as noted earlier) in terms of their countries of origin and nationality, time duration in the program, age, prior educational and work-related backgrounds, and other dimensions, the lack of significant numbers in this study prevent co-relating these factors with patterns in student responses (e.g., collectivistic practices and community support noted among Chinese women case participants), an activity that will be pursued in future research. The author recognizes differences in individual student experiences, yet the goal of this chapter is to generalize phases in case participants' cross-cultural learning process, while acknowledging some variations within the generalizations. This chapter presents the findings in a general manner indicating the commonalities in the experiences of a majority of case participants; where there were significant variations in experiences, those are duly noted. It is beyond the scope of the chapter to discuss similarities or differences between the experiences of international and American students in a doctoral program or other programs of study.

METHOD

This chapter is based on the author's doctoral dissertation titled "The Cross-Cultural Learning Process of International Doctoral Students: A Case Study in Library and Information Science Education" (Mehra, 2004) completed during 2004 in the Graduate School of Library and Information Science at the University of Illinois at Urbana–Champaign about international doctoral students' experiences in the U.S. Select findings that describe the affective dimensions and physical actions of case participants during their cross-cultural learning process are presented.

The dissertation research applied multiple data collection strategies in a case study to document the cross-cultural learning experiences of all LIS international doctoral students enrolled during the time of research in a premier American LIS institution. Methods included the following: semistructured narrative interviews along with informal discussions conducted during spring 2004; analysis of electronic interactions across a period of nearly five years from 1999–2004; and ethnographic participatory observations drawn from personal experiences as a participant researcher enrolled as an international doctoral student in the program. Apparent disadvantages as a participant researcher in terms of perceived unreliability, role limitations, loss of objectivity, interviewer effect, and time consumption have been addressed elsewhere and justified in extensive detail (Mehra, 2004); advantages documented in the research far exceeded the perceived limitations as a participant researcher (Labovitz & Hagedorn, 1981) and included the following: access to natural setting and emotions, accumulation of data over time, access to context, and development of rapport, among others. This chapter presents the primary analysis of interview data and informal discussions with case participants. Insights gained from the other secondary sources of information are beyond the chapter's scope.

In information science research, the case method has been used as a positivist, interpretive, and critical approach to understand human behavior and information seeking applications in information systems design and implementation (Benbasat, Goldstein, & Mead, 1987; Dubé & Paré, 2003; Markus, 1983; Myers, 1994). This research extends the case study method in past information systems research to deeply understand the cross-cultural learning experiences of international doctoral students in LIS education from a user-focused perspective instead of a systems-based approach. A case method was appropriate to this research since it allowed for in-depth qualitative understanding of case participants' experiences and perspectives. It facilitated the detailed and in-depth examination of one specific context of study. This made the whole experience of conducting research richer and complete, from documenting the process to analyzing the experiences and perspectives of case participants (as well as my own) to presenting the affective and action-oriented dimensions in case participants' cross-cultural learning process.

Qualitative, narrative interviews adopted in this research were useful to capture detailed nuances of learning experiences of case participants in one intercultural context. This extends the kind of cross-cultural information that was gained by use of mail surveys in previous research. Many researchers have tried to alleviate the lack of cross-national validity of theories and models in cross-cultural research by using mail surveys as "the only feasible data collection method for research in more than a few countries" (Harzing, 2000, p. 243). Mail surveys provided responses about merely simple and general cultural categorizations, such as Hofstede's (2001) four cultural dimensions of difference, namely: power distance, uncertainty avoidance, individualism/collectivism, masculinity/femininity, and Trompenaars' (1993) cultural dimensions that included universalism/particularism, individualism/collectivism, affectivity/neutrality, specific/diffuse cultures, status achievement/ascription, synchronous/sequential time, and relation to nature. These categorizations are insufficient to understand the complexities of experiences and issues associated with intercultural dimensions of study that call for precise and in-depth description and analysis of what is happening in cross-cultural environments (Fink, 2002). Narrative interviews and the case study method used in the research fill this missing gap. They also address methodological problems in international or cross-cultural environments owing largely to geographic and cultural distances that have attracted the attention of a considerable number of researchers in the past (for overview of issues to be considered in cross-cultural research, see Alder, 1984; Harpaz, 1996; Malhotra, Agarwal, & Peterson, 1996; Singh, 1995).

Implementation of data collection procedures involved facilitation of narrative interviews and informal discussions during structured interactions that were initially applied with five case-participants during a pilot study, following which revised methods were used to gather feedback from the entire international doctoral student body. Narrative interviews provided a suitable hermeneutic research method since they allowed for collecting case-participant feedback without any predetermined assumptions or theoretical framework beyond trying to broadly understand the cross-cultural learning experiences of international doctoral students.

This chapter summarizes select findings about the case participants' cross-cultural learning experiences in terms of their feelings (affective dimensions) and information seeking activities (information behavior) commonly undertaken during the cross-cultural learning process. The findings are briefly described in the following eight non-hierarchical phases: (1) post-admission before the first semester starts, (2) program initiation, (3) gathering experiences, (4) triggers—realization of differences, (5) dyslexic state of existence, (6) conditioned awareness and comparison-contrast to past experiences, (7) de-conditioning of expectations based on the past, and (8) enlightened adaptation (see Mehra, 2004, for details about the cross-cultural learning process). It is beyond the scope of this chapter to address in lengthy detail other related dimensions of the case participants' cross-cultural learning process such as their thoughts, resources and people consulted, and concerns and challenges encountered, and how they affected their emotional state and their information seeking activities during different phases in their cross-cultural learning process.

The data collection instrument used during the narrative interviews applied open-ended interview questions that yielded responses about the different phases in the model of the cross-cultural learning process. Affective and information seeking activities during each cross-cultural learning phase, as well as implications for future research and suggestions for interventions, were analyzed using grounded theory principles and application of open, axial, and selective coding practices that identified relevant concepts, categories and subcategories, and relationships between individual case participant feedback and their process of cross-cultural learning.

Questions were asked during the interviews in an order different from that presented in the listed questions in this section. During the actual interviews, questions were asked based on maintaining a flow of the interview, the social dynamics between the researcher and the case participants, and the communication interactions that took place. The interview questions presented are based on how they shed light upon the demographic variables associated with the case participants and their experiences during different phases in their cross-cultural learning process. They are identified by double quotation marks ("") and marked as "IQ" for Interview Question. Sometimes a series of questions follow "IQ" to show how questions were worded and used differently with individual case participants, based on contextual dynamics and social and communication interactions during particular interviews. Questions in square brackets following the word "Prompt" were asked during the interviews to prompt further feedback from the case participants. Even though information about the different phases in the model of the cross-cultural learning process was gathered throughout the interviews and other data collection methods employed, the indication before certain interview questions and phase titles identify the main phase about which case participants provided much information in response to that particular question. The questions are described in the following section.

Demographic Characteristics and Contextual Instrumentals

> **IQ**: What is your country of origin?
> **IQ**: How long have you been in the U.S. and in your LIS program?
> **IQ**: What is your educational background?

LIS CROSS-CULTURAL LEARNING EXPERIENCES
Post-Admission Before the First Semester Starts

IQ: How did you hear about this program? What made you decide to join this particular LIS program? What did you do once you got admitted and before you joined the school? [Prompt: Who did you talk to and what resources did you seek?] What were some key experiences and challenges?

Program Initiation

IQ: What have been stages in your progress in the LIS program? [Prompt: What is your current stage of progress?] For example, how did you get initiated into the program? What were your experiences when you started in the program?

Gathering Experiences

IQ: What are some (kind of) experiences you have had during your progress in the LIS program? [Prompt: What kinds of work (RA or TA) have you been involved in since you joined the program? Have these been helpful to you?].
IQ: How did you make sense of your experiences during those stages of progress?
IQ: What have been some memorable (good or bad) experiences in your LIS education in the U.S.?
IQ: Give examples of resources and/or people you have turned to in order to make sense of your LIS (academic) experiences.

Triggers—Realization of Differences

IQ: What was the biggest adjustment concern when you joined the program? [Prompt: How did you cope with adjusting when you joined the program?]
IQ: What have been some memorable (good or bad) experiences in your LIS education in the U.S.? Advice for others?
IQ: What have been some significant moment(s) in your LIS education in the U.S.?
IQ: What have been major challenges in your LIS education in the U.S.?

IQ: Any other concerns that you have had in terms of your LIS education in the U.S.? What were specific problems you faced and solutions you found?

IQ: Give examples of resources and/or people you have turned to in order to make sense of your LIS (academic) experiences. Suggest ways of improvements so that other LIS international doctoral students in the future may not face the same problems you faced.

Dyslexic State of Existence

IQ: Being from a different cultural background, how did you learn to perform the activities expected of you as a doctoral student to further your academic development?

IQ: Have you been able to use your cross-cultural experiences to further your academic development in LIS education in the U.S.? Why/why not?

Conditioned Awareness and Comparison-Contrast to Past Experiences

IQ: What are some (kind of) experiences you have had during your progress in the LIS program? How did you make sense of your experiences during those stages of progress?

IQ: What advice can you provide to others about how to make sense of their experiences?

IQ: What is your conceptualization of LIS education before you joined and since?

IQ: How have your non-U.S. experiences been helpful in performing the activities expected of you as a doctoral student in LIS?

De-Conditioning of Expectations Based on the Past

IQ: How did you make sense of your experiences during various stages of progress? What was the biggest adjustment concern when you joined the program? [Prompt: How did you cope with adjusting when you joined the program?]

IQ: What have been some significant moment(s) in your LIS education in the U.S.?

Enlightened Adaptation

IQ: Being from a different cultural background, how did you learn to perform the activities expected of you as a doctoral student in LIS?

IQ: How have your non-U.S. experiences been helpful in performing the activities expected of you as a doctoral student in LIS?

IQ: What are your future plans and what strategies have been helpful to you so far in reaching your goal?

FINDINGS AND DISCUSSION

This section briefly summarizes emotions and actions during different phases of the cross-cultural learning process based on the case participants' perceptions of their experiences and their willingness and abilities to mentally construct and communicate about these experiences. Scenarios in the form of personal narratives or "little stories" and comments shared by the case participants are also presented to exemplify their typical experiences, affective dimensions, and information behavior during various cross-cultural learning phases. Table 17.1 documents the affective dimensions and information seeking activities of the case participants during each phase in their cross-cultural learning process (see also Mehra, 2005).

Table 17.1   Affective Dimensions and Information Seeking Activities in the Cross-Cultural Learning Process

Sr. No.	Cross-Cultural Learning Phase	Affective Dimensions	Information Seeking Activities
1.	Post-admission before the first semester starts	Excitement, doubt, fear, uncertainty	Exploring all available sources (local/global, digital/nondigital) for any kind of information, support, or feedback; finishing prior work and/or academic obligations; completing official arrangements/procedures to travel (passport/visa/ticket purchases and health check-up).
2.	Program initiation	Feeling lost/isolated at personal/professional levels; uncertainty and frustrations in not knowing how to do well based on internalized expectations to succeed	Completing aspects related to moving to a new country and studying at a university in the U.S.; enrolling in classes; Attending LIS and university-level orientations

Table 17.1 (cont.)

3.	Gathering experiences	Overwhelmed by information overload and new cultural/academic experiences; do not know how to handle the information clutter; social isolation	Talking to other students and building initial social networks; experiencing new learning situations in classes (readings and lectures style)
4.	Triggers— realization of differences	Confusion and anxiety; doubtful about position in the program/culture	Finding help/support and talking to anyone who participants interact with
5.	Dyslexic state of existence	Need for complete picture; disconnect with culture/discipline; feelings of senselessness from provided isolated frames of reference	Adjusting to perceived U.S.-centrality in LIS education; taking classes in LIS and other disciplines; expanding breadth and depth of reading
6.	Conditioned awareness and comparison-contrast to past experiences	Internalize the "dominant" American way of doing things; feel disadvantaged when there is a lack of recognition/practice of earlier experiences; nostalgically romanticize or disregard past experiences	Getting involved in different research/teaching activities; judging their own experiences based on scrutinizing differences
7.	De-conditioning of experiences based on the past	Developing patience, hard work, and faith in ultimately finding the goal toward focused research	Attempting sense-making in different situations via analysis of own limited experiences; making slow progress to focus on specific research within larger discipline; discussing with different people about their own processes of work, thinking, and research; exploring avenues of job opportunities via conferences and networking
8.	Enlightened adaptation	Synthesizing and integrating; wanting to complete the doctoral program and get a job; wanting to move	Representing range of cross-cultural and academic experiences; searching and locating "best fit" for job; planning the move; developing and completing focused research

Source: Revised from Mehra (2005) and Mehra (2004).

During the *post-admission before the first semester starts* phase, international doctoral students are involved in planning and engaging in activities that eventually lead to their joining the LIS programs to which they have been admitted. For many international doctoral students, this entails preparation and travel across large geographic distances and national boundaries.

For example, 17 of the 21 case participants interviewed in this research were in their countries of origin or in other resident countries and had to make extensive financial and travel arrangements to come to the U.S., while four case participants were already in the U.S. and completed or transferred from their prior American programs to join the doctoral program under study.

Case participants reported feeling excited, mixed with fear and uncertainty in making the move to a new country and a new program of study. These affects shaped their information behavior that involved seeking information and support for their impending journey through all available sources (local and/or global, electronic and/or face-to-face) that they could find. Actions involved talking to others (e.g., remote distance communication with school authorities and faculty in the new program), seeking online resources (e.g., Web-based information about new city/program/faculty), finishing prior work and/or academic obligations, and completing the official procedures and arrangements to visit the U.S. (e.g., health requirements, obtaining passport, air ticket, and visa). As one participant noted:

> I contacted my earlier undergrad friends studying in the U.S. who gave me information about what they had done and their experiences ... I was scared and found information over the school's Web site and went to the professors' Web sites to see what projects they had related to my research interests.

Upon joining the LIS program, international doctoral students get involved in the *program initiation* phase during which formal and informal activities introduce them to the new cultural and educational environment. Social- and community-supported structured involvement in efforts like orientation events, class introduction sessions, and registration processes help them find relevant information, build social networks, and develop cultural acclimatization strategies. During this time, case participants reported feeling lost and isolated at personal and professional levels. Feelings of uncertainty were coupled with internalized expectations to succeed, though case participants felt frustrated since they did not know how they were going to achieve this goal and do well in the LIS program. This had a direct impact on their information seeking activities, where the case participants reported desperately contacting university and program administrators and faculty members to ensure that they were fulfilling necessary requirements for starting a doctoral program in a new country. For example, one case-participant noted the following:

> When I joined I did not know anything and I wanted to make sure about my status and what I have to do. And so I was talking to everybody: the LIS administrators, secretaries, international student office, my advisor, talking to several faculty here to find

what research they are doing and if I could do research with them, talking to other doctoral students who have been here longer both international and American, my friends and all.

The case participants reported that initial experiences of finding different information and getting to know where it could be found were not easy, especially because they could not find a consolidated place where such information was presented clearly and succinctly. Many of them stated that meeting with other doctoral students by chance, interacting with other team members from common research and/or teaching assistantships, and finding that if their work supervisor was their assigned advisor, had made it much easier for them to monitor their learning process. Mentoring and advising activities would have been much appreciated during this time since some of the case participants did not know who their advisor was or what to do during their program initiation period. One case participant offered the following suggestion:

> Whole new student group should be introduced first and give them time to get to know each other during orientation. Organized orientation should have faculty introduce what they are doing, who they are, etc. ... Coming from a different country it is not so simple. Other PhD students should become mentors and should take on the role to teach the ropes of adjusting and what has to be done during at least for first six months.

A significant activity for the case participants in cross-cultural learning environments involves a *gathering experiences* phase where students consciously and/or unconsciously, observe, mentally record, and try to make sense of their realities in order to navigate their journey in the LIS cross-cultural learning process. During this phase, the case participants' emotional responses were attributed to difficulty grasping the new cultural and educational environment, making sense of a new discipline, and trying to find relevance and validity in their experiences, especially in terms of connections with past, present, and future trajectories and goals. One case participant from China noted:

> I think there are general issues for any international student, including me, that you know in Asia we have such a different educational system and what they expect you to do in the classroom is much different from here. And they have a lot of discussion sections here and just like the academic structure is very different here and how you interact with your instructor and you have to end up spending a lot of time in adjusting and trying to figure out to know what you are supposed to do. And even when you know

what you are supposed to do, you need to try to talk more in the discussion section and class and it is kind of hard at first.

During the gathering experiences phase case participants reported being overwhelmed with information at every level. Often case participants spoke about the clutter of information and experiences that led to confusion and not knowing what was more important than the other. The difference in the entire socio-cultural experience (accentuated and marked in the context of the LIS academic learning process) led to a sense of social and psychological isolation and, after the initial state, case participants tried to overcome their sense of desperation by talking to other students and trying to build networks and support with whomever they interacted with.

An important feature in cross-cultural learning is the phase marked by occurrence of *triggers* (real or perceived experienced incidents or moments) that awaken the international doctoral student to the reality that things are different from their earlier expectations and practices. The following remark by a case participant captures the power of perception in generating an emotional response to a trigger in a cross-cultural situation:

> Hmm, quite a few times I think I am in good shape I am taking class everything is fine. After a month I just feel things cannot be so good, or if something I hear of unpleasant happened, and I say [to myself] 'oh, maybe something is wrong with me.' And then I really need feedback and I start asking my advisor, my supervisor, asking my friends about what should I do? Can you give me some feedback? Like I want to know where I am. If I want to make a big decision when should I take the qualifying exam? If I have a question I interact a lot, if I don't have a question then I stay by myself.

Experiences that initiate triggers can range from an innocuous comment by an instructor in class, perceived verbal and/or nonverbal behaviors of others, someone's response to something the international doctoral student says or does, or something she or he symbolizes to represent a certain meaning. Trigger experiences take place owing to personal, cultural, and/or educational differences that are perceived and internalized, and lead to much anxiety and confusion. Triggers are initiated via initial emotional recognition or reactions that are subsequently transmitted at a cognitive level. Case participants tried to respond to the triggers and understand the new cultural and educational experiences by locating any helpful sources that might shed light upon the nature of their (real or perceived) troubling experience. Feelings associated with triggers were being lost after trying to understand the meaning of the real or perceived experience and doubts about their position and role in the program and culture. Feelings of confusion and anxiety forced students to locate any helpful sources that they could identify as shedding light upon the nature of the trigger, finding support mechanisms to alleviate the doubt in their mind, and interacting with anyone to talk about the issue. Owing to socio-cultural differences in perceptions of faculty-student hierarchies and formal-informal distance maintained in interactions between faculty and students, case participants (especially those from East and South Asia) sensed that they would be troubling their advisors/supervisors during the occurrence of most triggers. Hence, they reported consulting with their advisors/supervisors only in situations that they perceived as emergencies. However, if there were several other students from the case participant's home country in the program, then the first option for the case participant was to get in touch with them to try and relieve their anxiety about a particular issue. This led to building of community narratives within the international doctoral student population where students passed down to newer students, stories of their experiences, or those heard from others, expressing similar situations to those encountered by them or other international doctoral students. Case participants revealed that sharing of such stories were most helpful to them in getting advice about tackling certain problematic issues in the academic process such as: boundary negotiation in research projects; opinion and authority to resolve co-authorship issues with faculty and other students; appropriate information about classes matching their specific interests; and resolving conflicts in different teaching and research situations.

The alienation owing to newness in the cross-cultural environment is accentuated by the *dyslexic state of existence* phase for international doctoral students in terms of their inability to make connections between incomplete and isolated pieces of information that are connected only through the cultural knowledge and experiential understanding that they lack. The following comment by one case participant expresses the feelings shared by all case participants for the need to see a complete picture stemming from a cultural and disciplinary disconnect:

> OK, if for a foundational LIS course for the whole bunch of readings, tell me why you choose this piece of text and what is the position of the text and why is it important and what is the big picture this article is going to address and tell us the whole picture and not just a point in the picture ... Ask more questions of the instructor, ask them to provide more background information like if the author is a big name like in the American history in the classical research or something, if the author is a big name then for us it is just a name. Like if I give you a name from Chinese history a Chinese person will come up with a whole picture even if he doesn't read the specific article he knows of the related things. But for us we cannot make the connections in the mental network. It is like a dyslexia you know a point is here and a point there but we cannot make all the connections for it is

> connected through the culture that is learnt from the high school
> or the elementary school everyday readings and so I think that is
> hard. So if the instructor does not fill the gaps, then it is lost.

The case participants' initial interaction with class materials and the discipline resulted in a dyslexic state. Adjusting to the perceived U.S.-centrality in LIS education and teaching materials, taking classes in LIS and other disciplines, and expanding understanding by increased readings from different areas in LIS helped them to overcome this dyslexic situation.

Some of the isolation and doubt faced during initial cross-cultural learning phases was overcome over time via a *conditioned awareness based on comparing and contrasting with past experiences* phase where international doctoral students began to see similarities and/or differences between their past and current cultural/academic experiences. For example, one case participant observed the following:

> Sometimes what happens when a person goes from country to
> another country they tend to spend a lot of time comparing "you
> know at home it is like this and here it is like this." I suppose hav-
> ing done that a variety of different times I don't spend so much
> time, I don't get bogged down trying to compare and see which
> one is better. You know when I was in [name of place] one year
> and the next year I went there I was really disappointed because
> it was not like that the first time and it was the second-event
> experience that was tough and by the time I went the third year I
> knew it was not going to be the same and knew it was going to be
> different for I had that experience base to build on.

During this phase, case participants stated that their feelings tended to either completely disregard or nostalgically romanticize their past experiences since they were comparing their past only in terms of the present, and because they were subjectively involved in trying to navigate their present experiences. Analysis of interview data gathered during this research revealed that all case participants internalized the dominant way of doing things in the U.S., and often, more than once, felt "marginalized" and disadvantaged during their cross-cultural learning when there was a lack of acknowledgement and practice of their earlier modes of cultural experience, knowledge, and interaction. Activities they were involved in during this phase included participating in different research and teaching settings that provided exposure to broader interconnections between various dimensions that went beyond analyzing in terms of similarities and differences between prior and current experiences. During this time, case participants often judged their experiences as "good" or "bad" based on an awareness that emerged from a lens of scrutinizing difference.

A *de-conditioning* phase, where international doctoral students develop abilities to not measure each and every present and expected future experience based on comparison and contrast to earlier experiences, eventually follows the *comparison-contrast* phase. Such understanding helped international doctoral students to recognize each experience on its own terms and to begin to draw broader connections between seemingly disparate experiences (cultural and/or academic). This phase was marked by a realization of a person's focused area and being able to place that in the context of the discipline and its global dimensions. According to one case participant:

> The biggest challenge I would say would be to figure out the exact point the exact research question you will explore for your dissertation. I will say that it is difficult it is hard to decide. You have a broad idea about research area but it is time to pick the exact piece of research question that is hard because sometimes you feel there are lots of research questions to pick and sometimes you feel there is not enough to go by. Thinking about the specific research questions come right in the beginning and all through the process.

Case participants talked about feelings of beginning to make connections with people and experiences. Patience, hard work, and faith in ultimately finding the goal of focused dissertation research kept them on track toward completion. Their actions revolved around sense making attempts in different situations via analyzing their own limited experiences, nurturing slow and steady progress to focus on specific research within larger discipline, discussing with various people about their own processes of work and thinking, and exploring avenues of job opportunities via conferences and networking.

The culminating *enlightened adaptation* phase at the cross-cultural and the academic levels of experience represents the temporal end of the cross-cultural learning process for it generally leads to the international doctoral student getting a job in the U.S., country of origin, or another country, based on individual goals and efforts. This period represents a phase of understanding the different cultural and/or academic experiences on their own terms where international doctoral students are able to see the similarities and differences between different experiences in the context of a larger understanding of the intersections between the individual, people, culture, and the environment (the context). It leads to "enlightenment" in drawing connections between the local and the global, home and host, and other realities of experience, as well as developing an understanding of the depth and breadth of the discipline, and even working in different areas within it, in addition to locating and identifying their own focused area of research and work within the discipline. As one case participant observed:

Our success is related to the survival of the field since you are a student here and you want a good future in the field. And positioning oneself in the field is important, finding my own area in the field as it is changing and how I can market my strength and interest and also make sure it can expand with the changing field.

Case participants recognized diverse experiences and hybridized identities and synthesizing and integrating, wanting to complete the doctoral program, and getting a job and planning to move. Actions represented acknowledgment of the significance of a range of cross-cultural and academic experiences that case participants encountered. This helped case-participants identify their niche in the discipline, as well as search and locate (or plan for) the kind of job they would like in the future. It led to identification of a "best fit" in terms of personal experiences and interests on one hand, and expectations of potential hiring agencies and institutions on the other.

IMPLICATIONS

The cross-cultural learning process is consciously expressed in terms of a "phase" that represents a non-sequential dimension with overlapping and intermixing elements, based on the experiences of different participants (as compared to a "stage"—a description that implies a more fixed and rigid dimension of temporal experience). Affective relationship with cognition and action acknowledges the four constituents of any cross-cultural learning process in terms of intersections between individual-people-culture-environment (context) factors. A study of these connections is intrinsic to an understanding of the nature and development of cross-cultural learning for it recognizes the complex nature of social interactions embedded in the experiences. It helps realize the role of mutually impacting variables associated with the discipline (for example, a lack of globally recognized name and function of the discipline that led to a confusion among students about how they could connect their past experiences to the current expectations of the program), program (educator behavior, policies, and procedures), education (pedagogical expectations, class format familiarity), socio-culture (language, social interactions), and individual (cognitions, personality types, learning styles) in shaping the cross-cultural learning process. The intersecting nature of participants' emotional experiences during cross-cultural learning with actions that they undertook draws attention to the need for holistic interventions (as opposed to isolated strategies) at the level of the discipline, program, faculty, doctoral student community, and individual student. This finding has significance in the context of future research that will identify holistically applied interventions in varied cross-cultural learning environments. For example, in order to address the experience of triggers during the cross-cultural learning process an intervention at the program and doctoral student community level may develop efforts (via possible electronic means) to make more permanent some aspects of stories developed as community narratives so that new students may find helpful information, guidance and support to address similar experiences that they may encounter in the future.

CONCLUSION

It is important to recognize the role of affect in information seeking during the cross-cultural learning process that make the learner the focus of attention and take into account her or his emotive experiences as integral to the analysis. For example, identifying and improving mechanisms and interventions in LIS that recognize the past cultural and academic experiences of international doctoral students will help them relate better to the discipline in the U.S. It will tap into the wealth of cultural knowledge and past experiences of LIS international doctoral students who can potentially act as gatekeepers to "other" worlds. This could facilitate cultural bridges across global distances and further internationalizing efforts in LIS education in the U.S. Moreover, strategies that seek to identify inter-related interventions made in conjunction with each other that do not view the international learner as the sole cause of the perceived "problem" in settings of cross-cultural learning are needed. Implementing such strategies could perpetuate global equality in international participation in world LIS education and project a more ecocentric perception instead of an egocentric world view, a relevant philosophical route in the contemporary context of global interconnectedness and interdependence since it acknowledges respect of the equality intrinsic to all human beings and the recognition of need for mutual cooperation and trust between nations. They could also provide potential options to develop globally dispersed knowledge networks by tapping into foundational social infrastructures that are in some ways already set in place. The development of such social infrastructures is essential to support the socially contingent technological infrastructure of globally networked information and communication technologies for appropriation and growth of a global economy and society in today's macro community (Best & Kellner, 2001; Gilder, 1989; Kaku, 1997).

The importance of understanding the affective factors of cross-cultural participants (e.g., international doctoral students) in terms of emotional drive and responses and their relationship to actions and activities is instrumental toward nurturing positive intercultural and global interactions in a globally intertwined environment as a tangible reality.

REFERENCES

Alder, N. J. (1984). Understanding the ways of understanding: Cross-cultural management methodology reviewed. In R. N. Farmer (Ed.), *Advances in international comparative management: Vol. 1* (pp. 31–67). Greenwich, CT: JAI Press.

Association of Library and Information Science Educators (ALISE). (2003). *Library and information science education statistical report 2003*. Oak Ridge, TN: ALISE.

Benbasat, I., Goldstein, D. K., & Mead, M. (1987). The case research strategy in studies of information systems. *MIS Quarterly, 11*(3), 369–386.

Best, S., & Kellner, D. (2001). *The postmodern adventure: Science, technology, and cultural studies at the third millennium.* New York and London: Guilford and Routledge.

Bilal, D. (2005). Children's information seeking and the design of digital interfaces in the affective paradigm. *Library Trends, 54*(2), 197–208.

Bruner, J. (1973). *Beyond the information given: Studies in psychology of knowing* (J. M. Arglin, Ed.). New York: W. W. Norton & Co.

Carnovsky, L. (1971). The foreign student in the accredited library school. *Journal of Education for Librarianship, 1*(2), 102.

Cveljo, K. (1996). International students in American library and information science schools. *Encyclopedia of Library and Information Science, 57* (supplement 20), 209–269.

Danton, P. (1957). *United States influence on Norwegian librarianship, 1890–1940.* Berkeley, CA: University of California Press.

Dervin, B. (1993). Verbing communication: Mandate for disciplinary invention. *Journal of Communication, 43*(3), 45–54.

Dervin, B. (1999). On studying information seeking methodologically: The implications of connecting metatheory to method. *Information Processing and Management, 35*, 727–750.

Dewey, J. (1933). *How we think.* Lexington, MA: Heath.

Dubé, L., & Paré, G. (2003). Rigor in information systems positivist case research: Current practices, trends, and recommendations. *MIS Quarterly, 27*(4), 597–636.

Endres, B. (1996). Habermas and Critical Thinking. *Philosophy of Education 1996.* Accessed December 05, 2006, from www.ed.uiuc.edu/EPS/PES-Yearbook/ 96_docs/endres.html.

Fink, G. (2002, August). *Issues of international intercultural research: The narrative interview process.* Presentation at the PDW Academy of Management Meeting 2002, Denver, CO. Accessed December 5, 2006, from www.harzing.com/download/ aom2002gf1.pdf.

Froomkin, M. A. (2003). Habermas@discourse.net: Toward a critical theory of cyberspace. *Harvard Law Review, 116*(3), 749–873.

Gagnon, G., & Collay, M. (2001). *Designing for learning: Six elements in constructivist classrooms.* Berkeley, CA: Corwin Press.

Gilder, G. (1989). *Microcosm: The quantum revolution in economics and technology.* New York: Simon and Schuster.

Goldman, A. (1995). Emotions in music (A postscript). *Journal of Aesthetics and Art Criticism, 53*(1), 59–69.

Habermas, J. (1993). *Justification and application: Remarks on discourse ethics* (C. P. Cronin, Trans.). Cambridge, MA: The MIT Press.

Harpaz, I. (1996). International management survey research. In B. J. Punnett & O. Shenkar (Eds.), *Handbook for international management research* (pp. 37–62). Cambridge, MA: Blackwell.

Harzing, A. (2000). Cross-national mail surveys: Why do response rates differ between countries. *Industrial Marketing Management, 29*(3), 243–254.

Hofstede, G. H. (2001). *Culture's consequences: Comparing values, behaviors, institutions, and organizations across nations.* Thousand Oaks, CA: Sage Publications.

Kaku, M. (1997). *Visions: How science will revolutionize the 21st century.* New York: Anchor Books.

Kellner, D. (1989). Boundaries and borderlines: Reflections on Jean Boudrillard and critical theory. *Current Perspectives in Social Theory, 9*, 5–22. Accessed December 5,

2006, from www.gseis.ucla.edu/faculty/kellner/Illumina_percent20Folder/kell2. htm.

Kelly, G. A. (1963). *A theory of personality: The psychology of personal constructs.* New York: W. W. Norton.

Kort, B., Reilly, R., & Picard, R. W. (2001). An affective model of interplay between emotions and learning: Reengineering educational pedagogy—building a learning companion. *Proceedings of the Second IEEE International Conference on Advanced Learning Technologies (ICALT'01),* 43–48.

Kuhlthau, C. C. (2004). *Seeking meaning: A process approach to library and information services* (2nd ed.). Westport, CT: Libraries Unlimited.

Labovitz, S., & Hagedorn, R. (1981). *Introduction to social research.* New York: McGraw-Hill.

Malhotra, N. K., Agarwal, J., & Peterson, M. (1996). Methodological issues in cross-cultural marketing research: A state-of-the-art review. *International Marketing Review, 13*(5), 7–43.

Markus, M. L. (1983). Power, politics and MIS implementation. *Communications of the ACM, 26,* 430–444.

Marques de Oliveira, S. (1990). The compatibility between American library and information science programs and foreign countries' needs: An exploratory study. In J. L. Tallman and J. B. Ojiambo (Eds.), *Translating an international education to a national environment* (pp. 83–104). Pittsburgh, PA: University of Pittsburgh, School of Library and Information Science.

Mehra, B. (2004). *The cross-cultural learning process of international doctoral students: A case study in library and information science education.* Unpublished doctoral dissertation, University of Illinois at Urbana–Champaign.

Mehra, B. (2005). A phase-model of the cross-cultural learning process of LIS international doctoral students: Characteristics and interventions. *Proceedings of the 68th Annual Meeting of the American Society for Information Science & Technology 2005, 42.*

Mehra, B., & Bishop, A. P. (2007). Cross-cultural perspectives of international doctoral students: Two-way learning in library and information science education. *International Journal of Progressive Education, 3*(1). Accessed July 9, 2007, from inased.org/v3n1/mehrabishop.htm.

Mehra, B., & Papajohn, D. (in press). "Glocal" patterns of communication-information convergences in Internet use: Cross-cultural behavior of international teaching assistants in a culturally alien information environment. *The International Information & Library Review, 39*(1): 12–30.

Myers, M. D. (1994). A disaster for everyone to see: An interpretive analysis of a failed IS project. *Accounting, Management and Information Technologies, 4*(4), 185–201.

Nahl, D. (1998a). Ethnography of novices' first use of Web search engines: Affective control in cognitive processing. *Internet Reference Services Quarterly, 3*(2), 51–72.

Nahl, D. (1998b). Learning the Internet and the structure of information behavior. *Journal of the American Society for Information Science, 49*(11), 1017–1023.

Piaget, J. (1990). *The child's conception of the world.* New York: Littlefield Adams.

Picard, R. W., Papert, S., Bender, W., Blumberg, B., Breazeal, C., Cavallo, D., Machover, T., Resnick, M., Roy, D., & Strohecker, C. (2004). Affective learning: A manifesto. *BT Technology Journal, 22*(4), 252–269.

Rochester, M. K. (1986). *Foreign students in American library education: Impact on home countries.* New York: Greenwood Press.

Sarkodie-Mensah, K. (1988). *Foreign students and U.S. academic libraries: A case study of foreign students and libraries in two universities in New Orleans, Louisiana.* Unpublished doctoral dissertation, University of Illinois at Urbana–Champaign.

Saye, J. D., & Wisser, K. M. (2003). Students. In E. H. Daniel & J. D. Sayer (Eds.), *Library and information science education statistical report 2003*. Oak Ridge, TN: ALISE.

Singh, J. (1995). Measurement issues in cross-national research. *Journal of International Business Studies, 26*(3), 597–620.

Tallman, J. I. (1990). International students in United States library and information science schools. In J. I. Tallman & J. B. Ojiambo (Eds.). *Translating an international education to a national environment* (pp. 13–22). Pittsburgh, PA: University of Pittsburgh, School of Library and Information Science.

Trompenaars, F. (1993). *Riding the waves of culture: Understanding diversity in business*. London: Economist Books.

References

Abbas, J., Norris, C., & Soloway, E. (2002). Middle school children's use of the ARTEMIS digital library. *Proceedings of the 2nd Joint Conference on Digital Libraries*, 98–105.

Agosto, D. E. (2001). Bounded rationality and satisficing in young people's Web-based decision making. *Journal of the American Society for Information Science and Technology, 53*(1), 16–27.

Alder, N. J. (1984). Understanding the ways of understanding: Cross-cultural management methodology reviewed. In R. N. Farmer (Ed.), *Advances in international comparative management: Vol. 1* (pp. 31–67). Greenwich, CT: JAI Press.

Allen, B., & Kim, K. (2001). Person and context in information seeking: Interaction between cognitive and task variables. *New Review of Information Behaviour Research, 2*, 1–16.

Altieri, J. L. (1995). Multicultural literature and multiethnic readers: Examining aesthetic involvement and preferences for text. *Reading Psychology: An International Quarterly, 16*, 43–70.

American Association of School Librarians. (1998). *Information power*. Chicago: American Library Association.

American Association of School Librarians. (1999). *A planning guide for Information Power*. Chicago: American Library Association.

American Psychiatric Association. (2000). *Diagnostic and statistical manual of mental disorders* (4th ed., text revision). Washington, DC: American Psychiatric Association.

Amsel, A. (1992). *Frustration theory*. Cambridge: Cambridge University Press.

Anderson, T. (2006). Uncertainty in action: Observing information seeking within the creative processes of scholarly research. *Information Research, 12*(1), Paper 283. Accessed July 8, 2007, from informationr.net/ir/12-1/paper283.html.

Ashkanasy, N. M., & Daus, C. S. (2005). Rumors of the death of emotional intelligence in organizational behavior are vastly exaggerated. *Journal of Organizational Behavior, 26*(4), 441–452.

Asselin, M. (2000). Reader response in literature and reading instruction. *Teacher Librarian, 27*(4), 62–63.

Association of College and Research Libraries. (2000). *Information literacy competency standards for higher education*. Chicago: American Library Association. Accessed December 3, 2006, from www.ala.org/ala/acrl/acrlstandards/standards.pdf.

Association of Library and Information Science Educators (ALISE). (2003). *Library and information science education statistical report 2003*. Oak Ridge, TN: ALISE.

Athenasou, J. A. (Ed.). (1999). *Adult educational psychology*. Katoomba, NSW: Social Science Press.

Baker, L. M. (2005). Monitoring and blunting. In K. E. Fisher, S. Erdelez, & L. E. F. McKechnie (Eds.), *Theories of information behavior* (pp. 239–241). Medford, NJ: Information Today, Inc.

Baker, L. M., Wilson, F. L., & Kars, M. (1997). The readability of medical information on Info Trac: Does it meet the needs of people with low literacy skills? *Reference and User Services Quarterly, 37*(2), 155–160.

Bandura, A. (1986). *Social foundations of thought and action: A social cognitive theory.* Englewood Cliffs, NJ: Prentice Hall.

Bandura, A. (Ed.). (1997). *Self-efficacy: The exercise of control.* New York: W.H. Freeman.

Baron, R. A. (1977). *Human aggression.* New York: Plenum.

Barr, T., Burns, A., & Sharp, D. (2005). *Smart Internet 2010.* Melbourne, Vic: Swinburne University of Technology, Faculty of Life and Social Sciences. Accessed November 28, 2006, from smartinternet.com.au/ArticleDocuments/123/Smart-Internet-2010.pdf.

Barsky, A., Thoresen, C. J., Warren, C. R., & Kaplan, S. A. (2004). Modeling negative affectivity and job stress: A contingency-based approach. *Journal of Organizational Behavior, 25*(8), 915–936.

Baym, N. (1997). Interpreting soap operas and creating community: Inside an electronic fan culture. In S. Keisler (Ed.), *Culture of the Internet.* Mahwah, NJ: Lawrence Erlbaum Associates.

Beer, J. S., Knight, R. T., & D'Esposito, M. (2006). Controlling the integration of emotion and cognition: The role of the frontal cortex in distinguishing helpful from hurtful emotional information. *Psychological Science, 17*(5), 448–453.

Beile, P. (2002, February). *The effect of library instruction learning environments on self-efficacy levels and learning outcomes of graduate students in education.* Paper presented at the Annual Meeting of the American Educational Research Association, New Orleans, LA.

Belenky, M. F., Clinchy, B. M., Goldberger, N. R., & Tarule, J. M. (1986). *Women's ways of knowing: The development of self, voice, and mind.* New York: Basic Books.

Belkin, N. J. (1980). Anomalous state of knowledge for information retrieval. *Canadian Journal of Information Science, 5,* 133–143.

Bellardo, T. (1985). An investigation of online searcher traits and their relationship to search outcome. *Journal of the American Society for Information Science, 36*(4), 241–250.

Benbasat, I., Goldstein, D. K., & Mead, M. (1987). The case research strategy in studies of information systems. *MIS Quarterly, 11*(3), 369–386.

Benson, P., Scales, P., Leffert, N., & Roehlkepartain, E. (1999). *A fragile foundation: The state of developmental assets among American youth.* Minneapolis, MN: Search Institute.

Berkowitz, L. (1978). Whatever happened to the frustration-aggression hypothesis? *American Behavioral Scientist, 32,* 691–708.

Bernard, M. (1990). Rational-emotive therapy with children and adolescents. *School Psychology Review, 19*(3), 294–303.

Bernard, M. (2003). *You can do it!* New York: Time Warner.

Bernard, M., & Cronan, F. (1999). The child and adolescent scale of irrationality: Validation data and mental health correlates. *Journal of Cognitive Psychotherapy, 13*(2), 121–131.

Bernard, M., & Laws, W. (1988, August). *Childhood irrationality and mental health.* Paper presented at the 24th International Congress of Psychology, Sydney, Australia.

Berryman, J. M. (2006). What defines 'enough' information? How policy workers make judgments and decisions during information seeking: Preliminary results from an exploratory study. *Information Research, 11*(4), Paper 266. Accessed November 28, 2006, from informationr.net/ir/11-4/paper266.html.

Best, S., & Kellner, D. (2001). *The postmodern adventure: Science, technology, and cultural studies at the third millennium.* New York and London: Guilford and Routledge.

Bilal, D. (1998). Children's search processes in using World Wide Web search engines: An exploratory study. *Journal of the American Society for Information Science, 35,* 45–53.

Bilal, D. (2000). Children's use of the Yahooligans! Web search engine: I. Cognitive, physical, and affective behaviors on fact-based search tasks. *Journal of the American Society for Information Science and Technology, 51*(7), 646–655.

Bilal, D. (2001). Children's use of the Yahooligans! Web search engine: II. Cognitive and physical behaviors on research tasks. *Journal of the American Society for Information Science and Technology, 52,* 118–136.

Bilal, D. (2002a). Children's use of the Yahooligans! Web search engine: III. Cognitive and physical behaviors on fully self-generated search tasks. *Journal of the American Society for Information Science and Technology, 53,* 1170–1183.

Bilal, D. (2002b). Perspectives on children's navigation of the World Wide Web: Does the type of search task make a difference? *Online Information Review, 26*(2), 108–117.

Bilal, D. (2003). Draw and tell: Children as designers of Web interfaces. *Proceedings of the 66th annual meeting of the American Society for Information Science and Technology, 40,* 135–141.

Bilal, D. (2004). Research on children's information seeking on the Web. In M. Chelton & C. Cool (Eds.), *Youth information-seeking behavior: Theories, models, and issues* (pp. 271–291). Lanham, Maryland: The Scarecrow Press.

Bilal, D. (2005). Children's information seeking and the design of digital interfaces in the affective paradigm. *Library Trends, 54*(2), 197–208.

Bilal, D., & Bachir, I. (2007a). Children's interaction with cross-cultural and multilingual digital libraries. I. Understanding interface design representations. *Information Processing & Management, 43,* 47–64.

Bilal, D., & Bachir, I. (2007b). Children's interaction with cross-cultural and multilingual digital libraries. II. Information seeking, success, and affective experience. *Information Processing & Management, 43,* 65–80.

Bilal, D., & Kirby, J. (2002). Differences and similarities in information seeking: Children and adults as Web users. *Information Processing and Management, 38*(5), 649–670.

Bilal, D., & Wang, P. (2005). Children's Conceptual Structures of Science Categories and the Design of Web Directories. *Journal of the American Society for Information Science and Technology, 56,* 1303–1313.

Blackford, H. (2004). Playground panopticism: Ring-around-the-children, a pocketful of women. *Childhood: A Global Journal of Child Research, 11*(2), 227–249.

Blimling, G. S. (1999). A meta-analysis of the influence of college residence halls on academic performance. *Journal of College Student Development, 40*(5), 551–561.

Bodi, S. (1992). Collaborating with faculty in teaching critical thinking: The role of librarians. *Research Strategies, 10*(2), 69–76.

Booth-Butterfield, M., & Booth-Butterfield, S. (1990). Conceptualizing affect as information in communication production. *Human Communication Research, 16*(4), 451–476.

Bostick, S. L. (1992). *The development and validation of the library anxiety scale.* Unpublished doctoral dissertation, Wayne State University, Detroit, Michigan.

Boyd, E. R. (2002). "Being there": Mothers who stay-at-home, gender and time. *Women's Studies International Forum, 25*(4), 463–470.

Brewer, W. F., & Lichtenstein, E. H. (1982). Stories are to entertain: A structural-affect theory of stories. *Journal of Pragmatics, 6,* 473–486.

Brewer, W. F., & Ohtsuka, K. (1988). Story structure and reader affect in American and Hungarian short stories. In C. Martindale (Ed.), *Psychological approaches to the study of literary narratives* (pp. 133–158). Hamburg: Buske.

Briggs, C. L. (1986). *Learning how to ask: A socio-linguistic appraisal of the interview in social science research.* Cambridge: Cambridge University Press.

Browne, M. (1993). *Organizational decision making and information.* Norwood, NJ: Ablex.

Bruce, C. (1997). *The seven faces of information literacy.* Adelaide: Auslib Press.

Bruner, J. (1973). *Beyond the information given: Studies in psychology of knowing* (J. M. Arglin, Ed.). New York: W. W. Norton & Co.

Bruner, J. (1986). *Actual minds: Possible worlds.* Cambridge: Harvard University Press.

Bunbury, R., & Tabbert, R. (1988). 'Midnite' and other bushrangers: Heroes for children or adults? A bi-cultural study of identification: Readers' responses to the ironic treatment of a national hero. *International Review of Children's Literature and Librarianship, 3,* 74–83.

Burke, A., Heuer, F., & Reisberg, D. (1992). Remembering emotional events. *Memory & Cognition, 20,* 277–290.

Burleson, W., & Picard, R. W. (2004, August). *Affective agents: Sustaining motivation to learn through failure and a state of "stuck."* Paper presented at the Social and Emotional Intelligence in Learning Environments Workshop in conjunction with the 7th International Conference on Intelligent Tutoring Systems, Maceio—Alagoas, Brasil. Accessed December 13, 2006, from affect.media.mit.edu/pdfs/04.burleson-picard.pdf.

Burnetta, G., & Bonnici, L. (2003). Beyond the FAQ: Explicit and implicit norms in Usenet newsgroups. *Library & Information Science Research, 25*(3), 333–351.

Burrell, D. (1997) *From sanctity to property: Dead bodies in American society and law, 1800–1860.* Accessed December 13, 2006, from www.historicalinsights.com/dave/bodyasproperty.html.

Butler, D., & Cartier, S. (2005, April). *Multiple complementary methods for understanding self-regulated learning as situated in context.* Paper presented at the American Educational Research Association conference, Montreal, Canada.

Cahoy, E. (2004). Put some feeling into it! *Knowledge Quest, 32*(4), 25–27.

Campbell, R. N. (1997). Expertise and cognitive development. In L. Smith, J. Dockrell, & P. Obeying (Eds.), *Piaget, Vygotsky and beyond: Developmental psychology and education issues for the future* (pp. 159–164). London: Routledge.

Canadian National Institute for the Blind (2005). *The status of Canadian youth who are blind or visually impaired.* Toronto, Canada.

Carnovsky, L. (1971). The foreign student in the accredited library school. *Journal of Education for Librarianship, 1*(2), 102.

Carter, R. F. (2003). Communication: A harder science. In B. Dervin & S. Chaffee (Eds.), *Communicating, a different kind of horse race: Essays honoring Richard F. Carter* (pp. 369–376). Cresskill, NJ: Hampton Press.

Case, D. (2002). *Looking for information: A survey of research on information seeking, needs, and behavior.* New York: Academic Press/Elsevier Science.

Chang, C. (2006). Beating the news blues: Mood repair through exposure to advertising. *Journal of Communication, 56*(1), 198–217.

Chatman, E. A. (1985). Information, mass media use, and the working poor. *Library and Information Science Research, 7*(2), 97–113.

Chatman, E. A. (1991). Life in a small world: Application of gratification theory to information-seeking behavior. *Journal of the American Society for Information Science, 42*(6), 438–449.

Chatman, E. A. (1992). *The information world of retired women.* Westport, CT: Greenwood Press.

Chatman, E. A. (1996). The impoverished life-world of outsiders. *Journal of the American Society for Information Science, 47*(3), 193–206.

Chatman, E. A. (1999). A theory of life in the round. *Journal of the American Society for Information Science, 50*(3), 207–217.

Chatman, E. A. (2000). Framing social life in theory and research. *The New Review of Information Behavior Research, 1*, 3–17.

Childers, T. (1975). *The information poor in America.* Metuchen, NJ: Scarecrow Press.

Choo, C. W., Detlor, B., & Turnbull, D. (2000). *Web work: Information seeking and knowledge work on the World Wide Web.* Boston: Kluwer Academic Publishers.

Christianson, S.-A., & Loftus, E. (1991). Remembering emotional events: The fate of detailed information. *Cognition & Emotion, 5*, 81–108.

Cohen, J. (Ed.). (1999). *Educating minds and hearts: Social emotional learning and the passage into adolescence.* New York: Teachers College Press.

Cohen, J. (Ed.). (2001). *Caring classrooms/intelligent schools: The social emotional education of young children.* New York: Teachers College Press.

Cohen, M. Z., Kahn, D. L., & Steeves, R. H. (2000). *Hermeneutic phenomenological research: A practical guide for nurse practitioners.* Thousand Oaks, CA: Sage Publications.

Collaborative to Advance Social and Emotional Learning. (2003). *SEL competences.* Chicago: Collaborative to Advance Social and Emotional Learning. Accessed November 25, 2006, from www.casel.org/about_sel/SELskills.php.

Collins, K. M. T., & Veal, R. E. (2004). Off-campus adult learners' levels of library anxiety as a predictor of attitudes toward the Internet. *Library and Information Science Research, 26*(1), 5–14.

Colorado State Library and Adult Education Office and Colorado Educational Media Association. (1997). Rubrics for the assessment of information literacy. In California Library Media Educators Association, *From library skills to information literacy* (2nd ed.). San Jose, CA: Hi Willow.

Condit, C. M. (2000). Culture and biology in human communication: Toward a multi-causal model. *Communication Education, 49*(1), 7–24.

Cooper, L. Z. (2005). Developmentally appropriate digital environments for young children. *Library Trends, 54*, 286–302.

Corcoran-Perry, S. & Graves, J. (1990). Supplemental-information-seeking behavior of cardiovascular nurses. *Research in Nursing & Health, 13*, 119–127.

Craven, J. (2004). Linear searching in a non-linear environment: The information seeking behavior of visually impaired people on the World Wide Web. *Lecture Notes in Computer Science, 3118*, 530–537.

Creswell, J. W. (1994). *Research design: Qualitative and quantitative approaches.* Thousand Oaks, CA: Sage Publications.

Creswell, J. W. (1998). *Qualitative inquiry and research design: Choosing among five traditions.* Thousand Oaks, CA: Sage Publications.

Cveljo, K. (1996). International students in American library and information science schools. *Encyclopedia of Library and Information Science, 57*(supplement 20), 209–269.

Dale, D. C. (1989). Content Analysis: A research methodology for school library media specialists. *School Library Media Quarterly, 18*(1), 45–48.

Dalrymple, P. W. (1990). Retrieval by reformulation in two library catalogs: Toward a cognitive model of searching behavior. *Journal of the American Society for Information Science, 41*(4), 272–281.

Dalrymple, P. W., & Zweizig, D. L. (1992). Users' experience of information retrieval systems: An exploration of the relationship between search experience and affective measures. *Library and Information Science Research, 14*(2), 167–181.

Damasio, A. (1999). *The feeling of what happens: Body and emotion in the making of consciousness*. San Diego, CA: Harcourt Press.

Danton, P. (1957). *United States influence on Norwegian librarianship, 1890–1940*. Berkeley, CA: University of California Press.

Davidson, R. J. (1994). Complexities in the search for emotion-specific physiology. In P., Ekman, & R. J. Davidson, (Eds.). *The nature of emotion: Fundamental questions* (pp. 237–242). New York: Oxford University Press.

Davidson, R. J. (2003). Affective neuroscience and psychophysiology: Toward a synthesis. *Psychophysiology*, *40*, 655–665. Accessed December 13, 2006, from www.sprWeb.org/articles/Davidson03.pdf.

Davidson, R. J., Scherer, K. R., & Goldsmith, H. H. (2000). *The handbook of affective sciences*. Oxford: Oxford University Press.

Davis, M., & Scott, C. (2002). Where does reading fit in citation theory and information seeking? Operalisation of reading: The "black box" of information use. In H. Bruce, R. Fidel, P. Ingwersen, & P. Vakkari, (Eds.), *Emerging frameworks and methods: Proceedings of the Fourth International Conference on Conceptions of Library and Information Science (CoLIS4)*, (pp. 301–304). Greenwood Village, CO: Libraries Unlimited.

Denzin, N. K., & Lincoln, Y. S. (2000). *Handbook of qualitative research* (2nd ed.). Thousand Oaks, CA: Sage Publications.

Department of Environment, Transport and the Regions. (2000). *Indices of Multiple Deprivation*. London: Department of Environment, Transport and the Regions. Accessed December 5, 2006, from www.odpm.gov.uk/index.asp?id=1128626.

Dervin, B. (1975/2002). *Communicating ideas: An adapted guide to Richard F. Carter's early picturing language*. Unpublished manuscript. Accessed November 24, 2006, from communication.sbs.ohio-state.edu/sense-making/art/artabsdervin75pic lang.html.

Dervin, B. (1977). Using theory for librarianship: Communication, not information. *Drexel Library Quarterly*, *13*, 16–32.

Dervin, B. (1983, May). *An overview of sense-making research: Concepts, methods and results*. Paper presented at the annual meeting of the International Communication Association, Dallas, TX.

Dervin, B. (1992). From the mind's eye of the user: The sense-making qualitative-quantitative methodology. In J. D. Glazier & R. R. Powell (Eds.), *Qualitative research in information management* (pp. 61–84). Englewood, CO: Libraries Unlimited.

Dervin, B. (1993). Verbing communication: Mandate for disciplinary invention. *Journal of Communication*, *43*(3), 45–54.

Dervin, B. (1994). Information <—> democracy: An examination of underlying assumptions. *Journal of the American Society for Information Science*, *45*(6), 369–385.

Dervin, B. (1999). On studying information seeking methodologically: The implications of connecting metatheory to method. *Information Processing and Management*, *35*, 727–750.

Dervin, B. (2003a). Human studies and user studies: A call for methodological interdisciplinarity. *Information Research*, *9*(1) paper 166. Accessed December 13, 2006, from InformationR.net/ir/9-1/paper166.html.

Dervin, B. (2003b). Sense-making's journey from metatheory to methodology to method: An example using information seeking and use as research focus. In B. Dervin & L. Foreman-Wernet (Eds.), *Sense-making methodology reader: Selected writings of Brenda Dervin* (pp. 133–164). Cresskill, NJ: Hampton Press.

Dervin, B., & Foreman-Wernet, L. (Eds.). (2003). *Sense-making methodology reader: Selected writings of Brenda Dervin*. Cresskill, NJ: Hampton Press.

Dervin, B., & Fraser, B. (1985). *How libraries help.* Sacramento, CA: California State Library (ERIC Document Reproduction Service N. 264857).

Dervin, B., & Nilan, M. (1986). Information needs and uses. *Annual Review of Information Science and Technology, 21,* 3–33.

Dervin, B., & Shields, P. (1999). Adding the missing user to policy discourse: Understanding US user telephone privacy concerns. *Telecommunications Policy, 23,* 403–435.

Dervin, B., Reinhard, C. D., Kerr, Z. Y., Connaway, L. S., Prabha, C., & Normore, L., et al. (2006, November). *How libraries, Internet browsers, and other sources help: A comparison of sense-making evaluations of sources used in recent college/university and personal life situations by faculty, graduate student, and undergraduate users.* Poster presented at the annual meeting of the American Society for Information Science & Technology, Austin, TX. Accessed November 24, 2006, from imlsproject.comm. ohio-state.edu/imls_papers/asist06poster_list.html.

Dervin, B., Reinhard, C. D., Kerr, Z. Y., Song, M., & Shen, F. C. (Eds.). (2006). *Sense-making the information confluence: The whys and hows of college and university user satisficing of information needs. Phase II: Sense-making survey.* Report on National Leadership Grant LG-02-03-0062-03, to Institute for Museums and Library Services, Washington, D.C. Columbus, Ohio: School of Communication, Ohio State University. Accessed November 24, 2006, from imlsproject.comm.ohio-state.edu/imls_reports_list.html.

Dervin, B., Zweizig, D., Banister, M., Gabriel, M., Hall, E. P., Kwan, C., et al., (1976). *The development of strategies for dealing with the information needs of urban residents: Phase 1: Citizen study.* Washington, DC: U.S. Office of Education. (ERIC Document Reproduction Service No. ED125640).

Desrosières, A. (1998). *The politics of large numbers: A history of statistical reasoning.* Cambridge, MA: Harvard University Press.

Dewey, J. (1933). *How we think.* Lexington, MA: Heath.

Diller, S., Shedroff, N., & Rhea, D. (2006). *Making meaning: How successful businesses deliver meaningful customer experiences.* Berkley, CA: New Riders.

Dimitroff, A., Wolfram, D., & Volz, A. (1996). Affective response and retrieval performance: Analysis of contributing factors. *Library and Information Science Research, 18*(2), 121–132.

Dollard, J., Doob, L. W., Miller, N. E., Mowrer, O. H., & Sears, R. R. (1939). *Frustration and aggression.* New Haven, CT: Yale University Press.

Dortins, E. (2002). Reflections on phenomenographic process: Interview, transcription and analysis. In A. Goody, J. Herrington, & M. Northcote (Eds.), *Proceedings of the 2002 Annual International Conference of the Higher Education Research and Development Society of Australasia* (HERDSA) (pp. 207–213). Canberra, ACT: HERDSA.

Drentea P., & Moren-Cross J. L. (2005). Social capital and social support on the Web: The case of an Internet mother site. *Sociology of Health & Illness, 27*(7), 920–943.

Druin, A. (2005). What children can teach us: Developing digital libraries for children with children. *Library Quarterly, 75,* 20–41.

Dubé, L., and Paré, G. (2003). Rigor in information systems positivist case research: Current practices, trends, and recommendations. *MIS Quarterly, 27*(4), 597–636.

Duda, A. E. (2005). *A content analysis of book reviews from a readers' advisory perspective.* Unpublished master's dissertation, University of North Carolina at Chapel Hill. Accessed November 28 2006, from, etd.ils.unc.edu/dspace/bitstream/1901/143/1/Paper.pdf.

Dunning, D., Johnson, K., & Ehrlinger, J. (2003). Why people fail to recognize their own incompetence. *Current Directions in Psychological Science, 12*(3), 53–57.

Eagan, N. (2004). The meaning associated with the experience of a sea kayaking adventure among adults with visual impairment. In P. Tierney & D. Chavez (Eds.). *The Fourth Social Aspects and Recreation Research Symposium, 2004 February 4–6.* San Francisco, CA: San Francisco State University. Accessed November 25, 2006, from www.fs.fed.us/psw/programs/recreation/pdf/2004_sarr_proceedings_session_08.pdf.

Elias, M., Zins, J., Graczyk, J., & Weissberg, R. (2003). Implementation, sustainability, and scaling up of social-emotional and academic innovations in public schools. *School Psychology Review, 32*(3), 303–319.

Elksnin, L., & Elksnin, N. (2003). Fostering social-emotional learning in the classroom. *Education, 124*(1), 63–76.

Ellis, A., & Bernard, M. (Eds.). (1983). *Clinical applications of rational-emotive therapy.* New York: Plenum Press.

Endres, B. (1996). Habermas and Critical Thinking. *Philosophy of Education 1996.* Accessed December 05, 2006, from www.ed.uiuc.edu/EPS/PES-Yearbook/96_docs/endres.html.

Erdelez, S. (1997). Information encountering: A conceptual framework for accidental information discovery. In P. Vakkari, R. Savolainen & B. Dervin (Eds.), *Information seeking in context: Proceedings of an International Conference on Research in Information Needs, Seeking, and Use in Different Contexts (Aug. 14–16, 1996, Tampere, Finland)* (pp. 412–421). London: Graham Taylor.

Ericsson K. A., & Simon, H. A. (1993). *Protocol analysis: Verbal reports as data.* Cambridge, MA: MIT Press.

Erikson, E. H. (1950). *Childhood and society.* New York: Norton.

Erikson, E. H. (1963). *Youth: Change and challenge.* New York: Basic Books.

Erikson, E. H. (1968). *Identity: Youth and crisis.* New York: Norton.

Etaugh, C., & Moss, C. (2001). Attitudes of employed women toward parents who choose full-time or part-time employment following their child's birth. *Sex Roles: A Journal of Research, 44*(9/10), 611–619.

Evans, D. (2001). *Emotion: The science of sentiment.* Oxford: Oxford University Press.

Facione, P. A., & Facione, N. C. (1992). *The California critical thinking dispositions inventory.* Millbrae, CA: California Academic Press.

Facione, P. A., Facione, N. C., Blohm, S. W., Howard, K., & Giancarlo, C. A. (1998). *The California critical thinking skills test. Form A and Form B test manual.* Millbrae, CA: California Academic Press.

Facione, P. A., Facione, N. C., & Giancarlo, C. A. (2000). The disposition toward critical thinking: Its character, measurement, and relationship to critical thinking skill. *Informal Logic, 20*(1), 61–84.

Fallows, D. (2005). *Search engine users: Internet searchers are confident, satisfied and trusting, but they are also unaware and naïve.* Washington, DC: Pew Internet & American Life Project. Accessed December 3, 2006, from www.pewinternet.org/pdfs/PIP_Searchengine_users.pdf.

Farmer, L. (2006). Degree of implementation of library media programs and student achievement. *Journal of Librarianship and Information Science, 38*(1), 21–32.

Feynman, R. P. (1999). *The pleasure of finding things out: The best short works of Richard P. Feynman.* Cambridge, MA: Perseus Publishing.

Fink, G. (2002, August). *Issues of international intercultural research: The narrative interview process.* Presentation at the PDW Academy of Management Meeting 2002, Denver, CO. Accessed December 5, 2006, from www.harzing.com/download/aom2002gf1.pdf.

Fisher, K. E. (2006, May). *The death of the user and other ruminations on information behavior research.* Paper presented at the School of Library and Information Studies, Oslo University College, Norway.

Fisher, K. E., Durrance, J. C., & Hinton, M. B. (2004). Information grounds and the use of need-based services by immigrants in Queens, NY: A context-based, outcome evaluation approach. *Journal of the American Society for Information Science & Technology*, *55*(8), 754–766.

Fisher, K. E., Erdelez, S., & McKechnie, L. (Eds.). (2005). *Theories of information behavior*. Medford, NJ: Information Today, Inc.

Fisher, K. E., Landry, C. F., & Naumer, C. M. (2006, July). *Social spaces, casual interactions, meaningful exchanges: An information ground typology based on the college student experience*. Paper presented at the *Information Seeking in Context VI* (ISIC) conference, Sydney, Australia. Submitted for publication.

Fisher, K. E., & Naumer, C. M. (2006). Information grounds: Theoretical basis and empirical findings on information flow in social settings. In A. Spink & C. Cole (Eds.), *New directions in human information behavior* (pp. 93–111). Amsterdam: Kluwer.

Fisher, K., Naumer, C., Durrance, J., Stromski, L., & Christiansen, T. (2005). Something old, something new: Preliminary findings from an exploratory study about people's information habits and information grounds. *Information Research*, *10*(2), paper 223. Accessed December 5, 2006, from informationr.net/ir/10-2/paper223.html.

Flick, U. (1998). *An introduction to narrative research*. London: Sage.

Flyvbjerg, B. (2001). *Making social science matter: Why social inquiry fails and how it can succeed again*. Cambridge: Cambridge University Press.

Forgas, J. P. (Ed.). (2000). *Feeling and thinking: The role of affect in social cognition*. Cambridge: Maison des Science de l'Homme & Cambridge University Press.

Forgas, J. P., & George, J. M. (2001). Affective influences on judgments and behaviour in organisations: An information processing perspective. *Organizational Behavior and Human Decision Processes*, *86*(1), 3–34.

Forgays, D. K., Ottaway, S. A., Guarino, A., & D'Alessio, M. (2001). Parenting stress in employed and at-home mothers in Italy. *Journal of Family and Economic Issues*, *22*(4), 327–351.

Foshay, A. W., Thorndike, R. L., Hotyat, F., Pidgeon, D. A., & Walker, D. A. (1962). *Educational achievements of thirteen-year-olds in twelve countries*. Hamburg: UNESCO Institute for Education. Accessed November 28, 2006, from unesdoc.unesco.org/images/0013/001314/131437eo.pdf.

Freire, P. (1970). *Pedagogy of the oppressed* (M. Bergman Ramos, Trans.). New York: Seabury Press.

Freud, S. (1921). Types of onset and neurosis. In J. Strachey (Ed. & Trans.), *The standard edition of the complete psychological works of Sigmund Freud: Vol. 12. Case history of Schreber, papers on technique and other works (1911–1913)* (pp. 227–230). London: Hogarth Press.

Friedman, B. (1997). *Human values and the design of computer technology*. Stanford, CA: CSLI Publications.

Frijda, N. H., Manstead, A. S. R., & Bem, S. (2000). *Emotions and beliefs: How feelings influence thoughts*. Cambridge: Cambridge University Press.

Froomkin, M. A. (2003). Habermas@discourse.net: Toward a critical theory of cyberspace. *Harvard Law Review*, *116*(3), 749–873.

Gagnon, G., & Collay, M. (2001). *Designing for learning: Six elements in constructivist classrooms*. Berkeley, CA: Corwin Press.

Galda, L. (1982). Assuming the spectator stance: An examination of the responses of three young readers. *Research in the Teaching of English, 16*, 1–20.

Galda, L. (1983). Research in response to literature. *Journal of Research and Development in Education, 16*(3), 1–7.

Galda, L., & Beach, R. (2001). Response to literature as a cultural activity. *Reading Research Quarterly, 36*(1), 64–73. Accessed November 28, 2006, from www.readinghall offame.org/Library/Retrieve.cfm?D=10.1598/RRQ.36.1.4&F=RRQ-36-1-Galda.pdf.

Geertz, C. (1973) *The interpretation of cultures*. London: Fontana Press.

Gibson, J. J. (1986). *The ecological approach to visual perception*. Mahwah, NJ: Lawrence Erlbaum Associates.

Gigerenzer, G., & Goldstein, D. G. (2000). Reasoning the fast and frugal way: Models of bounded rationality. In T. Connolly, H. R. Arkes, & K. R. Hammond (Eds.), *Judgment and decision making: An interdisciplinary reader* (2nd ed., pp. 621–650). Cambridge: Cambridge University Press.

Gilder, G. (1989). *Microcosm: The quantum revolution in economics and technology*. New York: Simon and Schuster.

Given, L. M. (2000, August). *Student life on the margins: Mature students' information behaviours and the discursive search for a 'student' identity*. Paper presented at the Information Seeking in Context: The 3rd International Conference on Information Needs, Seeking and Use in Different Contexts, Gotheburg, Sweden.

Given, L. M. (2002). The academic and the everyday: Investigating the overlap in mature undergraduates' information-seeking behaviour. *Library & Information Science Research, 24*(1), 17–29.

Glaser, B. G., & Strauss, A. L. (1967). *The discovery of grounded theory: Strategies for qualitative research*. New York: Aldine de Gruyter.

Glesne, C. (1999). *Becoming qualitative researchers: An introduction*. New York: Longman.

Goffman, E. (1959). *The presentation of self in everyday life*. Garden City, NY: Doubleday.

Gohm, C. L., & Clore, G. L. (2002). Affect as information: An individual-differences approach. In L. F. Barrett & P. Salovey (Eds.), *The wisdom in feelings: Psychological processes in emotional intelligence*. New York: The Guilford Press.

Goldman, A. (1995). Emotions in music (A postscript). *Journal of Aesthetics and Art Criticism, 53*(1), 59–69.

Goodin, M. (1991). The transferability of library research skills from high school to college. *School Library Media Quarterly, 20*, 33–42.

Gorman, K. A., & Fritzsche, B. A. (2002). The good-mother stereotype: Stay-at-home (or wish that you did!). *Journal of Applied Social Psychology, 32*(10), 2190–2201.

Granovetter, M. S. (1982). The strength of weak ties: A network theory revisited. In P. V. Marsden & N. Lin (Eds.), *Social structure and network analysis* (pp. 105–130). Beverly Hills, CA: Sage.

Green, W. S., & Jordan, P. W. (Eds.). (2002). *Pleasure with products: Beyond usability*. New York: Taylor & Francis.

Greenberg, B. S., & Dervin, B. (1970). *Use of the mass media by the urban poor: Findings of three research projects with an annotated bibliography*. New York: Praeger.

Grimsaeth, K. (2005). *Kansei engineering: Linking emotions and product features*. Accessed December 13, 2006, from www.ivt.ntnu.no/ipd/fag/PD9/2005/artikler/PD9%20Kansei%20Engineering%20K_Grimsath.pdf.

Grover, R., Lakin, J., & Dickerson, J. (1997). An interdisciplinary model for assessing learning. In L. Lighthall & K. Haycock (Eds.), *Information rich but knowledge poor?* Seattle: International Association of School Librarianship.

Guba, E. G., & Lincoln, Y. S. (1982). Epistemological and methodological bases of naturalistic inquiry. *Educational Communications and Technology Journal, 30*(4), 233–252.

Guillaume, L. R., & Bath, P. A. (2004). The impact of health scares on parents' information needs and preferred information sources: A case study of the MMR vaccine scare. *Health Informatics Journal, 10*(1), 5–22.

Gunn, H. (2002). Virtual libraries supporting student learning. *School Libraries Worldwide, 8*(2): 27–37.

Habermas, J. (1993). *Justification and application: Remarks on discourse ethics* (C. P. Cronin, Trans.). Cambridge, MA: The MIT Press.

Haghenbeck, K. (2005). Critical care nurses' experiences when technology malfunctions. *Journal of the New York State Nurses Association, 36*, 13–19.

Halász, L. (1991). Understanding short stories: An American-Hungarian cross-cultural study. *Empirical Studies of the Arts, 9*, 143–163.

Hall, S. (1997). *Representation: Cultural representations and signifying practices.* London: Sage.

Hanoch, Y. (2002). "Neither an angel nor an ant": Emotion as an aid to bounded rationality. *Journal of Economic Psychology, 23*, 1–25.

Hansen, R. A. (2003). *Coping with loss: The use of media and entertainment as a mood-management device.* Unpublished master's thesis, California State University, Fullerton.

Happy Medium Productions, Inc. (2006). *Spaghetti book club: Book reviews by kids for kids!* Accessed November 28, 2006, from www.spaghettibookclub.org.

Harada, V., & Yoshina, J. (1997). Improving information search process instruction and assessment through collaborative action research. *School Libraries Worldwide, 3*, 41–55.

Harpaz, I. (1996). International management survey research. In B. J. Punnett & O. Shenkar (Eds.), *Handbook for international management research* (pp. 37–62). Cambridge, MA: Blackwell.

Harris R., Stickney J., Grasley C., Hutchinson G., Greaves L., & Boyd T. (2001). Searching for help and information: Abused women speak out. *Library and Information Science Research, 23*(2), 123–141.

Harris, R. M., & Dewdney, P. (1994). *Barriers to information: How formal help systems fail battered women.* Westport, CT: Greenwood.

Harrison, E. F. (1999). *The managerial decision-making process* (5th ed.). Boston: Houghton Mifflin.

Hartson, H. R., Andre, T. S., Williges, R. C., & van Rens, L. (1999). The user action framework: A theory-based foundation for inspection and classification of usability problems. In H.-J. Bullinger & J. Ziegler (Eds.), *Proceedings of the Eighth International Conference on Human–Computer Interaction. September 24–29, 1999, Munich, Germany* (pp. 1058–1062). Mahwah, NJ: Lawrence Erlbaum Associates.

Harzing, A. (2000). Cross-national mail surveys: Why do response rates differ between countries. *Industrial Marketing Management, 29*(3), 243–254.

Hawkins, J., Smith, B., & Catalano, R. (2004). Social development and social and emotional learning. In J. Zins, R. Weissberg, W. Wang, & H. Walberg. (Eds.), *Building academic success on social and emotional learning: What does the research say?* New York: Teachers College Press.

Hayes, A. (2005). *Statistical methods for communication science.* Mahwah, NJ: Lawrence Erlbaum Associates.

Heinström, J. (2002). *Fast surfers, broad scanners and deep divers: Personality and information seeking behaviour.* Åbo, Finland: Åbo Akademi University Press. Accessed December 5, 2006, from www.abo.fi/~jheinstr/thesis.htm.

Heinström, J. (2003). Five personality dimensions and their influence on information behavior. *Information Research, 9*(1). Accessed November 25, 2006, from informationr.net/ir/9-1/paper165.html.

Heinström, J. (2005). Fast surfing, broad scanning and deep diving: The influence of personality and study approach on students' information-seeking behavior. *Journal of Documentation, 61*(2), 228–247.

Helliwell, M. (2003). Building information bridges between parents and health care providers in the neonatal intensive care unit. In W. C. Peekhaus & L. Spiteri (Eds.), *Bridging the digital divide: Equalizing access to information and communication technologies. Proceedings of the 31st Annual Conference of the Canadian Association for Information Sciene, May, 2003, Halifax, Canada.* Halifax, Nova Scotia: Canadian Association for Information Science. Accessed November 25, 2006, from www.cais-acsi.ca/proceedings/2003/Helliwell_2003.pdf.

Hepler, S. I., & Hickman, J. (1982). "The book was okay. I love you": Social aspects of response to literature. *Theory into Practice, 21*(4), 278–83.

Hersberger, J. (2001). Everyday life information needs and information sources of homeless parents. In P. Vakkari (Ed.), *The new review of information behaviour research: Studies of information seeking in context* (pp.119–134). Cambridge: Taylor Graham.

Heuer, F., & Reisberg, D. (1990). Vivid memories of emotional events: The accuracy of remembered minutiae. *Memory & Cognition, 18*, 496–506.

Heyneman, S. P. (2004). The use of cross-national comparisons for local education policy. *Curriculum Inquiry, 34*(3), 345–352.

Hofstede, G. H. (2001). *Culture's consequences: Comparing values, behaviors, institutions, and organizations across nations.* Thousand Oaks, CA: Sage Publications.

Holliday, W., & Li, Q. (2004). Understanding the millenials: Updating our knowledge about students. *Reference Services Review, 32*(4), 356–366.

Holsti, O. R. (1969). *Content analysis for the social sciences and humanities.* Reading, MA: Addison-Wesley Publishing Co.

Horowitz, A., Reinhardt, J. P., & Kennedy, G. J. (2005). Major and subthreshold depression among older adults seeking vision rehabilitation services. *The American Journal of Geriatric Psychiatry, 13*, 180–187.

Hsu, M.-H., & Chiu, C.-M. (2004). Internet self-efficacy and electronic service acceptance. *Decision Support Systems, 38*, 369–381.

Huang, G. H., Law, K. S., & Wong, C. S. (2006). Emotional intelligence: A critical review. In L. V. Wesley (Ed.), *Intelligence: New research* (pp. 95–113). New York: Nova Science Publishers.

Hudlicka, E. (2003). To feel or not to feel: The role of affect in human–computer interaction. *International Journal of Human–Computer Studies, 59*, 71–75.

Hyldeğard, J. (2006). Collaborative information behaviour: Exploring Kuhlthau's Information Search Process model in a group-based educational setting. *Information Processing and Management, 42*(1), 276–298.

Hynds, S. (1997). *On the brink: Negotiating literature and life with adolescents.* New York: Teachers College Press.

IFLA/UNESCO. (2002). *School library guidelines.* The Hague, Netherlands: IFLA.

Ingwersen, P. (1984). Psychological aspects of information retrieval. *Social Science Information Studies, 4*(2/3), 83–89.

Ingwerson, P. (1992). *Information retrieval interaction.* London: Taylor Graham.

International Association for the Evaluation of Educational Achievement. (n.d.). *Current studies.* Accessed November 28, from www.iea.nl/current_studies.html.

International Children's Digital Library Foundation. (2006). *International Children's Digital Library.* Accessed November 28, 2006, from www.childrenslibrary.org.

Irvine, J. R. (2002). *Ask them! Children's fiction book choices and the implications for libraries.* Working paper. Accessed November 28, 2006, from www.openpolytechnic.ac.nz/research/wp/res_wp302irvinej.pdf.

Isen, A. M. (2004). Positive affect and decision making. In M. Lewis & J. Haviland-Jones (Eds.), *Handbook of emotions.* New York: Guilford Press.

Isen, A. M., Daubman, K. A., & Gorgoglione, J. M. (1987). The influence of positive affect on cognitive organization: Implications for education. In R. E. Snow & M. J. Farr

(Eds.), *Aptitude, learning, and instruction. Volume 3: Conative and affective process analyses* (pp. 143–164). Mahwah, NJ: Lawrence Erlbaum Associates.

Jakobovits, L. A., & Nahl-Jakobovits, D. (1987). Learning the library: Taxonomy of skills and errors. *College and Research Libraries, 48,* 203–214.

Jakobovits, L. A., & Nahl-Jakobovits, D. (1990). Measuring information searching competence. *College & Research Libraries, 51,* 448–462.

Jarvela, S., Lehtinen, E., & Salonen, P. (2000). Social-emotional orientation as a mediating variable in the teaching–learning interaction: Implications for instructional design. *Scandinavian Journal of Educational Research, 44*(3), 293–306.

Järvenoja, H., & Järvelä, S. (2005). How students describe the sources of their emotional and motivational experiences during the learning process: A qualitative approach. *Learning and Instruction, 15*(5), 465–480.

Jiao, Q. G., & Onwuegbuzie, A. J. (2004). The impact of information technology on library anxiety: The role of computer attitudes. *Information Technology and Libraries, 23,* 138–144.

Johnson, D. (1994). *Cooperative learning in the classroom.* Alexandria, VA: Association for Supervision and Curriculum Development.

Johnson, J. D. (1997). *Cancer-related information seeking.* Cresskill, NJ: Hampton Press.

Johnston, D. D., & Swanson, D. H. (2003). Invisible mothers: A content analysis of motherhood ideologies and myths in magazines. *Sex Roles: A Journal of Research, 49*(1/2), 21–33.

Johnston, D. D., & Swanson, D. H. (2004). Moms hating moms: The internalization of Mother War rhetoric. *Sex Roles: A Journal of Research, 51,* 497–509.

Jordan, P. W. (2000). *Designing pleasurable products: An introduction to the new human factors.* Philadelphia: Taylor & Francis.

Julien, H. (1999). Barriers to adolescents' information seeking for career decision making. *Journal of the American Society for Information Science, 50*(1), 38–48.

Julien, H. (2005). Women's ways of knowing. In K. E. Fisher, S. Erdelez, & L. E. F. McKechnie (Eds.), *Theories of information behavior* (pp. 387–391). Medford, NJ: Information Today, Inc.

Julien, H., & Boon. S. (2004). Assessing instructional outcomes in Canadian academic libraries. *Library & Information Science Research, 26*(2), 121–139.

Julien, H., & Duggan, L. J. (2000). A longitudinal analysis of information needs and uses literature. *Library & Information Research, 22*(3), 291–309.

Julien, H., & McKechnie, L. E. F. (2005). What we've learned about the role of affect in information behaviour/information retrieval. In J. Gascón, F. Bruguillos, & A. Pons, (Eds.), *Proceedings of the 7th ISKO (International Society for Knowledge Organization)—Spain Conference. The Human Dimension of Knowledge Organization* (pp. 342–356). Barcelona, July 6–8, 2005.

Julien, H., McKechnie, L. (E. F.), & Hart, S. (2005). Affective issues in library and information science systems work: A content analysis. *Library and Information Science Research, 27*(4), 453–466.

Julien, H., & Michels, D. (2000). Source selection among information seekers: Ideals and realities. *Canadian Journal of Information and Library Science, 25*(1), 1–18.

Jungermann, H. (2000). The two camps on rationality. In T. Connolly, H. R. Arkes, & K. R. Hammond (Eds.), *Judgment and decision making: An interdisciplinary reader* (2nd ed., pp. 575–591). Cambridge: Cambridge University Press.

Kaku, M. (1997). *Visions: How science will revolutionize the 21st century.* New York: Anchor Books.

Kalbach, J. (2004). Feeling lucky? Emotions and information seeking. *Interactions, 11*(5), 66–67.

Kalbach, J. (2006). I'm feeling lucky: The role of emotions in seeking information on the Web. *Journal of the American Society for Information Science and Technology, 57*(6), 813–818.

Kautzman, A. M. (1998). Virtuous, virtual access: Making Web pages accessible to people with disabilities. *Searcher, 6*(6): 42–49.

Kavanagh, R. (1999). The virtual library for blind and visually impaired Canadians. *Feliciter, 45*(5), 296–299.

Kellner, D. (1989). Boundaries and borderlines: Reflections on Jean Boudrillard and critical theory. *Current Perspectives in Social Theory, 9,* 5–22. Accessed December 5, 2006, from www.gseis.ucla.edu/faculty/kellner/Illumina%20Folder/kell2.htm.

Kelly, G. A. (1963). *A theory of personality: The psychology of personal constructs.* New York: W. W. Norton.

Kernan, J., & Mojena, R. (1973). Information utilization and personality. *Journal of Communication, 23*(3), 315–327.

Knobloch-Westerwick, S., & Alter, S. (2006). Mood adjustment to social situations through mass media use: How men ruminate and women dissipate angry moods. *Human Communication Research, 32*(1), 58–73.

Kochen, M. (1989). *The Small World.* Norwood, NJ: Ablex.

Koenes, S. G., & Karshmer, J. (2000). Depression: A comparison study between blind and sighted adolescents. *Issues in Mental Health Nursing, 21*(3): 269–279.

Kort, B., Reilly, R., & Picard, R. W. (2001). An affective model of interplay between emotions and learning: Reengineering educational pedagogy—building a learning companion. *Proceedings of the Second IEEE International Conference on Advanced Learning Technologies (ICALT'01),* 43–48.

Kracker, J. (2002). Research anxiety and students' perceptions of research: An experiment. Part I. Effect of teaching Kuhlthau's ISP model. *Journal of the American Society for Information Science and Technology, 53*(4), 282–294.

Kracker, J., & Pollio, H. R. (2003). The experiences of libraries across time: Thematic analysis of undergraduate recollections of library experiences. *Journal of the American Society for Information Science and Technology, 54*(12), 1104–1116.

Kracker, J., & Wang, P. (2002). Research anxiety and students' perceptions of research: An experiment. Part II. Content analysis of their writings on two experiences. *Journal of the American Society for Information Science and Technology, 53*(4), 295–307.

Kraft, D. H., & Waller, W. G. (1981). A Bayesian approach to user stopping rules for information retrieval systems. *Information Processing and Management, 17*(6), 349–360.

Krathwohl, D. R., Bloom, B. S., & Masia, B. B. (1964). *Taxonomy of educational objectives: The classification of educational goals. Handbook II: Affective domain.* New York: David McKay.

Krippendorf, K. (2004). Reliability in content analysis. *Human Communication Research, 30*(3), 411–433.

Kuhlthau, C. C. (1985). *Teaching the library research process.* Englewood Cliffs, NJ: Prentice-Hall.

Kuhlthau, C. C. (1988a). Developing a model of the library search process: Cognitive and affective aspects. *RQ, 28*(2), 232–242.

Kuhlthau, C. C. (1988b). Perceptions of the information search process in libraries: A study of changes from high school through college. *Information Processing & Management, 24*(4), 419–427.

Kuhlthau, C. C. (1991). Inside the search process: Information seeking from the user's perspective. *Journal of the American Society for Information Science, 42*(5), 361–371.

Kuhlthau, C. C. (1993a). A principle of uncertainty for information seeking. *Journal of Documentation, 49*(4), 339–355.

Kuhlthau, C. C. (1993b). *Seeking meaning: A process approach to library and information services.* Westport, CT: Libraries Unlimited.

Kuhlthau, C. C. (2004). *Seeking meaning: A process approach to library and information services* (2nd ed.). Westport, CT: Libraries Unlimited.

Kurbanoglu, S. S. (2003). Self-efficacy: A concept closely linked to information literacy and lifelong learning. *Journal of Documentation, 59*(6), 635–646.

Kvale, S. (1996). *Interviews: An introduction to qualitative research interviewing.* Thousand Oaks, CA: Sage Publications.

Labovitz, S., & Hagedorn, R. (1981). *Introduction to social research.* New York: McGraw-Hill.

Lance, K. (2002). Proof of the power. *Teacher Librarian, 29*(2), 29–34.

Large, A., & Beheshti, J. (2000). The Web as a classroom resource: Reactions from the users. *Journal of the American Society for Information Science, 51,* 1069–1080.

Large, A., Beheshti, J., & Moukdad, H. (1999). Information seeking on the Web: Navigation skills of grade-six primary school students. *Proceedings of the 62nd annual meeting of the American Society for Information Science and Technology, 36,* 84–97).

Larsen, S. F., & László, J. (1990). Cultural-historical knowledge and personal experience in appreciation of literature. *European Journal of Social Psychology, 20,* 425–440.

László, J., & Larsen, S. F. (1991). Cultural and text variables in processing personal experiences while reading literature. *Empirical Studies of the Arts, 9,* 23–34.

Lather, P. (1991). Getting smart: Feminist research and pedagogy with/in the postmodern. New York: Routledge.

Lauria, A. R. (1979). *The making of mind.* Cambridge, MA: Harvard University Press.

Lawson, R. (1965). *Frustration: The development of a scientific concept.* New York: MacMillan.

Lazar, J., Jones, A., Hackley, M., & Schneiderman, B. (2006). Severity and impact of computer user frustration: A comparison of student and workplace. *Interacting with Computers, 18*(2), 187–207.

Leckie, G. J., & Pettigrew, K. E. (1997). A general model of the information seeking of professionals: Role theory through the back door? In P. Vakkari, R. Savolainen & B. Dervin (Eds.), *Information seeking in context: Proceedings of an International Conference on Research in Information Needs, Seeking, and Use in Different Contexts (Aug 14–16, 1996, Tampere, Finland)* (pp. 99–110). London: Graham Taylor. Accessed November 25, 2006, from projects.ischool.washington.edu/fisher/pubs/ISIC.1997.pdf.

Leu, L., & Lee, P. S. N. (2005). Multiple determinants of life quality: The roles of Internet activities, use of new media, social support, and leisure activities. *Telematics and Informatics, 22*(3), 161–180.

Leung, C. (2003). Bicultural perspectives and reader response: Four American readers respond to Jean Fritz's Homesick. *Canadian Modern Language Review, 60*(1). Accessed November 28, 2006, from www.utpjournals.com/product/cmlr/601/601_leung.html.

Lewis, C., & Fabos, B. (2005). Instant messaging, literacies, and social identities. *RRQ Reading Research Quarterly, 40*(4), 470–501. Accessed December 13, 2006, from www.reading.org/Library/Retrieve.cfm?D=10.1598/RRQ.40.4.5&F=RRQ-40-4-Lewis.html.

Li, X., & Hitt, L. M. (2004). *Self selection and information role of online product reviews.* Working Paper. University of Pennsylvania, Wharton School. Accessed November 28, 2006, from opim-sky.wharton.upenn.edu/wise2004/sat321.pdf.

Limberg, L. (1999). Experiencing information seeking and learning: A study of the interaction between two phenomena. *Information Research, 5*(1), paper 68. Accessed November 28, 2006, from informationr.net/ir/5-1/paper68.html.

Lincoln, Y. S., & Guba, E. G. (1985). *Naturalistic inquiry.* Beverly Hills, CA: Sage Publications.

Maatita, F. C. (2003). Mothers and playgroups: "Doing" motherhood in the social sphere. *Dissertation Abstracts International, A: The Humanities and Social Sciences, 64*(5), 1853-A. (UMI No. DA3089750.).

MacKinnon, N. J. (1994). *Symbolic interactionism as affect control.* Albany: State University of New York Press.

Malhotra, N. K., Agarwal, J., & Peterson, M. (1996). Methodological issues in cross-cultural marketing research: A state-of-the-art review. *International Marketing Review, 13*(5), 7–43.

Marchionini, G. (1995). *Information seeking in electronic environment.* Cambridge: Cambridge University Press.

Markus, M. L. (1983). Power, politics and MIS implementation. *Communications of the ACM, 26,* 430–444.

Marques de Oliveira, S. (1990). The compatibility between American library and information science programs and foreign countries' needs: An exploratory study. In J. L. Tallman & J. B. Ojiambo (Eds.), *Translating an international education to a national environment* (pp. 83–104). Pittsburgh, PA: University of Pittsburgh, School of Library and Information Science.

Martin, A., & Marsh, H. (2006). Academic resilience and its psychological and educational correlates: A construct validity approach. *Psychology in the Schools, 43*(3), 267–281.

Martin, L. L., & Tesser, A. (1996). *Striving and feeling: Interactions among goals, affect and self-regulation.* Mahwah, NJ: Lawrence Erlbaum Associates.

Martindale, C. (Ed.). (1988). *Psychological approaches to the study of literary narratives.* Hamburg: Buske.

Martinez, M., & Roser, N. L. (2003). Children's responses to literature. In J. Flood, D. Lapp, J. Squire, & J. Jensen (Eds.), *Handbook of Research on Teaching the English Language Arts* (2nd ed.). Mahwah, NJ: Lawrence Erlbaum Associates.

Martzoukou, K. (2005). A review of Web information seeking research: Considerations of method and foci of interest. *Information Research, 10*(2), paper 215.

Massey, S. A., Weeks, A. C., & Druin, A. (2005). Initial findings from a three-year international case study exploring children's responses to literature in a digital library. *Library Trends, 54*(3), 245–265.

Maxwell, J. A. (1996). *Qualitative research design: An interactive approach* (Applied Social Research Methods Series No. 41). Thousand Oaks, CA: Sage Publications, Inc.

Mayer, J. D. (2002). Forward. In L. F. Barrett & P. Salovey (Eds.), *The wisdom in meaning: Psychological processes in emotional intelligence* (pp. x–xvi). New York: Guilford Press.

McCown, K., Freedman, J. M., Jensen, A., & Rideout, M. (1998). *Self science.* San Mateo, CA: Six Seconds Press.

McCreadie, M. (1998). *Access to information: A multidisciplinary theoretical framework.* Unpublished doctoral dissertation, Rutgers, The State University of New Jersey, New Brunswick.

McGowen, K. (2003). Student choice: Empowering students with tools for reading. *Houston Teachers Institute, 7.* Accessed November 28, 2006, from www.uh.edu/hti/cu/2003/7/09.pdf.

McKechnie, L. (1996). *Opening the "preschoolers' door to learning": An ethnographic study of the use of public libraries by preschool girls.* Unpublished doctoral dissertation, University of Western Ontario, London, Ontario, Canada.

McKechnie, L. (2000). The ethnographic observation of preschool children. *Library and Information Science Research, 22*(1), 61–76.

McKechnie, L. (2004). "I'll keep them for my children" (Kevin, nine years): Children's personal collections of books and other media. *Canadian Journal of Library and Information Science, 27*(4), 75–90.

McKnight, M. (2004). Hospital nurses: No time to read on duty. *Journal of Electronic Medical Resources in Libraries, 1*, 13–23.

McKnight, M. (in press). A grounded theory model of on-duty critical care nurses' information behavior: The patient-chart cycle of informative interactions. *Journal of Documentation.*

McNee, S. M., Albert, I., Cosley, D., Gopalkrishnan, P., Lam, S. K., Rashid, A. M., et al. (2002). On the recommending of citations for research papers. In *Proceedings of the 2002 ACM Conference on Computer Supported Cooperative Work* (pp. 116–125). New York: ACM Press.

Mehra, B. (2004). *The cross-cultural learning process of international doctoral students: A case study in library and information science education.* Unpublished doctoral dissertation, University of Illinois at Urbana–Champaign.

Mehra, B. (2005). A phase-model of the cross-cultural learning process of LIS international doctoral students: Characteristics and interventions. *Proceedings of the 68th Annual Meeting of the American Society for Information Science & Technology 2005, 42.*

Mehra, B., & Bishop, A. P. (2007). Cross-cultural perspectives of international doctoral students: Two-way learning in library and information science education. *International Journal of Progressive Education, 3*(1). Accessed July 9, 2007, from inased.org/v3n1/mehrabishop.htm.

Mehra, B., & Papajohn, D. (2007). "Glocal" patterns of communication-information convergences in Internet use: Cross-cultural behavior of international teaching assistants in a culturally alien information environment. *The International Information & Library Review, 39*(1): 12–30.

Mellon, C. A. (1986). Library anxiety: A grounded theory and its development. *College & Research Libraries, 47*(2), 160–165.

Metoyer-Duran, C. (1991). Information-seeking behavior of gatekeepers in ethnolinguistic communities: Overview of taxonomy. *Library and Information Science Research, 13*(4), 319–346.

Moir, A., & Jessel, D. (1991). *Brain sex.* New York: Dell.

Morehead, D. R., & Rouse, W. B. (1982). Models of human behavior in information seeking tasks. *Information Processing & Management, 18*(4), 193–205.

Morra, S., & Lazzarini, S. (2002). A cross-cultural study of response to Icelandic and Italian folktales. *Empirical Studies of the Arts, 20*(1), 61–82.

Murdock, G. (1997). Thin descriptions: Questions of method in cultural analysis. In J. McGuigan (Ed.), *Cultural methodologies* (pp. 178–192). Thousand Oaks, CA: Sage Publications.

Murfin, M. E. (1980). The myth of accessibility: Frustration and failure in retrieving periodicals. *Journal of Academic Librarianship, 6*(1), 16–19.

Myers, M. D. (1994). A disaster for everyone to see: An interpretive analysis of a failed IS project. *Accounting, Management and Information Technologies, 4*(4), 185–201.

Nabi, R. L. (2003). Exploring the framing effects of emotion: Do discrete emotions differentially influence information accessibility, information seeking, and policy preference? *Communication Research, 30*(2), 224–247.

Nahl, D. (1993). *CD-ROM point-of-use instructions for novice searchers: A comparison of user-centered affectively elaborated and system-centered unelaborated text.* Unpublished doctoral dissertation, University of Hawaii, Honolulu. Accessed December 13, 2006, from www2.hawaii.edu/~nahl/articles/phd/phdtoc.html.

Nahl, D. (1995). Affective elaborations in Boolean search instructions for novices: Effects on comprehension, self-confidence, and error type. *Proceedings of the 58th ASIS Annual Meeting, 32*, 69–76.

Nahl, D. (1996a). Affective monitoring of Internet learners: Perceived self-efficacy and success. *Proceedings of the 59th ASIS Annual Meeting, 33*, 100–109.

Nahl, D. (1996b). The user-centered revolution: 1970–1995. *Encyclopedia of Microcomputing* (vol. 19, pp. 143–200). New York: Marcel Dekker.

Nahl, D. (1997). Information counseling inventory of affective and cognitive reactions while learning the Internet. In L. E. M. Martin (Ed.), *The challenge of Internet literacy: The instruction-Web convergence* (pp. 11–33). New York: Haworth Press.

Nahl, D. (1998a). Ethnography of novices' first use of Web search engines: Affective control in cognitive processing. *Internet Reference Services Quarterly, 3*(2), 51–72.

Nahl, D. (1998b). Learning the Internet and the structure of information behavior. *Journal of the American Society for Information Science, 49*(11), 1017–1023.

Nahl, D. (2001). A conceptual framework for defining information behavior. *Studies in Multimedia Information Literacy Education (SIMILE), 1*(2). Accessed December 13, 2006, from www.utpjournals.com/simile/issue2/nahlfulltext.html.

Nahl, D. (2004). Measuring the affective information environment of Web searchers. *Proceedings of the 67th annual meeting of the American Society for Information Science & Technology, 41*, 191–197.

Nahl, D. (2005a). Affective and cognitive information behavior: Interaction effects in Internet use. *Proceedings of the 67th annual meeting of the American Society for Information Science & Technology, 41*. Accessed December 13, 2006, from eprints.rclis.org/archive/00004978/01/Nahl_Affective.pdf.

Nahl, D. (2005b). Affective load theory (ALT). In K. E. Fisher, S. Erdelez, & L. E. F. McKechnie, (Eds.), *Theories of information behavior* (pp. 39–43). Medford, NJ: Information Today, Inc.

Nahl, D. (2006). *A symbiotic human-machine model for tracking user micro-attributes.* Paper presented at the Hawaii International Conference on System Sciences (HICCS), Kauai, Hawaii. Accessed July 9, 2007, from www.itl.nist.gov/iaui/vvrg/hicss39/HICSS-2006-Nahl1.doc.

Nahl, D. (2007a). A discourse analysis technique for charting the flow of micro-information behavior. *Journal of Documentation, 63*(3): 323–339.

Nahl, D. (2007b). Social-biological information technology: An integrated conceptual framework. *Journal of the American Society of Information Science* (JASIST), *58*(13): 1–26.

Nahl, D., & Harada, V. (1996). Composing Boolean search statements: Self-confidence, concept analysis, search logic, and errors. *School Library Media Quarterly, 24*(4), 199–207.

Nahl, D., & Jakobovits, L. A. (1985). Managing the affective micro-information environment. *Research Strategies, 3*(1), 17–28.

Nahl, D., & Tenopir, C. (1996). Affective and cognitive searching behavior of novice end-users of a full-text database. *Journal of the American Society for Information Science, 47*, 276–289.

Nahl-Jakobovits, D., & Jakobovits L. A. (1985). Managing the affective micro-information environment. *Research Strategies, 3*(1), 17–28.

Nardi, B. A., & O'Day, V. L. (1999*). Information ecologies: Using technology with heart.* Cambridge, MA: MIT Press.

Neuman, D. (2003). Learning in an information-rich environment: Preliminary results. In D. Callison (Ed.), *Measuring student achievement and diversity in learning: Papers of the Treasure Mountain Research Retreat #10* (pp. 39–50). San Jose, CA: Hi Willow Research & Publishing.

Neuman, D. (2004). The library media center: Touchstone for instructional design and technology in the schools. In D. H. Jonassen (Ed.), *Handbook of Research on*

Educational Communications and Technology (2nd ed., pp. 499–522). Mahwah, NJ: Lawrence Erlbaum Associates.

Newton, E., Stegmeier, G., & Padak, N. (1999). Young children's written response to text. *Reading Horizons, 39*(3), 191–208.

Nicholas, D., & Marden, M. (1998). Parents and their information needs. A case study: Parents of children under the age of five. *Journal of Librarianship and Information Science, 30*(1), 35–47.

Nielsen, J. (1993). *Usability engineering.* San Francisco: Morgan Kaufmann.

Nielsen, J. (1994). *Usability inspection methods.* New York: John Wiley & Sons.

Nodelman, P. (1988). *Words about pictures: The narrative art of children's picture books.* Athens, GA: University of Georgia Press.

Norman, D. A. (1981). Twelve issues for cognitive science. In D. A. Norman (Ed.), *Perspectives on cognitive science* (pp. 265–295). Hillsdale, NJ: Erlbaum, Basic Books.

Norman, D. A. (1990). *Design of everyday things.* New York: Doubleday.

Norman, D. A. (2004). *Emotional design: Why we love (or hate) everyday things.* New York: Basic Books.

Ogle, L. T., Sen, A., Pahlke, E., Jocelyn, L., Kastberg, D., Roey, S. et al. (2003). *International comparisons in fourth-grade reading literacy: Findings from the Progress in International Reading Literacy Study (PIRLS) of 2001.* Washington, DC: National Center for Education Statistics. Accessed November 28, 2006, from nces.ed.gov/pubs2003/2003073.pdf.

Onwuegbuzie, A. J., & Jiao, Q. G. (2000). I'll go to the library later: The relationship between academic procrastination and library anxiety. *College and Research Libraries, 61*(1), 45–54.

Onwuegbuzie, A. J., Jiao, Q. G., & Bostick, S. L. (2004). *Research methods in library and information studies: No. 1. Library anxiety: Theory, research, and applications.* Lanham, MD: Scarecrow.

Ortony, A., & Turner, T. J. (1990). What's basic about basic emotions? *Psychological Review, 97,* 315–331.

Ortony, A., Clore, G. L., & Collins, A. (1988). *The cognitive structure of emotions.* Cambridge: Cambridge University Press.

Osgood, C. E., Suci, G., & Tannenbaum, P. (1957). *The measurement of meaning.* Urbana, IL: University of Illinois Press.

Palmer, J. (1991). Scientists and information: II. Personal factors in information behaviour. *Journal of Documentation, 47*(3), 254–275.

Panksepp, J. (1998). *Affective neuroscience: The foundations of human and animal emotions.* Oxford: Oxford University Press.

Parker, N. (2004). Assignment information processes: What's 'enough' for high achievement? [Summary of a research note delivered at the Information Seeking In Context 2004 conference, Dublin, 1–3 September, 2004]. *Information Research, 10*(1), Summary 3. Accessed November 28, 2006, from InformationR.net/ir/10-1/abs3.

Parker, N. (2005). Diversity in high places: Variation in highly achieving students' experiences of course work assignments. In C. Rust (Ed.), *Improving student learning: Diversity and inclusivity.* Oxford: The Oxford Centre for Staff and Learning Development.

Patterson, P. K., Blehm, R., Foster, J., Euglee, K., & Moore J. (1995). Nurse information needs for efficient care continuity across patient units. *Journal of Nursing Administration, 25,* 28–36.

Pearce, L. (1997). *Feminism and the politics of reading.* New York: Arnold.

Petress, K., & Harrington, J. (n.d.). *List of emotions* [Internet document]. Accessed November 25, 2006, from www.umpi.maine.edu/~petress/feelinga.pdf.

Pettigrew, K. E. (1999). Waiting for chiropody: Contextual results from an ethnographic study of the information behaviour among attendees at community clinics. *Information Processing and Management, 35*(6), 801–817.

Pettigrew, K. E. (2000). Lay information provision in community settings: How community health nurses disseminate human services information to the elderly. *Library Quarterly, 70*(1), 47–85.

Pettigrew, K. E., Fidel, R., & Bruce, H. (2001). Conceptual frameworks in information behavior. In M. E. Williams (Ed), *Annual Review of Information Science & Technology: Vol. 35* (pp. 43–78). Medford, NJ: ASIST and Information Today, Inc.

Piaget, J. (1990). *The child's conception of the world.* New York: Littlefield Adams.

Piaget, J., & Inhelder, B. (1969). *The psychology of the child.* New York: Basic Books.

Picard, R. W. (1997). *Affective computing.* Cambridge, MA: MIT Press.

Picard, R. W. (1999). Affective computing for HCI. Accessed Dec. 15, 2006, from affect.media.mit.edu/pdfs/99.picard-hci.pdf.

Picard, R. W., Papert, S., Bender, W., Blumberg, B., Breazeal, C., Cavallo, D., Machover, T., Resnick, M., Roy, D., & Strohecker, C. (2004). Affective learning: A manifesto. *BT Technology Journal, 22*(4), 252–269.

Picard, R. W., & Klein, J. (2002). Computers that recognize and respond to user emotion: Theoretical and practical implications. *Interacting with Computers, 14*(2), 141–169.

Porter, T. M. (1995). *Trust in numbers: The pursuit of objectivity in science and public life.* Princeton: Princeton University Press.

Potter, W. J. (2004). *Theory of media literacy: A cognitive approach.* Thousand Oaks, CA: Sage Publications.

Powell, M. C. (2004). *To know or not to know? Perceived uncertainty and information seeking and processing about contaminated great lakes fish.* Unpublished doctoral dissertation, University of Wisconsin, Madison.

Preece, J., Rogers, Y., Sharp, H., & Benyon, D. (1994). *Human–computer interaction.* Boston: Addison-Wesley Longman.

Pritchard, R. (1990). The effects of cultural schemata on reading processing strategies. *Reading Research Quarterly, 25*, 273–295.

Probst, R. E. (2003). Response to literature. In J. Flood, D. Lapp, J. R. Squire, & J. M. Jensen (Eds.), *Handbook of Research on Teaching the English Language Arts* (2nd ed., pp. 814–824). Mahwah, NJ: Lawrence Erlbaum Associates.

Public Library of Charlotte & Mecklenburg County. (2006). *The BookHive.* Accessed November 28, 2006, from www.bookhive.org.

Purves, A. C. (1973). *Literature education in ten countries.* Stockholm: Almqvist and Wiskell.

Purves, A. C., & Beach, R. (1972). *Literature and the reader: Research in response to literature, reading interests and the teaching of literature.* Urbana, IL: National Council of Teachers of English.

Radford, L. (1999). *The reference encounter: Interpersonal communication in the academic library.* Chicago: American Library Association and the Association of College and Research Libraries.

Raghunathan, R., & Corfman, K. P. (2004). Sadness as pleasure-seeking prime and anxiety as attentiveness prime: The "different affect–different effect" (DADE) model. *Motivation and Emotion, 28*(1), 23–41.

Ramsden, P. (2003). *Learning to teach in higher education.* New York: Routledge Falmer.

Rapaport, D. (1950). *Emotions and memory.* New York: International Universities Press.

Rashley, L. H. (2005). "Work it out with your wife": Gendered expectations in parenting rhetoric online. *NWSA Journal, 17*(1), 58–92.

Raskin, J. (2000). *The humane interface: New directions for designing interactive systems.* Boston: Addison-Wesley.

Ratner, C. (1991). *Vygotsky's sociohistorical psychology and its contemporary applications*. New York: Plenum.

Redwood High School Research Study Group. (2000). *Research handbook*. Larkspur, CA: Tamalpais Union High School District. Accessed November 25, 2006, from rhsWeb.org/library/researchhandbook.htm.

Reisberg, D., Heuer, G., McLean, J., & O'Shaughnessy, M. (1988). The quantity, not the quality, of affect predicts memory vividness. *Bulletin of the Psychonomic Society, 26*, 100–103.

Ren, W. (1999). Self-efficacy and the search for government information: A study of small-business executives. *Reference and User Services Quarterly, 38*(3), 283–291.

Reuter, K., & Druin, A. (2004). Bringing together children and books: An initial descriptive study of children's book searching and selection behavior in a digital library. *Proceedings of the 67th annual meeting of the American Society for Information Science and Technology, 41*, 339–348.

Revelle, W., & Loftus, D. A. (1990). Individual differences and arousal: Implications for the study of mood and memory. *Cognition and Emotion, 4*, 209–237.

Richardson, L. (2002). Poetic representation of interviews. In J. F. Gubrium & J. A. Holstein (Eds.), *Handbook of interview research: Context and method* (pp. 877–892). Thousand Oaks, CA: Sage Publications.

Riday, J. D. (2003). "First and foremost, I'm a mom!": The experience of full-time and part-time stay-at-home mothering. (Doctoral Dissertation, Iowa State University, 2003). *Dissertation Abstracts International, A: The Humanities and Social Sciences, 64*(3), 1095-A.

Right brain/left brain thinking. (2001). From *Funderstanding.com* (Home–Engaging kids–Theories–About learning). Accessed November 25, 2006, from www.funderstanding.com/right_left_brain.cfm.

Roberts, J., While, A., & Fitzpatrick, J. (1995). Information-seeking strategies and data utilization: Theory and practice. *International Journal of Nursing Studies, 32*, 601–611.

Rochester, M. K. (1986). *Foreign students in American library education: Impact on home countries*. New York: Greenwood Press.

Roe, K. (1985). Swedish youth and music: Listening patterns and motivations. *Communication Research, 12*(3), 353–362.

Rosenblatt, L. M. (1978). *The reader, the text, the poem: The transactional theory of the literary work*. Carbondale, IL: Southern Illinois University Press.

Rosenblatt, L. M. (1991). Literature-S.O.S.! *Language Arts, 68*, 444–448.

Ross, C. S. (1991). Readers' advisory service: New directions. *RQ, 30*(4), 503–518.

Ross, C. S. (1994). Readers reading L. M. Montgomery. In M. H. Rubio (Ed.), *Harvesting thistles: The textual garden of L. M. Montgomery* (pp. 23–35). Guelph, Ontario: Canadian Children's Literature.

Ross, C. S. (1995). "If they read Nancy Drew, so what?": Series book readers talk back. *Library and Information Science Research, 17*(3), 201–236.

Ross, C. S. (1999). Finding without seeking: The information encounter in the context of reading for pleasure. *Information Processing and Management, 35*(6), 783–799.

Ross, C. S. (2001). What we know from readers about the experience of reading. In K. D. Shearer & R. Burgin (Eds.), *The reader's advisor's companion* (pp. 77–95). Englewood, CO: Libraries Unlimited.

Ross, C. S., McKechnie, L., & Rothbauer, P. M. (2006). *Reading matters: What the research reveals about reading, libraries and community*. Westport, CT: Libraries Unlimited.

Rothbauer, P. M. (2004a). *Finding and creating possibility: Reading in the lives of lesbian, bisexual and queer young women*. Unpublished doctoral dissertation, University of Western Ontario, London, Ontario, Canada.

Rothbauer, P. M. (2004b). The Internet in the reading accounts of lesbian and queer young women: Failed searches and unsanctioned reading. *Canadian Journal of Library and Information Science, 27*(3), 89–112.

Rothbauer, P. M. (2004c). "People aren't afraid anymore but it's hard to find books": Reading practices that inform the personal and social identities of self-identified queer and lesbian young women. *Canadian Journal of Library and Information Science, 27*(4), 53–74.

Rubin, D. C., & Kozin, M. (1984). Vivid memories. *Cognition, 16*, 81–95.

Sadl, Z. (1996). *The 'affective' revolution: Cognitive turn in contemporary social sciences. Emotiology in Slovenia (1850–1930). The European Legacy, 1*(3): 958–963.

Salovey, P., & Mayer, J. (1990). Emotional intelligence. *Imagination, Cognition, & Personality, 9*, 185–211.

Saracevic, T., Shaw, W. M., & Kantor, P. B. (1977). Causes and dynamics of user frustration in an academic library. *College and Research Libraries, 38*, 7–18.

Sarkodie-Mensah, K. (1988). *Foreign students and U.S. academic libraries: A case study of foreign students and libraries in two universities in New Orleans, Louisiana.* Unpublished doctoral dissertation, University of Illinois at Urbana–Champaign.

Saumure, K. & Given, L. M. (2004). Digitally enhanced? An examination of the information behaviors of visually impaired post-secondary students. *The Canadian Journal of Information and Library Science, 28*(2), 25–42.

Savolainen, R. (1993). The sense-making theory: Reviewing the interests of a user-centered approach to information seeking and use. *Information Processing & Management, 29*, 13–28.

Savolainen, R. (1995). Everyday life information seeking: Approaching information seeking in the context of 'way of life'. *Library and Information Science Research, 17*(3), 259–294.

Saye, J. D., & Wisser, K. M. (2003). Students. In E. H. Daniel & J. D. Sayer (Eds.), *Library and information science education statistical report 2003.* Oak Ridge, TN: ALISE.

Schacter, D. L. (1996). *Searching for memory.* New York: Basic Books.

Scheurich, J. J. (1995). A postmodernist critique of research interviewing. *International Journal of Qualitative Studies in Education, 8*(3), 239–252.

Scheutz, M., & Sloman, A. (2001). Affect and agent control: Experiments with simple affective states. In N. Zhong, J. Liu, S. Ohsuga, & J. Bradshaw (Eds.), *Intelligent agent technology: Research and development. Proceedings of the 2nd Asia-Pacific Conference on IAT Maebashi City, Japan 23–26 October 2001.* Singapore: World Scientific. Accessed December 13, 2006, from www.cs.bham.ac.uk/research/cogaff/scheutz.sloman.affect.control.pdf.

Schlosser, L. Z., & Sedlacek, W. E. (2001). The relationship between undergraduate students' perceived past academic success and perceived academic self-concept. *Journal of the Freshman Year Experience, 13*, 95–105.

Schutz, A., & Luckmann, T. (1974). *The structures of the life-world.* London: Heinemann.

Schwarz, N. (1990). Feelings as information: Information and motivational functions of affective states. In E. T. Higgins & R. M. Sorrentino (Eds.), *Handbook of motivation and cognition: Vol. 2. Foundations of social behavior* (pp. 527–561). New York: Guilford Press.

Schwarz, N. (2002). Situated cognition and the wisdom in feelings. In L. F. Barrett, & P. Salovey (Eds.), *The wisdom in meaning: Psychological processes in emotional intelligence* (pp. 144–166). New York: Guilford Press.

Scott, W. A. (1955). Reliability in content analysis: The case of nominal scale coding. *Public Opinion Quarterly, 19*, 321–325.

Seligman, M. E. P., & Csikszentmihalyi, M. (2000). Positive psychology: An introduction. *American Psychologist, 55*, 5–14.

Shamo, E. (2001). *University students and the Internet: Information seeking study*. Unpublished doctoral dissertation. University of North Texas, Denton, Texas.

Shaver, P., Schwartz, J., Kirson, D., & O'Connor, C. (1987). Emotion knowledge: Further exploration of a prototype approach. *Journal of Personality and Social Psychology, 52*, 1061–1086.

Shoemaker, S. (2005). Acquisition of computer skills by older users: A mixed methods study. *Research Strategies, 19*, 165–180.

Shorkey, C. T., & Crocker, S. B. (1981). Frustration theory: A source of unifying concepts for generalist practice. *Social Work, 26*, 374–379.

Simon, H. A. (1967). Motivational and emotional controls of cognition. *Psychological Review, 74*(1), 29–39.

Simon, H. A. (1997). *Models of bounded rationality: Volume 3. Empirically grounded economic reason*. Cambridge, MA: MIT Press.

Sims, R. (1983). Strong black girls: A ten year old responds to fiction about Afro-Americans. *Journal of Research and Development in Education, 16*(3), 21–28.

Singh, J. (1995). Measurement issues in cross-national research. *Journal of International Business Studies, 26*(3), 597–620.

Solomon, P. (1997). Discovering information behavior in sense making. III. The person. *Journal of the American Society for Information Science, 48*, 1127–1138.

Solomon, P. (2005). Rounding and dissonant grounds. In K. E. Fisher, S. Erdelez, & L. E. F. McKechnie (Eds.), *Theories of information behavior* (pp. 308–312). Medford, NJ: Information Today, Inc.

Solomon, R. C. (2004). *Thinking about feeling: Contemporary philosophers on emotions*. Oxford: Oxford University Press.

Spears-Bunton, L. A. (1990). Welcome to my house: African American and European American students' responses to Virginia Hamilton's House of Dies Drear. *Journal of Negro Education, 59*, 566–576.

Spears-Bunton, L. A. (1993). *Cultural consciousness and response to literary texts among African-American and European-American high school junior*s. Unpublished doctoral dissertation, University of Kentucky, Lexington.

Spink, A., Wilson, T. D., Ford, N. J., Foster, A. E., & Ellis, D. (2002). Information-seeking and mediated searching: Part 1. Theoretical framework and research design. *Journal of the American Society for Information Science and Technology, 53*(9), 695–703.

Spradley, J. P. (1979). *The ethnographic interview*. New York: Holt, Rhinehart and Winston.

Steinfirst, S. (1986). Reader-response criticism. *School Library Journal, 33*(2), 114–116.

Stempel, G. H. (1955). Increasing reliability in content analysis. *Journalism Quarterly, 32*, 449–455.

"Stay-at-home" parents top 5 million, Census Bureau reports. (2004, November 30). *U.S. Census Bureau News*. Accessed November 25, 2006, from www.census.gov/Press-Release/www/releases/archives/families_households/003118.html.

StoneSoup. (2006). *StoneSoup.com: For young writers and artists*. Accessed November 28, 2006, from www.stonesoup.com.

Strauss, A., & Corbin, J. (1998). *Basics of qualitative research: Techniques and procedures for developing grounded theory* (2nd ed.). Thousand Oaks, CA: Sage Publications.

Suler, J. R., & Phillips, W. (1998). The bad boys of cyberspace: Deviant behavior in multimedia chat communities. *CyberPsychology and Behavior, 1*, 275–294.

Sumara, D. J. (1996). *Private readings in public: Schooling in the literary imagination*. New York: Peter Lang.

Tallman, J. I. (1990). International students in United States library and information science schools. In J. I. Tallman & J. B. Ojiambo (Eds.). *Translating an international education to a national environment* (pp. 13–22). Pittsburgh, PA: University of Pittsburgh, School of Library and Information Science.

Tardy, R. W. (2000). "But I am a good mom": The social construction of motherhood through health-care conversations. *Journal of Contemporary Ethnography, 29*(4), 433–473.

Tardy, R. W., & Hale, C. (1998). Getting 'plugged in': A network analysis of health-information seeking among 'stay at home moms'. *Communication Monographs, 65*(4), 336–357.

Tashakkori, A., & Teddie, C. (Eds.). (2002). *Handbook of mixed methods in social and behavioral research.* Thousand Oaks, CA: Sage Publications.

Taylor, R. S. (1968). Questions-negotiation and information seeking in libraries. *College and Research Libraries, 29*(3), 178–194.

Tenopir, C. (1994). The emotions of searching. *Library Journal, 119,* 134–135.

Tenopir, C. (2003). *Use and users of electronic library resources: An overview and analysis of recent research studies.* Washington, DC: Council on Library and Information Resources. Accessed November 25, 2006, from www.clir.org/pubs/reports/pub120/pub120.pdf.

Thelan, L. A., Lough, M. E., Urden, L. D., & Stacy, K. M. (1998). *Critical Care Nursing Diagnosis and Management* (3rd ed.). St. Louis, MO: Mosby.

Todd, R. J. (2003). Adolescents of the information age: Patterns of information seeking and use, and implications for information professionals. *School Libraries Worldwide, 9,* 27–46.

Todd, R., & Kuhlthau, C. C. (2004). *Student learning through Ohio school libraries.* Columbus, OH: Ohio Educational Library Media Association. Accessed November 25, 2006, from www.oelma.org/StudentLearning/documents/OELMAReportof Findings.pdf.

Tomlinson, L. M. (1995). *The effects of instructional interaction guided by a typology of ethnic identity development: Phase one. Reading Research Report No. 44.* Athens, GA & College Park, MD: National Reading Research Center.

Towne, N., & Adler, R. B. (1996). *Looking out looking in* (8th ed.). Forth Worth, TX: Harcourt Brace.

Trompenaars, F. (1993). *Riding the waves of culture: Understanding diversity in business.* London: Economist Books.

Tufte, E. R. (1997). *Visual explanations: Images and quantities, evidence and narrative.* Cheshire, CT: Graphics Press.

Tuominen, K., & Savolainen, R. (1997). A social constructionist approach to the study of information use as discursive action. In P. Vakkari, R. Savolainen & B. Dervin (Eds.), *Information seeking in context: Proceedings of an International Conference on Research in Information Needs, Seeking, and Use in Different Contexts (Aug. 14–16, 1996, Tampere, Finland)* (pp. 81–96). London: Graham Taylor.

Turkle, S. (1995). *Life on the screen: Identity in the age of the Internet.* New York: Simon & Schuster.

Turner, M. M., Rimal, R. N., Morrison, D., & Kim, H. (2006). The role of anxiety in seeking and retaining risk information: Testing the risk perception attitude framework in two studies. *Human Communication Research, 32*(2), 130–156.

Tyszka, T. (1989). Information and evaluation processes in decision making. In N. Eisenberg, J. Reykowski, & E. Staub (Eds.), *Social and moral values* (pp. 175–193). Mahwah, NJ: Lawrence Erlbaum Associates.

University of Maryland & Internet Archive. (2002). *International Children's Digital Library: International research.* Accessed November 28, 2006, from www.icdlbooks.org/about/research/international.shtml.

Van Hout, M. (2004). Getting emotional with ... Donald Norman. *Design & Emotion*. Accessed December 13, 2006, from www.design-emotion.com/2004/12/15/getting-emotional-with-donald-norman.

Van Manen, M. (1990). *Researching lived experience: Human science for an action sensitive pedagogy*. London, Ontario: Althouse Press.

Van Oers, B. (1994). On the narrative nature of young children's iconic representations: Some evidence and implications. Accessed November 12, 2006, from www.psych.hanover.edu/vygotsky/vanoers.html.

Vandergrift, K. E. (1987). Using reader response theories to influence collection development and programs for children and youth. In J. Varlejs (Ed.), *Information seeking: Basing services on users' behaviors* (pp. 52–66). Jefferson, MD: McFarland.

Vandergrift, K. E. (1990). The child's meaning-making in response to a literary text. *English Quarterly, 33*(3/4), 125–140.

Vygotsky, L. (1978). *Mind in society: The development of higher psychological processes*. Cambridge, MA: Harvard University Press.

Vygotsky, L. (1982). *Collected works, vol. 1: Problems in the theory and history of psychology*. Moscow: Isdatel'stvo Pedagogika.

Vygotsky, L. (1962). *Thought and language*. Cambridge, MA: MIT Press.

Walsh, W. (2002). Spankers and nonspankers: Where they get information on spanking. *Family Relations, 51*(1), 81–88.

Wang, P., & Tenopir, C. (1998). An exploratory study of users' interaction with World Wide Web resources: Information skills, cognitive styles, affective states, and searching behaviors. In M. E. Williams (Ed.). *19th National Online Meeting Proceedings* (pp. 445–454). Medford, NJ: Information Today, Inc.

Warner, J. (2005, February 21). Mommy madness. *Newsweek, 145*(8), 42. Accessed November 25, 2006, from www.msnbc.msn.com/id/6959880/site/newsweek.

Watson, D., & Clark, L. A. (1984). Negative affectivity: The disposition to experience aversive emotional states. *Psychological Bulletin, 96*, 465–490.

Watson, J. S. (1998). "If you don't have it, you can't find it." *Journal of the American Society for Information Science, 49*, 1024–1036.

Watson, J. S. (2001). Making sense of the stories of experience: A methodology for research and teaching. *Journal of Education for Library and Information Science, 42*(2), 137–148.

Weigts, W., Widdershoven, G., Kok, G., & Tomlow, P. (1993). Patients' information seeking actions and physicians' responses in gynaecological consultations. *Qualitative Health Research, 3*, 398–429.

Weiss, R. P. (2000). Emotion and learning. *Training and Development, 54*(11), 45–48.

White, R. T. (1989). Recall of autobiographical events. *Applied Cognitive Psychology, 3*, 127–136.

Whitmire, E. (1998). Development of critical thinking skills: An analysis of academic library experiences and other measures. *College & Research Libraries, 59*(3), 266–273.

Whitmire, E. (2002). Academic library performance measures and undergraduates' library use and educational outcomes. *Library & Information Science Research, 24*, 107–128.

Whitmire, E. (2004). The relationship between undergraduates' epistemological beliefs, reflective judgment, and their information-seeking behavior. *Information Processing and Management, 40*, 97–111.

Wicks, D. A. (1999). The information-seeking behavior of pastoral clergy: A study of the interaction of their work worlds and work roles. *Library and Information Research, 21*(2), 205–206.

Wiegand, W. (1997). Out of sight, out of mind: Why don't we have schools of library and reading studies? *Journal of Education in Library and Information Science, 38*, 314–326.

Wilhelm, J. D. (1997). *"You gotta BE the book": Teaching engaged and reflective reading with adolescents.* New York: Teachers College Press.

Williamson, K. (1989). Discovered by chance: The role of incidental information acquisition in an ecological model of information use. *Library and Information Science Research, 20,* 23–40.

Williamson, K. (1996). The information needs and information seeking behaviour of older adults: An Australian study. In P. Vakkari, R. Savolainen & B. Dervin (Eds.), *Information seeking in context: Proceedings of an International Conference on Research in Information Needs, Seeking, and Use in Different Contexts (Aug. 14–16, 1996, Tampere, Finland)* (pp. 337–350). London: Graham Taylor.

Williamson, K., Schauder, D., & Bow, A. (2000). Information seeking by blind and sight impaired citizens: An ecological study. *Information Research, 5*(4). Accessed November 25, 2006, from informationr.net/ir/5-4/paper79.html.

Wilson, T. D. (1981). On user studies and information needs. *Journal of Documentation, 37*(1), 3–15. Accessed December 5, 2006, from informationr.net/tdw/publ/papers/1981infoneeds.html.

Wilson, T. D. (1997). Information behaviour: An interdisciplinary perspective. *Information Processing & Management, 33*(4), 551–572.

Wilson, T. D. (1999). Models of information behaviour research. *Journal of Documentation, 55*(3), 249–270.

Wilson, T. D., Ford, N., Ellis, D., Foster, A. E., & Spink, A. (2000). Uncertainty and its correlates. *The New Review of Information Behaviour Research, 1,* 69–84.

Wilson, T. D., Ford, N., Ellis, D., Foster, A., & Spink, A. (2002). Information seeking and mediated searching. Part 2. Uncertainty and its correlates. *Journal of the American Society for Information Science and Technology, 53*(9), 704–715.

Yankelovich, D. (1996). A new direction for survey research. *International Journal of Public Opinion Research, 8*(1), 1–9.

Yin, R. K. (1989). *Case study research: design and methods* (Applied Social Research Methods Series No. 5). Newbury Park: California: Sage Publications.

Zach, L. (2005). When is "enough" enough? Modeling the information-seeking and stopping behaviour of senior arts administrators. *Journal of the American Society for Information Science, 56*(1), 23–35.

Zillmann, D. (1988). Mood management: Using entertainment to full advantage. In L. Donohew, H. E. Sypher, & E. T. Higgins (Eds.), *Communication, social cognition, and affect* (pp. 147–171). Hillsdale, NJ: Lawrence Erlbaum Associates.

Zimmerman, T. S. (2000). Marital equality and satisfaction in stay-at-home mother and stay-at-home father families. *Contemporary Family Therapy, 22*(3), 337–354.

Zins, J., Weissberg, R., Wang, M., & Walberg, H. (Eds.). (2004). *Building academic success on social and emotional learning: What does the research say?* New York: Teachers College Press.

Zorn, T. E. (1993). Motivation to communicate: A critical review with suggested alternatives. *Communication Yearbook, 16,* 515–549.

REFERENCED CHILDREN'S BOOKS

Blume, J. (1998). *Summer sisters: A novel.* New York: Delacorte.

Burton, V. L. (1939). *Mike Mulligan and his steam shovel.* Boston: Houghton Mifflin.

Dahl, R. (1964). *Charlie and the chocolate factory.* New York: Knopf.

Farmaanfarmaaeeian, J., & Farjaam, F. (1984). [1363 by the Iranian calendar.] *Uninvited guests.* Iran: The Children's Book Council. Accessed November 28, 2006, from www.childrenslibrary.org/icdl/SaveBook?bookid=uninvit_00390064&lang=English.

Huseinovic, A. P. (2003). *Ciconia, Ciconia.* Croatia: Kašmir Promet. Accessed November 28, 2006, from www.childrenslibrary.org/icdl/SaveBook?bookid=baucico_00040009&lang=English.

Igus, T., & Wood, M. (1996). *Going back home.* San Francisco, CA: Children's Book Press. Accessed November 28, 2006, from www.childrenslibrary.org/icdl/SaveBook?book id=woogoin_00030021&lang=English.

Maillu, D. G. (2002). *The survivors.* Kenya: Sasa Sema Publications. Accessed November 28, 2006, from www.childrenslibrary.org/icdl/SaveBook?bookid=thesurv_004 60010&lang=English.

Molina, R., Fucio, H., & Popa, A. (2003). *Sandosenang kuya*/A dozen brothers. Philippines: Adarna House, Inc. Accessed November 28, 2006, from www.childrens library.org/icdl/SaveBook?bookid=molsand_00370010&lang=English.

Montgomery, L. M. (1908). *Anne of Green Gables.* Toronto: Ryerson Press.

Riddell, E. (1992). *My first day at preschool.* Hauppauge, NY: Barron's.

Robart, R. (1986). *The cake that Mac ate.* Toronto: Kids Can Press.

Samuel, N. (1994). *How to make peace.* Israel: Lilach. Accessed November 28, 2006, from www.childrenslibrary.org/icdl/SaveBook?bookid=smlhwtm_00190001&lang =English.

Ta'erpoor, F. (1986). [1365 by the Iranian calendar.] *The adventure of Ahmad and the clock.* Iran: Children's Book Council. Accessed November 28, 2006, from www. childrenslibrary.org/icdl/SaveBook?bookid=ahmadan_00390073&lang=English.

White, E. B. (1945). *Stuart Little.* New York: Harper Collins.

About the Contributors

Jennifer Berryman is a doctoral researcher at Australia's University of Technology, Sydney. Her research focuses on developing a deeper understanding of the concept of enough information as experienced by policy workers. She also works in policy and research at the State Library of New South Wales. Her recent projects include research into the implications of e-government for public libraries and the value of public libraries.

Brenda Dervin is Professor of Communication and Joan N. Huber Fellow in the School of Communication in the College of Social and Behavioral Sciences at Ohio State University.

Allison Druin is Associate Professor at the University of Maryland's College of Information Studies and is a member of the Human–Computer Interaction Lab. She is the lead Principal Investigator of the International Children's Digital Library and a Commissioner on the U.S. National Commission on Libraries and Information Science.

Lesley S. J. Farmer, Professor at California State University Long Beach, coordinates the Library Media Teacher program. She earned her MSLS at the University of North Carolina, Chapel Hill, and received her adult education doctorate from Temple University. A frequent presenter and writer, her research interests include information literacy, collaboration, and educational technology.

Karen E. Fisher is Associate Professor in the Information School of the University of Washington and Chair of the Library and Information Science program. She is currently a visiting researcher at Microsoft Research. Her specialty is information behavior in everyday life, particularly informal information flow in social settings. Her latest books include *Theories of Information Behavior* (2005) and *How Libraries and Librarians Help* (2005). Supporters of her research include the National Science Foundation, Microsoft, and the Institute of Museum and Library Services. She won the 2005 Shera Award for Distinguished Published Research, the 1999 ALISE Research Award, and the 1995 ALISE Jane Hannigan Award. She is a member of several editorial boards, as well as the Permanent Program Committee of the Information Seeking in Context (ISIC) Conference series, and she was the 2004–05 chair of ASIST SIG USE. She received her doctorate from the University of Western Ontario, and was a post-doctoral fellow at the University of Michigan.

Rich Gazan is Assistant Professor in the Library and Information Science Program in the Information and Computer Sciences Department at the University of Hawaii. His research interests center on the social and technical challenges of integrating knowledge from diverse sources, in digital libraries, online communities, and information-system design collaborations.

Lisa M. Given is Associate Professor in the School of Library and Information Studies at the University of Alberta. She teaches graduate-level courses in research methods, Web design, and information literacy. Her research interests include individuals' information behavior, Web usability, the design of library space, and information use in the context of higher education. Her current research project, The University as Information Space: Exploring Undergraduates' Information Behaviours, was awarded a 2003 SSHRC Standard Research Grant.

Susan Hayter currently teaches in the Faculty of Information and Media Studies at the University of Western Ontario in the areas of foundations of library and information science and information behavior. Her research interests focus on information needs and seeking, particularly relating to disadvantaged populations, everyday life, and the affective and social aspects of information behavior. Prior to moving to Canada in 2004, she completed her MA in Library and Information Management and her PhD at Northumbria University in Newcastle, U.K. She has also worked as a school library manager, reference librarian, and student library assistant at The British Library. She has published several articles and conference papers.

Wooseob Jeong is Assistant Professor in the School of Information Studies at the University of Wisconsin, Milwaukee. His research interests include human–computer interaction: multimodal interfaces, especially haptic and auditory displays; multilingual/multiscript information systems; information retrieval and image retrieval; digital libraries; information seeking habits of ethnic groups, such as immigrants and foreign students; and education for library and information science.

Heidi Julien is Associate Professor at the University of Alberta. Previously, she held academic appointments at Dalhousie University and Victoria University of Wellington, New Zealand. She holds a PhD from the University of Western

Ontario. Her research areas include information behavior and information literacy.

Nahyun Kwon is Assistant Professor in the Graduate School of Library and Information Science at the University of South Florida. Her research interests relate to the measurement of user needs and service effectiveness in various information contexts, including community information and communication technologies (ICTs), virtual reference services, and nontraditional library user services.

Carol F. Landry is a doctoral student in Information Science at the University of Washington's Information School, where she received her MLIS degree in 2005. Her research interests include human information behavior, information poverty, the digital divide, and the role of affect in information behavior. She has studied dentists' information behavior and is currently working as a research team member for Washington Information Network 211 (WIN 211) and Communities Connect Network (CCN).

Sheri Anita Massey is a doctoral student in the College of Information Studies at the University of Maryland where she also earned her MLS. She is a graduate research assistant on the International Children's Digital Library (ICDL) project.

Lynne (E. F.) McKechnie is Associate Professor in the Faculty of Information and Media Studies at the University of Western Ontario and Cleary Professor (Visiting) at the University of Washington. Her teaching and research centers on children's literature, library services, and information behavior.

Michelynn McKnight is Assistant Professor at the Louisiana State University School of Library and Information Science, and a Distinguished Member of the Academy of Health Information Professionals. A National Library of Medicine Medical Informatics Fellow, she was a co-author of *Mathematics Education Research* and wrote a chapter in *The Medical Library Association Guide to Managing Health Care Libraries*.

Bharat Mehra is Assistant Professor in the School of Information Sciences at the University of Tennessee. His work explores social justice and social equity concerns to meet the needs of minority and disenfranchised populations. His areas of focus include diversity and intercultural issues, community informatics, and international perspectives in library and information science.

Helena M. Mentis is a doctoral candidate in the College of Information Sciences and Technology at Pennsylvania State University. Her research interests are in the three related areas of emotion in interactive systems, the user experience, and design research. Her doctoral study is on designing for emotion in high-stress collaborative environments.

Nicola Parker is a doctoral researcher at Australia's University of Technology, Sydney. Her research focuses on the interplay of information and learning in a complex task. The study uses a phenomenographic approach combined with case studies to focus on the experiences of postgraduate coursework students. It explores highly achieving students' experiences of task processes and the concept of enough as well as the affective dimensions of information seeking and learning.

CarrieLynn D. Reinhard is a doctoral student in the School of Communication and research assistant for the Sense-Making the Information Confluence project at Ohio State University.

Catherine Sheldrick Ross is Professor and Dean of the Faculty of Information and Media Studies at the University of Western Ontario. Her research focuses on information behavior, the reference transaction, and reading for pleasure.

Paulette Rothbauer is Assistant Professor in the Faculty of Information Studies at the University of Toronto. Her current research project examines the information behavior, reading practices, and media uses of older rural teens.

Ann Carlson Weeks is Professor of the Practice in the College of Information Studies at the University of Maryland, where she teaches in the area of school library media program development. She is the Director of Collection Development for the International Children's Digital Library (ICDL), and a Principal Investigator on the research team.

About the Editors

Diane Nahl is Professor of the Library and Information Science program in the Information and Computer Sciences Department at the University of Hawaii. She holds a PhD in Communication and Information Sciences from the University of Hawaii. Her research areas encompass affective computing, information behavior, information problem-solving, human information interaction, human system interaction, and information technology literacy. Her research focuses on discovering how people approach, understand, value, react to, and interact with information systems. Her recent books include *Strategic Research Approaches for Reference Librarians* (2001, Kendall Hunt) and *Road Rage and Aggressive Driving* (2000, Prometheus Books). She is a member of several editorial boards and is a reviewer for the *Journal of the American Society for Information Technology* (*JASIST*) and ASIST annual meetings.

Dania Bilal is Professor at the University of Tennessee, School of Information Sciences, College of Communication and Information. She holds a BS in Communications and Documentation from the College of Communication and Information Management at the Lebanese University in Beirut, and an MSLS and a PhD in Library and Information Studies from Florida State University. Her research focuses on children and young adults' information seeking behavior, system design, human–computer interaction, cognitive and affective information seeking of children and adult users, and user-centered interface design, especially for young users.

Author Index

Subject Index

More Titles of Interest from Information Today, Inc.

Theories of Information Behavior

Edited by Karen E. Fisher, Sanda Erdelez, and
Lynne (E. F.) McKechnie

This unique book presents authoritative
overviews of more than 70 conceptual
frameworks for understanding how people
seek, manage, share, and use information in
different contexts. Covering both established
and newly proposed theories of information
behavior, the book includes contributions from
85 scholars from 10 countries. Theory
descriptions cover origins, propositions, methodological implications,
usage, and links to related theories.

456 pp/hardbound/ISBN 978-1-57387-230-0
ASIST Members $39.60 • Nonmembers $49.50

ASIST Thesaurus of Information Science, Technology, and Librarianship, Third Edition

Edited by Alice Redmond-Neal
and Marjorie M. K. Hlava

The *ASIST Thesaurus* is the authoritative reference
to the terminology of information science,
technology, and librarianship. This updated third
edition is an essential resource for indexers,
researchers, scholars, students, and practitioners. An
optional CD-ROM includes the complete contents of the print thesaurus
along with Data Harmony's Thesaurus Master software. In addition to
powerful search and display features, the CD-ROM allows users to add,
change, and delete terms, and to learn the basics of thesaurus construction
while exploring the vocabulary of library and information science and
technology.

Book with CD-ROM: 272 pp/softbound/ISBN 978-1-57387-244-7
ASIST members $63.95 • Nonmembers $79.95

Book only: 272 pp/softbound/ISBN 978-1-57387-243-0
ASIST members $39.95 • Nonmembers $49.95

Covert and Overt
Recollecting and Connecting Intelligence Service and Information Science

Edited by Robert V. Williams and Ben-Ami Lipetz

This book explores the historical relationships between covert intelligence work and information/computer science. It first examines the pivotal strides to utilize technology to gather and disseminate government/military intelligence during WWII. Next, it traces the evolution of the relationship between spymasters, computers, and systems developers through the years of the Cold War.

Covert and Overt is published in cooperation with Scarecrow Press, Inc. To order outside North America, please contact Scarecrow Press via phone: 44-1752-202-301 or fax: 44-1752-202-333. You can also e-mail orders@nbninternational.com.

256 pp/hardbound/ISBN 978-1-57387-234-8
ASIST Members $39.60 • Nonmembers $49.50

Information Representation and Retrieval in the Digital Age
By Heting Chu

This is the first book to offer a clear, comprehensive view of Information Representation and Retrieval (IRR). With an emphasis on principles and fundamentals, the author first reviews key concepts and major developmental stages of the field, then systematically examines information representation methods, IRR languages, retrieval techniques and models, and Internet retrieval systems.

264 pp/hardbound/ISBN 978-1-57387-172-5
ASIST members $35.60 • Nonmembers $44.50

To order or for a complete catalog, contact:
Information Today, Inc.
143 Old Marlton Pike, Medford, NJ 08055 • 609/654-6266
email: custserv@infotoday.com • Web site: www.infotoday.com